A History of Antigua

Also by Brian Dyde

Antigua and Barbuda: Heart of the Caribbean
Islands to the Windward: Five Gems of the Caribbean
St Kitts: Cradle of the Caribbean
Caribbean Companion: The A–Z Reference
The Empty Sleeve: The Story of the West India Regiments of the British Army

A History of Antigua

The Unsuspected Isle

Some unsuspected isle in far-off seas!
Robert Browning

Brian Dyde

*For Bill Frisken
with very best wishes
Brian Dyde*

CARIBBEAN

© Copyright text Brian Dyde 2000
© Copyright illustrations Macmillan Education Ltd 2000

All rights reserved. No reproduction, copy or transmission of this publication may be made without written permission.

No paragraph of this publication may be reproduced, copied or transmitted save with written permission or in accordance with the provisions of the Copyright, Designs and Patents Act 1988, or under the terms of any licence permitting limited copying issued by the Copyright Licensing Agency, 90 Tottenham Court Road, London W1P 9HE.

Any person who does any unauthorised act in relation to this publication may be liable to criminal prosecution and civil claims for damages.

First published 2000 by
MACMILLAN EDUCATION LTD
London and Oxford
Companies and representatives throughout the world

ISBN-13: 978-0-333-75169-5
ISBN-10: 0-333-75169-8

10   9   8   7   6   5   4   3
09   08   07   06

This book is printed on paper suitable for recycling and made from fully managed and sustained forest sources.

Printed in China

A catalogue record for this book is available from the British Library.

Illustrations by Brian Dyde and Tech Type

Cover illustration of the Mill Yard at Gambles Estate courtesy of Cambridge University Library

To my beloved wife
VERONICA JOSEPH DYDE
who has helped me to understand

Contents

List of Illustrations ix
List of Maps x
Acknowledgements xi

PART ONE: THE SETTLEMENT

1 Prelude 3
2 Discovery 8
3 Proprietary Rule 14
4 Hewing out New Fortunes 20
5 The Codrington Years 30
6 An Unfortunate Divel 48

PART TWO: SUGAR AND SLAVERY

7 Prospering at a Price 62
8 A Great Deal of Trouble in this Island 71
9 In the Service of their Country 78
10 Every Foolish Extravagance 85
11 Matters of Consequence 103
12 Immediate, Entire and Universal Freedom 124
13 A Private Governmency 137

PART THREE: NEITHER PLANTERS NOR PEOPLE PROSPER

14 Their Natural Portion 150
15 The Fortunes of the Planter 167
16 Great Misery and Distress 177
17 Deemed to be a Dependency 189
18 Always Incapable and Frequently Corrupt 201

PART FOUR: THE STRUGGLE AND THE CONQUEST

19 Bound to Succeed 214
20 Unrest in the Graveyard 231

21	In No Mood to be Dictated to	250
22	Removing the Pillars	264
23	For Good, or Come What May	276

Notes	294
Bibliography	307
Index	314

List of Illustrations

between pages 84 and 85

1. Reaping sugar-cane in the eighteenth century
2. An eighteenth century boiling-house and animal-powered sugar mill
3. Field slave on his way to work in the eighteenth century
4. The 'unfortunate divel' Governor Daniel Parke *c.*1705
5. The Martello Tower at The River landing in Barbuda, built in 1745
6. The Court House in St John's as completed in 1750
7. Horatio Nelson: a portrait painted in 1777 but altered in 1781 to show the insignia of a post-captain
8. The dockyard at English Harbour in 1803, with Shirley Heights in the background
9. The interior of the boiling-house at Delaps estate in 1829
10. Shipping hogsheads of sugar from Willoughby Bay in 1829
11. The Cathedral of St John the Divine, consecrated in 1848, photographed *c.*1910
12. Workers' housing on the outskirts of St John's *c.*1910
13. The city of St John's *c.*1910, viewed from the site of the present-day hospital
14. St John's Harbour as seen from the summit of Rat Island *c.*1910

between pages 228 and 229

15. Weighing phosphate on the Redonda in 1912
16. Work on the Body Ponds water scheme in 1913
17. The abandoned dockyard in a deserted English Harbour in 1913
18. High Street in St John's decorated for the visit of Princess Marie Louise in 1913
19. Governor Henry Hesketh Bell with a police guard of honour at the lower end of High Street in 1913
20. Governor Bell with members of the Antigua Cricket Club in 1913
21. High Street in St John's in 1928
22. Sir Eustace Fiennes Bt in retirement in England in 1931
23. Barclays Bank and the Court House in St John's in 1928
24. Governor Reginald St Johnston's model housing scheme at Clare Hall
25. Lord Baldwin in the process of upsetting the *Herrenvolk* by socialising with the workers in 1949
26. The swearing-in of Reginald St Johnston as Governor of the Leeward Islands in 1929
27. The Antigua Legislative Council pose with Princess Margaret in 1955
28. Vere Cornwall Bird, Prime Minister of Antigua and Barbuda in 1981

List of Maps

1	Antigua	2
2	The Leeward Islands	10
3	Mid-eighteenth century map of Antigua	64
4	Barbuda in 1848	138
5	Redonda	195
6	Mining operations in Redonda	197
7	Barbuda	269

Acknowledgements

I would first like to thank my wife, to whom this book is dedicated, for her forbearance, support and good humour during its preparation and writing. Antigua is her homeland, and without her advice and assistance I could not have undertaken the task. I must also thank Michael Bourne at Macmillan for so readily giving me the opportunity to fulfil a long-held ambition. Help and information were received from Richard Alexander, Dr Peter Bander-van Duren, Terry Barringer, Peter Bursey, David Druett, Sir Ranulph Fiennes, Bt., Gertrude Gerstle, Dr Martin K. Gordon, Major Edward Green, John K. Hughes, Charles Kidd, Philip Knights, Colonel John Lowles, Dr Eileen Scarff, Major George Stephens, Huw Thomas and Christopher Walker.

For their courtesy and efficiency in dealing with my enquiries and requests for material I would also like to thank the staff of the libraries at Cambridge University, the Institute of Commonwealth Studies, the Institute of Historical Research, the Foreign and Commonwealth Office, the Royal Geographical Society and the Commonwealth Institute. The archivists of the US Air Force Historical Research Agency, the US Army Corps of Engineers Office of History, and the US Naval Historical Center, all provided valuable assistance. The staff of the Pembrokeshire County Library at Haverfordwest were, as always, extremely helpful.

Part One:
The Settlement

The history of the Englishmen who settled on the islands of the Caribbean during the seventeenth century is a chronicle of an impressive material accomplishment that was overborne by social failure and human tragedy.

Carl and Roberta Bridenbaugh
No Peace Beyond the Line (1972)

ANTIGUA

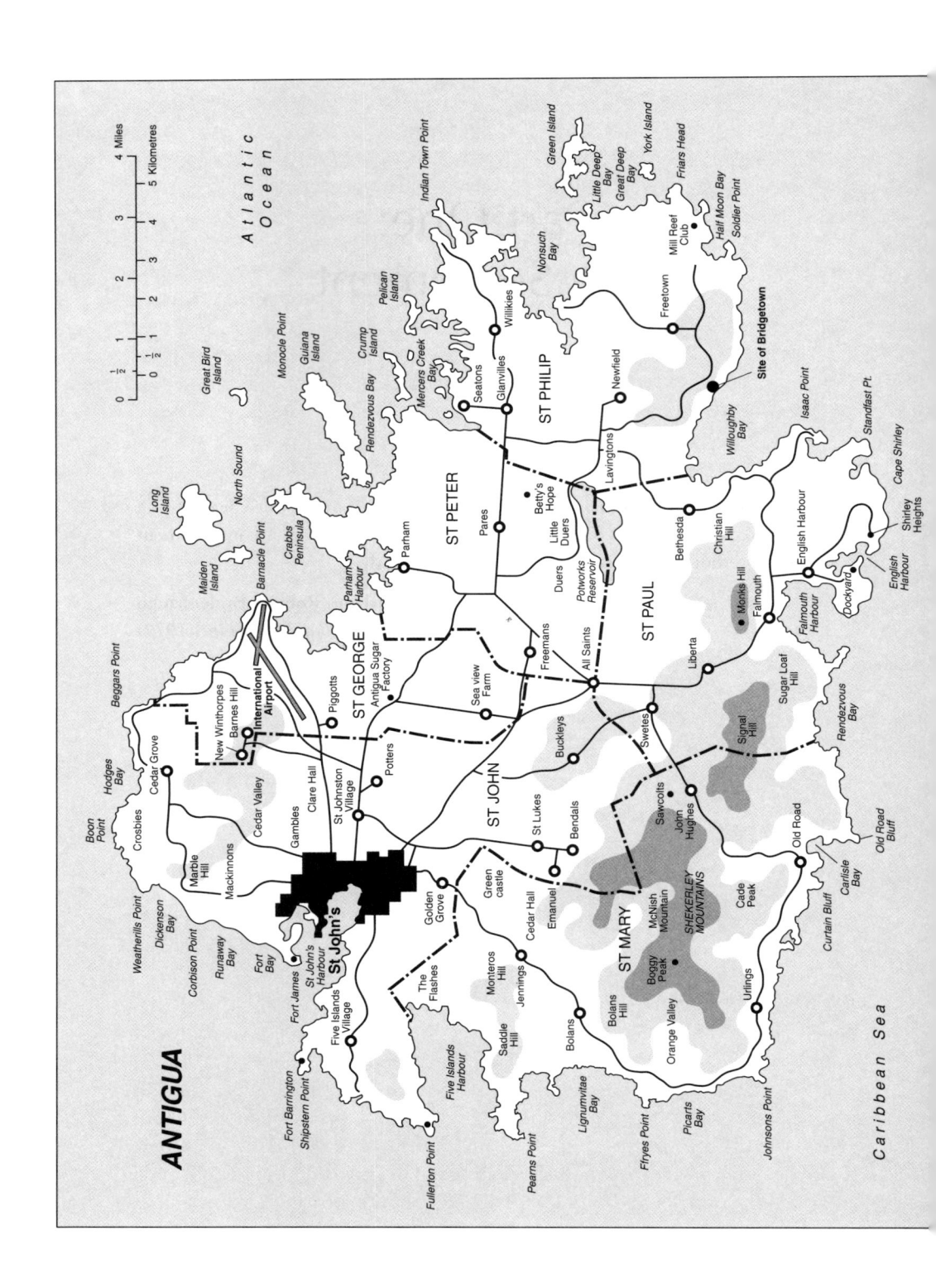

1
Prelude

Antigua is a fine Island, tho' it has not one Single Spring of Water in it: So that in times of drouth when all their Ponds are dry, and their Cisterns almost empty, they are obliged to fetch their fresh water from Montserrat, in times of War; or, in times of Peace from that and Guardaloup a Neighbouring French Island.

Emanuel Bowen
A note on his map of Antigua
(c. 1750)

Today the Arawaks are hardly even a memory. They had no writing; their only records took the forms of carving in wood and stone and of rude graffiti on natural rock faces. Our knowledge of them is derived partly from the accounts of sixteenth-century Spanish writers, and partly from examination of burial caves and middens. All the witnesses agree that they were a kindly and peaceful people. They had no reason to be otherwise.

J.H. Parry and P.M. Sherlock
A Short History of the West Indies (1956)

Antigua is only one of the many hundreds of islands and islets which make up that enormous archipelago which creates the Caribbean Sea out of one small corner of the North Atlantic Ocean; an island well over 400 miles north of the nearest point of the South American mainland, and more than 1300 miles southeast of the closest part of North America. For over 300 years it was a minor member of that selection of these islands owned by Great Britain and which, together with bits of South and Central America, were known as the British West Indies. Situated near the middle of the eastern group of small islands known as the Lesser Antilles, and as one of the northerly sub-group called, misleadingly, the Leeward Islands, it is well within sight of half a dozen of its neighbours.[1] With five of these in the past it was politically linked in the British Leeward Islands colony; with the sixth, the French island of Guadeloupe, it was frequently at war; and with two, Barbuda and Redonda, it now forms an independent state.

Barbuda, the larger of these two dependencies, gives its name to the large area of shallow water which separates it from Antigua, and from out of which both islands rise as above-surface peaks of a single, much larger geographical feature that, in turn, is separated by deep water from similar banks round about – out of some of which rise the other Leeward Islands.

Antigua is very roughly oval in shape, with a highly indented coastline, and a considerable number of offshore islets. Its approaches, particularly from the north and east, are well protected by large areas of coral reef. Although only just over 100 square miles in area (a little larger than Martha's Vineyard off Massachusetts, and considerably smaller than the Isle of Wight off the south coast of England) the island has three distinct geological regions. The most apparent and obvious of these is in the south-west, where the greatly eroded remains of the volcano which formed the foundation of the island are known as the Shekerley Mountains. This is an area of steep-sided hills cut into by deeply incised valleys, barely meeting the height criterion for mountains in half a dozen peaks and culminating at 1319 feet in one called Boggy Peak towards the western end of the region. The North-East Uplands are an area of carbonate rocks originating from ancient coral reef complexes which rise here and there into hills between three and four hundred feet high along an escarpment. They slope towards the north-east and face the island's largest area of reefs and islets. Between these hills and the Shekerley Mountains is a broad central plain with a few low rolling hills, formed from a mixture of marine and non-marine sediments, and pierced by large shallow bays in the north-west and south-east. The type and quality of the soil varies greatly throughout the island. That in the south-west, produced by the weathering of unstratified volcanic rocks, is probably the richest and most fertile, but because of the topography is mostly not suitable for intensive farming or any sort of plantation or estate development. The soils of the North-East Uplands are highly calcareous but are generally mixed with enough clay to be easily tilled and reasonably fertile. These contrast sharply with the sands and heavy clay soils of the central plain, which are derived from the weathering of the underlying stratified shales and require much fertilising and extensive tillage to be made into good farming land. This mixed geology gives a strange variety of agricultural conditions, with soils varying from patch to patch. In general, the most fertile tract lies along the junction between the north-east limestone uplands and the central plain, while the least fertile area is found on the opposite side of the plain where it abuts the Shekerley Mountains.

Barbuda is smaller than Antigua, with an area of between 62 and 68 square miles, the uncertainty being caused by extensive mudflats in the north, and also by whether or not the existence of the large lagoon on the western side is taken into account. The true land portion is made up entirely of limestone, deposited in and raised from the sea in stages over the past 2 million years or so. This is fairly recent in geological terms and there is evidence that the island is still rising from the sea. A low plateau along the eastern side – called The Highlands even though it rises no more than 128 feet above the sea – is the only topographical feature. The lagoon on the opposite side of the island was created by a narrow sandbar forming across the mouth of a large shallow bay. It is now almost totally enclosed, the only entrance being a meandering narrow channel through the northern mudflats. The water in the lagoon is generally less than six feet deep, and steadily becoming less as material is washed into it from the land, with natural flushing inhibited by the very small tidal range. At opposite ends of the sandbar are areas of sand dunes. Those to the south are constantly being added to by material brought by longshore currents from the north and east, resulting in the south-western corner of the island extending into the sea at a rate of about 150 feet every century. The northern part of Barbuda is made up of areas of dry land surrounded by swamp and mudflats, the actual boundaries between them being ill-defined, constantly changing, and almost impossible to map accurately. This area is protected by coral reefs a mile or so offshore, and deposits from these assist in gradually building up this end of the island. Similar reefs are found along the entire eastern coast and in great profusion around the south-eastern corner. The remaining part of the island, between The Highlands, the lagoon, the sand dunes in the south-east, and the northern mudflats, contains the only land on which farming can and ever did take place. Unfortunately, because it is only slightly above sea level, poorly drained and (as a 1937 survey report stated) 'The Barbuda soils have little or no agricultural value', it is – and always has been – mostly covered with wild vegetation.

Any discussion about the fertility or otherwise of either Antigua or Barbuda depends far more on the climate than on the quality of their soils. Both islands are situated between latitudes 17° and 18° north and directly in the path of the more or less constant north-east Trade Wind, but because of their low elevations both have always suffered from insufficient rainfall. Prolonged droughts, high evaporation, the absence of rivers and streams, and the presence of only one or two permanent springs in Antigua, and none at all in Barbuda, have all combined to give each island a constant shortage of fresh water: a factor which played a major part in the settlement of both.[2]

•

The pre-European history of the islands is not fully understood, nor has it been studied in any depth. It is thought that the first people in the Lesser Antilles may have been groups of paleo-indians from South or Central America who entered the region when sea levels were much lower than at present, perhaps around 10000bc. No evidence of their presence has ever been found in either Antigua or Barbuda (which at that time probably formed a single island), but this may be because any remains of their occupation, which would have been near the water's edge, are now lost beneath the sea.

The earliest date yet established for human occupation of Antigua is around 3100bc, from a site on Little Deep Bay on the east coast, but more substantial evidence of the presence of meso-indians around 1800bc exists on the opposite coast, at a site near Lignumvitae Bay. These originated in South America as 'maritime nomadic wanderers', and are now usually referred to as Ortoiroid people, after a site found at Ortoire in Trinidad. Very little is known about them, other than they used stone tools, did not practise agriculture, and had not invented pottery (the archaeologist's surest guide to the classification of pre-historic peoples). Further evidence of Ortoiroid use (occupation or settlement seem hardly appropriate) of Antigua may be unearthed but it is most unlikely that more remains to be discovered about how they got there, how long they stayed, where they went to, or what happened to them when the next lot of South American migrants, neo-indians known as Saladoid people, arrived.

Arawakan-speaking people from the Orinoco region probably reached the island shortly before the beginning of the Modern Era. As it is not known to which particular tribe or group they belonged they always have been, and most likely always will be, referred to simply as Arawaks. In addition to being hunter-gatherers like their predecessors, they were also cultivators, using the slash-and-burn method known as conuco to grow a variety of food crops, and made much use of decorated pottery. At least thirty settlement sites have been found, all around the coastline, with dates ranging from the first century to around AD 1100.

The Arawaks were the first people to produce any lasting effect on the island's landscape and its animal and plant life. While they settled only around the shoreline they fished and hunted extensively, and their shifting cultivation must eventually have degraded the vegetation and soils over sizeable areas as they worked inland. Such detrimental activities were counter-balanced by their introduction of many South American plants, including maize, manioc, peanut, pineapple, tobacco, cotton, guava and soursop; together with small animals such as the agouti, guinea pig and possibly the iguana. In general they were a peaceful, artistic people who appear to have been able to inhabit the island in such numbers, and in such a way, as to be able to make full use of its resources while coping with its very limited and erratic supply of fresh water.

This placid and harmonious existence, we may suppose, continued for over a thousand years, but what brought it to an end still remains to be discovered. Another group of Arawakan-speakers from the Orinoco region began to enter the Caribbean at some time during the fourteenth century, and had taken over all the Lesser Antilles well before 1500. Although identified by tribal names in some islands these new arrivals have never been called – in connection with Antigua – anything other than Caribs. From much the same background as the Arawaks and with many similarities in material culture, they were more aggressive and far more mobile, using bigger and better designed canoes to move between the islands. Following well-established mainland traditions of inter-tribal raiding and bride capture they had little difficulty in replacing their weaker and more passive forerunners. Once they reached Antigua they either drove out or assimilated the people they found there – or they found it deserted: no one knows. One reason for considering the possibility that the island may have been uninhabited, disregarding the fact that the paucity of fresh water must have made life precarious at the best of times, is that although there are indications that Caribs visited it frequently on hunting and fishing expeditions, nothing has ever been found which points to any sort of permanent settlement.

Evidence of any pre-European habitation of Barbuda is circumstantial only. Various finds have been made but no proper investigation has yet been carried out. As the island can be seen quite clearly with the naked eye from the Shekerley Mountains, and even from the tops of the modest northern hills, there is no reason to suppose that any of the early people did not find both islands at much the same time. However, it is difficult to believe that any of them could ever have attempted to live on Barbuda permanently. The Caribs, about whom we know most, as they played a part in the recorded history of the island, treated it as they did Antigua – as a suitable place to visit briefly from time to time; and this is all that any of the pre-historic people are likely to have done.

2
Discovery

He dreamed not that the ocean would bear ships
Heavy with slaves in the holds, to spill their seed
And fertilize new islands under whips

A.J. Seymour
'For Christopher Columbus'

Her Majesty does not understand why her subjects and those of other Princes are prohibited from the Indies, which she could not persuade herself are rightful property of Spain by donation of the Pope of Rome, in whom she acknowledged no prerogative in matters of this kind, much less authority to bind Princes who owe him no obedience, or to make that new world as it were a fief for the Spaniard and clothe him with possession.

Letter from Queen Elizabeth I to the Spanish Ambassador quoted by William Camden in *Annales Rerum Anglicarum et Hibernicarum 1589* (1615)

Antigua was first sighted by a European on 11 November 1493 during Columbus' second voyage to the New Word. It is unlikely that the man concerned was Columbus himself, even more unlikely that the island was then given the name it now bears, and inconceivable that he or anyone else landed there at the time.

The second voyage had begun in September of that year when over a thousand men in a fleet of seventeen vessels had left Cadiz in Spain. Nearly six weeks later a landfall had been made on the northern end of Dominica, and the Lesser Antilles entered recorded history for the first time. The fleet anchored off Guadeloupe for nearly a week before setting off towards that part of the Caribbean Columbus had discovered during his first voyage, and in particular for Hispaniola, where a small garrison had been left on the north coast. The eminent American historian and biographer of Columbus, Samuel Eliot Morison, on whose work most of the subsequent accounts of the discovery of the islands of the Eastern Caribbean are based, maintained that the entire fleet then sailed in a north-westerly direction, passing close along the western coasts of Montserrat, Redonda, Nevis, St Kitts, St Eustatius and Saba before ending up at St Croix. According to his account, the day after leaving 'Santa Maria de

Guadalupe', and from somewhere between 'Santa Maria de Monserrate' and 'Santa Maria Redonda' (an island which was to enter Antigua's history 366 years later) Columbus saw 'a large island to the north-eastward' which, with his abiding penchant for the Virgin, he named 'Santa Maria la Antigua'.[1] Unfortunately this account ignores too much other evidence to be wholly convincing.

Although Columbus kept a journal and presumably tried to make some sort of chart on which to indicate the islands as he found and named them, both have long since been lost. All details of his second voyage are based on the accounts of other people, primarily that of the Italian historian, Peter Martyr, who was a contemporary of Columbus and published his account of the discovery and conquest of the New World in 1511; but also that of Ferdinand Columbus, the explorer's son, who wrote his own *Historie*, published after his death in 1571. According to Martyr, after the fleet left Guadeloupe on 10 November:

> There appeared from the north, a great island which the captives that were taken in Hispaniola [on the first voyage, and who were now being returned to their homeland] called Madanino or Martinino, affirming it to be inhabited only with women . . . They could not at this time approach to this island by reason of the NNE wind which blew so vehemently from the same . . . After they departed from Mandanino and sailed by the space of forty miles they passed not far from another island which . . . they called Mons serratus because of was full of mountains.[2]

Three days later, having sailed past 'Santa Maria Rotunda' (Redonda) and 'Santa Martini' (Nevis), the fleet reached a third island which, because of the direction the ships were heading, could only have been what is now St Kitts but was then, Martyr tells us, given the name 'Santa Maria Antigua'.

This sequence of events is borne out by Ferdinand Columbus, who states:

> On Sunday, the tenth of November, the admiral weighed anchor and sailed with the whole fleet along the coast of the island Guadeloupe towards the north-west for Hispaniola and came to the island Montserrat . . . Thence he proceeded to St Mary Redonda . . . Next he came to St Marie la Antigua.[3]

From these accounts it would seem reasonably certain that the island we now know as Antigua *was* sighted during this voyage, but no less certain that it was *not* given this name at the time. Martyr's reference to Columbus bestowing the name on what is now St Kitts is reinforced by Ferdinand Columbus who states that the Carib name for the island he called 'St Marie la Antigua' was *Yamaca*, meaning a country with many springs – a description which could never have been applied to the Antigua we know – but which was very appropriate for mountainous St Kitts. Even the established Carib name for that island, *Liamuga*, has a similar derivation.

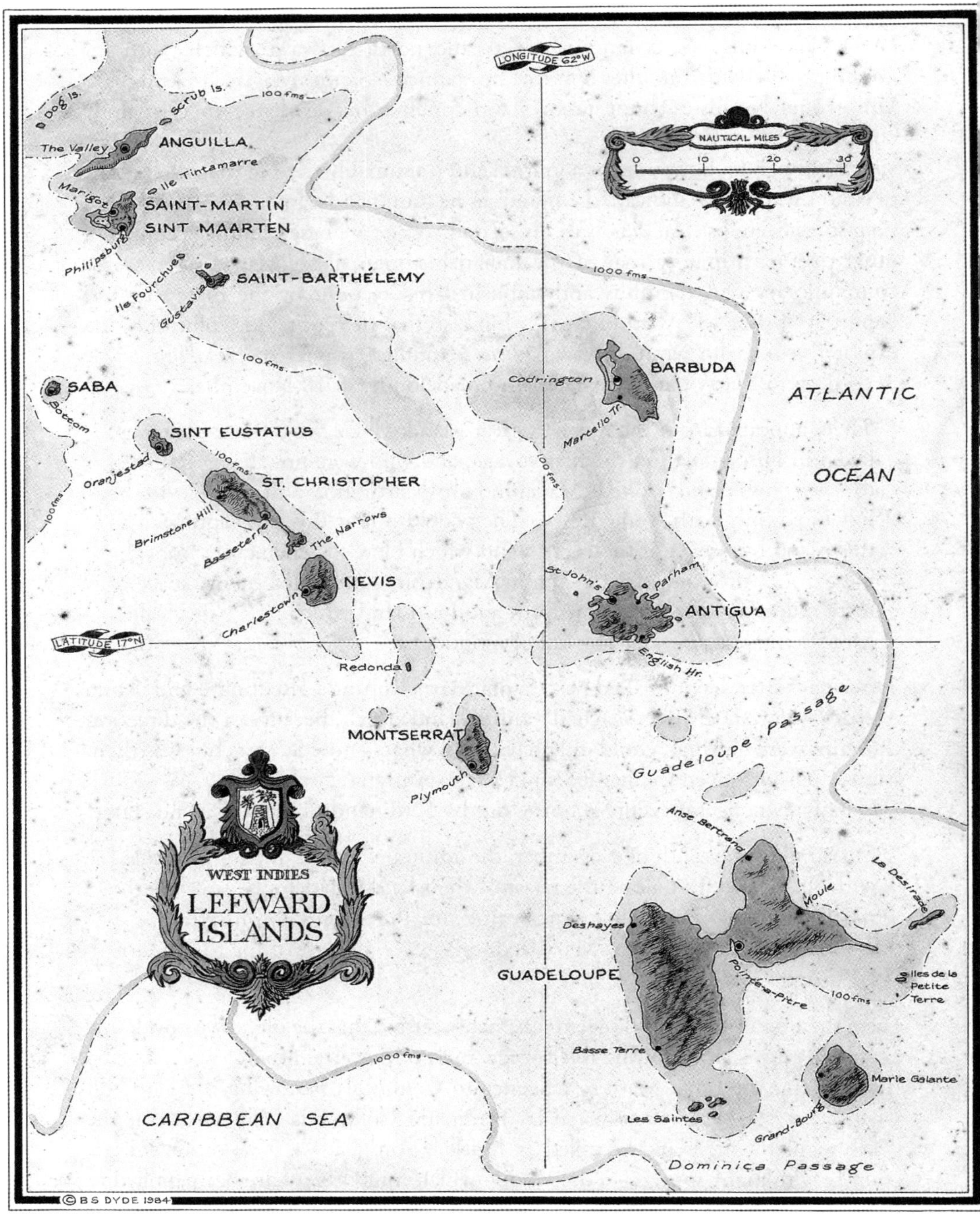
LONGITUDE 62°W
NAUTICAL MILES
0 10 20 30
Dog Is.
Scrub Is.
100 fms
The Valley
ANGUILLA
Ile Tintamarre
Marigot
SAINT-MARTIN
SINT MAARTEN
Philipsburg
Ile Fourchue
SAINT-BARTHÉLEMY
Gustavia
1000 fms
100 fms
SABA
Bottom
SINT EUSTATIUS
Oranjestad
100 fms
ST. CHRISTOPHER
Brimstone Hill
Basseterre
The Narrows
NEVIS
Charlestown
Codrington
BARBUDA
Marcello Tr.
100 fms
ATLANTIC
OCEAN
St John's
Parham
ANTIGUA
LATITUDE 17°N
English Hr.
Redonda
MONTSERRAT
Plymouth
Guadeloupe Passage
Anse Bertrand
La Desirade
Moule
Deshayes
GUADELOUPE
Pointe-a-Pitre
100 fms
Iles de la Petite Terre
WEST INDIES
LEEWARD ISLANDS
1000 fms
Basse Terre
Marie Galante
Les Saintes
Grand-Bourg
CARIBBEAN SEA
Dominica Passage
© B S DYDE 1984

It is possible that Columbus merely accepted his captives' name of Martinino for the island to the north of Guadeloupe, but unless his journal is one day found we shall never know for sure. The earliest map of the region is an inaccurate document drawn by Juan de la Cosa, who accompanied Columbus on his third voyage, and drew his map soon after his return to Spain in 1500. On this map no island to the north of Guadeloupe is shown at all, but a S. de Lanebo (which is surely not an impossible corruption of S. de Lantigua?) is shown in roughly the right position for St Kitts. Later map-makers made a better job of positioning all the islands in the area, but obviously then had to carry out a fair amount of guesswork with regard to which island bore which name. It was not until the second decade of the sixteenth century that an island called Antigioa or Lantigua began to appear on maps of the day in more or less its correct position, and Guadeloupe's northern neighbour has borne the name ever since.

With regard to Antigua's northern neighbour, nothing was shown on any map before 1512, when a Barbata or La Barbada started to appear. It is not known which European was the first to sight it or who named it, only that it was not Columbus nor anyone else who was with him on any of his voyages to the Caribbean.

Columbus had just as little time for, or interest in, the small islands of the Caribbean on his subsequent voyages as he had during the second. His main aims were to establish that he had reached Asia – by finding the mainland – and to obtain specimens of the riches of China and the fabulous island of Cipangu that would prove it. The Spaniards who came after him soon found out that the continent he had discovered, even though it was not Asia, had riches of its own, and Spain's interest became fixed on Central America and the Greater Antilles. The Lesser Antilles had nothing to offer by comparison, and as the majority were occupied by a race of people prepared to resist any attempted occupation, their incorporation into the Spanish New World empire was only nominal.

In 1520 Antonio Serrano was commissioned as governor of all the eastern Caribbean islands between Barbuda and Martinique, but his attempted settlement – probably in Guadeloupe – came to nothing. He visited Antigua and drove off the few Caribs he found there but, presumably because of the danger their return with reinforcements might present, combined with the limited supply of fresh water, his stay was only brief. After that the Caribs of Antigua and those of the neighbouring islands were left very much to their own devices, as a Spanish historian recorded in 1601:

> The Spaniards having such a vast extent of land to subdue, as is from the north of Mexico to the south of Chili, never had leisure to think of these inconsiderable islands, at which they only touch'd sometimes for fresh water, and set ashore on them some swine, which in process of time multiply'd prodigiously.[4]

During the sixteenth century Dominica remained the primary landfall for Spanish ships crossing the Atlantic. Like Guadeloupe this island had plenty of the fresh water these vessels needed after such a voyage but as both were very much Carib strongholds, it is possible that once it had been established that Antigua had a permanent source of water near a secluded bay on the south coast, this island became the preferred place to call. Even though after Serrano's visit no attempt was made to establish a settlement, cattle, sheep, goats and pigs were landed, as on all the other islands, 'for the better convenience of their [the Spanish] Navigations, and supply of their Ships in case of necessity.'[5]

The feral descendants of these animals would be of great value to Antigua's early settlers in due course, but long before this took place such livestock was also of use, along with the island's plentiful wood and limited water, to the pirates and privateers – French and Dutch as well as English – who began to frequent the Caribbean from the mid-1500s. Closer to home, their activities had grown steadily during the earlier Anglo-French wars, but once these had ended in 1564 the English pirates, Dutch 'sea-beggars' and French corsairs all turned their attention to the Spanish shipping plying between the Iberian peninsula and the New World. The rich pickings obtained as a result in turn stimulated interest in the establishment of non-Spanish settlements in the Caribbean. Drake's voyages to the region in the 1570s exposed the vulnerability of the main Spanish possessions to raiding and plunder, and an undeclared war existed between England and Spain from the mid-1580s until 1604. This period, which became the era of 'no peace beyond the Line' – of unlimited warfare anywhere south of the Tropic of Cancer and to the west of the longitude of the Azores – further encouraged Spain's enemies to attempt settlements in the Lesser Antilles. Early English attempts failed in St Lucia and Grenada, but eventually succeeded in January 1624, when Thomas Warner landed with his family and thirteen or fourteen other people at Old Road Bay in St Kitts.

Warner had first visited the island two years earlier after taking part in a failed attempt to found a settlement in the Guianas. Impressed by its natural attractions, and also by its proximity to other promising islands round about, he had then returned to England in order to obtain financial backing and to find potential settlers. As a former army officer and member of the royal bodyguard he was able, once the settlement was firmly established, to secure a commission from King Charles I in 1625 giving him 'full power and authority for us & in our name & as our Lieutenant to order and despose of any landes or other things' in St Kitts, Nevis, Barbuda, Montserrat and 'any other neighbour Islandes to them . . . not beinge in the possession or government of any other Christian Prince, State or Potentate.'[6]

This commission gave Warner status but not full security. In those days it was essential for a man of his rather humble birth – he was the younger son of a gentleman farmer – to have a powerful patron, and he needed a rich nobleman, preferably a courtier, to protect his interests by acquiring proprietary rights to the islands. This he acquired in July 1627 when the King granted Letters Patent to a court favourite and 'hopeless spendthrift' James Hay, the first Earl of Carlisle, giving him the proprietorship of all the 'Caribbee Islands'.

The Letters Patent promised far more than was in the power of Charles I to deliver, and the contents were based more on a desire to pre-empt any French or Dutch exploitation of the islands which the Spanish had by now more or less abandoned. Although by this time the English had established themselves on only two islands, St Kitts and Barbados, the grant covered 'St Christopher's [the full name for St Kitts – of which in fact only half was in English hands, the other half having been settled by the French at the same time as Warner was establishing his settlement], Grenada, St Vincent, St Lucia, Barbados, Mittalanea [Martinique], Dominico, Marigalante, Deseada, Todosantes [The Saintes], Guadaloupe, Antigua, Montserrat, Radendo, Barbuda, Nevis, Statia [St Eustatius], St Bartholomew, St Martin, Anguilla, Sembrera, Enegada, and other islands, before found to his great cost.' The proprietor was to bring these 'to a large and copious colony of English, to be hereafter named "the Carlisle or the islands of Carlisle province", reserving a yearly rent of [£]100, and a white horse when the King, his heirs and successors, shall come into those parts.'[7] In addition the King was to receive one-fifth of any gold or silver which might be discovered.

With regard to administering his province the proprietor, who had no intention of ever visiting it, was authorised to appoint his own governors and to make

> such laws as he the said Earl of Carlisle, or his heirs, with the consent, assent, and approbation of the free inhabitants of the said province or the greater part of them, thereunto to be called, and in such form as he or they in his or their discretion shall think fit and best.[8]

In return all the produce of the islands was to be exported only to England, where the duty it incurred – payable to Carlisle – was expected to make his fortune. It was in his interest therefore not only to make sure the duty imposed was a high as possible, but also, through his administrators on the spot, to ensure that all that the islands produced did in fact get sent to England. Fortunately for Warner large amounts of tobacco were already being shipped home from St Kitts, and Carlisle issued him with a new commission as governor in 1629.

By this time the English portion of St Kitts was already becoming overcrowded. The settlement which had been established a year earlier in Nevis, its close neighbour, prospered quickly and eased the problem for a while, but by the early 1630s Warner was forced into considering the colonisation of islands further afield. During the previous decade one or two half-hearted attempts had been made to establish small settlements in both Antigua and Barbuda – by both the English and the French – but none had come to anything because of fear of the Caribs in the former and the shortage of water in the latter. In 1632 Warner decided that a more determined effort was called for with regard to Antigua.

3

Proprietary Rule

> The early Leeward colonists will remain forever obscure – for the best of reasons, because they were obscure men at the time.
>
> Richard S. Dunn
> *Sugar and Slaves* (1972)

> They all be a company of sodomites that live here.
>
> Margaret Heathcoat, written in a letter from Antigua in 1665

The generally accepted date for the colonisation of Antigua is 1632 but, as with much else in the island's early history, this is based on tradition rather than on any documentary evidence. It may well have been a year or two later that a group of people led by Thomas Warner's son, Edward, made the crossing from St Kitts to become the first permanent European inhabitants, but until something comes to light to verify this 1632 remains the accredited year in which this took place. Just how many people came, how they were divided up between men, women and children, and even where they landed and set up their first encampment, are all matters about which it is only possible to speculate. There were about forty families on the island in 1640 which, even with an average of five to a family, would give a population of no more than 150. It is doubtful if Edward Warner brought even half this number with him, but it will never be known for sure. Their initial settlement must surely have been on Carlisle Bay, near the present village of Old Road on the south coast, as this was the closest anchorage to the best freshwater spring. Exactly when some – probably most – of those who arrived with Warner moved eastward around the coast, to found the town of Falmouth at the head of a much larger bay, is another question to which there is no answer other than probably well within that first year.

The original settlers came to an island which, apart from a few cleared areas along the windward coast previously used as Arawak *conucos*, was still wooded to the water's edge, and where an immense amount of backbreaking labour was needed before any sort of profitable crop could be planted. While a few among them would have been servants, each indentured to work for a master for a set number of years in return for a lump sum payment on completion of the period of indentureship, this could have meant very little in the early days. All who were among the first settlers, whether man, woman, child, master, mistress or servant, would have had to turn to as soon as they landed. Some sort of shelter was the first requirement and this could have consisted of little more than rough stick and palm-leaf huts to begin with. Food would hardly have been a problem once hunting and fishing had been organised. The island by this time was overrun with feral livestock, so much so that even in the 1670s it was still being described as 'naturally stored with wild Game as Hogs goats cattell etc.'

The gruelling work of hewing a settlement and its supporting agricultural base out of the virgin landscape and of catching enough game and fish to support the community, was made even harder by the constant need to be on the lookout for Caribs. None had been found living on the island when the settlers arrived, but those in Guadeloupe and the islands to the south soon learned of this further European intrusion into their territory. Raids began within a few months of the first landing and continued throughout the remainder of the seventeenth century. In the early days they presented an acute problem, as two or three of their war canoes or *piraguas* could carry enough warriors to outnumber the armed settlers. In 1640 they almost wiped out the settlement before carrying off Edward Warner's family (the first of many women and children abducted over the years), bringing about his early death as a result. Warner, who was only twenty-nine at the time, had had no official commission to act as governor when sent to Antigua by his father (possibly because it was not an island named in Thomas Warner's own commission of 1625) but he had managed to keep the new colony going through the crucial first years and led, as far as anyone knows, a fairly blameless life.

The same cannot be said of his successor. Following Warner's death the first of the many rogues who feature in Antigua's history was appointed by the proprietor (now the second Earl of Carlisle, who had succeeded his father in 1636) to take his place. Colonel Henry Ashton, a man who had been Thomas Warner's deputy in St Kitts, had been given his colonelcy by Carlisle (so becoming the first of the many placemen and   planters Antiguans were to see over the years swaggering about with an unearned and unjustifiable army rank), and he was to remain governor until 1655. Ashton epitomised the worst kind of early English settler in the Caribbean, the majority of whom were crude, uncouth adventurers. Such men came to the islands to make their fortunes, in much the same way as in the nineteenth century the same type of man rushed to the Klondike, to Ballarat or the Rand. None gave any thought to establishing a different sort of society from the one they had left behind, or to the possibility of creating a way of life to match the natural beauty with which they were now surrounded. In general, as one commentator recorded in 1693, the settlers were

> A sort of loose vagrant People, vicious and destitute of means to live at home, (being either unfit for labour, or such as could find none to employ

themselves about, or had so misbehaved themselves by Whoreing, Thieving, or other Debauchery, that none would set them on work).[1]

Nothing is known of Ashton's English background, or of how he became Thomas Warner's deputy in St Kitts by 1628. His attempt to murder the lieutenant-governor of Nevis in that year almost led to an outbreak of violence between the two islands, so it probably came as a great relief to Warner when Ashton was sent to Antigua. His character was not improved by his transfer and elevation, as was shown by his behaviour when a woman resisted his attempts to seduce her. This so annoyed him that he savagely cut off her hair, reducing her to a state of such distress and shame that she was forced to flee the island. In spite of his personal failings, however, he still managed to oversee a continuing, if very slow, development of the settlement in the face of repeated Carib raids. At the same time he was also able to help it to survive the far-reaching effects not only of the death of the first Earl of Carlisle, but also those of the English Civil War which broke out in 1642.

Just before Carlisle died, and because his son was then not legally of age, he had transferred his proprietary rights – along with his massive debts – to three trustees. His son, as might have been expected, did not get on with these too well, and his decision to make Ashton governor of Antigua in 1640 was only one of the many actions about which the Trustees and he did not see eye to eye. Their disagreements helped to build up waves of confusion about the proprietorship which, when the Civil War began, soon turned into a sea of trouble for all concerned – particularly as Carlisle wavered about which side to support.

The English Parliament took very little interest in Antigua or indeed any of the other Caribbean colonies during the first eighteen months of the war, having far more pressing matters to worry about. Those in charge of the various islands, such as Ashton and Warner, maintained a watchful neutrality while hoping to gain from the expected relaxation of proprietary rule. Having made no declaration for either King or Parliament, at the end of 1643 Warner was rewarded by having his commission as Governor and Lieutenant-General of the Caribee Islands renewed once again, and Ashton was confirmed in his governorship of Antigua. To their disappointment proprietary rule remained unchanged, and three years later Ashton wrote to Carlisle, urging him at least to visit his 'Province', and complaining that even though there were by now about 750 people on the island, less than half of them were capable of defending it by being 'serviceable in the feild [sic]'. He also made what was probably the very first of over 300 years' worth of gubernatorial references to Antigua's prime climatic defect:

> We have had soe long a drought that this tenn monethes past I have not made heere one hundred pounds of tobacco p[er] poll of all my family.[2]

Tobacco was the only cash crop for the early settlers in Antigua, as it was for those in St Kitts: it required very little investment in equipment, had a guaranteed market in England, and – provided there was a reasonable water supply – was very easy to grow.

Ashton's request that Carlisle visit the West Indies went unanswered, and early in the following year the Earl came out in support of the monarchy and fled to Holland. There he joined the refugee Royalists and, in return for half the revenue, leased his proprietorship for twenty-one years to Francis, the fifth Baron Willoughby of Parham, another deserter from the Parliamentary cause. After his English estates had been sequestered in 1649 Willoughby, armed with a commission from the exiled Charles II (whose father had been executed at the beginning of the same year), had more reason to visit the Caribbean: 'Since all is gone at home it is time to provide elsewhere for a being.'

Once he arrived in the West Indies most of the events which then transpired in his providing for 'a being' were centred on Barbados, and are not relevant here, but his presence in the region did have an effect on Antigua. He visited the island in 1650 and, once Ashton had proclaimed his support for the Royalists, he laid claim to a large area of land for future development in more settled times. Such times were not to return for Willoughby for some years, and they were never to come back for Ashton. When in the following year a fleet arrived from England to restore Parliamentary authority to the Caribbean possessions a few ships were detached to Antigua, causing support for the King to evaporate as quickly as it had arisen. Ashton was relieved of his post and taken back to England; seven years later, he was executed in the Tower of London.

His replacement, Christopher Keynell, arrived in 1652 to find that although loyalty to the home government was no longer in question there were plenty of other matters which needed to be addressed if the colony were to succeed. Even after twenty years Antigua remained 'the best wooded' of all the islands settled by the English, and still had a population of under 1000, consisting mostly of people of humble backgrounds scratching out a living with or without the help of indentured white servants. Such servants represented an outlay of capital and the colonists who could afford them – determined to get the most they could for their money – treated them as virtual slaves. They worked from sunrise to sunset, slept in hammocks, lived and worked in the same clothes until the garments fell apart, and had little or no access to leisure, recreation or women. The entire population was in any case predominantly male, with all the pressures on society that this created. Even so, the numbers were still too small to develop the island, to bring about the creation of a thriving community, and to deter the Caribs from their frequent and highly destructive raids.

The original Letters Patent had given the proprietor authority to make laws in each island and to summon the freemen to meet in an Assembly, with a few of the more important being appointed to a Council to advise the governor on administration. While the first recorded acts drawn up by such a body in Antigua date from 1644 the Assembly then, and for many years afterwards, could have been little more than a semi-informal meeting of the better-off settlers. It is not without interest that among the first laws to be passed was one 'against Carnall coppulation between Christian and Heathen', which declared that any child resulting from such a union was to be enslaved until the age of eighteen or twenty-one. As African slaves had hardly made their appearance in the Leeward Islands by this date, this perhaps indicates that rather more went on between the settlers and the Caribs in the early days than might be supposed from all the contemporary references to the latter's bloodthirsty activities. That it was also necessary to pass a law in the same year specifying the death penalty for incest presents another sad reflection on early Antiguan society. Sex, however, was not all the Assemblymen had on their minds at the time of Keynell's arrival. To add to the island's problems the market for West Indian tobacco had collapsed because of over-production, and in 1650 and 1651 Parliament had passed two Navigation Acts prohibiting trade between England or her colonies with the rest of the world other than in English ships – each of which had to be licensed, captained by an English master and crewed by a majority of Englishmen.

Keynell arrived to find Antigua in turmoil, with the Assembly not prepared to co-operate with him until their grievances regarding the state of the island's economy, trade and defence had been attended to. The Governor, as a keen Parliamentary supporter, would have little truck with men he considered Royalist sympathisers, and he and the Assembly were soon at loggerheads. The situation deteriorated steadily until, in 1655, Keynell clapped several of the more antagonistic and vociferous members in jail and took passage to England to seek advice and help. In London he laid his troubles before Cromwell, who was now Lord Protector, asking for free trade to be permitted, for foreigners to be allowed to become settlers, for arms and ammunition, and for more to be done to provide the island with additional labour. While Cromwell himself was sympathetic, a great deal of opposition was voiced by London merchants who were much against free trade, and who attempted to accuse Keynell of neglecting his duties. He eventually managed to get the Committee of Trade – a body established in 1650 – to support his plea for assistance and returned to Antigua to await the results. These turned out to be neither very extensive nor readily forthcoming. Dispensation was given for the admission of foreign nationals – provided they were Protestants – and a few Norwegians took advantage of this, but none of the other measures introduced did very much to stimulate the growth of the colony or to improve its society. By 1660, when the monarchy was restored in England, there were still no more than about 1300 people on the island, most of them with only modest landholdings and barely able to make a living.

The restoration of Charles II was 'the signal for the revival of the old controversies concerning the political status of the Caribees and their inhabitants.' Francis Willoughby, who survived his 1652 defeat at the hands of the forces sent out to reclaim the colonies for Parliament, had spent most of the intervening years as an active Royalist, and was confirmed in his proprietorship within a few weeks of Charles' return to the throne. His patent from Carlisle was immediately disputed by those in authority in Barbados, where he had not been seen for the previous eight years; by the creditors of the first Earl of Carlisle (who were still waiting for their money twenty-four years after his death); and by the heir to the second Earl of Carlisle (who had died bequeathing property he did not possess). The long legal battle which ensued ended three years later with Willoughby's appointment as Governor-in-Chief by the King for a period of seven years – which was the length of time the twenty-one year lease he had received from the second Earl of Carlisle still had to run. During this period he would be solely responsible for all the expenses of government in return for half the profits the islands under his control could be expected to produce; the other half being used to pay off all the creditors. Once those debts had been settled, and the second Earl of Carlisle's heir provided for, the second half of the profits would revert to the monarch.

Willoughby returned to the Caribbean in 1663 and within a month had persuaded the Assembly in Barbados, his seat of government, to pass the legislation he needed to start producing some of the revenue required. Under the act which was passed, and in return for confirmation of land titles and the abolition of existing rents and dues, a tax of 4½ per cent would be levied on the value of 'all dead commodities of the growth or produce of this island, that shall be shipped off the same.' At the beginning of the following year he visited each of the other islands under his authority in turn, and a similar act, levying a 4½ per cent export duty in return for confirmation of land titles, was passed in each Assembly. This marked the end of proprietary rule. It was now recognised that the Governor-in-Chief held his office by authority of the King, and that from now on the sovereign (and before long, his Government) had a direct interest in how the Caribbean colonies were governed, and in the amount of revenue they could be expected to generate.

In Antigua, where Keynell had been replaced soon after the Restoration by a Colonel John Bunckley, special provisions were included in the 4½ per cent Duty Act which paid some heed to the dismal state of the island. By this time many people had come, obtained land, and then either not bothered to do anything with it, or had tried, failed and given up. The act specified that the owners of such properties would forfeit their titles unless they were developed within two years. Another clause stated that for each acre he possessed the owner had to employ one white servant, a measure it was hoped would bring about an increase in the population. It was also intended, now that some of the better-off landowners had begun to import African slaves, to preserve an acceptable balance between white and black in society. No one living in Antigua at the time could have foreseen that, regardless of this or any other legislation concerning servants or slaves, society was soon to change out of all recognition.

4

Hewing out New Fortunes

Everything that fell in their way was devastated; and it has been remarked by an old author, that the French robbed the very shoes from off the feet of the inhabitants.

Mrs Lanaghan
Antigua and the Antiguans (1844)

I have deserted our unfortunate colony of Surinam, war and pestilence having almost consumed it. As it is to revert to the Dutch, I have with great loss removed to Antigua, where I am hewing a new fortune out of the wild woods.

Captain William Byam, in a letter to a friend from Antigua (1668)

The first West Africans to be brought to the Leeward Islands as slaves were landed in St Kitts in 1626, almost as soon as the island was settled, but black slavery was not to become important there – or in any of the adjacent islands – for many years. It is not known when the first slaves were brought to Antigua: one or two may just possibly have come with Warner in 1632, but generally they were an insignificant part of society there until after the middle of the century. In the early days they were obtained mainly from Dutch traders using the nearby island of St Eustatius as their base, but this source dried up after 1660, when another Navigation Act was passed which prohibited Dutch trade with the English colonies, and a company called Royal Adventurers into Africa was subsequently given the monopoly of supplying these colonies with slaves. This monopoly was much resented in the small islands of the eastern Caribbean where, as they offered such poor markets in comparison with places like Jamaica and Surinam, the price of a slave more than doubled. This then made the market even worse, particularly in Antigua where many landowners already could barely afford to engage white servants. However, there were some who could afford both, and during the 1660s it was these who were already planting the crop with which Antigua was to be linked for the next 300 years, and for the cultivation of which it seemed that only slaves could provide the necessarily large labour force.

Sugar had been produced in Barbados as early as 1642, and in St Kitts from around 1648, but there is no mention of it in connection with Antigua before 1655. After the collapse of the market for tobacco there, other crops such as ginger and indigo had been planted, with no great success; by this time it must have seemed that the only salvation for the still-minute population lay in a crop which was proving to be very profitable elsewhere. Although few men had the capital needed to purchase both the equipment and the workers sugar production required, those that did were soon buying slaves and opening up cane-fields. By the middle 1660s at least a few of Antigua's landowners were all set to take advantage of a land formation which lent itself to the creation of sizeable plantations, and to produce and export something for which there appeared to be an insatiable demand in Europe. However, no sooner had these planters, as we can now call them, started to produce than the Second Dutch War – a conflict between England and Holland – broke out in March 1665. When the French sided with the Dutch in the following January this ruined everything, and threatened to change the course of Antiguan history for ever.

By this time the French, like the English, had spread out from their original settlement (in what they chose to call Saint Christophe) and had colonised both Guadeloupe and Martinique, making the potential for warfare between the English and French islands just as great as between their mother countries. When Willoughby was informed at the end of 1665 that France was about to join Holland by honouring her treaty obligations he recognised the danger to the Leeward Islands, but could do little about it until the following April, when he mustered a scratch force of 600 militia in Barbados under the command of his nephew, Henry Willoughby, and despatched it to St Kitts in a homeward-bound merchant fleet. They arrived too late, to find the French in possession of the whole island and well prepared to fight to retain it. Henry Willoughby had no option but to withdraw, divide his troops between Nevis (where he himself remained) and Antigua, and allow the fleet to proceed on its way.

In July Lord Willoughby rounded up another thousand or so militiamen in Barbados and sailed north with eight ships, only to be caught in a hurricane off Guadeloupe. One or two of the ships managed to survive and struggle to Montserrat, but the remainder were wrecked and most of the troops – along with Willoughby – were never seen again. This disaster gave the French command of the sea and opened the way for them to capture the remaining English colonies, of which Nevis would be the main prize and Antigua the softest target.

Three months later they were ready to begin their campaign. With the Governor-in-Chief, Antoine Le Febvre de la Barre, in overall command, and with the governors of Martinique and Guadeloupe and about 900 troops embarked, a fleet of eight ships sailed from St Kitts for Antigua on 23 October 1666. Using information supplied by two Frenchmen who had been living on the island until earlier in the year, the fleet entered Five Islands Harbour on the west coast two days later. The defences there were rudimentary, and the small batteries which had been set up on either side of the entrance were quickly blown apart. One company of troops, having looted and burnt the few houses they came across after landing, were then led overnight by one of the informers to where the Governor's house was situated, overlooking St John's Harbour and the small group of buildings which represented the beginnings of the town of St John's. The spirited fight which then ensued ended when Colonel Robert Carden (who had relieved Bunckley as Governor in 1664) and most of the 150 men he had with him were taken prisoner; the house they had been defending was looted and destroyed. The victorious French then returned with their prisoners and plunder to Five Islands Harbour.

The next day more troops were landed and another attack launched on the embryo town of St John's. By now some 200 of Willoughby's Barbadian militia, under the command of a Lieutenant-Colonel Guest, had taken up a defensive position in the house and sugar-works belonging to Bastien Baijer, one of the island's wealthier planters, and it was necessary for this to be taken before anything else. The fight for Baijer's property (the site of which can no longer be identified) lasted rather longer than that of the previous day and cost the French fifty or sixty casualties, but ended in the same way. Guest was badly wounded early on, and once their ammunition began to run out the defenders were soon overpowered. Many were killed, while the rest – leaving Guest now mortally wounded – escaped as best they could. Retreating inland in great disorder, most of them 'haueing now no other place left for defence', eventually ended up at the house of Samuel Winthrop, another of the richer planters, just to the north of where the present-day airport terminal is situated. The French meanwhile destroyed all that they could not remove from Baijer's house and other properties in the vicinity before returning once again to their ships.

An ultimatum was sent ashore the next day, in which the French threatened that unless there was a complete surrender, 'we will distroy by fire the whole Iland & will not give quarter to any person.'[1] Two days later the Council, assuming responsibility in the enforced absence of Carden, and having discussed the alternatives, sent six representatives to sign the capitulation on board a ship in St John's Harbour. They had been influenced in their decision to give up the island by 'finding themselves not able to resist ye French & ye cruell Indian who lay burning and massacaring vpon ye windward while ye French were to leward.'[2] There is some evidence that the Caribs attacked in conjunction with the French, but they were always prepared to take advantage of any dispute between the white men who were gradually taking over their islands to carry out yet another raid on Antigua. In the end their depredations were made only less effective than those of the French because their *piraguas* could not carry away anywhere near as much spoil as the French ships.

Under the terms of the treaty signed at the beginning of November the inhabitants of Antigua either had to swear allegiance to the King of France or leave the island (for anywhere other than Nevis). Those that stayed would then have to pay an indemnity of 200 000 pounds of sugar and renounce any claim to possession of the whole of Barbuda. Carden was released in order to carry a warning to the colonists that unless these terms were generally accepted within ten days, punitive action offering no quarter would be taken against the entire population.

They were given rather more than ten days to consider their future as, having re-embarked and departed for Saint Christophe on 4 November, the French did not return for another three weeks. In the interim Henry Willoughby in Nevis, when informed of the invasion and capitulation, had sent a Colonel Daniel Fitch to take Carden's place and to prevent any acceptance of the terms of the treaty. His arrival with these orders caused considerable dissension. So much so that when the French troops returned, now under the command of M. de Clodoré, the Governor of Martinique, they found Carden and most of the population prepared to stick to the agreement which had been signed, but Fitch and the troops he had mustered – mostly belonging to the Barbadian militia – ready to fight. Any hope that the French might be deterred from landing because of the prospect of more fighting ended after an exchange of letters had taken place, with receipt of a missive from de Clodoré announcing:

> I am landing and coming to you, to teach you your duty by force of arms: those who will lay down their arms will have good quarter from me, and the others shall be treated according to the rigour of war.[3]

It all ended ignominiously for the colonists. Once they were ashore the French troops were met with a flag of truce, the bearer of which offered the island's surrender provided Fitch and his militiamen were included under the terms of the treaty. De Clodoré refused to consider this and marched northwards towards the area then known as Pope's Head (Crosbies and Hodges Bay today) to where Fitch and his men had retreated. What happened next was described in a letter sent by Samuel Winthrop to his brother some months later:

> Daniel Fitch . . . called ye people in armes & drew them vp against ye French; but seeing them to be stronger than he thought for, & seeing ye Indians fireing on ye other side, he ran away from ye companyes, gott into a little boat, & made his escape. When ye soldiers perceiued it, they faced about & fled also.[4]

As most of them ran in the direction of Winthrop's house and the French followed, de Clodoré soon found a suitable place to establish temporary headquarters. He 'possest himselfe of 24 of my slaues (ye rest escaped), & most of ye slaues in ye island' Winthrop complained to his brother before adding that he also 'destroyed most of my stock, his soldiers plundering ye country round about.' After everything of any use or value had been removed the property of anyone who refused to swear allegiance to the King of France was destroyed, as was that of anyone who had already fled the island. Looting and burning were accompanied by the rounding up of the island's slaves and the winkling out of the Barbadian troops from their hiding places; all ended a week after it had begun.

The return of de Clodoré and his men with their loot and captives to Saint Christophe did not mark the end of suffering for the Antiguan population as 'added to our afflictions were ye murthers & rapes wch ye Indians com'itted vpon ye inhabitants after ye French departed, haueing, as they said, liberty so to do for fiue days.'[5] Among those so murdered was the unfortunate Robert Carden, whose wife and children, like those of his earlier predecessor Warner, were taken away by the Caribs – and never seen or heard of again. The Caribs also very probably helped some of the planters' slaves to escape from the island, something they seem to have made a habit of doing on all their raids. The majority of those slaves not assisted in this way or seized by the French very sensibly made themselves scarce by disappearing into the undeveloped parts of the island, particularly the Shekerley Mountains. Some managed to hold out there for years, in spite of later determined attempts to recapture them, but most were probably forced to give themselves up through hunger, or caught when trying to steal supplies from the planters; not that there could have been very much left for anyone to eat or steal for some considerable time after the French and Caribs had left.

Even though Antigua was not occupied by the French it remained in danger of being so until the war ended with the Treaty of Breda in July 1667. During this period the islanders suffered great distress, receiving no assistance from the representatives of the sovereign to whom they had all, with the exception of a few Quakers,[6] sworn allegiance; nor any aid or support from Henry Willoughby, who had too many troubles of his own in Nevis to deal with, that island being under constant threat of invasion from Saint Christophe. Recovery after return to English rule was very slow, and made no easier by the lack of a resident governor and a functioning legislature. There was also a widespread feeling of dissatisfaction, in St Kitts, Nevis and Montserrat as well as Antigua, that the Governor-in-Chief in Barbados had not done enough for the Leeward Islands during the war. Petitions to London, which began to be forwarded as soon as peace returned, asking that these islands to be placed under a separate administration, were to bear fruit three years later.

In February 1668 Lord William Willoughby, who had inherited the title and been commissioned as Governor-in-Chief on the death of his brother Francis – and who was undoubtedly aware of the criticisms which had been levelled against him – found it prudent to visit Antigua. Appalled by what he saw of the results of the French depredation, and recognising the pressing need for leadership, he re-established the Council and summoned his son from Nevis to become the new governor.

On his arrival Henry Willoughby was faced with many problems, not least of which concerned the size of the popuation. Even before the French invasion there had not been enough people on the island to develop it properly; now there were even fewer. With many of their fellows having left, and with nearly all their slaves either carried off as booty or at liberty in the hills, subsistence farming was about all that the landowners who remained could manage. Among the complaints which were now addressed to the revived Legislature was one that the island could not progress because 'some Men will never setle their Land, but kiep it till land be growne scarce', and because there were 'great proportions of Land taken up by severall Persons & never settled': a complaint which resulted in the passing of an 'Act for the Encouraging and Promoting the Settling of this Island.'[7] This annulled all the land grants made before the French invasion, except for those made to owners who had taken possession and were now working the land, and promised that 'every labouring person brought hither shall be given 10 acres of good land to own & hand on to his heirs.' Samuel Winthrop was then appointed as registrar of all new land claims. Except for those people already resident, all such claims were limited to a maximum of 600 acres, with the proviso that for every ten acres taken up one labouring person, free or slave, had to be employed.

The act had wide appeal, attracting not just people from nearby islands who were not particularly well-off and able only to take up small amounts of land, but several very wealthy planters from Barbados who wanted as much land as they could get in order to create new sugar plantations. A few other equally rich men came from Surinam, the colony which had been set up by Lord Francis Willoughby in South America, but which had been ceded to the Dutch in the Treaty of Breda. Such men, like those from Barbados, also had the means to buy large numbers of slaves, who were easier to come by than the poor whites willing to become indentured servants. As a result, the size of the black population overtook that of the white in the mid-1670s, the number of slaves increasing from about 600 in 1672 to nearly 3000 six years later. Such a rapid increase, leading as it did to the dominance in Antiguan society of black people, could not take place without causing the white community some concern. Issues arose such as those concerning the loss of property occasioned by slaves running away, or the possibility of a slave rebellion, which were to continue to trouble the white population until slavery was abolished in 1834; one issue – sexual relations between the races – continued for many years after that. Early signs of these concerns may be seen in the contents of Acts passed in 1669 and 1672. The former, in an attempt to try and prevent slaves from escaping from the island, ordered the owners of boats to remove masts, sails, oars and rudders before leaving them unattended, while large vessels had to be guarded in port. The latter re-issued the earlier law prohibiting 'Carnall Coppullation' between whites and blacks, now specifying that the offspring of any such illicit activity would be enslaved for life.

Meanwhile, as the Antiguan planters were laying down the foundations of a slave-based society, the petitions they and their counterparts in other islands had sent to London at last achieved their effect. In January 1671, Charles II commissioned Sir Charles Wheler as Governor-in-Chief of 'St Christopher's, Montserrat, Antego, Barbuda, Anguilla, Nevis and the other Leeward Islands, which His Majesty thought fit to separate from the Government of Barbados.'[8] He established his headquarters in Nevis, and appointed a deputy or lieutenant-governor in each of the other islands (other than Barbuda, which was generally accepted as being a ward of Antigua and still at this time more or less deserted). Unfortunately he quickly fell foul of the inhabitants of St Kitts over arrangements made about their return from French rule, and was replaced in the following February by William Stapleton, formerly Lieutenant-Governor of Montserrat, and the man who would now oversee the development of the Leeward Islands for the next twelve years. While each island was to retain its own Council and Assembly, Stapleton was authorised to 'call General Assemblies of the Freeholders and Planters within every of the respective islands under your government in manner and form according to the custom and usage of our other Plantations.' Such an Assembly was called for the first time in 1674, meeting as a purely consultative body. Once it acquired legislative powers, which it did soon afterwards, it went out of favour in all the islands, fell into disuse after 1705, and was only called once more – in 1798 – before being abolished.

A body which was set up in London in 1675, a year after the General Assembly met for the first time, was of far more importance to the future of the islands, being established in order to exercise royal authority over them. Members of the Privy Council, called the Lords of the Committee of Trade and Plantations, were given wide-ranging powers over such matters as the appointment of governors, the issuing of instructions and royal proclamations, the granting of approval to parliamentary legislation, the hearing of colonial legal appeals, and the reviewing of all laws passed by colonial Assemblies. This last function was carried out with such great care that within a few years each island began to feel the need for a representative in London, to act on its behalf to get legislation approved. The Antigua Assembly led the way among the Leeward Islands, and in 1683 William Barnes became the first of the island's long line of colonial agents, occupying a post which was not abolished until 1851 (by which time such an agent had been made redundant by the development of the Crown Colony system and the creation of the Crown Agents).

•

The man appointed under Stapleton as Lieutenant-Governor of Antigua was Philip Warner, another of Thomas Warner's sons; he had inherited his brother Edward's estate to the east of Falmouth Harbour and married the only daughter of Henry Ashton. He is remembered today mainly for the drastic action he took to curb the Carib attacks which continued to be made on the island. In November 1674 Stapleton was informed in Nevis that the Caribs of Dominica were preparing yet another raid on Antigua, but received the news too late to be able to alert the island before it took place. As a result he afterwards authorised Warner to carry out a retaliatory attack on Dominica, to take revenge 'on those heathens for their bloody and perfidious villainies'. This expedition, consisting of perhaps 100–150 armed men in several small sloops, set off early in 1675, led by Warner himself. Details of the subsequent killing of more than 80 Caribs, in or near the village which today is called Massacre on the west coast of Dominica, are scanty and conflicting. This is especially so with regard to how their leader Thomas 'Indian' Warner, the son of a Carib woman sired by the Governor of St Kitts, met his end. At some point in the proceedings, whether as part of a plan, an incident in a drunken brawl, or because he resented their kinship, Philip Warner is supposed to have stabbed his half-brother to death.

While this action did not put an end to Carib raids, as was shown in Barbuda six years later, it certainly lessened the frequency and severity of their attacks on Antigua. After it had taken place Warner and his men returned home well pleased with themselves. Regrettably, as far as Warner was concerned, other people were not so pleased. The Governor of Barbados, who considered Dominica to be within his sphere of interest, had not been informed about the expedition. As he had been depending on 'Indian' Warner to help persuade the Caribs to allow an English settlement on the island, he was only too ready to accept the story of the master of one of the expedition's sloops that Philip Warner had murdered his half-brother in cold blood. When this version of events was reported to London Warner was summoned there, charged with murder, and put in the Tower of London. Fortunately for him, before he could suffer the same fate as his father-in-law, it was decided to send him back to the Caribbean to stand trial: an event which took place in Barbados and resulted in his acquittal. In spite of petitioning the King, he was not afterwards allowed to resume his duties as Lieutenant-Governor; the post went instead to another planter, Rowland Williams, reputedly the first white man to have been born in Antigua. This move did not meet with the approval of the other planters and, as some sort of compensation, they elected Warner as Speaker of the House of Assembly.

Having – it was hoped – dealt with the Carib problem, the Assembly now turned its attention to matters closer to home. By this time the great influx of slaves, which went with the clearance of more and more land for the planting of sugar-cane, was beginning to be seen as a possible threat. In an attempt to maintain what was thought to be a reasonable ratio between blacks and whites an act was passed in 1677, stating that in future every slaveowner had to employ one white servant for every ten of his slaves.

At the time, such servants fell into one of three categories: young free men and women from poor backgrounds, offenders given the option of prison or becoming indentured, or political prisoners sent out to the West Indies as slaves in all but name. Most belonged to the first category, and men were in the majority. Not too many employers wanted women who, if they became pregnant, had to be given time off for childbirth and rearing. Those that did made it a condition that female servants, who were normally employed as domestics and not as fieldhands, could not marry without consent. Servants under sixteen years of age had to serve for seven years, those between sixteen and twenty for five, and those over twenty for four years. All were fed, clothed and accommodated during their service, and each received £10 worth of sugar on completion of his or her indentureship. The shippers of such servants were paid in amounts of sugar: 1700 pounds for anyone under sixteen, otherwise 2000 pounds.

That these figures – all from an act passed in Antigua in 1679 – are quoted in terms of sugar is because for most of the seventeenth century this commodity was the normal currency in the Leeward Islands. Very little money was in circulation and everything, from salaries to fines, was reckoned and paid in sugar. When both tobacco and sugar were being grown they were considered to be equal in value, but by the 1670s sugar predominated and had become the regular medium of exchange, being passed from hand to hand in settlement of claims. For most of a twenty-year period after 1654 such exchanges were made through certificates issued from a public storehouse set up:

> For the propagation of Trade Ease of the [merchants] and ready payment of the Planters. Who Havering His Storehouse Notes can Passe them in all places of the Island like ready money.[9]

It was an excellent institution but, the society of the time being what it was, the general dishonesty of the storehouse keepers brought about its closure in 1675. From then on, until money became more readily available, trade took place by barter.

Regardless of whether white servants were to receive sugar or cash, or even land, when their indentures expired, they could never be obtained in the numbers needed to maintain the one-to-ten ratio, and few of the planters made more than a nominal effort to obey the law. White men were not suited to the hard physical life of a tropical plantation; servants by no means all came from rural backgrounds, and even those who did were totally unsuited by experience or temperament for the gruelling, monastic existence expected of them. African slaves, on the other hand, besides being cheaper (provided, that is, they did not live long enough to become too old or feeble to work – something many of the early planters made sure never happened by literally working them to death), were much better able to adjust to the diet and housing they were given, and to the work they were required to carry out. The production of sugar was labour intensive, and any planter intending to become rich not only needed a large area of land but a large and disciplined workforce to go with it. White servants were never going to provide the numbers required nor submit to the regimen. Slaves could and did, and that was all that really mattered to the large-scale planters who, by the last quarter of the seventeenth century, were the leaders of Antiguan society; and one family among them was soon to dominate all the rest.

In 1668 Lord William Willoughby, while he still retained authority over the Leeward Islands, gave the title to a large estate in Antigua to a young man from Barbados. The estate, in the eastern part of the island, was in the most fertile zone where the central plain abutted the northern uplands; it was called Betty's Hope, and the new owner, Christopher Codrington, was the elder son of another Christopher Codrington – a rich sugar planter who had emigrated to Barbados from England in 1649. The fact that Betty's Hope was at the time the property of the Keynell family was ignored (Keynell, after all, had been a Parliamentarian and his title to the land had become void under what may be thought of as the Reconstruction Act of 1668).[10]

Codrington arrived in Antigua to take over his new property in 1674. Although he is popularly credited with the establishment of sugar in the island from this date, this is far from the case. Sugar was already being grown successfully by men like Warner, Baijer, Winthrop and Byam, but only on a scale which someone like Codrington, fresh from an island where sugar production flourished, would have considered derisory. His aggressive attitude towards plantation management, combined with his introduction of Barbadian production methods, soon inspired other planters to follow his lead, and his arrival in Antigua must be seen as a major turning point in the island's development.

5

The Codrington Years

Everyone that is able is working upon sugar, which is a certaine gaine.

Christopher Codrington (1675)

We are the more Sensible of the expediency of a Law for restraining inhumane Severity not only towards Christian Servants but Slaves, which you are directed . . . to endeavour to procure.

Letter to Governor Codrington
from the Board of Trade (1702)

At the beginning of the last quarter of the seventeenth century the total white population of Antigua's 550 or so registered households numbered about 2300, with twice as many men as women. Some lived in the six small communities of Falmouth, St John's, Carlisle Road [Old Road], Parham, Bridgetown and Bermudian Valley which had been designated as official trading places, with more resident in Falmouth than in any of the others. Falmouth itself was hardly more than a small village, while none of the others could have consisted of more than a few dwellings and storehouses around a landing place. Bridgetown, on the north-east side of Willoughby Bay, never developed into anything very much, and had ceased to be of any significance long before it was finally abandoned in the nineteenth century. The landing place on Picarts Bay in the south-west, which took its name from Bermudian Valley (now called Orange Valley) behind it, never developed at all. The remainder of the population were scattered around the island, living on plantations ranging in size from just a few acres to – as in the case of Betty's Hope – over 700 acres, nearly all on or close to the coast. Although most of the buildings they lived in, whether in town or country, were according to a report by Stapleton in 1676 'of ordinary timber, covered with thatch, very few shingled', this was already changing: in 1690, after a severe earthquake had shaken all the Leeward Islands, the *London Gazette* reported that Antigua had suffered the greatest losses because most of its buildings, unlike those in the other islands, were built of stone.

The various communities were joined by a few narrow roads, with those through the interior still running through uncleared woodland, but it was probably still easier and quicker to sail rather than to ride or walk from, say, Falmouth to St John's. The smaller, poorer landowners, if they were not just raising provisions, grew cash crops such as indigo, cotton, ginger or tobacco. The better-off, with more land available, had already moved away from these crops and were planting, or preparing to plant, sugar-cane – for which they needed the labour of the island's constantly increasing slave population. Less than half the householders possessed slaves, but among those that did there were some who owned dozens and one or two, like Christopher Codrington and Philip Warner, with over a hundred.

Slaves were obtained from the Royal African Company which, having replaced the Royal Adventurers in 1672, had been given the monopoly of supplying all the British colonies. The price was fixed at £16 a head provided delivery was contracted for in London, otherwise slaves were sold at the best price obtainable. In the first fourteen years after it was set up the Company brought some 8000 slaves to the Leeward Islands. Nearly all of them were sold through from a depot established in Nevis, much to the annoyance of the Antigua Assembly which complained that this was

> very prejudicial to his Majesty's subjects the inhabitants of this Island, in regard this is the Windermost of his Majesty's Islands, so that the Negroes that are brought to Nevis are sold and disposed of, before any notice can be given us.[1]

In spite of this disadvantage, and the fact that during the same fourteen-year period only one shipment by the Company was made direct to Antigua, the island's planters seem to have had little trouble in obtaining all the slaves they wanted. The black population doubled during the 1680s, reaching 6000 at the end of the decade, by which time the Royal African Company's monopoly had disintegrated under pressure from independent traders willing to bring shipments of slaves to wherever there was a market. From then on, while there were occasional shortages, especially in wartime, more Antiguan planters probably suffered from lack of the means to buy than from any scarcity of slaves for sale.

While the Royal African Company still enjoyed its monopoly the slaves it carried were all obtained through forts maintained at various places along the West African coast between Cape Coast and Accra, and nearly all belonged to one or other of the two largest ethnic groups, the Fanti and the Asante. After the monopoly had ended Antiguan planters continued for many years to prefer slaves from the same Gold Coast origin, claiming that 'Coromantees' were both hard-working and tractable, but the traders of later years took their cargoes from wherever they could on the western side of Africa. As a result it is impossible to say with any certainty where the majority of all those who ended up in the island originated.

The ratio between the sexes is better established and it is known that about one-third of all slaves brought to Antigua – as to the rest of the colonies – in the seventeenth century were female. As a result, the Antiguan planter who needed labour, even if he did not particularly want women (for the same reason he did not want female white servants), had little option but to buy them. There were compensations, however, both for the planter and his male slaves. For the planter, females were generally cheaper to buy, could do much the same work as men, and any child a woman might have – if it survived – only added to his assets. For the male slaves, the mere fact of having access to even a limited number of women meant that they were not totally deprived of all creature comforts along with their liberty. Only for the unfortunate female slaves themselves was there no alleviation, subject as they became to the sexual attentions of their owners as well as the male inhabitants of the slave quarters, being forced to add virtual prostitution by night to their labours by day.

The long, hard, backbreaking labour of men and women alike, in conjunction with close supervision and careful timing, was required for every aspect of sugar production. The operation of a sugar plantation, which was still being worked out in Antigua in the 1660s, was soon perfected once Codrington had moved to Betty's Hope. Sugar-cane takes from fourteen to eighteen months to ripen, and planting had to be staggered so that it could be harvested over a period of several months. Account had to be taken of the climate, to ensure that planting took place during the months from June to November, when rain was most likely, and to produce full-grown cane which could be harvested during the driest months of January to May, when the sugar content was at its maximum. It was soon found that dividing a plantation into 'pieces', all of a similar size, and then planted to mature at intervals produced the best results. As each piece was cleared cuttings from old cane, each about two feet in length, were planted in holes about three feet square and one foot deep, under a mixture of soil and manure. A field gang of about thirty slaves could plant about two acres a day in this manner, and provided the entire operation was completed between October and December of one year – and given the right weather conditions in between – a harvest could be reaped starting in January two years later. In between each piece had to be constantly weeded and fertilised, using animal dung and cane trash, and as far as possible kept free of vermin. Manuring, which involved carrying baskets weighing up to 80 pounds when full on their heads, was for obvious reasons the most detested task. Harvesting was just as laborious as planting and weeding. The cane was cut with bill-hooks, stripped of its leaves – the 'trash' – before being made up into large bundles, and then carted to the mill. The trash was collected later, either to be dried and used as fuel, or carried to cattle pens for use as litter (later to be returned to the fields as part of the manure).

To begin with all sugar-mills were driven by oxen, and even though wind-driven versions based on the standard European model began to be built around

1690 animal-powered mills did not disappear completely for another hundred years. The cattle-mill consisted of an arrangement of three vertical rollers through which the cane was passed twice to extract the maximum amount of juice, which was then piped to an adjacent building where it was boiled, clarified and evaporated to produce crystallised sugar. This work required far fewer hands than in the fields, but was just as hard. In addition, because of the heat and the nature of the various operations required, it was dangerous. The juice was boiled in a series of different-sized copper kettles, being skimmed of its impurities before each transfer between them until, in the smallest and hottest of them all, it turned into a thick, dark brown sludge. This then had to be 'tempered' with lime to promote granulation.

All of these operations were carried out under the supervision of a skilled 'boiler', the man responsible for judging when the contents of the final kettle were on the point of crystallising, and ordering the 'strike'. Once this had been called the contents were rapidly ladled into a cistern, cooled, and then packed into earthenware pots to be cured in a heated drying shed. After two days each pot had to be unplugged in order to drain off the accumulated molasses, and after a month emptied completely. The top and bottom of each hard block of golden-brown muscovado sugar was cut off and re-boiled, while the remainder – having been spread out in the sun for a while – was packed into huge barrels called hogsheads. As each of these held a nominal 1000 pounds of sugar their storage, handling, cartage and eventual shipment for export all combined to add one more punishing, hernia-inducing aspect to the life of the plantation slave.

Every stage of these operations, from preparing the pieces for planting to the shipping of the final product – if sugar production was to be profitable – required close and constant supervision; and in the early days profits must have varied greatly as this aspect of plantation slavery was being worked out. The use of servants and slaves working side by side in the fields was not something that lasted longer than it took for the latter to be shown by the former what they had to do and to glean enough English to be able to understand orders. The slaves' mastering of the work required of them was accompanied by the servants' almost automatic adoption of lighter supervisory duties with an accompanying elevation in status. It is difficult to believe that on any plantation, once enough slaves had been trained, that any white man of whatever class or background was ever again employed on the same sort of work and under the same conditions as the slaves. Racial sentiment became an ingrained part of plantation life long before the close of the seventeenth century, and provided the basis for the fears and the accepted privileges which were to keep the white population of Antigua united for the next 200 years or more.

•

As well as now living in a racially divided society, the population of late seventeenth-century Antigua also lived in a fairly godless one. Although a Church of England clergyman had arrived within a couple of years of the first settlement he appears not to have stayed for very long, and certainly no provision for any church to be built was made before 1671. Such a building was erected at Falmouth the following year, being finished at much the same time as Wheler, during his brief term of office as Governor-in-Chief, complained to the Privy Council that although there were by then over 10 000 supposedly Christian inhabitants under his care in the Leeward Islands, there were only two ministers in Holy Orders, 'both scandalous livers, and one a notable schismatic'. Which, if either, of this pair lived in Antigua is not recorded, but in 1676 Wheler's successor Stapleton reported:

> There is but one [c]hurch, and that at Falmouth, which serves also for a Court House. No register of births, deaths or marriages are kept, there being no Ministers and no Churches.

This was a sad reflection on a society in which, in the absence of any other authority, the Assembly controlled ecclesiastical affairs and the Governor had power to license clergymen, and was only marginally improved the next year when the Bishop of London sent six ministers to the Leeward Islands. Two of these, named Jones and Lambert, took up residence in Antigua. Jones eventually managed to persuade the Assembly to build a church in St John's of which he became the rector in 1683, two years after the island had been divided into five parishes. His stipend was 16 000 pounds of sugar a year. Lambert went to Falmouth, with the same stipend and a strong urge to persecute the island's few Quakers – subsequently his only known claim to fame. The Bishop of London took no further interest in the religious affairs of the far-off appendages his diocese had been landed with, and it was well into the next century before religion played anything but a nominal – and often quite un-Christian – part in the life of Antigua's white community.

As for the slaves, once Lambert and later Jones's successor, the Reverend James Field, had begun to victimise the Quakers, there was no one much interested in their moral or spiritual welfare before the Society for the Propagation of the Gospel in Foreign Parts (the SPG) was founded in 1701. Even then it was a very tepid kind of interest, and a genuine, wholehearted desire to bring Christianity to the slaves had to wait until the first Moravian missionaries arrived over fifty years later.

•

Given the conditions under which the slaves were forced to live and work it is hardly surprising that they put up some resistance from the very beginning. During the troubled times caused by the French and Caribs in 1666, many took the opportunity to take to the hills, or to escape from the island with the aid of the Caribs, if they could. Even if most of those who fled into the Shekerley Mountains at this time either had to surrender, or were killed or recaptured, the region offered a chance of freedom of a sort to runaways for many years afterwards. Running away was relatively easy when much of the island remained undeveloped and under-populated, and soon became so much of a problem that the Assembly was forced to pass an act for 'Restrayneing such Runnawayes' in 1680. Under its provisions rewards were offered for their recovery, and penalties laid down for varying lengths of absence. Anything under a month was treated as a misdemeanour and dealt with accordingly, with flogging, confinement or some other punishment devised at the whim of the aggrieved master. A longer period at large was a felony which could carry the death penalty, depending on what the absconder had got up to while free or other circumstances. Any slave who was caught after being on the run for over three months faced immediate execution, as he (or much less frequently, she) was generally considered to have made a conscious decision to live a life in the wild, completely divorced from anything to do with society, and become a maroon.

The only part of the island where maroons could hope to survive was in the south-west and gradually, in spite of all the inducements offered for their capture, a sizeable community began to form in the Shekerley Mountains. The Legislature's appointment of bounty hunters in 1684, with rewards of 500 pounds of sugar for each maroon taken alive, and 200 pounds for any killed, made little difference. Three years later, according to the nervous owners of the surrounding plantations, such fugitives were coming out of the hills 'to Excite and stir up the Negroes to forsake their masters, and . . . to make them selves masters of the Country.' In February 1687, with the Council having now decided that there was evidence of a plot among the maroons to incite the slaves to 'force their freedom by Destroying their Masters, and other Christian people', the Governor ordered an investigation to be carried out. At the same time, having increased the bounties to 1000 and 600 pounds of sugar, several parties of militia 'Well fitted with Arms and Ammunition' were ordered into the field 'in psuite of the runn away Negroes that are gathered Together Toward the Mountains on the South Seide . . . and them to follow and psue to Death In Case they cannot bee Taken alive.'[2]

A month later they found and attacked a fortified encampment of about twenty dwellings. While only a few of the inhabitants were killed, and none of the others captured, this did have significant longer term effects. The maroons could no longer consider living in any sort of permanent community, and were forced into a much less settled existence, their raids on the surrounding plantations increasing as a result. This in turn had the effect of bringing some of the plantation slaves under suspicion as possible supporters of a plot to revolt.

Such a plot was all very much in the minds of the planters only but, given the way of these things, evidence of something untoward had to be found somewhere, and after a cursory investigation it was a slave named George, from an estate near Falmouth, who was brought to trial in order to provide it. Based on the flimsiest of evidence he was judged to have been involved in something which, even if it was not a plot, was serious enough to warrant his being made an example of, and he was condemned to be 'burned to ashes'. Nothing much could be found to incriminate anyone else, but two suspects ended up in confinement while poor Philip, a slave belonging to Sir Nathaniel Johnson (who had bought an estate in Antigua as soon as he had taken over as Governor-in-Chief in 1686), was sentenced to have 'one of his legs . . . Cutt off, and that if the governor should afterwards see Cause he should Cause his Toung to be cutt out and that hee might remaine as a Living Example to ye rest.'

At the time George, Philip and the others were being tried it was believed there were at least twenty-seven runaways, ten of them women, living as maroons in the mountains, some having been there for three years or more. During the next twelve months some of them were caught, while regular patrols made the lives of the rest increasingly difficult. The number of runaways committing a felony as opposed to a misdemeanour soon decreased and, while a few still considered life as a maroon preferable to the rigours of the plantation, the prospect of their inciting any kind of rebellion decreased at the same rate. Within another year or two maroons were no longer seen as a threat but more as a nuisance: something they remained until the last were found and executed in 1723.

•

Sir Nathaniel Johnson, who had been appointed by King James II to relieve Stapleton as Governor of the Leeward Islands in 1684, transferred his seat of government to Antigua from Nevis four years later. Ignoring the fact that he owned a large plantation there, he used as his reason for the move the not totally convincing argument – given the relative sizes of their populations and economies – that Antigua now paid the greater amount of customs duty into the royal exchequer. Although an ardent Protestant himself, he acknowledged his debt to the Catholic monarch who had appointed him by carrying out the King's pro-Catholic and pro-French policies to the best of his ability. In doing so it seems far more likely that his departure for Antigua was prompted by the distress these policies caused in Nevis, so close to the waft of Popery and the threat of invasion from Saint Christophe. The transfer did not do him a great deal of good, as within a year James had been replaced by the Protestants, William III and Mary; something with which Johnson could not come to terms, feeling his loyalty still lay with the King to whom he had sworn allegiance. A renewal of fighting between England and France followed the Glorious Revolution, in what could be termed the 'War of the British Succession', but is better known as King William's War. This naturally involved the West Indian colonies and, after six months of confusion during which the French once again took control of the whole of St Kitts, Johnson was forced to resign. Before leaving Antigua he nominated as his successor the man who by this time, as well as being the wealthiest of the island's planters, also owned or controlled more land, and possessed a larger number of slaves, than anyone else – Christopher Codrington.

During the fifteen years since his arrival on the island Codrington had played a leading part in bringing about the rapid domination of its economy by sugar, while ensuring his and his family's wealth and status improved at the same rate. As well as starting the acquisition of the other five estates the family would own in addition to Betty's Hope by 1740, he and his brother John negotiated a fifty-year lease of the entire island of Barbuda for a peppercorn rent. A number of attempts had been made to settle this island since the 1620s but none had met with any lasting success, mainly because of the depredations of the Caribs, whose raids included one in 1681, four years before the Codringtons had taken over, when over 200 warriors had landed and killed eight of the twenty people they found living there. In 1689, when Johnson was forced out of office, there could have been few men in any of the Leeward islands better qualified than Christopher Codrington in terms of wealth, influence and administrative ability – before moving to Antigua he had been deputy governor of Barbados for several years – to take his place, and his appointment received royal approval well before the end of the year.

It was hardly a propitious time to take over, with St Kitts already in enemy hands, the Irish settlers in Montserrat threatening to rebel, and the people of Nevis daily expecting a French invasion, but Codrington quickly seized the initiative. The Irish threat was dealt with by disarming and deportation, soldiers were requested from Barbados to stiffen the resolve of the Nevisians, and in May 1690 he took advantage of the arrival of a naval squadron carrying 700 troops from England to plan an attack on St Kitts. Using these troops, together with those from Barbados and others raised in Antigua, Nevis and Montserrat, the island was invaded the following month. Within three weeks the French had surrendered and the whole island was in British hands, where it remained for the next seven years. In his leadership of the invasion Codrington proved that his military prowess matched his administrative ability; in the restructuring of St Kitts which followed he showed, in his seizure of a large former French plantation and its attendant slaves, that it was also equalled by his rapaciousness. For the next seven years, until the island was once again divided under the terms of the treaty which ended King William's War in 1697, the profits from this property were added to those he drew from similar plantations in Barbados and Antigua, and to the revenue produced by his virtual ownership of Barbuda.

Since he and his brother had been given their lease Barbuda had been settled and developed as an adjunct to the Codrington plantations in Antigua. A fortified house had been built around a well about halfway along the eastern shore of the lagoon, which could only be reached after a lengthy trek overland, or by sea via the narrow channel through the lagoon's northern end, and so was removed from the danger of a surprise attack. Apart from this, which together with the surrounding slave quarters and a few other buildings represented the foundation of the future village of Codrington, the remainder of the island was still wild. The cattle, horses, sheep and other animals which had been introduced, other than those required for breeding purposes, were allowed to run free. The slaves, working under a resident overseer and one or two assistants, were able to supply Betty's Hope and Codrington's other Antigua properties with draught animals, fresh meat, leather and ground provisions, as well as fish and turtles. But this was not all that was derived from the island.

It had been realised by others long before the Codringtons' lease was granted that Barbuda was totally unfitted for development as a sugar-producing island, and only suitable for the raising of livestock and ground provisions – neither of which promised any great return on the capital and effort needed to provide and maintain the appropriate labour force. What the Codringtons saw, however, that others did not (and perhaps Christopher more than his brother, a shadowy figure about whom little is known), was that the island possessed the equivalent of a goldmine; the exploitation of which required little capital investment and no extra workforce. This came about through a special set of natural circumstances: the island's low-lying topography, its abundance of shallow coral reefs off the north and east coasts, and its geographical position as the most north-easterly of all the Caribbean islands. Ever since Europeans had first entered the Caribbean, this combination had made Barbuda a potential hazard for shipping, and especially for any vessel making a landfall after crossing the Atlantic. The potential goldmine lay in such disasters and the money which could be obtained from salvage operations. All that was needed was a team of salvors and a boat, plus – of course – the right to carry out such operations. For the Codringtons it was easy; the island's slaves would be there to do the work when needed, boats were already available for fishing and communicating with Antigua, and as they were leasing the whole island who else could be given the 'Right to Wreck'? Accordingly, in the original grant of 1685, the lessees were given the sole rights of 'Flotsam and Jetsam, and Wrecks which shall be found within the low water mark of the said Island.' This innocuous-sounding clause had begun to pay off straight away when, in the same year, a Spanish ship, *Santiago de Cullerin*, ran aground on what from then on was known as Spanish Point in the south-east of the island. In so doing she became the first of over 100 such losses which took place between then and when the Codrington family's lease was terminated nearly 200 years later. Ships ran aground at a rate which was unaffected by war or peace, although numbers decreased after an accurate means of determining longitude had been found in the latter half of the eighteenth century. In spite of this, making a precise landfall after a passage of 3–4000 miles remained far from easy, and ships continued to be wrecked on Barbuda long after the Codringtons had ceased to profit from such events.

The reputation of Christopher Codrington was very much affected by the fact that nearly the whole of his period as Governor of Leeward Islands – he died in July 1698, only nine months after the end of King William's War – was in wartime. His military and administrative abilities were hardly in doubt, and had he received better support from the Navy and from among the leading inhabitants of the islands he might well have achieved more against the French than he did. Unfortunately, the manner in which he conducted his public life was not matched by the way in which he led his private life.

Before leaving Barbados in 1674 he and his brother had been notorious for the scope of their illegal trading – buying slaves from any source in contravention of the Royal African Company's monopoly, and blatantly ignoring the Navigation Acts in order to increase their profits. By this time there were three such acts in force. The first, specifying that all trade had to be carried out by English ships, had been renewed in 1660. The Staple Act, passed three years later, prohibited anything from being shipped from Europe to the West Indies without first passing through, and incurring customs duty at, an English port. The third, passed in 1673, imposed 'plantation duty', payable at source, on sugar and other produce being shipped from the West Indies to anywhere other than England. All three were greatly resented in all the colonies, nowhere more so than in Antigua and, if the Codringtons' actions were anything to go by, in Barbados.

With regard to protecting and profiting from his investments, once he was established in Antigua Christopher Codrington continued to behave much as he had in Barbados. His rapacity, combined with his licentiousness at Betty's Hope – where he sired a number of children by different slave women – probably incited no more than jealousy among his fellow planters, most of whom were prepared to trade illegally if they could and were busy producing their own illegitimate offspring. What they did find hard to take, particularly after he became Governor, was his overbearing manner – something which soon led to his being referred to as 'Divus Augustus' or the 'high and mighty sultan'.

Towards the end of the war, and largely because of the imperious way in which he dealt with a lawsuit brought by one planter against another, he was exposed not only as having continued to contravene the Navigation Acts since becoming Governor, but as having traded on occasion with the French under flags of truce. His activities then came under the scrutiny of the Board of Trade and Plantations (the body which had replaced the Lords of the Committee of Trade and Plantations in 1696).[3] The Board's investigation determined that Codrington had carried out acts of oppression, amounting almost to tyranny, in order to try and prevent any hint of his illegal activities reaching London, and that nothing could excuse him 'for omitting to do many things which his duty required of him'. Altogether it was a damning indictment, but fortunately for his family he died before any action could be taken and their future was not affected. So much so that in May 1699 his eldest son, then aged thirty and yet another Christopher, was appointed to succeed him as Governor.

•

The new Governor, who had been educated in England, was far more cultured and less of a libertine than his father, and surprisingly enlightened for his day and age in admitting soon after his appointment that he had long 'thought it very barbarous that so little care should be taken of the bodies and so much of the souls of our poor slaves.' He was perhaps rather too sensitive an individual for the post he took up in September 1700, and it can have been of little consolation to him that the amount of corruption he found in the public life of Antigua was largely a legacy from his father. 'The dissorder in our Trade is so great', he reported to the Board of Trade the following year,

> yet I almost depair of doing any good in it, there is so much ignorance, laziness or Corruption in Naval and Customhouse officers, and so generall a Conspiracy in People of all ranks and qualitys here to elude ye Acts of Trade, yet I have ye Mortification of Knowing a hundred things are done every day (which I cannot possibly prevent) prejudicial to ye trade and interest of England.[4]

The reason for this, together with other difficulties he experienced in trying to administer the island, stemmed mainly from developments which had taken place since the Restoration in the way Antigua and the other islands were governed.

A royally appointed governor in 1660 had been given full executive, judicial and legislative authority in his colony. He could call and dissolve the elected Assembly at will, veto any legislation, and was responsible for selecting the men who, as members of the Council, formed his executive advisory group. By the time the younger Codrington took over in Antigua, the Council consisted of prominent citizens who, although they had been nominated by his father and previous governors, had not only been appointed by the Board of Trade but had been appointed for life. Because of this, over time, the Council had acquired a right to assist and, if necessary, check the powers of the Governor in the exercise of his authority. Decisions concerning matters such as land grants, the appointment of judges, the hearing of legal appeals, and the disbursement of public money could no longer be taken by the Governor in isolation, but only in conjunction with the Council. In addition he now also had to accept that the Assembly not only had prime responsibility for legislation and local taxation, but had a considerable say in concerns such as public accounts and expenditure, the salaries and fees of royal officials, and in the filling of a whole range of colonial offices. In a small society such as the one Codrington encountered in Antigua in 1700, this gave the planters and merchants who dominated both the Council and the Assembly control of virtually every aspect of life on the island, encouraging the corruption about which he was in 'depair of doing any good'. Because of this, after hinting several times that he wished to be relieved, he made a formal request to retire in 1702, only to have its acceptance postponed by the outbreak of another war between England and France. Before being replaced two years later, in addition to taking an active (and as far as the history of Antigua is concerned irrelevant) part in the West Indian aspects of the War of the Spanish Succession, Codrington oversaw a number of changes affecting the lives of both the free and slave inhabitants of the island. During the same period he quickly lost any vestige of the unworldliness he had brought with him from England, and in the end proved to be almost as authoritarian and grasping as his father had been.

In the year he became Governor, as the number of slaves in the island approached 10 000, another attempt was made to increase the white population from a figure which remained stubbornly less than 3000. An act was passed to enable private land which had not been developed, and on which no taxes had been paid, to be seized by the Crown and divided up into ten-acre lots. These were then made available to discharged servants or soldiers, or other poor people, in the hope that – with a handout of £3, a few provisions, and exemption from taxation – this would encourage the formation of a body of peasant farmers. The scheme got off to a reasonable start but was not a long-term success. Farming even ten acres was more than one man, or one family, could achieve without assistance. Ex-servants and ex-soldiers were hardly in a position to hire their own servants, and for them to have bought slaves – even if they could have afforded them – would clearly have defeated the object of the exercise. Even though, as a result, the creation of a 'buffer' class of small-scale farmers was never achieved, and many of the grants later reverted to the Crown or were incorporated into adjoining plantations, at the beginning of the eighteenth century every 'ten-acre man' was welcomed both for his addition to the white population and for the contribution he could make to the defence of the island.

•

How Antigua could best be defended had exercised the minds of successive governors and the Legislature since the earliest days. During the first three decades of the settlement, with such a small population, little could be done other than to insist that all able-bodied men maintained arms and made themselves available to respond to any threat, be it from Caribs, privateers or enemy troops. The events of 1666 had shown up the island's vulnerability to attack by even a modest military force, but it was not until many years after this that the administration was in a position to begin to take proper measures to prevent a repeat. To deter an invader coastal fortifications were needed, but with so many bays and harbours to protect the cost, even if the manpower had been available to carry out the work, was prohibitive. The uselessness of a few light field-guns stuck here and there around the coast having been demonstrated all too clearly by the French incursion into Five Islands Harbour twelve years earlier, there was little alternative to the suggestion made by the Council in 1678 that, away from the coast, 'some secure plot of land be fortified for the preservation of women, children and important persons', which could then be held until outside help arrived to drive away the invading forces.

The flat-topped Monks Hill which overlooked Falmouth, then still the main town, offered the most suitable site and the construction of a large fortified refuge began there a year or two later. Because of the lack of manpower – the planters proving most unwilling to provide the slave labour needed – and the cost involved, work progressed very slowly and was not completed until 1713. While this was going on, other means of defence were not totally ignored. As the island developed under the Codringtons, father and son, and more money and labour gradually became available, about twenty forts of one kind or another were built along the coastline. Some, like those erected to guard the harbours of Falmouth and St John's, were reasonably substantial and well-armed, but most were little more than one or two cannons and a small powder magazine behind a low stone wall. Once the inland refuge was completed and given the name Fort George these shore batteries were only intended to delay an invasion force long enough to enable all those who needed or wanted to seek the safety it afforded to make their way to Monks Hill.

Cannons and forts without troops were however purely ornamental, and an act passed in 1680 'for ensuring a better martial discipline throughout the island' established a militia from among the indentured servants. When King William's War began nine years later the Legislature, fearing another French invasion and recognising that such compulsory service was highly unpopular, rushed to announce a string of benefits which would accrue to those valiant, wounded or killed in defence of the island, including freedom from indenture for anyone who 'shewed deeds of valour', an annual award of 3000 pounds of sugar for life for anyone disabled, and state support for life for any widows or children.

Whether any of these awards would ever have been granted is open to question, and such provisions were not included when the militia was reorganised in 1702. Under the act passed in that year all white males between the ages of fourteen and sixty-five were required to register and to turn out for one day each month to exercise either as infantrymen or as a type of mounted infantryman called a carbineer. A scale of fines was laid down for absence and various other offences, and all were required to take part in an annual parade. The planters, merchants, professional men and anyone else with any pretension to a position in society refused to consider joining the rank and file and demanded officer status. The plethora of military titles which ensued, while continuing a tradition of fairly bogus captaincies and colonelcies stretching back to Edward Warner's day, and adding to the self-esteem of the recipients, did little for the militia as a whole except to subject it to the ridicule of the professional soldiers who had arrived to garrison the island a year earlier.

In anticipation of the start of the War of the Spanish Succession, both England and France had built up their naval and military forces in the Caribbean during 1701. The first four regiments ever to be sent to provide garrisons for the English colonies were brought to the West Indies in a fleet under Vice-Admiral John Benbow in November, and by the end of the year one of these, Tiffin's Regiment, had arrived in Antigua.[5] While it must have been comforting for Codrington and the planters to know that London was at last taking more interest in the island's security, and a great relief for the 500 or more men of the regiment to get ashore after several months of being cooped up in Benbow's ships, any euphoria this produced soon disappeared.

At this time in the history of the British Army, forty years after its accepted date of origin in 1661, proper support services hardly existed, and even such basic needs as barracks and medical comforts were unknown. Once a regiment had left the British Isles it was more or less obliged to fend for itself, trusting that the money needed for its pay, accommodation and other needs would be forthcoming from London. Tiffin's Regiment (which changed its name in August 1702 when Colonel Tiffin died and Colonel Thomas Whetham assumed command) remained in Antigua for five years, other than when taking part in an abortive invasion of Guadeloupe led by Codrington in 1703. For nearly three of these years neither the officers nor the men received any pay, and had to depend throughout on their commanding officer's ability to obtain credit, and even more on the forbearance of the citizens on whom many of them were billeted. Work on Monks Hill had probably progressed enough by this time for one or two companies to be accommodated in Fort George, and some troops must have been in Falmouth, but the rest surely would have been in St John's.

Following a steady decline in the importance of Falmouth during the previous twenty years or so St John's was recognised as the capital around the turn of the eighteenth century. The street grid which still forms the heart of the city – between North and South Streets, and between the harbour and East Street (Independence Avenue since 1981) – was laid out in 1702, in the same year that a public market was established and a number of wharves constructed. Given the speed at which legislative resolutions were implemented at the time, this probably means that the decision to make St John's the capital had been taken a year or two earlier. The other appurtenances of early eighteenth-century town life which made their appearance at the same time – 'a cage, pillory, stocks, whipping-post, and ducking-stool, put up at the public expense' – provided more grisly evidence of the new status of St John's.

•

Objects such as the cage, pillory and whipping-post, which would have been found in any British town of the day, were not erected with the punishment or even the intimidation of slaves in mind, although in time they would serve very well in both capacities. When they were erected slave owners had little need of public means of punishment. No law had yet been passed or even considered concerning a master's powers of life and death over his slaves; other, of course, than the one seemingly ignored by every white man from the Governor downwards which forbade 'Carnall Coppullation' between them.

Whether Major Samuel Martin, the owner of Green Castle plantation (and as such not content with anything less than a majority in the militia) engaged in such unlawful pursuits is not known (although the number of Antiguans bearing the name today might indicate that even if he did not his descendants almost certainly did), but he so mistreated his slaves in one way or another that he was killed by a group of them on Christmas Day 1701. The murder took place inside his house, and was carried out by men so enraged by something he had done that they not only beheaded him, but made every effort to hack his body to pieces. This act of butchery ceased only when men from a neighbouring plantation rode up, having been summoned by Martin's wife and family, who were left completely unharmed. One of the murderers was shot dead as he tried to escape, two more were chased and captured, and the others were arrested later. How they all met their fate is not known, any more than the precise reason for Martin's slaughter. In his report on the affair to the Board of Trade, Codrington recorded that 'I'm afraid he was guilty of some unusual act of Severity, or rather Some indignity towards [them]',[6] implying something rather more than the reason given in *Antigua and the Antiguans*, the very readable history published anonymously in 1844. In this the author, now known to have been a Mrs Lanaghan, stated that Martin met his death because he 'had for some reason or the other refused his slaves their usual Christmas holiday, and compelled them to work throughout the day'[7]: an explanation which seems to have been widely accepted every since.

There is no doubt that by the time the murder took place, at least fifty years after they had begun to be imported into Antigua, the slaves had, through sheer determination and persistence, managed to temper the constant, sordid grind of their daily existence; first of all by 'earning' what the planters considered to be privileges, and then subtly – with nothing in the way of laws or regulations to back them up – transforming such privileges into rights. Among these, and perhaps the most important, was the right to time off. If they were to survive and have any kind of family or social life they could not be worked from sunrise to sunset, day in and day out, from one year's end to the next: something many owners would have liked, and which we may be sure some of the cruder expected. Fortunately, because of the particular emphasis placed on the observance of the Sabbath in early colonial days, whether there were clergymen around or not, a six-day working week became accepted for all labourers, whether free or slave. On the seventh day the slaves quickly claimed a right to amuse themselves or carry on their own affairs as they saw fit. A day or two off at Christmas took a little longer to be introduced, but once such a holiday had been granted – perhaps by just the odd more kindly master – it was soon turned into something to which all slaves considered they had an inalienable right. This was certainly the case by Christmas 1701 when Martin met his end, but it is still difficult to accept that his cancellation of a day's holiday 'to take a crop he thought would perish if not got in' was enough to drive more than a dozen men into such a paroxysm of rage that they apparently wanted to obliterate his entire being. What the genuine, underlying and no doubt deeply disturbing motives were remain a matter for speculation.

The manner of the retribution handed out to the perpetrators of the murder also remains a matter for conjecture. That it was probably carried out in an even more gruesome and savage way than the crime itself can be assumed from the Board of Trade's response to Codrington's report, in which they enjoined:

> We are the more Sensible of the expediency of a Law for restraining inhumane Severity not only towards Christian Servants but Slaves, which you are directed . . . to endeavour to procure, And we therefore recommend it to your particular care.[8]

Codrington may well have been willing to give this his attention, but for the war which now intervened. As a result, during the remainder of his time in office, the only legislation passed merely updated an act of 1697 'for the Better Government of Slaves', which had been mostly concerned with the problem of runaways, the rewards payable for their recovery and the amounts of compensation to be paid for those executed.

In order to reduce the amount of public money being paid out, the amended act specified that death need no longer be the only punishment for a runaway caught after three months: the cutting off of a leg or a flogging would do just as well. Other sections dealt with matters such as the outlawing of fights among slaves and the prevention of their drinking in grog shops. No mention was made of a specific penalty for the killing of a white person, but there was hardly any need as under another clause, if a slave struck a white person, and in any way hurt or disfigured him, the slave could be executed, have 'his nose slit', or suffer having 'any member cut off' (a useful catch-all phrase intended to include the frequent practice of castration).

In addition to legislating for such barbarities, the new act, passed in 1702, also contained provisions intended to govern the life of a new class of inhabitants: black people who were not slaves. There had been a few such for many years (including John Preemer, a freeman who had lived with the

Shekerley maroons in the 1680s): men and women manumitted in someone's will or rewarded with freedom for some special act; a few who, if their mothers were free, were themselves born free; and even one or two who had somehow managed to buy their freedom. All were considered by the planters to be 'slaves without masters'.[9] There were probably no more than a dozen or two free blacks or mulattoes in the whole island when the act was passed, but it was felt they should be firmly linked to the slaves and regulated accordingly. Under its provisions 'all free Negroes, Mulattoes, or Indians, not having land' were required to choose a master or mistress to live with, while any free black who did possess land was prohibited from owning more than eight acres and denied the right to vote, to hold a public or parochial office, or to serve as a juror. There was no restriction on the amount of land which could be owned by a mulatto who, once he had the ten acres needed to be counted as a freeholder, would also be allowed to vote. In order to curb any increase in their numbers as much as possible both free blacks and mulattoes were forbidden to marry slaves.

The sharp division drawn between the landed and the landless, while it must have caused a lot of heartache initially, was capable of being ignored or circumvented and as such had no long-term effect. On the other hand, the discrimination between freemen of mixed or unmixed black ancestry was to have very long-lasting consequences: some perhaps not fully resolved even today. As well as the 1702 Act making it clear that some 'Free Negroes' were more free than others, it also made it equally clear that, regardless of how much land or property some of them might aspire to own, their status in society was all precisely the same. The earlier act which it had amended had laid down that:

> If any Free Person, not being a White, shall presume to strike a White Person, he shall be by Order of the next Justice (on proof of his striking) severely whipped.

The amended act, by promising the same punishment to any non-white who dared strike, not a 'White Person' any more, but a 'White Servant', now made it clear that even if a non-white owned a hundred acres and had received a university education he would still be considered the social inferior of any penniless, illiterate tatterdemalion sweating out his indentureship. But even so, the same 'Free Person, not being a White' was still able to live and work within defined boundaries of a kind, and with some sort of legal recognition of his identity, whereas the slaves from among whom he had emerged remained entirely without the law.

Another twenty years were to go by before the act which Codrington had been urged to procure 'for restraining inhumane Severity' towards slaves was actually passed by the Assembly, and even then they were not afforded a great deal of protection. Slaves were to remain subject, with no more than a nominal means of redress, to whatever cruelty or indignity their owners might inflict upon them until an Amelioration Bill was passed into law in the closing years of the eighteenth century.

•

The War of the Spanish Succession dragged on for more than a decade but, as far as the Leeward Islands were concerned, once the initial fighting in St Kitts in 1702 and in Guadeloupe the following year was over, it had little impact for several years. This gave the Board of Trade the opportunity to take Codrington at his word, and accept his much-proffered resignation. His departure from office in February 1704 did not bode well for Antigua. A professional soldier, Brigadier-General Sir William Mathew, seemed just the right choice to take over under wartime conditions, but he died within five months of his arrival on the island. John Johnson, the Lieutenant-Governor of Nevis who then took over the administration until a replacement for Mathew was appointed, could do very little but sit tight and watch the war turn into a conflict dominated by naval activity. For the next nine years the fortunes of the Leeward Islands rose and fell as supremacy in the Caribbean passed back and forth between British and French fleets, but for Antigua events which had already taken place in England and on the continent of Europe were to prove just as important.

6

An Unfortunate Divel

If I have my brains knokt out the Queen must send some other unfortunate Divel here to be roasted in the sun, without the prospect of getting anything.

Colonel Daniel Parke (1706)

The year 1706 is celebrated in the annals of Antigua as that in which that abominable and atrocious governor, Daniel Parke, arrived to blast for a time with his unhallowed breath this beautiful little island.

Mrs Lanaghan
Antigua and the Antiguans (1844)

The Battle of Blenheim, fought early in August 1704, was the first of the Duke of Marlborough's decisive victories in the War of the Spanish Succession. It was such an astonishing victory — the first major defeat of a French army in forty years — that an officer on the staff was despatched immediately to carry the news personally to Marlborough's patron, Queen Anne, who had succeeded to the throne two years earlier. On receiving the news the Queen was so delighted, and so taken with the bearer's fine presence, that she not only gave him a substantial cash gift but promised to honour the Duke's request that he be rewarded with a royal appointment.

The officer concerned was Daniel Parke, a Virginian who had had to abandon his wife and family and leave the American colonies in some haste six or seven years earlier on account of 'a crime at a gaming-table'. His somewhat shady background, violent temper and reputation as a libertine had not detracted from his ability to pursue a military career with distinction, any more than they did from his ability to beguile the Queen — who soon proved as good as her word when informed of the untimely death of General Mathew; Parke was offered the governorship of the Leeward Islands in his place. Although he would have preferred that of his home colony of Virginia, this had already been given to someone else, and so it was the Leeward Islands — 'the hardest taske of all the Queen's Governors, tho' the least sallary' as he complained — or nothing.

Parke took up his appointment in 1706, arriving in July of that year to find that St Kitts and Nevis had been devastated by the French several months earlier: the planters of both islands had had their property destroyed, their cane-fields burned and their slaves carried away, and the whole of Antigua lived in fear of a similar catastrophe. Although Parke was welcomed at first – the Assembly, reassured to some extent by his military reputation, voted him a sizeable annual sum to allow him to rent a suitable residence – this soon changed. His overbearing manner, disagreeable nature and lack of breeding, together with his obvious desire to use his position for profit, combined to make him increasingly unpopular. Within a year or so, through the growing misuse of his powers – mostly in efforts to make sure he did get something out of the job – he had antagonised more or less everyone who mattered. As a royally appointed governor, in order to exercise his full authority in executive, legislative and judicial matters he also served as the island's Vice-Admiral and military Commander-in-Chief. Any less self-seeking individual would have recognised that he could only govern through the island's Council and Assembly, and accepted that his admiralty powers were in judicial matters only. He also would have done his utmost to make sure he retained the support of the officer in command of any regular troops that were on the island, as control of these was not within the Governor's remit. Parke accepted none of this, but took his appointment to mean that he had carte blanche in every aspect of civil, naval and military affairs, and proceeded to act accordingly.

He began not too badly by trying to put the island's defences in better shape, and to do something for the remaining soldiers of Whetham's Regiment – those who had not been carried off by disease and general neglect, that is – while waiting for the replacements he had requested to arrive. His first priority was to complete the work at Monks Hill, the only fortification it was thought could be held if the island suffered an enemy invasion. While the prospect of a French incursion remained a possibility he had no difficulty in obtaining enough slaves for the work, each earning his owner one shilling a day, but once such a threat receded and the sugar-cane harvest began it was a different story. In March 1707 Parke complained to the Board of Trade that while the danger existed 'the People Sent me Negroes to fortyfie Monks Hill, but being Over I can't gett a Negroe to finish what I had begun, but they promise to doe it when the Crop is over.'[1] Not only were the planters' promises never fully honoured, causing the construction of Fort George to proceed in an unsatisfactory, piecemeal fashion, but a lot of the work carried out was of poor quality. This was hardly the fault of the slaves involved, but came about from not having a qualified military engineer, or even just one person, in overall charge of the project. A glimpse of the terrible conditions under which the labourers worked, hauling materials and equipment to the top of a steep-sided 700-foot hill, is provided in a claim submitted to the Assembly in 1707 by an owner asking for compensation for a slave who was most unmercifully used, by carrying burthens from the Waterside up the Hill; and that by kicking, beating, and hard usage from the Overseer . . . languished for about seven days, and afterwards dyed.[2]

Parke had more cause for complaint in the same year, but this time in connection with events which had taken place long before his arrival, involving Christopher Codrington, the former Governor who had since returned to his life as a planter. In 1701 the Admiralty Court in Antigua had dismissed a charge of illegal trading brought against a ship-owner, Samuel Baron, only to have its decision overturned by Codrington, who had then confiscated both the ship and its cargo. Although subsequently Baron had won an appeal to the High Court of Admiralty in London, and Codrington had been ordered to make restitution, this had still not happened by the time Parke took up his appointment. He now made an enemy of Codrington by not only serving him with a document, signed by the Queen in Council, ordering the return of Baron's ship, but by demanding details of what had happened to other ships and cargoes taken as legitimate prizes of war before his arrival.

By refusing to supply this information, or to give any account of his period of administration, Codrington added to the new Governor's growing dislike of the richer planters and the way he felt they were running, and in his opinion ruining, the island. His particular resentment of the way in which they were constantly adding to their holdings by buying out the smaller landowners led to his questioning some of the titles they held: a move which served to make the infuriated planters view him with increasing contempt. Codrington himself became even more enraged when his rights to Barbuda were challenged. His lease had been renewed in 1705 'in consideration of [his] service . . . and of his having built a castle on the said Island which was defended at his own cost and expense', and in return for the payment 'unto Her Majesty yearly and every year one Fat Sheep if demanded'.[3] The knowledge that this renewal had taken place during the Johnson interregnum, long before it was due, and for a period of ninety-nine years, was anathema to Parke, and reinforced his view that men like Codrington could seemingly operate above the law. His suspicion that he himself was seen as no more than an irritating, penniless place-hunter was not allayed by Codrington's refusal to justify his actions while Governor, his claim to Barbuda, or indeed anything else.

Their confrontation ended in August 1707 when Codrington, presumably deciding to leave while the going was still good, decamped for Barbados, where he remained until his death three years later. In his will he left a legacy to endow a library at All Souls' College, Oxford, and another to found what was to become Codrington College in Barbados. A request in the will, that his father's body 'be Carryd to England and buryed in Westminster Abbey', although rightly ignored, provides an indication of the position the Codringtons felt they deserved in society, and of why their imperiousness was so much resented over the years by many of their fellow planters. The third Christopher was the last of the family to reside in Antigua, and on his death his estates there passed into the hands of his cousin, William Codrington (later Sir William, first Baronet of Dodington).

With the departure of the proprietor of Betty's Hope from the island in 1707 Parke saw the back of his *bête noire*, but this by no means brought about any improvement in his standing with the majority of the white population, including most of the planters, the Legislature and, in due course, the military command.

The replacement garrison, Colonel Luke Lillingston's Regiment, had landed in May.[4] Following the custom of the day, two companies of Whetham's Regiment (which was about all that remained of that regiment by this time) were incorporated to bring the total number of troops to about 500. As Lillingston himself had not accompanied his men – perhaps understandably as according to Parke he had managed to recruit few other than 'old men, or boys fit for nothing' – the command devolved to the next most senior officer, Lieutenant-Colonel James Jones; a man with whom before very long the Governor had fallen out. Their dispute, largely brought about by Jones's dishonesty, avarice and mistreatment of his troops, was made worse by Parke's constant interference in the running and disposition of the regiment. It was to come to a head in 1710, but long before then Parke had also fallen foul of an even wider cross-section of the population.

He began by appointing 'a common foot soldier' named Michael Ayon as Provost Marshal over the objections of Jones, and much to the disgust of the inhabitants of St John's, where Ayon was quickly recognised as the Governor's stooge and tale-bearer. He followed this up by scandalising the townspeople with his own progress as a debauchee. Whether he seduced the wife of Edward Chester, the Speaker, before or after he set about disputing the rights and privileges of the House of Assembly is not known, but either way it did little to bring the Governor and Assembly together again after the altercation between them began towards the end of the year, following the introduction of a bill in which the Assembly claimed the right to fine or imprison anyone who did anything of which they disapproved, or which brought discredit on the House. Parke rejected this, as he did another bill under which the Assembly claimed the right of veto over the appointment of the Speaker. In retaliation the infuriated members withdrew the Governor's rent subsidy, and drew up a petition asking for his recall.

This petition – 'signed by eighty of the principal inhabitants' – carried to London by one of their number and received by the Queen in Council the following April, was too premature. By the time it had been dismissed nearly a year later as being 'groundless and vexatious' Parke had the whole island in an uproar. Having already decided, as he would record later, that the white inhabitants were 'a mungrill race liveing witnesses of their unnaturall and monstrous lusts', and that his fortune was not to be made among them, he turned towards the sea. Taking advantage of his vice-admiralty appointment he issued letters of marque to the masters of two privately owned ships. Armed with these licences they were permitted not only to seize enemy vessels as prizes, but also to trade on his behalf with the French islands, during visits supposedly made for the return of prisoners under flags of truce. The same ships also provided him with the means to suppress – much to the distress of those among the 'principal inhabitants' who were involved – the smuggling and illegal trading activities which had been carried on from Antigua ever since the war began. Whether the rector of St John's, the Reverend James Field, was one of the distressed is open to question, but he was certainly responsible for an attempt on Parke's life in September 1708. His aim with a gun, however, being even worse than his knowledge of the sixth Commandment, he shot and wounded a naval officer he had mistaken for the Governor.

This state of affairs could not be allowed to continue and at the beginning of 1709, with the help of testimony and cash from Codrington in Barbados, the Assembly prepared a detailed indictment of Parke. In it he was accused not only of irregularities in connection with his public duties, and of inhumane and immoral conduct, but also of such inappropriate activities as:

> It has been his common practice to ramble at night up and down the streets of St Johns and from house to house, list'ning and eavesdropping, and that in different disguises, tho' very well known in all of them, and so exposed to all the world, bringing thereby his person and authority in contempt.[5]

This document was sent to London in March and resulted eleven months later in Parke's recall. The planters' joy at hearing the news proved to be short-lived, however, as Parke was not a man to give in so easily. Through his sponsorship of privateering and illegal trading, and through his control of the vice-admiralty court which dealt with prizes and prize money, his efforts to make his fortune were now beginning to pay off, and he ignored the order to return to England.

His refusal to leave inspired Field, the 'drunken, quarrelsome, fighting parson' as Parke called him, to make another attempt at assassination, this time forcing one of his slaves to do the dirty work. The aim of the slave, Sandy, was no better than that of his master, and he only managed to wound the Governor as he rode past the would-be assassin's hiding place. What happened to Sandy as a result is not known, but he was undoubtedly executed. As Field had a sinister reputation for mistreating his slaves, having not only castrated but cut a leg off one unfortunate he owned, it is most unlikely that he would have hesitated in making Sandy pay the price of failure, any more than he would have delayed in making him the scapegoat had the assassination succeeded. Parke lost much of the use of one arm, but otherwise survived the attempt on his life.

To the increasing distress and disgust of all who, if they had not wished to see him dead, certainly wanted to see the back of him, the Governor then used the length of time it took for correspondence to pass to and fro across the Atlantic to further postpone his departure by arguing piecemeal about the misdoings of which he stood accused. One or two of his rejoinders may have carried some validity, but it is difficult to believe the Board of Trade found any merit in the justification he provided for combining the role of Governor with that of nightwatchman in his 'rambles' through St John's:

> You may easily imagine that a sea-port town in the West Indies full of punch-houses and taverns, crammed with soldiers and privateers, to be very licentious and the greatest care and pains is wanted to make it habitable. This fault they accuse me of, has so reformed the town that wheras formerly allmost ever night somebody was wounded or murder was cryed out in their streets, they are now as quiet as London within her walls.[6]

That many sailors and soldiers could have been seen in St John's during his midnight wanderings was undoubtedly true. The former were probably well able, because of Parke's keen interest in their seagoing activities, to drink and carouse, but whether many of the latter could have kept up with them is another question. By this time Jones's Regiment (which had assumed this title when Colonel Lillingston left the Army in 1708) had been spread around the Leeward Islands for three years. During this period Jones, from his headquarters in Antigua, had been quietly enriching himself at the expense of his troops, by drawing pay for men who had long since perished or deserted, and by withholding it from those still alive. Parke, who was well aware of what was going on but involved in too much nefarious activity himself to do anything about it, took no notice until he received a petition from members of the regiment stationed in St Kitts. Signed by well over a hundred NCOs and men led by Sergeant Charles Bowes, this petition complained of the 'great misery' which had befallen them

> since Colonel Jones had the Regiment, for before we had some money and some clothes; but since he was our Colonel, which is about 2 years, we have had neither clothes nor money. Our officers told us they received none from their Colonel . . . We had long since laid our condition before your Excellency, but for fear of our officers, from whose fury we now beg protection.[7]

Taking up the soldiers' cause now provided Parke with an excellent diversion from his own predicament, and in May 1710 he was writing to the Board of Trade about the 'deplorable condition of Colonel Jones's Regiment' and of his intention to court-martial the colonel for 'false musters, and not paying, clothing, or recruiting his Regiment; the greater part for want of which have perished, and are reduced to about one third of a Regiment, and many of them want arms.'[8] But one rogue could put pen to paper as readily as the other, and Jones lost no time in presenting his side of the story, arguing that he was being

> made an anvil of affronts by a man notably distinguished for the worst of character. He has carried his insolence so far that, upon receipt of the most mannerly and dutiful messages to call me a scoundrel and liar. He takes upon him to serve his own purpose, not only to do the duty of Colonel of the Regiment, but of every other officer, even [shades of his nightwatchman role] to that of a sergeant, so that I can no longer consider myself accountable for the miscarriages of my Regiment.[9]

Jones also drew attention to the effect that this had had on the loyalty of some of his men, accusing the Governor of having 'picked out a set of men both Officers and soldiers, abandoned to all his black and gloomy designs, who he has used as tools to trample under foot all discipline, etc.'

This breakdown in discipline was to grow worse, causing the men suborned to become involved in tragic events before the end of the year, but in the meantime Parke had more enemies to make, and more antagonism to arouse. While, in the words of the historian of the South Staffordshire Regiment, 'further complaints from both scoundrels flowed across the ocean to the authorities in London, who by this time must have been tired of the pair of them', the Governor made the mistake of trying to come between the Navy and its much-cherished right to prize money.

In early September an enemy ship which had been captured by HMS *Lark* was brought into St John's Harbour to be sold as a prize through the vice-admiralty court on behalf of the commanding officer, a Captain Norbury, and his crew. Once again overstepping the authority carried by his vice-admiralty appointment, Parke demanded the prize be turned over to him, and threatened to relieve Norbury of his command if this was not done. The angry exchange of letters which followed Norbury's refusal to comply ended abruptly with Parke's somewhat hysterical assertion that his 'power was above the Admiralty . . . or any flagg officers, that his Instructions was from the Queen and that [Norbury] should obey them.'[10] The captain argued no more but merely sent the prize to Barbados to be sold and reported the affair to the Admiralty; producing yet more shudders among authorities already weary of dealing with complaints about Parke.

In Antigua by this time his attempts to continue exerting his authority could only have been seen as ignominious and provocative. Everyone knew he had been recalled and probably viewed his refusal to leave the island as cowardice. He had long since fallen out with the Assembly, having brought things to a head earlier in the year when, ignoring convention, he had appointed one of his cronies as Clerk to House, and by November the members had had enough. At the end of the month Parke received a letter from them asking that he remove himself to some other island of the government; thereby to afford us the opportunity and means, in conjunction with the lieutenant-governor and council, to provide for the public security, to heal our divisions, restore discipline, and our broken constitution, after the best manner we can.

Should he refuse to go, they warned,

> we shall be under the unhappy necessity of withdrawing our obedience from you in order that the colony, our persons and estates, may no longer be exposed to such unhappy conduct and administration, which seems entirely – we must say, foully – devoted to the ruin and destruction of all.[11]

The Governor's response was to inform the Assembly that it was adjourned, and to request its members to attend a meeting with the Council and himself at 8.00 a.m. on 7 December.

Parke was now at loggerheads with the Queen, the Privy Council and the Board of Trade in London; he was feared and distrusted by the governments and people of all the Leeward Islands; and had a rebellious Assembly on his hands in an island which was under immediate threat of an attack by French privateers. On top of all this, once he and half a dozen of his few remaining supporters – including Michael Ayon – had withdrawn into his official residence, he found he could no longer depend on the full loyalty or co-operation of either the Army or the Navy. Calling on Jones's Regiment to provide him with a guard, only three officers and forty or fifty soldiers (including Sergeant Bowes and some of his fellow petitioners, recently transferred from St Kitts) rallied to his aid. The remainder of the garrison refused, while Jones made himself scarce by finding a reason to visit Nevis.

Parke's next move was to order HMS *Lark* to sea, and to cruise off the island in order to deter the French from carrying out raids on the coast or from seizing any more shipping, but first of all to land the contingent of troops recently embarked to make up crew numbers. This gave Captain Norbury his chance for revenge: he needed the soldiers to work the ship, he informed the Governor brusquely, and because he was short of provisions which were only obtainable in Barbados nothing could be done until he had been there. He then 'went away in hast . . . entered a pinnis and rowed away . . . put the ship under sails', and within a few hours was gone; leaving Parke to face new denunciations. Because of the troops he had guarding his residence he had already been accused of being 'in arms against the inhabitants'; with the departure of HMS *Lark* the rumour spread that he was now preparing to surrender the island to the French.

What he hoped to achieve at the meeting he had ordered for 7 December, or what action he intended to take against the Assembly, will never be known. By the time that day dawned his authority extended no further than the walls of his residence, and was exercised over no more than the fifty or so people –

soldiers and civilians – crowded inside. Many of the rest of the white inhabitants of the island had decided to take matters into their own hands, and by daybreak St John's was already filled with men under arms. A proclamation ordering them to disperse, which was read out and then nailed up in the marketplace by the Provost Marshal, had no effect and was countered by an address from the Assembly. This was delivered to Parke by a former Speaker, Nathaniel Crump, and a Council member, George Gamble, 'desiring him, in the name of the inhabitants, to discharge his guards, and quit the government, without any further contest.' His refusal to consider this, or even acknowledge that his authority had in any way been affected by his recall and by subsequent events, only served to turn what had been a noisy rabble into a purposeful mob under two vengeful leaders.

Captain John Piggott, the Speaker, and Captain John Painter a member of the Assembly, now set about dishonouring their all-but-worthless ranks in the militia as well as their privileged positions in the Legislature, by dividing the better-armed of the mob into two groups and marching on the Governor's residence. While Painter's band covered the rear of the building, Piggott's men attacked the front, with the first shot being fired by a man named Kerby. This attack was held off for some time by a field-gun firing grape and partridge shot, which had a devastating effect until the ammunition ran out. After that it was only a question of time before 'the assailants burst open the doors, and rushed into the dwelling' to begin hand-to-hand fighting. Amid the mayhem which followed Parke managed to kill Piggott, but was then wounded in the thigh before being dragged into the street, where he was stripped, humiliated and tortured before being left to bleed to death in the sun.

His seizure marked the end of the assault, but by the time the fury of the mob had abated one of the officers and fourteen of the soldiers who had stood by Parke were dead, and the other two officers and another twenty-six men had been wounded. All of the Governor's civilian supporters had in addition been injured. Among those who carried out the attack, Piggott and another three had been killed, and over thirty others had been wounded. Ayon, who may have assisted in the death of Piggott, survived only to be summarily shot after he had surrendered. Sergeant Bowes, who had done his best to protect Parke until he himself was wounded, was resourceful enough not only to escape from the ruined residence, but also from the island.

Some of those who took part in the attack also had cause to flee Antigua. Kerby and one or two others went to Barbados, where they managed to remain in spite of later efforts to get them sent to England to stand trial. That luminary of the Anglican Church, James Field, also found it expedient to remove himself and left for England 'under cover of dark'. His subsequent career, presumably free of any further desire to kill or castrate, was such that he managed to get himself buried eighteen years later in St George's Chapel, Windsor. As for the rest – men like Painter who had shot, slashed and slaughtered with the best of them, those like Crump and Gamble who had stood and watched, or Jones and Norbury who had merely turned their backs – all they could do was wait for the inevitable repercussions.

With Parke's death the administration of the colony passed briefly into the hands of John Yeamans, the Lieutenant-Governor, until such time as he could inform his opposite number in Nevis, Walter Hamilton, of what had taken place. Hamilton, who was the most senior of all the individual island governors, then took over until Parke's replacement was appointed. Some idea of what he may have thought of the affair can be gained perhaps from knowing that he received the men who brought him the news 'with great urbanity and kindness', and that after he had accompanied them back to Antigua 'he took up residence, for the time being, with Dr Mackinnon, one of the actors in the late affray.' It was also Hamilton who had Sergeant Bowes arrested and returned to Antigua, where Colonel Jones incarcerated him in a tiny cell in Fort George for two weeks in an attempt to make him swear that Parke had intended to turn the island over to the French. In this he was unsuccessful. Bowes refused to traduce the dead governor in this way, and Jones only managed to save his own skin by pleading ill-health, returning to England, and disposing of the regiment to another officer. Some of his subordinates were not so fortunate, and in 1711 three officers were sent back to England in, of all ships, HMS *Lark*, to be court-martialled for aiding and abetting the murder of Parke. As Captain Norbury initially kicked up a fuss about taking them on board, possibly feeling that his own actions had done nothing to prevent the murder, they cannot have enjoyed the most pleasant of Atlantic crossings. In the event, only one of the officers, the most junior, was brought to trial and he was acquitted 'for want of evidence'.

Queen Anne was incensed when, after several weeks, the news of the events in Antigua reached London, 'but, after hearing the catalogue of Parke's crimes, and in order to prevent any further effusion of blood, her majesty was graciously pleased to send a general pardon to all that were concerned in that transaction.'[12] This was to be carried to the island by the new Governor, Colonel Walter Douglas, a man who was to turn out to be no more worthy of the appointment than his dead predecessor. He arrived in July, with orders to dissolve the Council and Assembly, to investigate the happenings of the previous December – during which he was 'to try, and send home not fewer than three nor more than six, of the ringleaders implicated in the Murder of Governor Parke' – and to proclaim the Queen's pardon.

He landed to find the white population in a state of trepidation, concerned not only about the consequences of Parke's murder but also about the continuing threat of a French attack. When it became apparent that there was widespread sympathy for those involved in the murder, and he learned of the ambivalent attitude which had been adopted by the military and naval commanders, Douglas decided it might be wiser and safer to delay carrying out his orders to the letter – or better still, to reinterpret them to his own advantage. He did this by postponing the proclamation of the general pardon, and letting it be known that a suitable donation to his private exchequer from those involved in Parke's death could ensure their being included under its provisions in due course.

This worked so well that by February 1712, when the pardon was announced – following Douglas' receipt of a reprimand from the Queen for delaying it so long – the only men who had been arrested were the three army officers who had been sent back to England the year before, and only two of the civilians involved had refused to pay up. This pair, Dr Daniel MacKinnon and Chief Justice Samuel Watkins, avoided arrest by escaping to England.[13] Once there, even though they were briefly imprisoned 'from advices received from Governor Douglas', they successfully pleaded that they were covered by the pardon and were released without trial.

Having proclaimed the pardon on 21 February, and in spite of the shady dealings which had taken place beforehand, Douglas ordered that the same day in the following year should be kept as 'a Day of Publick Fast and humiliation'. The people of the island, he declared, were not to regard the pardon as a vindication of rebellion, and on the anniversary should 'abstain from party-making and opprobrious language'. Such hypocrisy from a man who had been busy making his fortune out of the aftermath of the rebellion and humiliation of the main participants must have been very hard to accept. The moves which were soon being made to get rid of him were brought to a halt in July when a large squadron of French privateers appeared off the island.

Fortunately the French chose to make their appearance in the south-east, in the invitingly sheltered and wide-mouthed Willoughby Bay. According to Sir Alan Burns in his majestic *History of the British West Indies*, no attack took place because 'the militia appeared in force ready to oppose a landing'. As the militia at this time consisted only of such units as a 'regiment' of one hundred 'carbinieres' under no less than three colonels and ten other officers, and a 'company' of three officers and a single private, it is difficult to believe that such forces could really have deterred the 3000 or more men the French ships are reported to have carried. A far more likely explanation is surely to be found in the bay itself – a large expanse of shallow water greatly encumbered by reefs and rocks, especially across its entrance – and no place for ships to linger in late July at the beginning of the hurricane season. Having had little more than a quick look round the enemy soon departed, no doubt as much to the relief of the militia as it was to the rest of the population. While the French turned their attention to Montserrat, where they did considerable damage and made off with 1200 slaves and much plunder, the planters of Antigua returned to the business of producing sugar, while joining with the rest of the white population in considering how best to rid themselves of their simoniacal governor.

By the time he had been in office for two years complaints about Douglas were already beginning to cross the Atlantic. When these began to include accusations of his 'ammassing a prodigious fortune by compounding with the murderers' in selling the Queen's pardon, and of defrauding the island's treasury by diverting certain customs duties to his own use, alarm had overtaken weariness at the Board of Trade. It then only needed the inevitable petition, signed by Walter Hamilton among others, 'praying the queen to recall him', for action to be taken. He was recalled in March 1714, and put on trial for bribery and for 'having exacted £10000 from the Island of Antigua before publishing the Queen's Pardon.' Following his conviction he was ordered to pay a fine of £500 and sent to jail for five years. After serving his sentence he disappeared to France – something he was then able to do quite freely, the war having ended some six years earlier.

•

For nineteen of the twenty-four years between the start of King William's War in 1689 and the signing of the Treaty of Utrecht (under the terms of which, incidentally, the French renounced any further claim to St Kitts) in 1713 there was no peace in the West Indies. Although Antigua, unlike St Kitts, Nevis and Montserrat, had suffered no invasion or direct attack of any consequence, the war years had caused plenty of hardship and suffering. They also had brought about some far-reaching changes in the life of the island. In spite of the constant disruption of trade, and the shortages of materials and foodstuffs caused by years of unrestricted naval warfare – not to mention the amount of time and effort the planters had had to devote to preparing fortifications and to militia activities (and even to the disposing of venal governors)– Antigua emerged from those years in altogether better shape than she went in. By 1713 she was pre-eminent among the Leeward Islands, and producing more sugar than the rest of them put together.

This was achieved at the expense of many of the smaller farmers whose lands were bought and incorporated into existing large estates, the proprietors of which, now sure of the backing of the British Government (changed from English to British with the 1707 Act of Union), had established a network of merchants and attorneys, with agents and lobbyists in England, to assist them in business. Even more, the success of the planters was achieved at the expense of the wretched men, women and children brought in the endless procession of ships crossing the ocean from Africa, regardless of war or peace, to provide the necessary labour.

Part Two:
Sugar and Slavery

The history of the West Indies is governed by two factors, the sugar plantation and Negro slavery

C. L. R. James
The Black Jacobins (1963)

7

Prospering at a Price

From the Negroes' Labour all produce must Come.

Clement Tudway, owner of Parham Hill plantation, in a letter to his agent in Antigua written in 1716

Slavery is among us not of choice but of necessity, and unless (as it is not to be imagined) our mother country should quit the trade of the sugar-colonies Englishmen must continue to be masters of their slaves.

Governor William Mathew (1736)

After peace had returned to Antigua with the signing of the Treaty of Utrecht the white population began to increase rapidly, reaching a figure of just over 5000 – the highest it was ever going to be – around the year 1725. Among those who helped swell the figure were white servants brought in to meet new regulations introduced in 1716, which specified that anyone owning fifteen slaves also had to employ one white man capable of serving in the militia, and one more for every twenty slaves owned in excess of fifteen. The revised rules and penalties for non-compliance proved to be rather more effective than those they replaced, and within four years nearly 20 per cent of the white population consisted of indentured servants.[1] The clause which allowed the merchants who imported them to claim from the Treasury for any not 'sold' within twenty days of being landed gave the unprincipled among them another opportunity to make easy money. Suitable young men who were prepared to work and serve in the militia for seven years, in return for a small cash sum and 400 pounds of sugar, were not that easy to find, but with a guaranteed price per head once they were in Antigua it hardly mattered to the importers, or their British agents, what quality or condition of man was sent out. As a result a sizeable proportion of the men landed were quite unsuitable as servants, and many slaveowners preferred to pay fines rather than employ them.

Although the influx of indentured servants was considerable it was not the only reason for the increase in the white population. Many other men, some with capital to invest, and others with mercantile or professional skills, came at the same time; all hoping, in a world where sugar was in ever-increasing demand, to make their fortunes. Among them were a number of Scotsmen who, following the 1707 Act of Union between England and Scotland, were free to export their considerable entrepreneurial abilities and professional expertise to the colonies. One of these, a young doctor named Walter Tullideph, arrived in 1726 and showed how it could be done. Ten years later he wrote home to announce he had

> married an agreeable young Widow by whom I have gott Possession of a very fine Estate to which I am making additions & improvements and am likely to have a heir of my Own.[2]

The estate which he acquired along with his 'agreeable young Widow' consisted of 127 acres worked by sixty-three slaves. Within twenty years he had turned it into a plantation of well over 500 acres with 271 slaves, and was able to retire to Scotland worth nearly £30 000.

Tullideph was one of the more fortunate. Even before he married, many of those who had arrived during the great influx had already gone again. In 1734 Governor William Mathew[3] (son of the Sir William Mathew who had been Governor for a few months thirty years earlier), tried to explain to the Board of Trade why the white population was by then decreasing; one reason he gave was that time-expired servants were not being replaced. The planters in his opinion were ignoring laws which

> hitherto procure Such unwilling, Worthless, Idle Vagabonds, as from whom but Little Service can be hop'd for, on Military Emergencys. Most of these Serve for a Term of Years, without wages, poorly Cladd, hard fedd, a worse State here than a Common Soldier, if possible.[4]

At the same time in London the Colonial Agent, John Yeamans (who had been the Lieutenant-Governor of Antigua during Parke's regime), gave as his opinion:

> The decrease of white men in the island I apprehend to be due to various causes. Epidemical Distempers have destroyed numbers. Dry weather, Want of Provisions, and Inability to pay the Taxes have caused others to go off. Land has been at so high a price from the Smallness of the Quantity in the said Island, that the settlers of ten or twenty acres, who formerly raised only Provisions have been tempted to sell their Possessions to the Sugar Planters, and have therupon quitted the Island.[5]

Mathew and Yeamans wrote at a time when the plantation system, and the dominance of the leading planters in all aspects of life in Antigua, were firmly established. Each estate was a family-owned concern, some with names such as Betty's Hope or Green Castle, but the majority – like Winthrop's or MacKinnon's – being called (even if they soon lost their apostrophes) after their original owners. Many of the more prominent planters, those who owned the

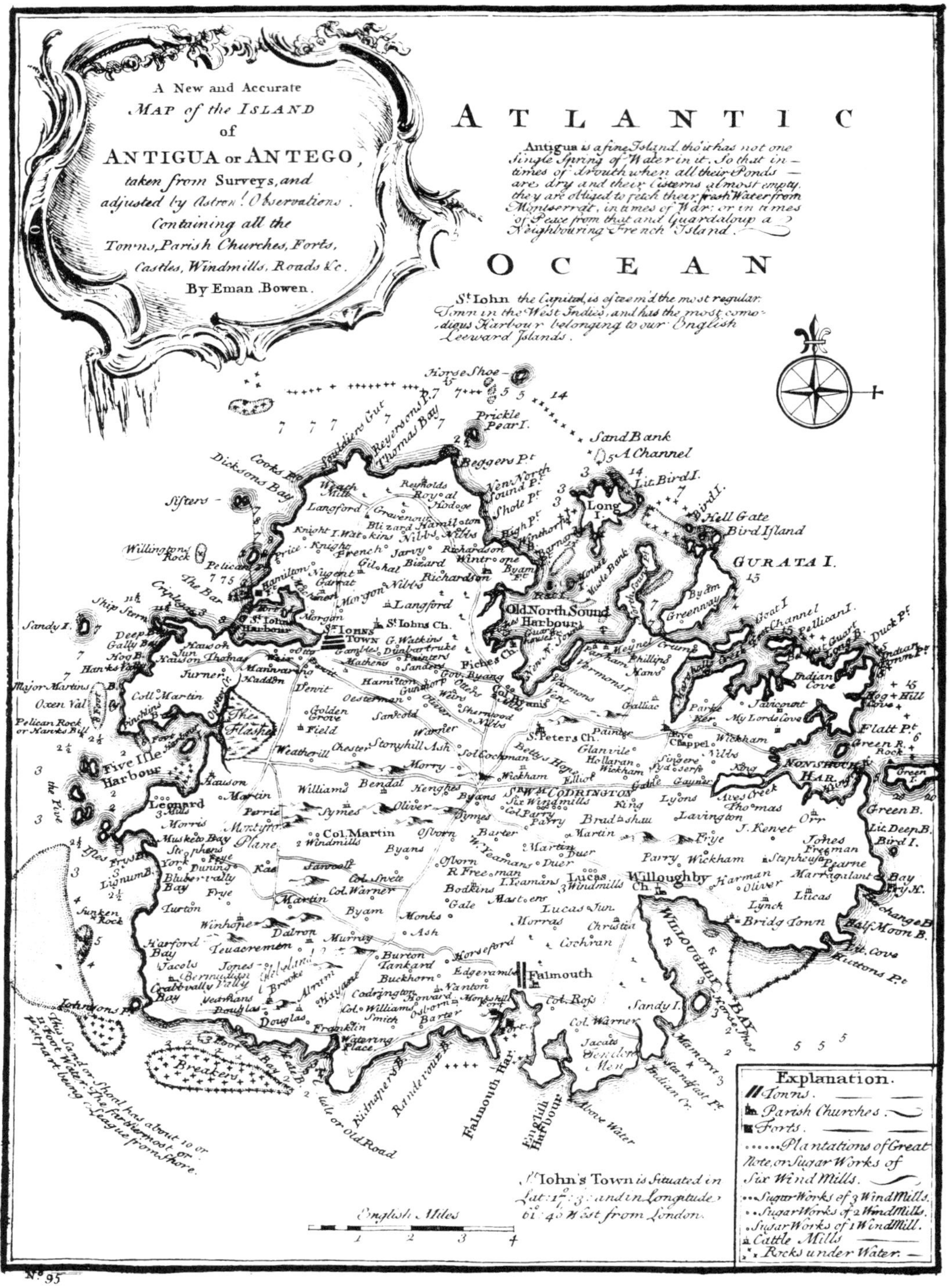

A New and Accurate
MAP of the ISLAND
of
ANTIGUA or ANTEGO,
taken from Surveys, and
adjusted by Astron! Observations.
Containing all the
Towns, Parish Churches, Forts,
Castles, Windmills, Roads &c.
By Eman. Bowen.
ATLANTIC
OCEAN
Antigua is a fine Island, tho' it has not one Single Spring of Water in it, So that in times of drouth when all their Ponds are dry and their Cisterns almost empty, they are obliged to fetch their fresh Water from Montserrat, in times of War: or in times of Peace from that and Guardaloup a Neighbouring French Island.
St. Iohn the Capital, is esteem'd the most regular Town in the West Indies, and has the most commodious Harbour belonging to our English Leeward Islands.
Horse Shoe
Prickle Pear I.
Sand Bank
A Channel
Lit. Bird I.
Long I.
Hell Gate
Bird Island
GURATA I.
Old North Sound Harbour
St. Iohns Ch.
St. Iohns Town
Five Isle Harbour
Willoughby
Falmouth
Falmouth Har.
English Harbour
NON SUCH HAR.
Willoughby Bay
St. Peters Ch.
Fiches Ch.
Sisters
Willingtons Rock
Sandy I.
Dicksons Bay
Cooks Pt.
Pelican Rock or Hawks Bill
Sunken Rock
Breakers
This Sand or Shoal has about 10 or 12 Foot Water, the farthermost part being 2 League from Shore.
Rendevous B.
Indian Cr.
Green B.
Half Moon B.
Explanation.
Towns.
Parish Churches.
Forts.
Plantations of Great Note, or Sugar Works of Six Wind Mills.
Sugar Works of 3 Wind Mills.
Sugar Works of 2 Wind Mills.
Sugar Works of 1 Wind Mill.
Cattle Mills
Rocks under Water.
St. Iohn's Town is Situated in Lat: 17°. 3'. and in Longitude 61°. 45' West from London.
English Miles
1 2 3 4
No. 95

largest estates and the most slaves, were from families resident in the island since the first Codrington's time or earlier. They had been joined by others who had arrived during the war years, and had added to their number a few who, like Tullideph, had come even later. Although estates frequently changed hands or were merged, such transactions usually took place between these same families, perhaps sixty or seventy in all by the middle of the eighteenth century, and often as a result of inter-marriage. As time went by it became increasingly difficult for an outsider to make a fortune without marrying into one of these families, even if he had been able to obtain enough land for a plantation in the first place.

By the time Tullideph left in the middle of the eighteenth century to become an absentee proprietor (the condition to which more and more planters aspired as the years wore on), his plantation was one of over 300 into which virtually all the island's arable land was divided. Although well above the average in size, his holding was nowhere as big as those of some of his fellow planters, several of whom had already been in possession of over a thousand acres each by the time he had first set up his practice as a doctor. By mid-century this size of holding had become almost commonplace, with perhaps a dozen planters each owning between 1000 and 2000 acres, and many more with 500 to 1000. As it was generally accepted that to be run efficiently and profitably a sugar plantation needed an average of one worker for every two acres, the ownership of such vast areas of land – in Antiguan terms – also meant the possession of huge numbers of slaves. There were many men like Tullideph with two or three hundred, and several, including Sir William Codrington (the second Baronet of Dodington who had succeeded his father the first Sir William in 1738), who owned nearly a thousand.

•

From a figure of about 12 500 in 1713 the slave population increased steadily for the next sixty years, to reach a maximum of almost 37 500 in the mid-1770s, by which time the white population had fallen below 3000. The number of slaves imported was never enough to satisfy the demand, and complaints similar to that voiced by a planter in 1758, that 'a plantation Cannot be Carried on without Negroes Accustomed to that Business & these are very seldom to be bought', were being voiced forty years earlier, and were still to be heard thirty years later. In the 1720s the demand was such that several of the richer planters, including the Lieutenant-Governor, Edward Byam, Edward Chester (who had been cuckolded by Parke), and an absentee proprietor, the first Sir William Codrington, had bought their own ships to trade for slaves. As a medium of exchange they used rum, made on their plantations for a fifth of what it could be sold for on the West African coast.

That the number of slaves in one small island increased by some 25 000 between 1713 and, say, 1775 is impressive enough at first sight, but not really that remarkable in the light of other statistics. Even when added together the slaves landed by Byam, Codrington and the rest of the Antiguan slavers represented only a tiny fraction of the total number imported in a period of just over sixty years. More than 50 000 arrived between 1720 and 1755, often at a rate of over 2000 a year, and it is likely that another 30–40 000 followed between 1755 and 1775.[6] That such numbers, in addition to the natural increase which took place as slave family life developed, only managed to triple the black population in this same period of a little more than sixty years must surely be seen as an indictment of the way in which such 'property' was used and treated by the planters.

In the pre-industrial era the sugar plantation was probably the nearest thing to an industry: 'a factory in the field' according to the historian Richard Pares.[7] Sugar, rum and molasses were all produced in the equivalent of a factory, and at the height of the harvest – with the mill and boiling-house working day and night – the amount of activity, heat and noise could have borne little resemblance to that of any other farming activity. A huge labour force was needed because human beings did the work of animals, and were often treated as such. At the same time no plantation could be worked by a large unthinking gang of slaves, with individuals or groups being detailed off for any job daily or seasonally. A great deal of knowledge was needed in order to carry out each of the different operations, from preparing a 'piece' to packing the hogsheads, and each slave – once he or she had been 'seasoned' – was trained out carry out a specific task or group of related tasks.

The seasoning process, by which 'salt-water slaves' as they were called, were acclimatised to plantation life and all the attendant horrors of slavery, was made as short as possible, but many failed to survive even this. The physical and psychological problems with which they were left after a traumatic transatlantic crossing under foul and harrowing conditions often proved fatal, and something like one in fifteen died soon after arrival on a plantation.[8] Having been given the names by which they would be known thereafter, those who survived were introduced into the routine of the work expected of them, and given a grounding in the pidgin English used to enable the whites to communicate with men and women from diverse linguistic and tribal groups. Those that got this far were still at risk, as about a third of all slaves died within the first three years, either from disease or from the wretchedness and torment of their condition. Female slaves succumbed just as easily to disease, but not being so prone to *taedium vitae* their death-rate during these early years was much lower than that of the males.

The great majority of plantation slaves were employed as field-workers, of whom there were usually just as many women as men. They did the hardest physical labour, using no more than simple tools, in a never-ending cycle of hoeing, planting, manuring, weeding and harvesting. Women who became pregnant were made to work until six weeks before delivery and had to resume three weeks later. All wore the minimum of clothing: the men worked in loincloths or drawers, and the women in skirts or smocks; hats and shoes were almost unknown. Children up to the age of puberty, unless they were employed indoors, went naked. Working hours stretched from sunrise to sunset, with a mid-morning break of half an hour and an hour's rest at noon, six days a week. All laboured under the general supervision of a white overseer, with each gang of between forty and fifty slaves under the eye of a black 'driver'. The drivers were themselves slaves, often creoles (that is, born in Antigua), chosen not only for their intelligence, strength and knowledge of the work required, but also because they had the respect of their fellows. Like the overseer each driver carried a whip, and was expected to use it. The work they supervised was monotonous, degrading and made harder than it need have been by the planters' refusal to consider the use of any of the labour-saving machinery and methods which had been introduced into European agriculture. The axe, bill-hook and hoe were the only tools used, and the most laborious task of all, that of preparing the ground for planting, was carried out with hoes in spite of the obvious difference the use of ploughs would have made. During harvest or 'crop' time, the work required of slaves at the mill and in the boiling-house, as well as being very hard was also dangerous. The round-the-clock operations often ordered increased the risk of accidents brought about by tiredness, and as the workers had no change of clothing any activity which involved moving to and from between the hot, steamy boiling-house and the cool night air introduced a risk to health.

In addition to gangs of field-workers a plantation also needed skilled tradesmen such as masons, carpenters, wheelwrights, coopers and sugar-boilers, and these positions had begun to be filled by slaves from early on in the century. The boilerman was the leading tradesman, highly skilled and greatly trusted as the quality of the sugar depended entirely upon his experience and judgement, but even this could not alleviate his condition. No matter how much depended upon him, his skill merely made him a more valuable piece of property, and should the sugar he produced not be up to standard for some reason he could be punished just like any other slave.

As all such skilled and semi-skilled positions were only open to men this soon led to an anomalous situation whereby the female slaves were in the majority in the field gangs, and obliged to do an even greater share of the hardest work. At Betty's Hope in 1751 – where there were equal numbers of men and women – women outnumbered men in the fields by three to two, because of the number of tradesmen. On the same estate thirty years later it was even worse, as the manager reported to Sir William Codrington, the absentee proprietor:

> We are at present so weak in Negroes that the women are Obliged to do the Labour of men, such as making fire, Carr[y]ing Potts of Sugar of 100 Weight which often occasions Violent Disorders & Miscarriages, and tends greatly to the Detriment of the General Interest.[9]

Not all women, however, had to suffer in this way, but even those who were fortunate enough to be given lighter duties frequently found that their employment brought its own forms of distress.

The planter (or his manager in the case of an absentee proprietor), in the way of the *nouveau riche*, invariably felt his position warranted the keeping of a host of domestic servants. Some of the females amongst them would have been indentured servants to begin with, but as their numbers decreased they were replaced by slaves. By the 1730s the occupant of even a modestly sized plantation house would take it for granted that he and his family needed the services of cooks, maids, nurses, seamstresses and washerwomen, while his grander neighbour would probably also require a butler, footmen, grooms and coachmen. All of these were selected from among the more presentable slaves, presumably chosen in the first place for some appealing physical characteristic, a markedly servile attitude or a pleasant disposition. Once trained for whatever positions they were to fill they could look forward to an easier life than any of the field-workers, with better food and a much better standard of dress; in some cases the males were decked out in fancy livery. At the same time they remained constantly under the eye of the planter and his wife, and at the beck and call of anyone in the house.

When it came to choosing the females amongst them, the owner's reasons for selecting a particular slave could be very different from those of his wife; and many a young maid or seamstress must have had to suffer both from the sexual attentions of her master, and from acts of victimisation carried out by her aggrieved mistress. There is no reason to suppose that the female slave servants of owners who were unmarried, or whose wives lived elsewhere, were much better off: life in a harem or under the thumb of a favourite concubine could well have been just as unpleasant. One result of such shenanigans was that, well before the end of the eighteenth century, the majority of domestics were of mixed blood. Most planters, even if they could not bring themselves to manumit their illegitimate offspring, were generally unwilling to commit them to the rigours of field work and, regardless of the feelings of their wives, kept them in or around the house.

Besides having to work to produce sugar the slaves were also expected to grow much of their own food. On each estate a certain area of land was set aside for the growing of corn and the ground provisions which, supplemented by a few imported foodstuffs such as dried fish, formed the bulk of their diet. While making the slaves grow most of their own food made good sense to the planters, their crops could not be raised without a regular water supply, and this was something which was never to be depended upon in Antigua. Any one of the island's frequent droughts could presage a disaster of the sort Governor John Hart[10] reported to the Board of Trade in May 1726:

The Dry weather . . . has continued for Eight months past; there having been no Rain fallen . . . till within this three days. So that [the planters] have not only lost their Crop for this Year and the next, But have been oblig'd to bring all their Water, from Guardeloupe and Mountserrat; which was sold at fifteen Shillings a Hogshead, which has occasion'd the loss of many of the Cattle and Negroes.[11]

A similar catastrophe was reported, in rather more charitable terms, twenty years later by Walter Tullideph, in his capacity as the attorney for an absentee proprietor, Sir George Thomas:[12]

> I must now inform you of very bad news here, no rains yet, all ye Guinea Corn burn't up & too late now to plant again, no prospect of a [Sugar] Crop & a probability of Provisions being very dear. Corn is now at 8/– & hardly to be gott . . . Most of ye Ponds in ye Island are drie, your negroes are reduced to drink ye Spring water at Vogan's. I wish they may not suffer by ffluxes.[13]

It is not known how many slaves on this estate or any other were lost from 'ffluxes' or just plain starvation on this occasion, but there can be little doubt that many were. Two years later, in August 1748, Tullideph wrote again to Thomas:

> We have planted Yams & Guinea Corn enough at Winthorpes to feed all ye negroes & at North Sound a large Yams piece, & always a good Potatoe piece by which your expence in feeding is greatly lessened . . . I hope negroes will now be imported here in greater plenty, that there may be an addition of 10 or 20 Young ladds . . .[14]

In the following June he was still asking for replacements for lost slaves, informing Thomas that he had enough cash in hand to 'purchase 5 or 6 young People for [Winthrops] Estate', adding 'You really want them, indeed the negroe Men are craving for wifes and therefore would advise Girls to be bought for that Estate and boys for North Sound.'[15]

Such matters were the subject of a great deal of the correspondence which passed between absentee owners and their attorneys throughout the years of slavery. 'Ladds' and their prospective 'wifes' were often discussed with little more feeling than if they had been cattle or horses, and the losses occasioned by trauma, psychological maladjustment, starvation, accidents, exhaustion or 'Violent Disorders & Miscarriages' usually meant nothing more than entries on the debit side of a plantation account book. The men who exchanged the letters and maintained the accounts were not all stony-hearted tyrants or depraved profligates, but none could conceive a plantation that was not worked by slaves. Nor could any of them visualise how such a workforce could be controlled except by constant close supervision, and the equally constant threat of harsh punishment for any wrongdoing.

Corporal punishment held a central position in plantation slavery, and all slaves from the oldest and most skilful creole to the newest 'salt-water' arrival, were subject to what can only be described as institutionalised violence. Even minor transgressions were punished with a whipping, often delivered before or after involving the victim in some degrading or disgusting act. For more serious offences – and anything could be so considered by a sadistic or malevolent overseer – a slave could lose an ear, have his nose slit, or be branded on the face. Should a slave retaliate in any way, an even worse punishment such as castration or the loss of a limb could follow. But the whip ruled the day to day life of all slaves, with the amount and frequency of its use entirely at the discretion of individual masters who, because it was they who controlled the Legislature and the judicial machinery, were immune from any legal reprisal for their sanction of unlimited brutality. At the same time, as Samuel Martin's murder in 1701 had shown all too clearly, they were not totally safe from retaliation.

Legislation which went some way towards restraining the violence of the slaveowners, which Codrington had been told to 'endeavour to procure' after Martin's death, was eventually passed in 1723. The 'act for attaining several slaves now run away from their Master's Service, and for the better Government of Slaves' which became law in December was, according to Governor Hart, intended 'to prevent the Inhumane Murdering Maiming and Castrating of Slaves by Cruel and Barbarous Persons (as has been too much practiced).' In reality it was more concerned with preventing slaveowners from inflicting punishments which might cause slaves to resist or rebel, rather than trying to curb inhumanity for its own sake. According to the preamble, although owners 'frequently kill, destroy, or dismember their own and other Persons' Slaves', they had not in the past been punished because, even if a law had existed under which they could have been tried, it 'would be too great a Countenance and Encouragement to Slaves to resist White Persons, to set Slaves so far upon an Equality with the free Inhabitants, as to try those that kill them for their Lives.' In future, however, any free person who killed a slave, caused the death of one through inflicting excessive punishment, or who gelded or dismembered a slave, would face prosecution.

In forwarding the act to London for approval, Hart stressed that there was 'no law before this, that laid any Penalty on Offenders for the Crimes mention'd', and while he had used his 'utmost Endeavours to make the Murdering a Slave Punishable with Death' he had been unable to 'gett it past in such a Manner, nor in any other than as It is now set.'[16] All the Assembly had agreed to were fines: between £100 and £300 for anyone found guilty of killing a slave; and from £20 to £100 for anyone convicted of 'Gelding or Dismembering'. It was hardly an eye for an eye, let alone a life for a life, but it did make the worst offenders less immune from legal retribution for their cruelty. At the same time it did little to make the owners generally less susceptible to slave retaliation, as events later in the century would demonstrate.

8
A Great Deal of Trouble in this Island

The events of the year 1736 were such as to strike horror into the hearts of all the white inhabitants of Antigua.

Mrs Lanaghan
Antigua and the Antiguans (1844)

We are in a great deal of trouble in this island; the burning of negroes, hanging them up on gibbets alive, racking them upon the wheel, etc., takes up all our time; that from the 20th of October to this day, there have been destroyed sixty-one intelligent negroes, most of them tradesmen, as carpenters, coopers and masons.

Walter Tullideph, in a letter to his brother,
15 January 1737

Much of the 1723 Slave Act was concerned with the problem of runaways: those slaves who had (because the existing laws had proved 'too mild and gentle to curb and restrain them')

> deserted the Service of their Masters, and fled to the Mountains and Rocky Parts of this Island, and have armed and assembled themselves in Bands to oppose their Masters and any that come in pursuit of them.[1]

By the time the act was published some fugitives had been at large for considerable periods of time; men like Papa Will, Sharper, Africa and Frank were believed to be responsible for enticing 'other Negroes to desert their Master's Service, and join with them'. These four were actually named in the act, and large rewards offered for their capture, dead or alive. At the same time encouragement was given to the hunting down of all other runaways. Any slave who, after being on the island for a year, ran away and remained at liberty for over three months was considered a felon, and would be executed after recapture. Anyone assisting or concealing such a fugitive would, if free, be fined heavily, and if a slave, suffer a flogging. The owners of runaways who were caught and executed were to be compensated from public funds.

The new act brought about little change in the numbers of slaves who decided that a life on the run was preferable to that of a field-hand. In 1730, although Sharper, Frank and the others had by then been tracked down and killed, the Assembly was still complaining about the 'great number of Runaway negroes [who] harbour themselves in a Body in the Mountains called Sheckerleys and about the Road Mountains & commit great Insults and Roberes in the Neighbourhood.' There was also alarm at the cost involved in their recapture. Three years earlier the Lieutenant-Governor, a planter named Edward Byam,[2] had criticised the 'excessive charge the Publick has been at in Executing Negros for running away', and had suggested that perhaps this could be lessened by allowing the magistrates to 'shew mercy to those that are less Culpable by taking of a limb or disabling them some other way.' The Council went along with him on this, proposing that if a recaptured runaway were 'hamstringed in one legg' he would be 'incapable of running away' again while remaining of use to his owner, and there would be 'a great expense saved to the publick'. None of this made much impression on the Assembly, composed of the sort of men who preferred to be compensated for property destroyed rather than having to cope with recalcitrant cripples of little or no value, and no change was made in the law until 1739. In that year, its members having taken over a decade to think about it, the Assembly decided that if recaptured slaves were 'Condemned to Chains, and Kept upon the Public Works, and the Owner paid for them as if Executed It would not only be of Service to the Country, but a greater Terror to Runaways than by being Executed.' Although such a long reluctance to consider any relaxation of the death penalty for runaways might give the opposite impression, it was not entirely to do with money and the devaluation of property. It also rose out of fear of a slave rebellion, something which had preyed on the minds of the white population since 1729.

In that year nearly half of all the claims submitted for compensation for executed slaves concerned those who had been convicted of involvement in a conspiracy to revolt. The plot had originated in the north-east of the island among a few slaves at Coconut Hall, an estate belonging to Nathaniel Crump, a planter who had been a minor participant in the Parke affair. It gradually involved slaves from six of the surrounding plantations, and in the end was betrayed by a slave from a seventh. A total of fourteen were arrested and – although there was little solid evidence to support the charge – accused of conspiring to kill Crump and his family and then, in a 'design laid much deeper than is yet imagined', bring about a general uprising. At their trial five were found guilty of acts which were thought to deserve the death penalty, but of these only four were executed. Hercules, one of Crump's slaves, was hanged, drawn and quartered before being beheaded and his head put on display.[3] Three others from Coconut Hall, Hanniball, Prurry and Boquin, were burned to death. Cuffy, another of Crump's men, had his sentence reduced to transportation, and joined the other nine who had been sentenced to be sent 'to some place from whence they cannot carry on a Correspondence with the Negros of this Island.' This was supposed to be one of the colonies in South or North America, but in the end they seem to have been sent no further than St Kitts.

Crump and all the other owners whose slaves had been involved, among them Sir William Codrington and Edward Byam, received compensation for their losses, while the appropriately named Tom, the slave who had informed the authorities of the plot, was not only set free but awarded a lifetime annuity from public funds. Lord Londonderry,[4] who had replaced Hart as Governor in 1727, reported to the Board of Trade that he considered many more than fourteen slaves had been involved, but had ordered no further investigation 'because everything is perfectly quiet', and because he felt the results would not justify 'the great Expence it would bring on the country'. A strange decision, considering that a slave uprising was the chief anxiety of the white population throughout the days of slavery, and the thought of disaffected slaves going not only unpunished but undetected could only have increased the general paranoia. With the benefit of hindsight, the Governor's decision was mistaken and unwise.

While nothing has ever been established to link the slaves involved in a conspiracy which took place in 1736 with anything that went on with Hercules, Hanniball and the rest seven years earlier, it would be surprising – had the earlier plot been as widespread as Londonderry alleged – if some slaves did not play a part in both. But by 1736 Londonderry had long since gone to his grave, and Governor Mathew was the man who, in the middle of October, was informed that a plot had been discovered 'whereby all the White Inhabitants . . . were to be murdered, & a new form of Government . . . Established, by the Slaves, among themselves, and they intirely to possess the Island.'[5]

Earlier, on Sunday 3 October, and on the only day of the week on which they were able to gather in large numbers, a huge crowd of slaves had assembled in a pasture outside St John's. In the middle of the afternoon they had watched what many of them, together with all the 'Great many White People [who] were present', could only have taken to be a noisy and colourful pantomine. During this, a very presentable, middle-aged slave called Court, in what had appeared to be fancy dress and surrounded by other outlandishly clad slaves, had been 'Crown'd King of the Coromantees'. The whole ceremony, with drumming, dancing, stamping and shouting, had passed off without incident, and was later recalled by some of the bemused white spectators as 'Only an Innocent Play of Courts Country'.

In fact it was anything but innocent, being nothing less than a ritual declaration of war on the whites conducted according to the Akan customs of that part of West Africa from which most of the onlookers had been taken. It was carried out in order to mobilise and inspire those slaves who had already entered into a plot to rebel, and to demonstrate to the rest that they had a leader prepared to take on their masters. Had any of those slaveowners who had stood and gawped in the afternoon sun known or cared anything about the background and culture of their slaves, they might not have been so sanguine in their opinion 'that no harm Could be meant by it, More Especially as it was Represented before so many White People.'

Suspicion was eventually aroused eight days later, during the arraignment in St John's of a group of slaves charged with gambling. In the course of his investigation the magistrate, Robert Arbuthnot, was told of the existence of some sort of list of slave officers and soldiers, and after making more enquiries this led him to voice an opinion that 'the Island appeared to him to be in Utmost Danger from the slaves'. Those to whom he spoke then began recalling unusual events such as Court's 'coronation' and strange sights and noises heard around the town, and owners began questioning some of their more trusted slaves. Within twenty-four hours Arbuthnot had heard enough about slaves gathering 'in the Pastures and Out Skirts of the Town', and of conch shells being blown during the night, to be sure that something untoward was going on, and had gathered enough information from two coopers to have a very good idea of just what it was. When one of his informants, Jack, admitted that he had a major role in a plot being led by Court, it was in the magistrate's opinion 'beyond all Doubt that a Conspiracy was formed and near ripe for Execution'. He reported his findings to the Assembly on 15 October, and four days later he and three other Justices of the Peace were appointed to carry out a full investigation. Later the same day Court, Jack, and ten other slaves were arrested and a few days later a special act was passed giving the investigators authority to gather and use the testimony of slaves, even if to obtain it they first had to inflict 'pains or Tortures not extending to Loss of life or limb'. This was not necessary in the case of Court and the others already under arrest, as they had already been interrogated and full details of the plot revealed.

To their horror the four justices discovered that an uprising had been planned to take place on the very day that Arbuthnot's suspicions had first been aroused. This had involved blowing up the governor's residence during a ball to celebrate the anniversary of the coronation of King George II, and the subsequent massacre of the rest of the white inhabitants of St John's by armed slaves coming in from the surrounding plantations. The plot had been brewing since the previous November, and had only been foiled by a last-minute decision to postpone the ball until 30 October. Although extremely fortuitous for the Governor and the gentry who would have attended it, the delay proved the undoing of the conspirators by giving enough time for disagreements to break out among the ringleaders, and for an inkling of the plot to reach Arbuthnot.

The main instigators were found to be Court and a slave called Tomboy. The former was the 45-year-old 'waiting-man' or valet of Thomas Kerby, the Speaker, and so well trusted that he had been permitted 'to carry on a Trade and many other greater Indulgencies than were allowed to any Slave in the Island.' Tomboy, who was probably about the same age, was a master carpenter owned by a merchant named Thomas Hanson. He too was highly thought of, and allowed to work for himself, taking on apprentices to help him in business, and 'paying his Master only a monthly Sum, far short of his usual Earnings.' Both were convicted within a day of being arrested and sentenced to be broken on the wheel.[6] Court was executed the next day in order to lose no time in demonstrating that the conspiracy had been uncovered, and that the authorities remained firmly in control.

> King Court was brought to the Place of Execution, there was laid extended on a wheel, seiz'd by the Wrists and Ancles, and so laid basking in the Sun for the full Space of an hour and a Quarter, or more, when he begg'd Leave . . . and . . . acknowledged every Thing that was alledged against him.[7]

After then being crushed and beaten to death his head was cut off and displayed on a pole near the prison door, while his body was taken to be burned in Otto's Pasture to the south of the town.[8] Tomboy had to wait until the following day, 21 October, to meet his end in the same way. He expired after having 'received 35 strokes with a large Iron Bar as hard as a lusty Negroe Fellow could strike upon the Breast', and he too was beheaded before being burned. Another carpenter, Hercules, suffered the same death after 'above four hours torture' on 22 October, while four other convicted slaves – all 'valuable Tradesmen and Sensible Fellows' – were burned alive on the same day. It took a few more days to convict the remaining five of those who had been apprehended, but eventually they too were burnt to death on Otto's Pasture.

Arbuthnot and his fellow investigators then ran out of suspects, or at least of any they could convict. Neither Court nor Tomboy had given away too much in their 'imperfect Confessions', and it was not until information was let slip by a female slave that the justices began to appreciate the full extent of the conspiracy. When they also received word that many of the as yet unidentified slaves who had joined the plot had now added vengeance for Court's death to their intentions, the search for all of those involved was renewed with greater intensity, and a further descent into barbarity. It was decided that burning alive and being broken on the wheel were 'too lenative and not Sufficiently Exemplary because the Criminals were not long enough under their Sufferings', and that other methods were needed to strike 'greater Terror into the Slaves that may see their Suffering'. Any suspect convicted in future would be gibbeted, 'hung up alive with proper Iron Work about their Bodies in the Publick Market Place', and left suspended without food or water until they expired.

During the first two weeks of November six more slaves were killed in this way, before being beheaded and burned. After that the justices never looked back. Such were the number of suspects they managed to convict of involvement in the plot that gibbeting as a means of creating terror became unnecessary. By 20 December forty-seven executions by burning or being broken had taken place, and the investigators were forced into asking to be relieved, 'being quite fatigued & wearyed out by a Long Attendance'. They were replaced by Governor Mathew with two members of the Council and three from the Assembly with any three, provided one was a Council member, able to constitute a court. They swung into action immediately, and another twenty slaves had been put to the torch by the middle of January 1737, causing Mathew to lament to the Board of Trade that 'I hope they will in good time put an end to these Executions, I think they are very numerous.'

Numerous or not they continued until the final eight pyres were set alight on Otto's Pasture on 8 March. By then a total of eighty-eight slaves, the majority of them craftsmen or drivers, had been executed. In addition another four dozen had been, or were about to be, banished either to North America or to one of the Spanish colonies. The slaves of some sixty owners, including the Governor himself, were involved. The majority had lived in St John's, and the rest came from plantations in every part of the island. The total amount of compensation claimed by the owners for slaves executed or banished approached £10 000 (compared with the £662 which seven years earlier had caused Londonderry to refuse to sanction any further expenditure on investigating the 1729 plot). This was an enormous sum which, when added to the costs of the investigation and rewards for informants, saddled the island with a financial burden it took more than a decade to clear.

Among the few suspects who had in the end to be released were four free men, John Corteen, Thomas Winthorp, and two brothers, Benjamin and William Johnson. Three were former slaves who had been given their freedom, while Winthorp, who was generally referred to as 'Mulatto Tom', may have been born free. Fortunately for them all, and to the great discomposure of the Legislature, the only evidence of their involvement in the plot came from slaves, and such evidence was not admissible in the trial of free persons, whether black or white. An attempt to charge them with high treason, by passing a law specifically to allow the evidence of slaves in their case, failed when the law was disallowed in London because it threatened to 'open a door to the greatest Oppression and Injustice'. After spending a considerable time in custody all four men were released towards the end of 1738.

There is reason to believe that they, as well as one or two other free blacks who were not pursued so vigorously, were indeed involved in the plot in one way or another, but at the time nothing more could be done about it. The law denied the unfree any right to give court testimony against the free, mainly in order to protect masters from being made accountable for the cruelty they inflicted on their slaves, and this had to be preserved. Continuing freedom for whites to treat their property more or less as they liked was far more important than carrying on with an attempt to twist the law in order to execute a few more blacks. And in any case, as the Assemblymen probably murmured to each other, there were plenty of other means for teaching people like the Johnson Brothers the error of their ways.

Once all those who could in any way have been involved in the conspiracy, and who could be convicted, had been disposed of, life eventually returned to what in a slave-based society passed for normal. As the report of the investigating justices laid much of the blame for the plot on owners who had let so many slaves like Tomboy work for themselves, or engage in 'Occupations truly proper only for Freemen' such as distillers, sailors or hawkers, some attempt was made to enforce the existing laws:

> After the suppression of the insurrection . . . it was resolved in future to keep a better watch over the negroes, and be more strict in the government of them. Slaves were not to be allowed to congregate about the streets of St John's; and if they refused to disperse, when ordered to do so, it was justifiable to fire upon them: the country paying for those who were shot.[9]

It was a short-lived resolution. Life and business in St John's could by this time no longer go on without the presence of a large number of slaves working as servants, craftsmen, traders and porters, any more than a plantation could operate without its field gangs, drivers and tradesmen. Even an act passed in 1739 prohibiting slaves from hawking or retailing could not be strictly enforced: too many owners in town and country alike were able to profit in some way from the numerous, unsupervised activities undertaken by their slaves. This, together with a widespread, unspoken acceptance among slaves that if they could not hope to alter their condition by force, they could at least alleviate it by continually pressing to turn every privilege into a right, soon returned life to very much what it had been before discovery of the planned revolt.

9

In the Service of their Country

H.M. Ships of warr careen, and English Harbour is an excellent safe one in the most violent stormes. Here is full room for ten or twelve men of warr or more of any rate, store-houses too are provided . . . and here the sea stores are laid up, and careening places close to the shore as to a wharf, and many more such careening places may be made in this harbour.

Governor William Mathew (1734)

I am told it has strangely prevailed among the poorer sort, that if in this Cause or any of Warr they are Called upon, tis to defend the Rich and wealthy only, and this at the Expence of their Lives, therefore that such a duty does not belong to them. But we ought all of us to Cure them of this Refractory Error by letting them know that the articles of Warr Established by Law will Certainly bring them to an Ignominious punishment or Death for their avoiding an uncertain Honourable One in the Service of their Country.

Governor William Mathew (1739)

The 1736 slave conspiracy, followed by the start of the War of Jenkins' Ear three years later, brought about a much-needed overhaul of the island's defences. By March 1737, when the full extent of the foiled revolt was known, Governor Mathew and the Legislature were conscious that both internal security and the general defence arrangements left a great deal to be desired.

The militia had been called out when martial law was declared soon after the discovery of the plot. Although within three months of this Mathew was able to inform the Board of Trade that 'Out of this Evil Antigua has gained an Advantage I long laboured for in vain', and that 'The whole Militia now is armed & with bayonets, & have been taught the use of them', as a force it was still top-heavy with officers and, given the numbers who were by law supposed to belong to it, grossly undermanned. Exemptions had been obtained by some of the better off, while others could always find an excuse to avoid service. This had created a reaction among the poorer whites, and among the indentured servants who had no option but to serve, causing them to grumble, as Mathew observed, that they were required 'to defend the Rich and wealthy only, and this at the Expence of their Lives.'

The garrison of regular troops hardly made up for the militia's shortcomings, having been reduced through long neglect to about 150 men divided into five pitifully undermanned companies: 'much too small a force for security'. The officers and men of what from now on it is easier to refer to as the 38th Foot[1] had been badly treated throughout their time in Antigua. In 1712 Governor Douglas had complained that the troops had no suitable accommodation and were being denied proper provisions, while their officers were being reduced to a state of poverty by having to feed their men from their own pockets. Fifteen years later Lord Londonderry had been urged by London

> to lay before the legislature . . . the necessity of building barracks for the accommodation of the regiment of foot stationed in the island, or else assign them quarters, by billeting them upon the several estates, or in the towns.[2]

But nothing had been done until 1735, when some rough and ready buildings were put up to the east of St John's. The tables were turned when in March 1737, as a result of the slave plot, a request for a larger garrison was made on behalf of the Legislature by the colonial agent, Yeamans, in London. This was turned down very smartly and nothing more was done until two years later, when the commanding officer of the 38th Foot, Lieutenant-Colonel Valentine Morris, went to London to make his own case for more troops.

Besides being an army officer, Morris, who had been born in Antigua, was also the owner of four large plantations and some 600 slaves. The fact that he was also a member of the Council may have helped his cause, but it is more likely that British knowledge of the approach of another war was the reason that a request for a larger garrison was now granted. In return, however, the Antiguan authorities were required to build proper barracks capable of accommodating at least 600 men, together with a military hospital, and to undertake to contribute an annual amount of 'additional subsistence' to enable the troops to be able to afford to buy the island's provisions. The Assembly had no choice but to accede, but insisted that the barracks could only be built 'with a contribution from the King', and if an assurance was given that there would never be less than 400 soldiers stationed on the island.

The site chosen for the barracks was on an islet in the middle of St John's Harbour with the unappealing name of Rat Island. This was connected to the shore by a rough causeway, so that using a grant of £2000 from Britain (about half the total cost), work could begin in 1740 and was completed the following year. The finished barracks, designed to accommodate eight officers and 240 men, came nowhere near meeting the needs of the 600 men specified by London, or even the 400 insisted upon by the Legislature, and extra accommodation had to be found elsewhere. Work had already begun on enlarging Fort James at the entrance to the harbour, and within a couple of years the barracks there, together with those in Fort George on Monks Hill, were able to hold another 250 soldiers. In the 1750s yet more barracks, complete with a military hospital, were built on the eastern outskirts of St John's, replacing the temporary quarters which had been built earlier.

Reinforcements for the 38th Foot began to arrive before the Rat Island barracks were finished, and during the next five years over 900 recruits were sent out from the British Isles – enough to provide garrisons for St Kitts, Nevis and Montserrat, as well as maintain the 400 minimum in Antigua. Morris did not return from England and command of the regiment passed to Major George Lucas, another estate owner who combined his duties as an army officer with those of a planter. The Rat Island barracks were not universally popular, being considered by the men to be too close to a large swamp to be good for their health, and by the officers as being too close to the grog shops and other low-life attractions at the shady end of St John's to be good for discipline.

A conflict between Britain and Spain – the War of Jenkins' Ear – broke out in the middle of 1739, but this had little effect on Antigua until February 1743, when most of the garrison were removed to take part in an attack mounted by the Navy on two ports in Venezuela. The Legislature had never been very happy about troops being sent to the other Leeward Islands, and had grown increasingly concerned as the numbers of those left in Antigua were steadily and inexorably reduced by disease. With the departure of Lucas and a sizeable proportion of the garrison the Assembly considered the British Government's undertaking to keep 400 troops on the island had been broken, and so ceased payment of the soldiers' additional subsistence money. Governor Mathew, who as well as being the British Government's representative was also a professional soldier with the rank of lieutenant-general, came in for blame from the Assembly and garrison alike, but could do nothing to resolve the situation. After the return of Lucas with a much-reduced number of troops in the middle of the year, he withdrew the Montserrat garrison and brought other men from St Kitts, but such had been the losses in the failed expedition to Venezuela that it was no longer possible to keep 400 men in Antigua and provide adequate garrisons elsewhere in the colony.

Even though Lucas, now a lieutenant-colonel, had been made Lieutenant-Governor in 1742, he could do no more than Mathew to improve matters – particularly as the colonel of his regiment, Lieutenant-General Robert Dalzell, was an unprincipled rogue. At the same time as the Assembly was robbing the troops in Antigua by withholding their very necessary subsistence money, Dalzell in London was defrauding the Government by pocketing the cash he had been given to supply his regiment with uniforms. As a result, long before he was eventually cashiered and prosecuted in 1750, his men in the Antigua garrison who had not already died 'like rotten sheep' were being forced to find civilian occupations in order to survive. The War of Jenkins' Ear ended in 1748 with the regiment in a worse condition than ever, and with Dalzell unwilling or unable to find recruits to send out to make up the losses. Pleas like the one sent to him in March of the following year – 'For God's Sake Sir, send Us over 40 or 50 Recruits that we may compleat, and discharge some real Invalides' – proved ineffective and usually went unanswered. By the middle of 1752 it was reported that 'there is not a regiment in His Majesty's service whose condition is more to be lamented', and even the junior officers were either living on charity, or had 'betook themselves to employments which elsewhere would not be thought compatible with their rank or duty.' None of this made any difference until, once again, the threat of war made both the Army authorities and the Antigua Assembly reconsider the value of the garrison.

Long before the outbreak of the Seven Years' War in 1756 Governor Mathew had asked the Assembly to consider the possibility of arming slaves for the defence of the island, arguing that

> from among our Negroes, we certainly may arm a thousand sturdy faithful fellows, that with a little encouragement, will I know do eminent service.[3]

As a result, when a new Militia Act was passed at the start of the war, it contained a provision under which all slaveowners were required to provide the commanding officer of the militia with a list of all slaves aged between eighteen and forty, and each planter had to nominate one-twentieth of his most able male field-hands for duty with the militia as required. The war, another conflict between Britain and France, only began to affect Antigua in 1759 after the Governor, George Thomas,[4] had been asked to contribute troops, both black and white, to a planned invasion of one of the French islands. He managed to soothe the planters' fears by informing them that any slaves taken for this purpose were 'to be transported, victualled and armed at the King's Expense, and to be paid for, in case they shall be killed or disabled.' The Assembly cautiously agreed to let 300 take part. In the end, although probably more than this number were involved in the successful capture of Guadeloupe in May, they were not armed, but were used as pioneers or 'as Rangers, to supply the camp with Cattle'. Similarly, in early 1762, having been requested as:

> Pioneers, drawers of cannon, or such other services, as from their accustom'd Labour and exposure to the Sun, they shall be judged better able to undergo, than the natives of other Climates . . .[5]

Two or three hundred slaves took part in the equally successful invasion of Martinique.

The 38th Foot took part in both of these operations, suffering even further losses from death, wounds and disease. The ragged and unkempt appearance of the regiment, which can have been little better than that of the slaves, and which compared very unfavourably with the fighting ability that had earned it two Battle Honours, must have been very evident to the generals and other senior officers taking part. It seems likely that their reports played a large part in the recall of the regiment after the war ended. When they eventually left Antigua in 1764, a modern regimental history poignantly relates, 'to make their ragged and faded clothing more presentable, other ranks wore sackcloth, normally used for packing sugar, in place of the official facings.'[6] They were replaced by another British regiment, but long before this, or before any debate about arming slaves had taken place, it had become obvious that the defence of the island, as with that of all the other British West Indian islands, was primarily a matter for the Navy.

•

From the beginning of the eighteenth century the Navy had maintained a squadron at Port Royal in Jamaica, except during the hurricane season when it moved to North America. This was of little comfort to the islands of the eastern Caribbean, as Jamaica was nearly 1000 nautical miles downwind; and while news of an attack could be sent to Port Royal in days, help would take weeks to arrive. Any ships which then did operate among the smaller islands had no access to stores or equipment, no harbour with proper repair facilities, and none of the base support and safety found at Port Royal.

By the 1720s the Antigua Assembly had become highly critical of the lack of naval protection, and knowing that when they did visit the island naval vessels made much use of English Harbour on the south coast, began to press for it to be developed as a base. The captains of some of the ships which had sheltered in this harbour over the years had also argued for its development, but nothing was done before 1725 when Captain Arthur Delgarno of HMS *Southsea Castle* reported that

> English Harbour might be made a very proper place for careening and refitting, and so save H.M. ships the trouble of going to the Northern Colonies for that purpose.[7]

His views were supported by the Legislature's purchase of twenty acres of land which were presented to the Admiralty and, once Delgarno's report had been accepted, by their funding of the construction of a careening wharf on the eastern side of the harbour and a proper fort to replace the small battery which guarded the entrance.[8] The associated capstan-house and storage sheds, together with cannons and equipment for the fort, were provided by 'His Majesty in his great wisdom' and within three years the first dockyard, called St Helena, was already in use. Captain Delgarno, who seems to have had much to do with the planning and supervision of the construction, was rewarded by the Assembly at the beginning of 1728 with the sum of 200 guineas for his services.

The actual construction work was of course carried out by slave labour, and a great deal of the £1250 which had been spent by the Legislature on the creation of the dockyard by 1729 went on paying their owners for their services. What they constructed proved to be too small and rudimentary, and other buildings and facilities were soon required, both at St Helena and at another site immediately opposite, on the large peninsula which formed the western side of the harbour. Work on creating a base and dockyard big enough to meet the needs of an increasing number of ships continued for most of the eighteenth century, with slaves being employed throughout. They not only did most of the heavy construction work, with the occasional assistance of prisoners of war (as in 1744 when about 100 Spanish captives were so employed), but also gradually became involved in assisting in all aspects of running the base. In 1749 the Commodore of the Leeward Islands Squadron (formed six years earlier as soon as the base was functional) informed the Secretary of the Navy that 'I find by General Mathew they [the Assembly] cheerfully lend us any Negroes we want for the Support of this Harbour.' Within a few years slaves were being used to heave down ships for cleaning, and had become involved in the more demanding aspects of ship repair; one or two tradesmen were already in the process of being converted into shipwrights.

Even though English Harbour was developed in this way it was never entirely suitable as a naval base. For one thing it proved to be very unhealthy, especially when – as during the hurricane season – it harboured numerous ships and any outbreak of disease was likely to run through all of their crews. Being almost completely landlocked it was a difficult place to enter and leave, and it proved to be too shallow for the largest men-of-war. Because of this, and much to the distress of the island legislatures, the larger ships on the station were always sent away for refitting or to escape the hurricane season. As the Leeward Islands Squadron rarely consisted of more than three or four ships of the line, with perhaps half a dozen frigates and a few sloops, their absence made a considerable difference to its strength. In wartime the Antigua Assembly led the way not only in complaining that the squadron never had sufficient ships to deter an invasion, but also in criticising its senior officer for not properly utilising those he had.

The War of Jenkins' Ear between Britain and Spain, which had begun in 1739, had little effect on the Leeward Islands until events in Europe caused the French to enter it on the side of Spain five years later. It was then a different story altogether, with the islands once again in danger of being attacked, and their trade at risk from privateers. The prospect of an invasion disappeared when a French fleet, which had entered the Caribbean when France entered the war, returned to Europe in 1745; but this was offset by the large number of privateers which soon appeared. Protection of British shipping from their depredations – together with disruption of the enemy's trade – now became the main concerns of the Commodore of the Leeward Islands Squadron. Because of the size of the squadron, however, these two activities were not totally compatible.

Defence of British trade, which meant cruising to windward, outside the arc of the eastern Caribbean islands, was boring and unrewarding in the days when the prospect of prize money was the only thing which made naval life tolerable; but to operate in areas where French prizes were to be taken meant abandoning British shipping to the mercy of privateers. The Antigua Assembly's constant demands that the squadron remain close to the island clashed with the desire of its captains for prize money, and the Commodore's dispositions rarely pleased either the Assembly or his subordinates. During 1746, when Commodore Fitzroy Lee was in command, the Assembly's complaints reached a new level. That Lee was a 'free liver' and 'a man of debauched habits and foul tongue' was hardly here or there, as many of the most vociferous members who dubbed him 'Commodore Bottle' or 'the Bacchanalian Commodore' were hardly renowned themselves for rectitude and sobriety. It was Lee's inept handling of his squadron which caused the storm of criticism. The ships he deployed around the island were never there at the right time to prevent the seizure of a sugar-laden merchantman, and those he sent after prizes rarely found any. At the end of the year, after eliciting support from Barbados as well as the other Leeward Islands, the Legislature informed the Admiralty 'that their whole trade would be sacrificed if Mr Lee was continued in the command', and accused him of drunkenness, incivility and general neglect of duty. Such accusations could not go unanswered and in February 1747 Commodore Edward Legge was sent out to take over the squadron and bring Lee to a court-martial on charges of misconduct and dereliction of duty. In the end though, having been found guilty of nothing but inefficiency, Lee returned home to continue his career, leaving Legge (who died within the year) to mollify the Assembly with the orders he had been given to concentrate henceforward on the protection of trade.

Commodore Lee was probably not the first naval officer to have been found wanting in Antigua, and he was certainly not to be the last. Only eight years after he had been relieved one of his successors, Commodore Thomas Pye, was sent home in disgrace, charged with peculation and neglect of duty. Both men suffered no lasting harm to their careers: Lee eventually rose to become a vice-admiral, while Pye not only made full admiral, but managed to acquire a knighthood on the way.[9]

•

Dishonourable or disreputable men, whether naval, military or civilian, were nothing new in Antigua in the middle of the eighteenth century. By this time, as the island entered what would be recognised later as its golden age, sugar completely dominated the economy just as slavery pervaded every aspect of society. Over the next twenty-five years or so the rich planters would become even wealthier, partly at the expense of the poor whites who were driven out, but even more so at the expense of the shiploads of slaves which were brought in, and no one would have much time for virtue or matters of honour and reputation. There would be few transient visitors, whether in a ship at English Harbour, in the officers' mess at Rat Island, on the verandah of some plantation house, or even at the Governor's table in St John's, who would not be corrupted or debased in one way or another by all that was going on around them.

1 Reaping sugar-cane in the eighteenth century (Topham Picturepoint)

2 An eighteenth century boiling-house and animal-powered sugar mill
(Topham Picturepoint)

3 Field slave on his way to work in the eighteenth century
(Topham Picturepoint)

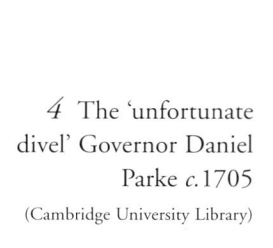

4 The 'unfortunate divel' Governor Daniel Parke c.1705
(Cambridge University Library)

5 The Martello Tower at The River landing in Barbuda, built in 1745
(Nicole Mouck Photography)

6 The Court House in St John's as completed in 1750
(Cambridge University Library)

7 Horatio Nelson: a portrait painted in 1777 but altered in 1781 to show the insignia of a post-captain (Popperfoto)

8 The dockyard at English Harbour in 1803, with Shirley Heights in the background (Hulton Getty)

9 The interior of the boiling-house at Delaps estate in 1829
(Cambridge University Library)

10 Shipping hogsheads of sugar from Willoughby Bay in 1829
(Cambridge University Library)

11 The Cathedral of St John the Divine, consecrated in 1848, photographed *c.*1910 (Cambridge University Library)

12 Workers' housing on the outskirts of St John's *c.*1910 (Cambridge University Library)

13 The city of St John's c.1910, viewed from the site of the present-day hospital (Cambridge University Library)

14 St John's Harbour as seen from the summit of Rat Island c.1910 (Cambridge University Library)

10
Every Foolish Extravagance

The Caribbean plantocracy constituted the most crudely philistine of all dominant classes in the history of Western slavery. Even Labat, worldly realist that he was, lamented that everything had been imported in the Indies but books.

Gordon K. Lewis
Main Currents in Caribbean Thought (1983)

To be manager of an estate, in this isle, I am well satisfied is one of the best situations in it, altho' their stipends amount to no more than eighty to one hundred pounds sterling per ann., and notwithstanding the necessaries and superfluities of life are considerably dearer than at London; yet, however paradoxical it may appear, when I tell you that this description of men sport several dishes at their tables, drink claret, keep mulatto mistresses, and indulge in every foolish extravagance of this western region, it is nevertheless strictly true.

John Luffman
A Brief Account of the Island of Antigua (1789)

In 1751 it was reported that Antigua had 'improved to the utmost, there being hardly one Acre of Ground, even to the Top of the Mountains, fit for Sugar Cane and other necessary Produce, but what is taken in and cultivated.' On the 300 or more estates which covered the island the way in which the land was worked, and the manner in which sugar was produced, had barely changed in a hundred years. Each plantation was divided into arable and pasture land, with the former in almost continuous use, its fertility maintained by the use of manure produced by the animals in the pasture. The process of making sugar was as it always had been, except that wind-driven mills had by now largely replaced those worked by animals. Other innovations in farm implements, land use and animal husbandry, which had already revolutionised agriculture in Britain, had hardly been noticed. To most of the planters none of this seemed to matter; the price of sugar was high and steady, and there was a ready market for all they could produce. The average annual production was nearly 10 000 tons, double what it had been twenty years earlier.

The prosperity this brought to the island, and which was to last for little more than a couple of decades, was obtained only at a high cost to human life, and to the detriment of land which, in spite of constant fertilising, was already 'getting impoverished by long Culture'. As the number of slaves required to keep the plantations in full production constantly increased, the limited amount of land made available to them for growing provisions became less able to support them. The resulting increase in price both of land and of imported foodstuffs brought about another change in society. Many of the smaller landowners sold out and departed, and by 1775, when the start of the American War of Independence brought about the end of the 'golden age' of sugar, there were hardly more than 2500 white people left on the island. Among them the planters still exercised the most power, but were increasingly obliged to admit merchants and professional men into the political structure. Together, in addition to being councillors, Assemblymen, officers of the militia, vestrymen, churchwardens, judges and justices of the peace, they also filled most of the main offices of government.

The Governor shared his political authority with the 'local notables' who formed the Council, and depended on the elected House of Assembly to provide the revenue needed to run the island, but had no civil service to assist him. All the senior officials, people like the Colonial Secretary, the Treasurer, Customs Collector, Attorney-General, Clerk of the Court, and Clerk of the Market, were appointed by Letters Patent issued in London – granted by government ministers to relatives, friends or political supporters who were felt to deserve some reward. No salaries, other than perhaps token ones, went with these appointments, as the rewards came from the fees or commission each office-holder charged for his services. No appointee was required to carry out his duties in person, or even to live on the island, and his position was normally filled by a local man, renting the post in return for a proportion of the money to be made from it. As none of these deputies could be removed from office except by the patentee, and as the majority rented their positions for financial reward only, their loyalty to the governor and commitment to the good of the community were nothing if not suspect. Their over-riding concern, as of the planters, merchants, lawyers and doctors – from among whose families of course many of these officials were drawn – was to make enough money to enable them to retire with a fortune to the British Isles.

Matters to do with the effect that concentrated sugar-cane cultivation was having on the land and slavery on society were of no consequence. Soil exhaustion, the spread of crop diseases, the constant wastage of human life in degrading circumstances, were accepted or ignored by all but a very few. Nor did it help that as the century wore on, and more and more proprietors retired while the going was good, that many estates were left to be run by managers under the general direction of attorneys. Such men had even less reason to consider the introduction of new methods or to contemplate any change in the way plantations were run. In the rate at which the planters turned themselves into absentee proprietors Antigua remained more fortunate than many another island, as Governor Sir Ralph Payne[1] noted in 1773:

> The number of Proprietors of these Colonies, who live in Europe, is . . . infinitely superior to the very few who are left . . . Antigua has much the advantage of the other Islands, with respect to Men of Fortune and Education, and in Point of an independent and respectable Inhabitancy.[2]

Whether the behaviour and lifestyle of the entire planter class entitled them to this description is perhaps open to question, but there were one or two proprietors at least who managed to live reasonably respectable lives and to demonstrate some independence of thought and action concerning both the operation of their estates, and the treatment of their slaves.

Among these the one who led the way was Samuel Martin, the owner of Green Castle plantation and the son of the man of the same name who had been so violently murdered by his slaves in 1701. He was unusual in a number of respects, not the least being that, after thirteen years as a member of the Assembly, followed by another twenty in England as an absentee landlord, he returned to the island at the age of fifty-seven to resume his proprietorship. He found his estate, which had been managed by his brother, 'ten fold worse than it was naturally' with the sugar-works 'all tumbling down', and was faced with the need not only to carry out repairs and re-stock with animals, but also to buy a large number of slaves. While carrying out this work and obtaining the animals and slaves he gave considerable thought to ways in which the estate's productivity and sugar quality could be improved, coming to the inescapable conclusion that this would only come about if both the land and the slaves received better treatment.

His experiments with different fertilisers and planting methods, in draining the land in different ways to suit differing soil conditions, and in using ploughs instead of hand-hoes, were matched by measures he took to improve the health and wellbeing of his slaves. Although he remained a stalwart defender of slavery, he was sensible and humane enough to realise that he would get better results if his slaves were fed, clothed and housed properly, trained correctly, and if each was employed in a manner appropriate to his or her age, strength, general ability and temperament. The measures he introduced included the services of a doctor, treatment of the sick in a specially built hospital, and basic instruction in Christianity. His policy of purchasing young males and females in equal numbers in order to increase the birth rate, although it initially put him into debt, paid off very quickly and for at least twenty years after 1755 he had no need to buy any more.

In connection with his development of what one historian has called a 'rudimentary system of agronomy'[3] Martin was so gratified by the results that in

1754 he published details of his methods in *An Essay on Plantership*. This proved to be so popular that it ran into seven editions and remained in print until 1802, with its precepts being adopted by many of the resident planters in all of the English-speaking islands. It proved less popular among those managing plantations on behalf of absentee owners, as few of these men had the time to experiment with new methods, or the incentive to ask an owner to invest in labour-saving devices like ploughs. Nor did they have the inclination to alleviate the lot of the slaves for whom they were responsible – except, as sometimes happened, in the case of particular individuals among them.

Samuel Redhead, a contemporary of Samuel Martin, was besides being a planter and a member of the Assembly also the attorney for Sir William Codrington, in charge of the latter's estates in both Antigua and Barbuda. His concern for the good of Codrington's slaves lasted no longer than they retained their ability to work, as he demonstrated in 1769 when he suggested that those who had grown too old or feeble to be of use should be manumitted, thereby relieving the estate of any further need to support them, and in effect sentencing them to death from starvation. Codrington, to his credit, did not agree. While the conduct of Redhead's wife – a virago who had 'art enough to make him believe he is the father of a tribe which is undoubtedly the offspring of others' – was possibly not that of too many of her contemporaries, his own behaviour once out of sight of this Jezebel was very much that of his peers. His visits to Barbuda obviously combined business with pleasure as he sired children there by at least two slaves. One, who bore him a son, he bought from Codrington and freed in 1771. Another, the mulatto half-sister of a Godfrey Davy in Antigua, had to wait until Davy purchased her freedom eight years later, by which time she had 'borne many children for Mr Redhead and now wishes to retire'.[4]

Men with the character and morals of Redhead had always outnumbered the more upright and humane such as the younger Martin since the earliest days of the settlement. Regrettably, as the white population continued to decrease (eventually falling below 2000 in the early 1820s), it was their values which came to predominate, much to the detriment not only of the slaves but of society in general.

The situation was not helped by the continuing existence of a law specifying that every slaveowner had to employ a certain proportion of white men, even though by the mid-1750s the ratio had been amended to one indentured servant for every thirty slaves, or payment of an annual fine of £40 in lieu. Such servants were now required to serve for four years in return for their transportation, 'sufficient meat drink washing and lodging' during the period of employment, and £20 a year in the 'current money of Antigua'. This was not unattractive in rural Britain where a farm labourer could expect to earn an average of £20 a year with nothing found. By becoming indentured he not only ended up with the same amount of money 'all found', but probably for doing less strenuous work and certainly with enhanced status. No white man at this period was going to be considered just another kind of slave, nor was he going to be made to work alongside slaves except in some kind of supervisory capacity. As all indentured servants would be only too keen to preserve the elevation from the bottom of the class structure which their entry into a slave society brought them, it is hard to believe that any in the employ of men like Redhead would not have adopted the same outlook and attitudes as their employers.

For the owners of smaller estates and fewer slaves there was little to choose between hiring a servant or paying the annual fine, as many could barely afford either. In 1767, in an attempt to slow down the rate at which such men were selling up and leaving, the Assembly modified the law once again.

> The cause of these persons emigrating, it appears, was on account of their not being allowed to reckon the female members of their family, in the place of a white servant to so many slaves, as the law required, as was the case in Jamaica and St Vincent's; it was therefore deemed expedient this year to give way in this respect, and permit two women to count as one man.[5]

This made so little difference that seven years later the Assembly, in desperation, changed the regulations again to permit Roman Catholics to be hired. Prior to this no one who was not prepared to swear he was a Protestant – in addition to taking an oath of allegiance – was accepted, but under the new law the first requirement was dropped. Eight years later still the number of slaves for whom one white man or two white women had to be employed was increased from thirty to forty, with an increase in the deficiency tax of £13 a year. None of these measures did more than bring about a temporary halt in the rate at which the white population continued its inexorable decline.

•

The slave population reached its maximum of about 37 500 in the middle of the 1770s, at much the same time as, through a combination of factors, the planters' golden years came to an end. By this time, in spite of all the work they had to do and the way in which they were regimented, the slaves were able to work the system in such a way as to give them some life of their own and to alleviate the worst aspects of bondage. Malingering had become a fine art and, with the huge disparity in numbers between those who laboured and those who supervised, there were many opportunities to avoid work. In 1774 the manager of Parham Hill plantation complained to the absentee owner about the current state of affairs on the island:

> There are a great many superannuated and Infant Slaves, who cannot do anything, which, with the Sick, Stock keepers, Watches, Tradesmen, attendants at the Sick House, and upon the white people in the Estates,

and now and then run away, reduce the numbers of Negroes working in the Field very considerably.[6]

Such was the number of slaves by this time that it had become entirely possible for one to run away and, if he could keep his wits about him and had already acquired a trade or some particular skill, to live as a free man. This had been recognised as early as 1757 when an act was passed in an attempt to control the increasing numbers of slaves found away from the plantations:

> A Custom hath prevailed for several Years past of permitting Slaves to go about Towns and Country to hire themselves out, or take their own Liberty and pay their Masters and Mistresses for their time, by which Means many Negroes, who were actually runaways, under Pretence of working out, or being at Liberty to hire themselves, have been employed in the Towns and Country unknown to their Masters and Mistresses.[7]

Under the new regulations a slave could not hire himself out as anything but a porter in the towns, and only then if he wore a special badge and could produce a pass signed by his owner giving consent to such employment. Slaves were also forbidden to go about as pedlars or hawkers, or to sell 'Goods, Wares, and Merchandizes of any Sort' without express, written permission.

These restrictions were not strictly enforced, any more than those introduced in 1773 which were intended to prohibit trade between slaves and the crews of ships in St John's Harbour, on account of 'divers Felonies and Frauds . . . committed, by Means of Boats, commonly called Bum Boats . . .'; or those of 1780 'for preventing the practices of slaves vending sugar, rum, molasses, and sugar canes and . . . for preventing abuses in carrying on the inland trade of the Island.' By the time this last act was passed it was all too late. Something like one-third of all the slaves no longer worked on the plantations, and there were slave artisans, pedlars, porters, hucksters and boatmen in profusion. The vast majority of course still belonged to owners who were only too willing to profit from their various activities, but among them were a sizeable number who had liberated themselves by running away from plantation life.

For the other two-thirds of the island's slaves, those who remained condemned to a plantation existence, other than when some respite could be obtained by swinging the lead, life in the latter years of the eighteenth century remained just as harsh and unpleasant as it always had been. Although by now it had come to be accepted that, except during the busiest periods of the harvest, slaves had both Saturday afternoon and Sunday free, the former was when they were required to tend their provision grounds. These could be either an allocated part of the estate where they worked under supervision or individual small plots in the 'Negro Ground', where they grew such crops as yams, eddoes, potatoes, corn and plantains to supplement the weekly rations of imported foodstuffs. During the same day and a half they also had to carry out their own chores and to make whatever enjoyment they could. The only slave holidays which had the force of law were Christmas Day and the two succeeding days, as ordained in an act of 1723 as 'Play-Days for their Recreation', and for violation of which an owner faced a fine of £20. Clothing was still as basic as ever, something which caused a visitor in 1787, John Luffman, to lament:

> It is my opinion, were the slaves to go quite naked it would have no more effect on the feelings of the major part of the inhabitants of this country than what is produced by the sight of a dog, cat, or any other domesticated quadruped.[8]

The way in which a large proportion of the indoor slaves were dressed was little better, and the gross insensitivity and crudeness of many of those who lorded it over these domestics is revealed in another of Luffman's observations:

> The tables of the opulent and also of many, who can ill afford it, are covered with profusion, known only in this part of the world; their attendants numerous, but it is not uncommon to see them almost destitute of clothing, and the little they have mere rags. Even in the first houses, where an attendant slave may possibly have a shirt, jacket, and breeches, they are always without stockings, and generally wanting shoes.[9]

Not all of the 'opulent' got away with treating their slaves in this way, as was the case with Giles Blizard, the owner of a plantation in the north of the island. Blizard well lived up to the description of him given by the author of *Antigua and the Antiguans* as 'a true planter of the olden time' living in an estate house 'where the polished surface of the mahogany furniture mocked the unwashed walls and darkened roof of the apartments, whose protruding beams afforded safe protection to innumerable hordes of insects.' He was both wealthy and coarse:

> Everything in his dwelling was conducted upon a scale of heavy munificence; his table groaned beneath the weight of its various viands; but there was no order, no delicacy . . . A stranger would have been surprised at having wines of the choicest vintage handed to him by a bare-footed butler, or his every movement attended to by a host of half-naked negroes.[10]

In 1774, at just about the time his fellow planter Samuel Redhead was busy adding to the population of Barbuda, Blizard was murdered, shot to death by two slaves amid his gleaming mahogany furniture. According to Mrs Lanaghan, from whose book these details are taken, he was killed in the course of a robbery while attempts were being made to force him to disclose the wherabouts of 'a noble portion of hard cash' – a reason which seems just as improbable as that given by the same author for Samuel Martin's murder in 1701. A more likely explanation is that the plantation's slaves had a longstanding grievance, not just against Giles, but against the entire Blizard family. Stephen Blizard, Giles's father, had been a slave dealer as well as a planter, and must have been well hated. Giles, as an infant in 1723, had been the victim of an attempted poisoning, carried out by two slaves who had then run away to join the Shekerley Mountain maroons. It seems probable that his murder, like that of the elder Martin, was carried out as an act of revenge rather than in the heat of the moment as part of some lesser crime, especially as one of the two murderers was Geoffry, 'the natural son of the old man'. He and his unknown collaborator made no effort to carry out the attack in secrecy, or to go into hiding once it was over. They were both apprehended the following day, and beheaded two days later.

•

Up until the closing years of the eighteenth century the greatest, if not the only, change for the good in the condition of the slaves was brought about through the work of sectarian Christian missionaries, of whom the first to arrive in Antigua came from St Thomas in 1756. Samuel Isles belonged to the Moravians or United Brethren, a Protestant Church which had been committed to missionary activity from the time of its foundation in Germany twenty-nine years earlier. As this Church had been at work among the slaves in the Danish West Indies since 1732, and because its missionaries concentrated solely on converting them to Christianity and teaching acceptance of the rule of both the temporal and the spiritual Master, Isles was permitted to take up residence in St John's and begin the same work among the slaves of the surrounding estates, as well as that of Samuel Martin at Green Castle. He baptised his first convert, a female slave on Gambles Estate, in January 1757, the year after his arrival, but progress in building up a congregation was very slow. The first Moravian chapel, a small hut at Spring Gardens on the northern outskirts of St John's, was not built until 1761, and there were probably no more than a handful of converts at any time during the first fifteen years of the mission.

This all changed in the 1770s, by which time Methodism had been introduced and the planters were able to see that the missionaries posed no threat to the social order, but rather that their teaching served to make the slaves more tractable and industrious, and less inclined to challenge their condition. By 1775 a proper chapel had replaced the earlier rough building at Spring Gardens, and out of some 2000 'hearers' some ten to twenty were baptised every month. Within another fifteen years there were five Moravian preachers at work, another chapel had been erected at Grace Hill (around which the village of Liberta would grow up in the next century), and there were well over 5000 converts.

William Warrener, the first missionary ever to be appointed by the Methodist Church to minister to non-Christian black people, arrived in the island in 1786, Antigua having been chosen as the base for his mission because of the earlier activities there of a number of white converts. The first of these was Nathaniel Gilbert, a lawyer and planter who had met John Wesley, the founder of Methodism, while on a visit to England in 1758. Two years later, soon after his return to Antigua, he had begun preaching to his family, servants and friends in his house in St John's, and a few weeks afterwards to the slaves on his estate in the east of the island. Thereafter, having resigned his position as Speaker of the House of Assembly and given up his law practice, he combined preaching with running his plantation until his death in 1774. His brother, Francis Gilbert, had joined him in 1763 in order to conduct a hectic, year-long evangelistic crusade among both whites and blacks, as he informed Wesley in June of that year:

> I preach in St John's every Sunday afternoon, and every Tuesday and Thursday at sunset. At Parham . . . I preach one Sunday in the morning, the other in the afternoon before I preach at St John's. Here I also preach on a Wednesday evening. I preach at my brother's house every Monday, Friday and Saturday night, and the congregation is increasing . . . Once a week I meet all the family as also the white servants; and once a week I meet my brother's children, also the house-Negroes, and a class for the other Negroes beside.[11]

Not surprisingly perhaps his health had broken down as a result of all this activity and, having been forced to go home to England, he did not return for another nine years. His second sojourn lasted until 1775 when, a year after his brother's death, his health failed once more and he departed again for England. The death of Nathaniel followed by the departure of Francis left the 200-strong Methodist Society they had formed without a proper leader, but it was kept going by the devoted efforts of two women, the free black, Sophia Campbell, and the free coloured, Mary Alley, who ran classes and prayer meetings as best they could. Their efforts were rewarded in 1778 when John Baxter, a Methodist lay preacher, was sent out from England as the Chief Shipwright of the dockyard at English Harbour. He immediately took up where the Gilberts had left off and within a year, by preaching each evening and every weekend, had increased the Society's membership to over 600. He was joined by Francis Gilbert's widow three years later and with her help, and that of his wife, raised enough money to build the first Methodist chapel in St John's in 1783. The following year, after being appointed an 'Elder' or Presbyter, he resigned from his dockyard post in order to work full-time for the Society, which by now had nearly 2000 members. He had written to Wesley soon afterwards, asking for an ordained minister to be sent to the island, and it was in response to this request that Warrener eventually stepped ashore on Christmas Day 1786.

Once he began work the number of Methodists increased rapidly and, even though he had been sent specifically to preach to the slaves, he even managed to convert some of the white population. By 1793 there were 6570 Methodists on the island, of whom about three dozen were white. Another hundred or so belonged to that growing section of society made up of people of mixed ancestry and blacks who had either earned or been given their freedom – all of whom, black or brown, it is perhaps more convenient from now on to refer to as 'free coloured'. Warrener's work, like that of Samuel Isles, was mainly concerned with converting and 'civilising' the slaves. In this they concentrated on the saving of souls, and in teaching the acceptance of the present while preparing for a better afterlife. Their efforts, although mocked and obstructed by many of the slaveowners, were to the benefit of society as a whole: the slaves were re-introduced to concepts of proper family and community and given new spiritual values, while the planters were provided with a more docile and fatalistic workforce.

•

When Baxter erected the first Methodist chapel in 1783 St John's had already acquired the layout, much of the extent, and some of the character it was to retain from then on until around the middle of the twentieth century. St John's Parish Church stood on the site of the present Anglican Cathedral[12] on the north-eastern edge, and an imposing stone courthouse (today a museum) had been built thirty years earlier in the centre close to the town arsenal (now the police station). The remainder of the town, apart from the barracks (which became the prison in due course) to the east of the church, mostly consisted of wooden buildings on either side of a pattern of streets which, although they were considered 'spacious', were unpaved and dirty:

> The prickly pear bush and other shrubs are suffered to grow therein, to the annoyance of the passenger, and secreting of every species of nastiness; and, to the great increase of vermin, insects, and reptiles, with which this place abounds.[13]

To the west, in an unsavoury area known as The Point, through which it was necessary to pass to reach the inshore end of the Rat Island causeway, was the burying ground for the slave and free coloured population, whose dead were all denied any resting place in consecrated ground. The barracks on Rat Island, which were never very well built in the first place, were out of use and 'suffered to go to ruin' by 1786. Elsewhere in the town, in positions which can no longer be identified but were probably not too far removed from The Point, or an equally insalubrious area to the south around the slaves' marketplace at Otto's Pasture, the gibbet and pillory remained very much in evidence. Punishment in the latter was not confined to the non-white population, as was observed in 1788 when according to Mrs Lanaghan, a Jew was sentenced to be pilloried for robbery:

This punishment, however, did not appear to make due impression upon the guilty Israelite, for a spectator of the exhibition (in a letter to a friend) describes him as standing there with the utmost assurance, 'holding, with one hand, his hat before his face, and with the other, supporting an umbrella to prevent the sun warming his head.'[14]

While the outward trappings of religion and the law were very much in evidence, anything to do with matters such as education, the care of the sick, culture or charity was totally absent. Apart from the occasional ball held in honour of some important visitor or to celebrate a royal occasion (and one can only wonder about the standard of music played), the entertainment of the white community – other than indulging in the pleasures of the flesh – consisted of little more than cockfighting, dicing and playing cards.

The leisure pursuits of the rest of the town's population were equally, but more understandably, philistine, mostly taking place on Sunday at Otto's Pasture. There, 'an assemblage of many hundred negroes and mulattoes' bought and sold at the market which had been held on the site each Sunday morning since the beginning of the century. The fresh produce was brought from well outside St John's, carried to town by plantation slaves with or without the passes the law required them to obtain from their owners, while less perishable articles were brought by the town slaves. According to John Luffman in 1788, 'The noise occasioned by the jabber of the negroes, and the squalling and cries of the children basking in the sun' were at their height by mid-morning, as – understandably in view of what the slaves wore and how they were fed – was the odour:

> The smell is also intolerable, proceeding from the strong effluvia, naturally arising from the bodys of these people, and from the stinking salt-fish and other offencibles sent for sale by hucksters, which the negroes will buy, even when in the last stage of rottenness, to season their pots with.[15]

As trading ended well before midday the afternoon gave plenty of opportunity to socialise, and for plantation slaves to enjoy the pleasures of town life. Some forms of entertainment were innocent enough, but others less so. While 'the principal dancing time is on Sunday afternoons, when the great market is over', the same afternoons also provided time to gamble, frequent 'Disorderly houses' and grog shops, and to take part in fighting – sometimes in pre-arranged matches. Needless to say, although the law turned a blind eye to most of what went on, this was not the case with the missionaries, for whom what took place at Otto's Pasture was an unholy abuse of the Sabbath. But even if their preaching could do little to curb the slaves' enjoyment of Sunday, it was just as well that under their zeal the Moravian and Methodist Churches began to flourish when they did, as the prosperity of the island and the condition of the slaves began to suffer at much the same time. This was brought about by the start of the American War of Independence in 1775 and a prolonged period of dry weather which caused Governor Sir William Burt[16] to compare the island five years later with the 'desert of Arabia'.

•

When the war began many of the planters in the British islands had great sympathy for the rebels in North America, and must have been tempted to join them. They had, after all, many of the same grievances, including taxation without representation, interference in their legislative freedom, and trade restrictions imposed by the British Government. At the same time an island like Antigua lacked any ability to defend itself, and as the many absentee landowners who were then living in Britain were in no position to support a rebellion any such feelings in the island were soon repressed. Instead the merchants and planters all complained vociferously about the effect the war was having on their ability to make a decent living, and turned to smuggling.

Until 1775, the North American colonies had been the main source of estate supplies such as lumber and staves for making hogsheads, as well as cattle and horses. They also supplied the foodstuffs – rice, flour, salted fish, corn and pulses – needed to help feed the slaves. Once war was declared all these supplies were cut off and could only be obtained by Antiguan merchants and planters by trading, in contravention of the prevailing trade laws, with neutral islands such as St Eustatius where they were still available – at a price. For the slaves, the result of such shortages and high prices, combined with the effects on their own provision grounds of the prolonged drought of the late 1770s and early 1780s, was disastrous. On one estate alone, between the summer of 1779 and the following autumn, one-tenth of the slaves died from a combination of insufficient food and dysentery caused by the lack of clean drinking water. They represented only a fraction of those who perished from starvation and sickness during the war years, of whom an estimated 8000 succumbed in 1780 alone.[17]

While losses on this scale caused great concern to the planters, even if for no other reason than that replacements were now not only scarce but considerably dearer, it was the effect that the war had on the trade with Britain which produced the greater distress. American privateers appeared in the Caribbean in 1777, and once France declared war on Britain the following year, sugar shipments were under increased threat. Freight and insurance rates shot up, British rates of duty were increased, and by 1780, after Spain and The Netherlands had joined in the war on the side of France, the planters were facing ruin. The amount of sugar arriving safely in Britain was only half what it had been before the war started, and there was no longer any certainty of even covering production costs.

•

The British Navy did all it could to protect the trade of Antigua and the other islands, but as it was having to fight a war against all the other major naval powers from 1780 onwards, commercial shipping remained at considerable risk until peace returned in 1783. Any danger of an invasion had ended the year before with the destruction of a French fleet in the Battle of the Saintes, but this had made no difference to the disruption of trade, which remained unabated until the end of the war. The Legislature and planters of Antigua remained aggrieved throughout, convinced that even though they provided the Navy with its eastern Caribbean base enough was never done to safeguard their interests. As a result, by the time the war ended, the Navy and its senior officers in the region were held in even less esteem than in the days of Commodore Lee. The dockyard had of course come into its own since 1775, with storehouses, workshops, a boat-slip and accommodation for dockyard officials all being built or enlarged. Its greatly increased use had not, however, been without its drawbacks. 'The men who are employed in . . . English Harbour suffer considerably from the heat and closeness of the situation, the access of the regular breeze being intercepted by the elevated ground which environs this spot', a visitor had noted in 1781, before going on to add:

> The quantity of rubbish and filth daily discharged from the ships must tend, by quick putrefaction, in some measure to corrupt the water into which it is thrown . . . This is therefore considered as the most unhealthy part of Antigua, and many have here suffered by putrid distempers.[18]

One man who quickly came to endorse this view, and to return in full the antipathy expressed towards naval officers by the Assembly and planters, was the twenty-five-year old Captain Horatio Nelson, who arrived there in July 1784 in command of the frigate HMS *Boreas*, and as senior officer of the Northern Division of the West Indies Station.

As the war had drawn to its close the British Government had taken steps to try and exercise firmer control over the West Indian colonies. The Board of Trade had been abolished and the main responsibility for colonial affairs placed in the hands of the Secretary of State for Home Affairs (where it remained until being transferred to the Secretary of State for War in 1801). Not long afterwards, in order to deal with commercial matters, he set up a Committee of Trade and Plantations, a body which made continuing observance of the Navigation Laws one of its main concerns. This followed an Order-in-Council in 1783 which banned all United States vessels from West Indian ports, and gave the sole right to supply the islands with foodstuffs to Canadian and Irish merchants. Anything else the islands required could be imported from the USA, but only in British ships.

This was a devastating blow to the revitalisation of the islands' economies after the long depression caused by the war, and was bitterly resented – nowhere more so than in Antigua where, after public protests, the merchants and planters set about getting around the Navigation Laws by selling British registrations to American ships, organising the transfer of cargoes at sea, and allowing American vessels into port under the pretence of their being in distress. At the same time a petition was sent to the Governor, who by this time was Major-General Thomas Shirley,[19] demanding that the Order-in-Council be suspended. Shirley was not prepared to accept this, but did admit the future looked bleak and made no effort to try to prevent the blatant illegal trading which was taking place. Such was the state of affairs when Nelson arrived at English Harbour, fully aware of the importance the British Government attached to the Navigation Laws and determined to enforce them.

Soon after Nelson's arrival an uproar ensued when a ship of his squadron, HMS *Mediator*, intercepted an American vessel as it was about to enter St John's Harbour; an act which caused Governor Shirley to complain to Nelson's superior, the Commander-in-Chief of the West Indies Station, who preferred to live in Barbados. 'An amiable, easy-tempered man, without much energy or force of character',[20] Rear-Admiral Sir Richard Hughes was not prepared to do anything one way or the other, and issued Nelson with the obfuscating instruction to 'let the residents of the various Islands decide the various cases'. This was the last thing a man of Nelson's temperament wanted to be told, as he complained in a letter he sent to a naval friend in January 1785:

> I, for one, am determined not to suffer the Yankees to come where my Ship is; for I am sure, if once the Americans are admitted to any kind of intercourse with these Islands . . . They will become first the Carriers, and next have possession of our Islands, are we ever again embroiled in a French war. The residents of these Islands are Americans by connexion and by interest, and are inimical to Great Britain . . . I am determined to suppress the admission of Foreigners all in my power.[21]

His actions were as good as his words and he set about preventing any further landing of American cargoes, not only in Antigua but in all the Leeward Islands, a move which caused him to be ostracised by island society wherever he went. It also brought him into increasingly bad odour with Governor Shirley, to whom in due course he found it necessary to appeal for support in ending illegal trading. This was unavailing as Shirley was just as much an 'American by connexion and interest' as any of the infuriated islanders he was trying to govern. The high-handed tone of Nelson's request only served to make him reply with asperity that 'old respectable officers of high rank, long service and of a certain life are very jealous of being dictated to in their duty by young gentlemen whose service and experience do not entitle them to it.' Whether this majestic rebuke really did produce the much-quoted and equally choice rejoinder, 'I have the honour, sir, of being as old as the Prime Minister of

England, and think myself as capable of commanding one of His Majesty's Ships as that Minister is of governing the State', is open to question, but in any case their exchange of correspondence altered nothing. Nelson remained at odds with Antiguan society throughout his time in the Caribbean, and his enforcement of the Navigation Laws continued to bring distress of one sort or another to all who lived on the island.

The odium in which the Navy was held as a result was alleviated to some extent in December 1786 when HMS *Pegasus*, under the command of the twenty-one year old Captain His Royal Highness Prince William Henry, arrived to join Nelson's squadron. The presence of one of the sons of King George III in English Harbour threw island society 'into a ferment':

> Addresses were immediately presented to him from the legislative body, and likewise from the merchants, expressive of loyalty to his royal father, and of the happiness and honour his highness had conferred on them by his gracious visit.[22]

Nelson was practically forgiven and the Navigation Laws almost forgotten in the excitement. Two grand balls were held at which 'The ladies put their best smiles upon their faces, and their best adornments upon their persons; indeed, every individual seemed emulous of shewing respect to the royal visitor.' The excitement continued over Christmas and into the new year, as Nelson confided on 13 January to Fanny Nesbit, the young widow in Nevis he was to marry two months later:

> I was in hopes to have remained quiet all this week: but today we dine with Sir Thomas; tomorrow the Prince has a party; on Wednesday he gives a dinner at Saint John's to the Regiment; in the evening is a Mulatto ball; on Thursday a cockfight, and we dine at Colonel Crosbie's brother's and a ball: on Friday somewhere, but I forget; on Saturday at Mr Byam's, the President. If we get well through this, I shall be fit for anything.[23]

To the besotted ladies of St John's, for whom the Prince was a pleasant and agile dancing partner, and to planters like Byam and the Crosbie brothers, for whom a meeting with any member of the royal family could be turned to who knew what advantage in the future, William could do no wrong. 'How long he means to honour this isle with his presence, I cannot with certainty learn', John Luffman noted later on in January, 'it will probably be several months; the people here, I believe, hope and *wish it may be for years*.'[24]

Those who did look forward to the Prince living amongst them for such a period might not have been so sanguine had they had any idea, as Nelson surely had, of his true nature. Besides being a bad-tempered naval officer who drank too much, and a brutal martinet as the commanding officer of a ship, he was also an habitual fornicator. The black and coloured women of the islands had proved irresistibly attractive to him as soon as his ship entered the Caribbean, and he had had several bouts of venereal disease before he reached Antigua. This caused him no concern, and made so little difference to his womanising that in May 1787 he could joke in a letter to one of his brothers about 'a sore I had contracted in a most extraordinary manner in my pursuit of the *Dames de Couleurs.*' Fortunately for Antiguan womanhood he spent very little time in English Harbour, even though a house was built for his use overlooking the dockyard.[25] He left for Canada in the autumn but was back in England in disgrace before the end of the year, on account of an affair with a married woman and the size of his debts: neither of which prevented him from being created Duke of Clarence two years later. Nor, regrettably, did his experiences among the *Dames de Couleurs* then do anything to prevent him from voicing his fervent opposition to the anti-slavery movement which was coming into its own around the same time.[26]

After Nelson's departure from Antigua, which also took place in 1787, and even though his successors were perhaps not quite so zealous in enforcing the Navigation and Trade laws, the general condition of the island continued to deteriorate. By 1792 things were so bad that the Council and Assembly petitioned George III, complaining of being 'reduced to the utmost distress by successive years of dry weather, and the devastation of insects formerly unknown in the Colony; whereby the labour of the planter has been rendered unprofitable and many families reduced from affluence to want', and requesting the granting of free port status

> as the only means of restoring our expiring commerce, of preventing our remaining inhabitants from quitting the Island, of inducing those who have left it to return, of encouraging new settlers among us, and of saving the Colony from ruin.[27]

Such ports already existed in Jamaica, Dominica, Grenada and the Bahamas and, even though under the provisions of the Free Port Act plantation stores from the USA would still not be admitted, it was considered that some benefit at least would accrue from increased trade. The petition met with success and free port status was granted the following year – just in time for the start of another war to ensure that it made no difference whatsoever to the declining fortunes of the island.

•

During the ten years which had elapsed since the end of the American War of Independence Governor Shirley had fought a running battle with the Legislature about the state of the island's defences and the money needed to improve them, a battle which had become more and more rancorous as the economy declined. Under the existing arrangements, Britain provided a naval force and a garrison of troops; in return, the Legislature was required to provide funds and labour for the upkeep of the dockyard, quarters and a local allowance for the troops, and a contribution towards the construction and maintenance of new fortifications. The last, unless imminent danger threatened, was something the Assembly was always finding excuses not to provide.

Because of the importance English Harbour had assumed during the American war a scheme had been drawn up in 1782 to protect it by fortifying the high ground overlooking it from the east, a scheme which even three years later had barely been started through lack of funds. Writing to the Secretary of State, Shirley complained that it had 'always been a matter of astonishment' to him that the French had not attacked Antigua during the war, before adding 'I have not the least doubt, in case of another war, if it is as defenceless as it was then, that it will be one of the first objects of their attention.' In order to speed up construction and reduce the cost he proposed that the slaves needed to carry out the work should be fed on army rations:

> It will induce the Legislature here to be more liberal in their allowance of negroes for labour which is attended with great fatigue from the situations of the Posts being upon eminencies, and the distance for bringing materials being generally very great. The hire of artificers and mechanics of all sorts are very dear. Masons and Carpenters will not be procured for less than four or five shillings per diem and Blacksmiths rather higher as they are very scarce. The allowance of Rations would lower these prices.[28]

After first of all announcing that they refused 'to spend one penny more on forts' the Legislature eventually relented and provided both funds and labour to enable the work to proceed until 1788. Having then been brought to a halt by the Assembly's refusal to provide further funds or to sanction any further hiring of slaves, work was not resumed for another two years. The fortifications were eventually finished only with the help of a massive British subvention, being completed more or less as the French Revolutionary Wars began in 1793. Shirley, whose name was given to both the main fort and the heights on which it was built, had already left the island by this time, leaving the administration in the hands of the senior of the Leeward Island lieutenant-governors.

During the interregnum before Major-General Charles Leigh arrived to take up the post of Governor in 1795 the Militia Act was renewed and revised. Under its grandiose provisions the militia was reorganised into 'one squadron of light dragoons, who were to serve on foot and horseback; two regiments and one independent company of foot; and one battalion of artillery', giving ample scope for an impressive corps of officers. The inclusion of free coloureds in the ranks was formalised but only to provide 'the under services of artillery, and to act as pioneers.' That as much as possible of the hard and dirty work of soldiering was to be given to non-whites was only to be expected: the act also forbade militiamen from entrusting 'their Firearms and Ammunition to Slaves, to be by them carried to and from the Alarm-posts and Places of Parade, whereby some fatal Accident through the Negligence or Licentiousness of the Slaves carrying the same may happen.'

In the event, at no time during the war years which were to last until the signing of the Treaty of Amiens in 1802, was the militia ever required to do more than drill or occasionally man the 'Alarm-posts', and Antigua was never in any danger of being attacked. This was probably just as well, as for much of this period the Leeward Islands were without a Governor-in-Chief. Leigh stayed for less than two years before 'becoming disgusted with the West Indies, he determined to return to England, and accordingly embarked on board a vessel bound for that place, on 3 July, 1796, without permission from his majesty.'[29] His disgust probably had a lot to do with frustration brought about by his dealings with the Legislature, with whom he was constantly at odds about the funds needed to administer the island in wartime. It is also possible that it had just as much to do with his distaste for the effect on the Council and Assembly of the words and actions of the anti-slavery movement in Britain.

11
Matters of Consequence

I find we are soon to know the fate of the Abolition Slave Bill, surely the Enthusiastic Rage of Mr Wilberforce and his Party can never prevail in a matter of such consequence to the Colonies and Mother Country.

> Langford Lovell, the Codrington attorney in Antigua,
> in a letter to Christopher Bethell written in 1791

The Act . . . for Ameliorating the Situation of the Slaves in this Government has received the approbation of the King in Council and is therefore now a law . . . It increases expences in feeding and clothing, as you are now bound to give equal to 9 pints of Grain p[er] Week to each Negroe and one Wand and half of fish or herrings this to be divided as we please and in course the greater portion will still be given by me to the Effective working field Strength. I must however request you to order out two Bales of Oznaburgs and 20lbs. coarse thread . . . Each Male is to have a pair of Trowsers, each female one petticoat twice a year; besides to the former a Jacket the latter a wrapper.

> Samuel Byam Athill, the Codrington attorney in Antigua,
> in a letter to Christopher Bethell Codrington written in 1799

The world of the Antiguan plantocracy (a word which – although it did not enter the language until the 1840s – could well have been coined a hundred years earlier, and which it is not inappropriate to now begin using), which had started to crumble when the North American colonies revolted, was undermined even more in April 1792 when the British Parliament approved a motion 'that the slave trade ought to be gradually abolished'. Ruin, as the planters saw it, was then averted by the opposition which arose in Britain as a result of the combined effects of the French Revolution, the slave rebellion in Saint-Domingue (the French half of Hispaniola), and the outbreak of yet another war with France. As a result, while the Abolition movement lost some of its momentum, the West Indian interest in Parliament was given time to mount, if not a counter-campaign, at least a holding operation. In April 1797 one of the interest's members, Charles Ellis, managed to get a motion passed to the effect that the governors of the West Indian colonies should be instructed to encourage their respective legislatures to improve the conditions for slaves, in order that the natural increase in their numbers which would result would in turn make the slave trade unnecessary.

That this was intended to be no more than a ploy to discredit the abolitionists by putting any initiative towards amelioration firmly in the hands of the plantocracy was spelt out in a letter another MP, the absentee Antiguan proprietor Sir William Young, sent to Edward Byam, the President of the Council and, in the absence of a replacement for General Leigh, the acting Governor of Antigua.

> It appears to me indispensably necessary to take steps by Legislative provisions, touching the situation of Negroes in Society, and to promote a natural increase in their population, and thus not only stop for the present, but gradually supercede the very pretensions at a future period, to a measure of direct abolition of the Slave Trade by the Mother Country, a measure which would blast the root of all our settlements of property.[1]

After Leigh had departed the West Indies so precipitously in 1796 his place as Governor-in-Chief had been filled in succession by three members of the Council of St Kitts. The third of these, Robert Thomson, took over in 1797 and it was to him, following receipt of Young's letter, that Byam wrote in October, arguing that the time had come for concerted action by all of the Leeward Island legislatures. His proposal that the General Assembly be convened, something which had not taken place for seventy-five years, was welcomed by Thomson, who then had to inform the Secretary of State of what was intended before taking any action.

•

While the correspondence between St Kitts and London was making its way back and forth across the Atlantic, in Antigua yet another naval officer managed to upset the equanimity of the Legislature; not this time by any action or lack of action at sea, but by shooting dead a fellow officer in the dockyard. The man responsible was the temporary commanding officer of HMS *Favourite*, Lieutenant Thomas Pitt, the second Baron Camelford, who while in command had been given the rank of 'acting commander and master'. The victim was Lieutenant Charles Peterson, the first lieutenant of HMS *Perdrix* who, until a few days before, had been the first lieutenant of the *Favourite*. The two men had detested each other. In Peterson's case it was because as a lieutenant two years senior to Camelford he had resented being made the latter's subordinate until his transfer to the *Perdrix*. In that of Camelford (a nephew of the Prime Minister, William Pitt) it was because he was an arrogant, nasty-tempered eccentric who could get on with no one, whether his junior or senior, for very long.

The circumstances which led to the shooting arose in January 1798 when only the *Favourite* and *Perdrix* were in harbour, and Peterson, in the absence of his captain on leave, was left in temporary command of the latter. Both he and

Camelford then claimed the title of 'senior officer present' – a dispute which led to considerable toing and froing between their ships, not to mention a great deal of alarm among their crews. It ended when Camelford, armed with a pistol, accosted Peterson outside the dockyard capstan-house and, having asked him three times whether he was prepared to obey an order without receiving a reply, accused him of mutiny and shot him at point-blank range.

The verdict of the coroner's inquest carried out the next day was that Peterson's death did come about because of mutiny, '*but on which side* such mutiny did exist, they cannot pretend to say.' Much to the relief of the Legislature, the dockyard authorities and the crews of the two ships, another warship, HMS *Matilda*, arrived the same day. Two days later, having no doubt heard a number of versions of the event, the captain of the *Matilda* had Camelford arrested and sent him to Martinique,[2] where he was court-martialled and acquitted. He was soon back in Antigua where, although he had made himself highly unpopular, probably nothing more would have been heard of him had he not once again taken the law into his own hands.

In March, while the *Favourite* was undergoing repairs, he became convinced that the Dockyard Superintendent, George Kittoe, was delaying completion of the work, and ordered members of his crew to seize the poor man and have him flogged. It is not clear how badly Kittoe was treated, but he had no hesitation in getting Camelford indicted for assault and summoned to appear before the magistrates in St John's. The summons was answered but, when ordered to post a large bond to ensure his appearance at the next session of the High Court, Camelford rushed out of court, stole a horse, and rode off towards English Harbour. He was caught somewhere in the vicinity of the modern-day village of Buckleys, brought back to St John's under arrest, and bound over to find £5000 bail. He drew bills for this amount but then, rather than stand trial, surrendered his command, forfeited his bail, and left the island. His family connections obviously stood him in good stead, for he was soon given command of another ship and returned to England at the end of the year. His appearance on his arrival there was noted as being 'extremely remarkable' by a contemporary:

> All the hair is shaved off his head, on which he wears a monstrous large gold laced cocked hat, which, by its appearance, one would think had seen service with Sir Walter Raleigh. He is dressed in a lieutenant's plain coat, the buttons of which are green with verdegrease as the ship's bottom; and with this all the rest of his dress corresponds.[3]

He left the Navy soon afterwards and 'for the next few years . . . lived principally in London, where he achieved an extraordinary notoriety by disorderly conduct',[4] before being killed in a duel in 1804.

•

At just about the time Camelford was jumping bail, delegates from all the Leeward Islands were meeting in St Kitts to convene the long-awaited General Assembly. Their discussions lasted for eight weeks and, being the sort of men they mostly were, these were not confined solely to considering how best to improve the life of the slaves. The draft of 'An Act more effectually to provide for the Support, and to extend certain Regulations for the Protection of Slaves, to promote their Increase, and generally ameliorate their Condition', which was sent to London for approval in May, was accompanied by two others. In order to try once again to increase the white population of the islands, the delegates thought 'An Act to admit upon Conditions, White Persons professing the Catholic Religion in the Leeward Islands to all the Rights and Privileges enjoyed by Protestant Subjects within the same' might do the trick. To ease their own distress, and that of the plantocracy they represented, they also tried an act 'to restrict the collection of the $4\frac{1}{2}\%$ Duty granted to His Majesty on the Exportation of the Produce of the Leeward Charibee Islands'.

The Amelioration Act was approved the following March, but the other two were doomed. The 'Catholic Relief' laws introduced in Britain some years earlier had precipitated riots, and the Government was hardly prepared to extend rights to colonial Catholics in 1799 which would not be allowed their co-religionists in Great Britain for another thirty years. As for remitting the duty on sugar – something which had been levied since 1663 – this was equally unthinkable. The money raised not only paid the salaries of governors and some other officials, as well as their pensions, but after all these years was still providing the heirs of the original seventeenth century proprietors with healthy incomes (see page 19), and it would not be abolished until 1838.

Under the provisions of the Amelioration Act slaves were to be given a specified quantity of provisions each week, a set amount of clothing each year, and were not to be made to work for more than fourteen hours a day (with meal breaks of two and a half hours) 'unless in crop time, or from evident necessity'. They were not to be imprisoned or flogged without good reason, and the use of 'unnecessary severities' such as chains, iron collars and weights could make an owner liable to a fine. It was obligatory for each plantation to provide a 'commodious' sick-house or hospital, and to arrange for regular medical attendance, while the manumission of disabled slaves was prohibited. A two-room house or a bed in a lying-in section of the hospital had to be provided for each pregnant woman, and during pregnancy she was not to be given heavy work or corporal punishment. An annual return of births and deaths was required from each owner.

Other clauses were intended to discourage what the planters always thought of as the undue licentiousness of the slaves, by the encouragement of monogamy and childbearing. As marriage would confer no rights, and in the planters' opinion would probably not be respected, it was considered 'unnecessary and even improper to enforce the Celebration of any religious

Rites among the Slaves'. Instead the act instructed owners to encourage lasting monogamous partnerships by recording such nominal 'marriages' in a special register, and rewarding each couple who then lived together faithfully with £1 for each year of their 'marriage'. In addition the female partner was to receive a larger cash sum for each child produced of the union. Any mother of six or more children, with the youngest being under seven years old, was to be further rewarded by being given only light work. Any white man convicted of having criminal intercourse with a 'married' slave would face a fine of £100. To encourage morality slaves were to be allowed to attend church services on Sundays, and the beneficed clergy were obliged to baptise, without fee, any who wished it once they had been properly instructed. Added together these measures represented a very significant advance in the legal protection of slaves throughout the Leeward Islands, even though some of the provisions – such as those concerning food, clothing and working hours – only translated what had become accepted practice into law.

For Antigua's slaves an equally important change had taken place in the year before the General Assembly had convened, when the 1723 Act 'for the better Government of Slaves' had been revised. Under its amended provisions the crimes of killing or maiming a slave were now dealt with as if they had been committed against free persons, with offenders facing 'Death, or such other Punishment as by the Laws of England such Persons would be sentenced to suffer, for the Murder of, or for the maiming or wounding a Free Person.' In addition it was specified that the body of any slave who died suddenly had to be seen by a coroner, and any owner not reporting such a death within six hours of it taking place faced a fine of £100. Its one great weakness was the same as that of the 1798 Amelioration Act.

A proposal to appoint a 'guardian' of slaves in each parish had been discussed in Basseterre but rejected by the General Assembly, as the delegates 'were a little apprehensive of loosening the Bond between Master and Slave, and thereby introducing Insubordination in the latter.' In the absence of such officials, and because the testimony of a slave in respect of a free person was not acceptable in court, there remained no way of enforcing the new laws in a wholly reliable and impartial manner. The system of courts which dealt with civil and criminal cases was almost entirely in the hands of untrained justices. Rowland Burton, who had been appointed Chief Justice of Antigua in 1786, was the first lawyer in the history of the island ever to hold the position. Because salaries were so poor, few lawyers ever applied for the subsidiary legal posts, leaving them to be filled by members of the plantocracy more interested in the status they afforded than in dispensing justice. As slaveowners themselves, whose fortunes and position in society rested on a way of life they were determined to preserve, they were hardly likely to investigate or prosecute contraventions of the new laws with any great vigour.

The prospect of the slaves reaping the full benefit of these laws was hardly improved when, at long last, a new Governor-in-Chief was appointed, and Lord Lavington arrived to take up the post in February 1801. He was not unfamiliar with the office, having already held it for four years in the early 1770s when he was still Sir Ralph Payne. During the intervening years he had been a British Member of Parliament until 1795 when, in return for his support of the Government, he had been rewarded with an Irish peerage as Baron Lavington. During his previous tenure as Governor he had been very popular with the plantocracy: not surprisingly perhaps, as having been born in St Kitts and his family owning an Antiguan estate he was very much one of their own. He now reappeared, not only with an elevated title, but with an unusually high opinion of his own importance.

The Legislature and planters in turn, just as they had bowed and scraped when Prince William Henry had 'honoured Antigua with a visit' earlier, allowed themselves to be carried away by the lustre they considered was attached to Payne's barony:

> Soon after his arrival, it was agreed for the country to allow him an annuity of £1000 to be paid quarterly out of the public treasury of the island; and a further sum of £300 to be paid in like manner until a government house was built for his reception. And that his excellency might better support his dignity, another annuity of £700 was granted him, as long as he remained within his government.[5]

The residence he eventually occupied, and which remains Government House to this day, was already under construction on the eastern side of St John's, conveniently situated on open land between the parish church and the barracks. Once he had moved in Lavington fully lived up to expectations as not only 'a very hospitable man, and very fond of splendour', but as 'a great stickler for etiquette, and a firm upholder of difference of rank and *colour*.' According to the *Dictionary of National Biography*:

> He was attended by an army of servants, but he would not allow any of the black servitors about him to wear shoes or stockings, their legs being rubbed daily with butter so that they shone like jet; and he would not, if he could avoid it, handle a letter or parcel from their fingers. To escape the indignity he designed a golden instrument, like a tongs, with which he held any article which was given him by a black servant.[6]

All this ostentation and the degrading business with butter and tongs inside Government House bore little resemblance to life outside where, following the short-lived peace brought about by the Treaty of Amiens, hostilities between Britain and France were resumed in May 1803, and Antigua was once again under threat of invasion.

This was demonstrated all too clearly four months later when a French fleet of schooners packed with troops sailed from Guadeloupe to attack English Harbour. Although they were intercepted by a British warship and easily dispersed, the threat of another attempt did not disappear for several years afterwards. Dominica, St Kitts, Nevis and Montserrat were all attacked in the first few months of 1805; Antigua was fortunate to escape the same treatment, as Samuel Athill, the attorney for the Codrington estates, reported in April:

> We were thrown into a state of great anxiety and alarm by the arrival of a very large force in line of battle Ships and Troops from France which immediately attacked Dominica and have since visited St Kitts, Nevis and Montserrat burning Shipping and laying the Islands under Contribution. We have hitherto escaped, thanks to our Rocks, I believe for it, as there is no doubt an attack was intended but the Pilots were afraid, had the French acted with enterprize they might at first have burnt plunder'd or taken all and every Island but we are now in a state of preparation and it is not a small force that would carry Antigua, the Garrison is strong in Regulars and the Militia in a state of high Discipline.[7]

As the war continued fears of an invasion only added to the general distress brought about by higher costs, shortages of food for the slaves and supplies for the plantations, the loss of ships and cargoes to privateers, and increased duties; in addition to a steadily decreasing share of the market for sugar in Britain. 'Bankruptcy is universal', Lavington reported in July 1805, 'and is not confin'd to the Public Treasury, but extends to the Generality of Individuals resident in the Colony.'[8] With conditions made even worse by the inevitable drought which reduced the crop by a third, so many people were unable to pay their taxes that the Government itself was indeed insolvent, and an emergency loan of £10 000 from Britain was needed to stave off disaster. The situation was to remain critical for some years to come but even so, within a year of Lavington's death in 1807, and in spite of the state of the island's finances, 'the Antiguans, out of respect to their late respected governor . . . agreed to allow his widow an annuity of £300 sterling during her life, which was to be paid out of the treasury.'[9]

•

In the closing year of his life, Lavington's health would not have been improved by receipt, whether handed to him with the golden tongs or not, of the news from England that after many years of trying William Wilberforce had finally managed to get Parliament to pass a bill to end the slave trade. This received royal assent some four months before the Governor expired, and from 1 January 1808 all trading in slaves was utterly abolished, prohibited and declared to be unlawful.' One of its provisions, concerning slaves who were employed as servants accompanying their owners from one colony to another, or from a colony to Britain, was to have particular relevance in Antigua some years later. Another, laid out in an Order in Council soon after the act came into effect, which specified what was to happen to the slaves found in foreign ships captured by the Navy in wartime, had more immediate application. Under its terms any such slaves landed in a colony like Antigua were to be made the responsibility of the Collector of Customs who, once he had listed and described them all, was to give each one a name 'if the African name is not sufficiently clear'. After that he was instructed to make the males available either to serve in the army or navy or to be apprenticed, along with the females, 'to prudent and humane masters and mistresses, to learn such trades, etc. as they may seem most fit for.'

Seven such cargoes of what were generally called 're-captives' were landed at St John's between 1808 and 1820. Details of the unfortunates making up one of these, found on board the Spanish schooner *San José y Anemas*, which was captured in 1811, are not without interest and well illustrate what happened to all the rest.

The 211 slaves who were released from the schooner consisted of 134 males aged between four and forty, and seventy-seven females whose ages ranged from seven to thirty. No fewer than forty-five were children under ten years old. Sixty of the males, a third of them aged fourteen or less, were drafted into the Army as recruits for the 3rd West India Regiment, while all the rest were given fourteen-year apprenticeships as masons, carpenters, coopers, tailors, gunsmiths, printers, sailmakers or sailors. Two of them were thought to be forty years old. One, given the name Briggs, who was described as 'cross eyed, almost blind', was sent to be trained as a cooper by a merchant in St John's. The other, King, who was thought to be a 'kind of priest' with a 'high forehead', was apprenticed to a carpenter also in St John's. The youngest boy, four-year-old Morson, died within a few weeks of landing, as did Briggs and eighteen others. All the females, other than nine who died within the first two years, became domestic workers. The oldest, Newbold, joined several others as the house servants of a Mrs Colquhoun in the country, while the youngest, Barnwell, along with two other girls and two boy apprentices, entered the service of the merchant Samuel Sheriff in St John's.

A rider to the instructions given to the Collector of Customs about providing each re-captive with a name, was that the name he chose would then be borne until such time as the bearer had been 'sufficiently instructed for baptism, when the same shall become the surname; the name of baptism being prefixed thereto.' The chief customs officer was never the most popular man on the island at the best of times, and some idea of who were the enemies of the incumbent in 1811 is perhaps to be seen in the names he selected for the 211 souls rescued from the *San José y Anemas*, which included those of various planters, Assemblymen and Council members together with 'Lavington' and 'Elliot' – the latter being the name of the man who had replaced the former as Governor in 1808.[10]

Hugh Elliot[11] could not have been more unlike his predecessor, being a man with no personal connection whatsoever with Antigua or the West Indies, and having served for the previous thirty-five years as a professional diplomat in various European countries. He took over a colony in which the economies of all its constituent islands were greatly depressed and in which, because of the interminable war with France, the white population was constantly shrinking. Small businessmen were being ruined and many planters were returning to Britain, abandoning their debt-ridden estates to the care of attorneys. Conditions in Antigua were rather better than in the other islands, but still enough people had left by 1810 to reduce the number of white inhabitants to less than 2500. In November of that year Elliot felt constrained to put pen to paper about the state of the islands, and to lambaste the type of men who were left to run them – the plantocracy and Legislature of Antigua along with the rest:

> The fact is, the governments of [these] Islands were formed in times when many of the proprietors lived upon their estates, and the white population was, in some instances, perhaps ten times as numerous as it is now. Of the few white inhabitants who remain, managers, overseers, self-created lawyers, self-educated physicians, and adventurous merchants, with little real capital and scanty credit, compose the greatest part. The acquirements of education among many of this description of persons, are very unequal to the task of taking a share in the government . . .
>
> To collect from such a state of society, men fit to be legislators, judges or jurymen, is perfectly impracticable. Individual interest – personal influence – animosity of party feuds, weigh down the scale of justice, and divert the course of legislative authority into acts of arbitrary and unjustifiable power, cloaked under the semblance, and dignified with the name, of constitutional acts.[12]

The arrival of such a vitriolic and, in comparison with much of the correspondence of previous governors, elegantly written missive on the desk of the Secretary of State for War (whose department had assumed responsibility for the colonies in 1801) cannot have been a common event, particularly coming from someone administering the Leeward Islands. Whether Lord Liverpool was impressed by the prose, concerned by the contents, or merely wanted Parliament to have a better appreciation of the difficulties he faced in trying to run the colonies, he had Elliot's dispatch published in May 1811 as a House of Commons Paper. This created an immediate uproar among the MPs representing the West Indian interest, and once details were relayed to the Caribbean whatever popularity the Governor may have enjoyed amongst the plantocracy instantly evaporated. Life for Elliot was then made so difficult that he resigned in the following November, and departed to a more congenial post in India.

Any views the slaves may have held of him can only have been enhanced by two measures he saw introduced into Antiguan law before he left the island. He first tackled the 'self-educated physicians' who, through their selling of 'deleterious drugs', he considered responsible for 'numerous cases of poisoning among the negroes', and persuaded the Assembly to ordain that in future no one would be licensed to practise medicine who could not produce 'a certificate from the Surgeons' Hall, or from one of the universities in Great Britain shewing his admittance in them.' Next, and of more importance in the days when doctoring, whether licensed or not, consisted of little more than purging, bleeding and various degrees of quackery, he was responsible for a crucial amendment to the Amelioration Act. Although the act prohibited excessive cruelty towards slaves no limit had been placed on the number of lashes which could be administered for one offence, an omission which was taken advantage of by more than one malicious manager or overseer. Elliot's despatch in 1810 had been written after he had been informed of a particularly barbarous flogging given to a slave in Nevis, and as a result of all the publicity which followed the act was amended two years later. Under the new provisions no more than thirty-nine lashes could be given at any one time, and such a punishment could not be repeated within fourteen days.

Another important change concerned summary punishments, reducing the number of lashes a driver could inflict to a maximum of six; with the proviso that if more were considered necessary they had to be delivered in the presence of the owner, his attorney, or an overseer. Previous to this, incidents of the kind witnessed by a young army officer 'a few days after landing in Antigua' in 1804 must have been commonplace:

> A huge slave-driver [was] flogging most unmercifully an old decrepit female negro, who appeared bowed down with misery and hard labour. I know not what her offence was, but she was one of a gang, as they are termed, of negroes of different sexes and ages, working with spades under a midday tropical sun.

Although such a scene cannot have been unusual, this one brought about a reaction which was far from typical:

> A brother-officer, who was with me on a shooting excursion, felt as astonished and indignant at this unnatural and inhuman proceeding as myself; and our first impulse was to threaten to shoot the driver if he did not desist. I am not ashamed to say, that, after drawing off to such a distance that our small shot could not seriously injure the vagabond, we peppered his legs pretty handsomely. That we should have adopted so summary a mode of punishment, had we lived twice as long in the world, I will not say; but my conscience has never reproached me for the steps we took to shew our disapprobation of the diabolical act.[13]

The amended Amelioration Act did not offer such immediate and satisfying deliverance from mistreatment, or even attempt to abolish corporal punishment, but it did at least bring the slaves a little further under the protection of the law.

•

The long years of war ended in June 1815 with the Battle of Waterloo. For the Antiguan plantocracy, although this meant that sugar production could now continue without wartime losses to add to those occasioned by natural disasters, peace brought its own concerns. During the war the excesses of the French Revolution and the bloody events of the Haitian slave rebellion had done much to mute the anti-slavery campaign in Britain. With the return of peace all the humanitarian, economic and religious objections to slavery were bound to be heard again and, now that the actual trade in slaves had been outlawed, with even more vigour and conviction. As none of the planters believed sugar could be produced without slave labour, it was obvious that their troubles were by no means at an end. For the more aware amongst them news of two documents which had been published in London well before the war ended would have given a clear idea of things to come. The first was an Order-in-Council of March 1812 which applied to Trinidad, the Spanish island that had come under British rule in 1797. In order to prevent any clandestine importation of slaves into the new colony, and to provide some measure of protection for those already there, the order made it compulsory for all slaveowners to register their slaves by a certain date. The second was a similar order concerning the slaves of St Lucia which was made two years later.

As could only have been expected this led to a demand by the Abolitionists for compulsory registration to be extended to all the colonies, and in June 1816 the Secretary of State (now Earl Bathurst) circularised the West Indian governors, asking them to bring pressure on their respective Assemblies to introduce the necessary legislation. In the Leeward Islands he now wrote to two governors, as three months earlier the Letters Patent of 1671 which had brought the colony into being had been revoked and the group divided: St Kitts, Nevis, Anguilla and the Virgin Islands into one colony, and Antigua, Barbuda and Montserrat into another.[14] Major-General George Ramsay had been appointed to govern the latter and it was he who now had to deal with the objections of the plantocracy to any suggestion of registering their slaves. His task was made all the harder in August, when he received another letter from Bathurst asking him to find out 'the disposition of the Legislature . . . with respect to providing for the subsistence of such a proportion of British troops, not of colour, as they may deem adequate for the maintenance of tranquility in the colony', and indicating that Britain could no longer afford to maintain the West Indian garrisons 'unless some part of the charge be defrayed by the colonies themselves'.

This merely added to the hullabaloo caused by the earlier letter, and in October the Council and Assembly in a joint resolution informed Ramsay that they were 'utterly unable to comply' with such a demand, and blamed the need to keep troops on the island in peacetime as rising 'solely from that dangerous spirit of interference with our domestic concerns on the part of individuals in England, and the public agitation of questions and measures there, which by their consequences have already deeply shaken our credit and happiness, and by their continuance must ultimately prove fatal to our safety and existence.' After blaming the Abolitionists in this way and then going into a long discussion about the effect the war had had on the island, 'the vast amount of heavy duties' they had to pay, and the difficulties facing them because of the poor market for sugar, they ended by prophesying that if the troops were withdrawn as a result of their inability to pay, 'the mischievous designs and insidious machinations of their avowed enemies in Great Britain' would seal their fate and bring about the island's inevitable ruin. Such doom-mongering paid off and British troops continued to garrison Antigua for another fifty years or more, but it did not prevent the Legislature, with a great deal of reluctance, from having to pass the other act Bathurst had requested 'for establishing a Register of Slaves' in less than six months.

The act of 1817, which set up 'an office of public registry for the registration of the names and descriptions of all negroes, mulattoes, or other persons, who now are, or shall or may be at any time hereafter held in a state of slavery', was intended 'more effectually to prevent the illicit introduction of slaves, and bar all possibility of encroachment on the rights of freedom.' This was to be ensured by the compilation of a full list of all the slaves held on the island on the first day of October of that year, and by a 'Triennial Return of Slaves' thereafter. Every owner was required to enumerate each slave by name, sex, age and colour: '"Black, or Coloured," including under the term Coloured, all who are not black.' In the triennial return he was to account for how any additions to the original return had been acquired, and also for any reductions, 'whether the same shall have happened by, or have been owing to death, sale, or other transfer of property, permanent desertion, manumission, or other cause of decrease.' While the act did nothing to ease the burden of bondage it did bring the slaves even further under the protection of the law, and one of the clauses – specifying that any slave not registered would be 'forfeited to the use of His Majesty . . . unless the person claiming title thereto' could provide proof that the slave had not been imported illegally – was to be at the centre of a *cause célebre* some eight years later.

•

Another document which caused unease and annoyance in Antigua before the end of the Napoleonic War, by providing another small but useful piece of ammunition in the fight against slavery, had nothing to do with the British

Government. This was a pamphlet issued by a charitable concern connected with the Moravian Church, published in London in 1814, and soliciting donations to a fund established for the relief of 'the Neglected and deserted Negroes in the Island of Antigua'. It consisted mostly of letters which had been received from the island over the previous decade, containing graphic accounts of the plight of slaves who had been abandoned by their owners. The most heartrending dwelt at length on the sufferings of those with leprosy, euphemistically referred to as 'a species of scurvy, or contamination of the system', as in a letter concerning a woman seen in St John's in 1808:

> Being out on business at a remote part of the town, I heard in an adjoining yard some cries, which I conceived proceeded from some poor creature who was being tied up to be flogged; I rode up, and was struck with horror at the sight of the object before me; – almost naked, exposed to the burning sun, lay a poor wretch, who appeared half consumed with the horrible disease I have spoken of . . . crowds of flies hovered round . . . [her] whole body appeared to be literally full of sores: I asked her who she belonged to, and found it was to a lady living in the town, who had long since discarded her on account of her complaint: she said she had been four days without food, the woman who had attended her having left her.[15]

Copies of the pamphlet soon found their way across the Atlantic and into the hands of men and women who, even if they were already hardened to such sights as those it described, were outraged at the anonymous editor's concluding indictment:

> Such are the facts in an Island where a fine of £300 is incurred upon conviction of such neglect and desertion: but prosecution must precede conviction, and no one could commence such a prosecution, without raising himself a host of enemies.[16]

A committee of the Assembly was set up to look into the matter; nominally to rectify the situation concerning such abandoned slaves, but with more interest in discovering those responsible for supplying the charity with information, and in suppressing any further revelations of a similar kind. Among those called to testify was Joseph Phillips who, as the Moravian Secretary and the only white member of that Church then on the island, fell under immediate suspicion. His involvement was more or less confirmed when he refused to turn over the Church records and papers demanded by the committee – something for which he was punished by being sent to jail for a year.

Another person called to testify, but who was treated more leniently as she had nothing to hide, was Elizabeth Thwaites, a prominent Methodist and one of a remarkable pair of sisters. She and the younger Anne were the daughters of Barry Conyers Hart, a coloured slaveowner who, until he moved to Trinidad soon after it had been captured from the Spanish, had farmed in the north of the island. Elizabeth had been born in 1772 and her sister a year later; soon after William Warrener arrived in 1786 both girls became Methodists and were inspired to begin teaching the family's slaves to read while giving them religious instruction. Well before the turn of the century both had become confirmed abolitionists.

In 1798 Anne became engaged to another Methodist, John Gilbert, a cousin of the late Nathaniel Gilbert, who not only held a responsible position as a naval storekeeper in the dockyard, but was a notary public and an officer in the militia. As interracial marriage was unheard of their intended union was bitterly opposed by the entire white community. It was also condemned by their fellow Methodists, including Gilbert's colleague in the dockyard, John Baxter, who warned him that he would be 'committed to jail as a madman'. His relatives pleaded with all the Anglican clergy not to perform the marriage, and the Naval Commander-in-Chief was written to, asking that he forbid any chaplain from taking part. The President of the Council considered Gilbert should lose his job as he 'had so basely degraded himself as to be unworthy of that office', while the officers of the militia thought he ought to be court-martialled 'for acting in a manner inconsistent with his rank and station, and the character of an officer, if he proceeded with this marriage.' In the end he lost both his commission in the militia and his position as a notary public, but the marriage did go ahead (although it is not known who performed it) and he did retain his job as a storekeeper. 'If I had determined upon seducing and degrading the object of my regard and esteem', Gilbert commented many years later, 'I should have been considered by the ungodly aristocracy of the country as having acted quite properly, and incurred no reproach from them, as she was a woman of colour.'

When in 1805 Elizabeth Hart also married a white man it caused less of a sensation, mainly because Charles Thwaites did not belong to Antiguan society, but like Baxter had been sent out from England to work in the dockyard; it still, however, caused a lot of resentment. 'Whatever obloquy attached itself to the union of a white person with a coloured lady Mr Thwaites bore with magnanimous patience', a local Pecksniff observed later, 'his amiable consort being both deeply pious and of a cultivated mind.' Regardless of what others may have thought Charles and Elizabeth Thwaites, once they were married, set up house at English Harbour, and joined forces with the Gilberts and Baxter in spreading Methodism. The two sisters opened a Sunday School; Gilbert gradually took over the regular meetings begun by Baxter at which he preached to slaves; and Thwaites became increasingly caught up with teaching slaves to read.

By 1813 there was such a demand for education among the slaves in the eastern part of Antigua that Thwaites built a schoolroom near the head of Willoughby Bay, giving it the biblical name for a house of mercy, and so laying the foundation of the present village of Bethesda. Four years later, having proved so adroit an educator, he was appointed by the Church Missionary Society – set up by the Anglican Church in 1799 in a belated attempt to catch up with the Moravians and Methodists – to a paid position as catechist and Superintendent of Sunday Schools in the eastern parishes. He and his wife then continued with this work for ten years before the Bishop of Barbados, in whose diocese the Leeward Islands had by then been placed, 'imperatively required that Mr Thwaites should either abandon his membership with the Wesleyan body, and be a thorough-going Churchman, or resign his situation.' He immediately resigned, only to be given an equivalent position at the same pay by the Wesleyan Missionary Society a few months later. He and Elizabeth then worked tirelessly for the good of the slaves for the rest of their lives, as did Anne and John Gilbert. Of the four only Thwaites lived to see the end of slavery; his wife and Gilbert both died in 1833, and Anne Gilbert only a month before emancipation day.

At the time of the Hart sisters' marriages, around the beginning of the nineteenth century, the free coloured population was about 3000 (much the same as that of the whites), having risen from a mere handful in a hundred years. The rise was brought about by a combination of manumission and natural increase: the former by slaves buying or receiving their freedom from male and female owners alike; the latter much aided, as a prissy female visitor to the island noted in 1774, by the white male population:

> Tho' children of the Sun, they are mortals, and as such must have their share of failings, the most conspicuous of which is, the indulgence they give themselves in their licentious and even unnatural amours, which appears too plainly from the crowds of Mullatoes, which you see in the streets, houses and indeed every where; a crime that seems to have gained sanction from custom tho' attended with the greatest inconveniences not only to Individuals, but to the publick in general.

As was to be expected from someone whose views of West Indian life were published as those of 'a Lady of quality', even if the 'children of the Sun' were mortal they were not really to blame:

> The young black wenches lay themselves out for white lovers, in which they are but too successful. This prevents their marrying their natural mates, and hence a spurious and degenerate breed, neither so fit for the field, nor indeed any work, as the true bred Negro.[17]

In the early years of the nineteenth century the number of free coloureds rose sharply, reaching 4000 in 1820 and 5500 ten years later, aided by men like the overseer at Betty's Hope who, in January 1816, requested permission to buy the freedom of the children he had fathered by 'a Mustee woman' (children who, according to Codrington's attorney in forwarding the request, 'had arrived at *that colour*'). Assuming these were freed, by the time they reached maturity in, say, 1825 they would have been members of that section of society which contained people not only of every gradation of skin colour, but of all levels of prosperity and respectability. The majority were town dwellers, although a few like Barry Conyers Hart (who was not unique in being a coloured slaveowner) had property in the country and one at least owned a sugar plantation. Among those in St John's were many who owned houses and business premises, and some of the wealthier, well established in commercial life, had been educated abroad. Below them were a host of shopkeepers, tradesmen, small businessmen, and clerks working in both public and private offices; and beneath all of these was the inevitable layer made up of the indigent, the disabled, the abandoned, and people suffering from disfiguring diseases such as leprosy, yaws and elephantiasis. Two coloured men owned the island's main newspaper, the *Antigua Weekly Register*, which was edited by one of them, Henry Loving, of whom much will be heard later. Many served in the militia, although prevented from holding commissioned rank in an organisation which remained as top-heavy as ever, with fifteen staff officers and between eighty and ninety regimental officers responsible for about 800 other ranks. For coloured men holding the necessary property qualifications their right to vote in Assembly and vestry elections had been recognised by law in 1822, after being accepted as a custom for the previous fifty years.

In the absence of any interest among the plantocracy, except when forced to act through changes in the law brought about by pressure from London, the coloured community was particularly active in the area of social welfare. In 1817 in St John's, Elizabeth Lynch had founded the 'Distressed Females' Friendly Society', intended to keep 'Young females in the humbler walks of life . . . from the grasp of the destroyer, and from the polluting effect of parental example and influence', while at English harbour around the same time, the 'Female Orphan Society' had been established by Anne Gilbert. Some time later the two amalgamated into the 'Female Refuge Society', an institution which then continued to try to save young women from a fate worse than death for another forty years or so. Other friendly societies with more prosaic aims, as well as a 'Society for Aiding the Education of Poor Children' were set up a little later, and support was provided for the Moravian and Methodist missionaries at work among the slaves. Regardless of their support for this work not all who contributed were themselves Nonconformists. 'The free mulattos in the West Indies would naturally incline rather to the side which elevates than to that which degrades them in society', noted Henry Nelson Coleridge in 1825 when he 'was particularly struck with the extreme neatness of the dresses, and the devout behaviour of the coloured classes who attended divine service at St John's Church.' Not that the professing of Anglicanism necessarily carried with it acceptance of all the tenants of Christianity:

The leading persons among the coloured inhabitants often give it as a reason for not attending the established service, that they cannot be sure of finding room for their wives and children with themselves, and are always liable to the intrusion of other people who may easily happen to be such both in demeanour and apparel, as to render contact with them a serious inconvenience.[18]

The concern shown by the Methodists and Moravians for the slaves and the less fortunate members of the coloured community was not completely lost on the Anglican Church, as had been shown by the employment of Charles Thwaites by the Church Missionary Society, and was further demonstrated in 1828 by the founding of the 'Daily Meal Society' in St John's. This was set up by the Reverend Robert Holberton, who had been appointed Rector of the parish church a year earlier, with the intention of providing such a meal to 'the sick and needy of St John's and its neighbourhood.' It started off as little more than a soup-kitchen in the yard of a house near the church which was owned by the woman appointed as superintendent, but soon developed into a shelter for the infirm. Ten years later the Society, with the support of the Legislature and public subscriptions, had moved its operations into a large building near the Rectory, with accommodation for twenty-four 'cases of distress', and a separate lazaretto with room for three dozen cases had been put up 'by the sea-side' well away from the town.

Before Holberton founded this Society there had been no interest among those who ran the island in providing relief for any other than white people. Local government was based on the parishes, each with a vestry made up of the Rector and a board elected from among the freeholders. Churchwardens elected from among the board members were then responsible for collecting and managing parish taxes, for the maintenance of roads and bridges, for distributing poor relief – provided those in need were of the right colour – and for maintaining law and order. No proper policing was carried out before 1813 when, in St John's, five 'reputable white men . . . assisted by about as many discreet black or coloured persons' were formed into a rudimentary police force. As well as attending at the magistrates' courts they were also used to patrol the streets, 'taking up slaves who were found selling . . . on working days, unless they could produce a pass from their owners.' They also were responsible for imposing a curfew on the slaves at 9.30 each night, chasing the 'country negroes' out of town, and obliging 'such as resided in the capital to return to their houses'. How effective they were, considering how many rules and regulations the slaves had managed to flout over the years, is open to question. Whether such constables were ever employed, or indeed needed, to replace the 'night watches' used in places like Parham or Falmouth is also open to doubt, and probably depended largely on the state of the parish funds.

•

In the early 1820s one of the slaves the town constables would have chased back to where she lived, had she been abroad after half-past nine at night, was a young domestic owned by a resident of St John's named John Allan. This was Grace Jones who, in spite of a blameless and otherwise anonymous life as Mrs Allan's nursery maid, was destined to become the unwitting cause of a contentious lawsuit and to enter legal history as – with all the sensitivity the English legal profession of the day could muster – 'The Mongrel Woman, Grace'.

In 1822 Grace travelled with her mistress to England, a common enough occurrence in the days when slaves acting as servants were often transported to and fro between the West Indies and Europe. At the end of their stay the following year Grace raised no objections with Mrs Allan about leaving 'and accompanied her voluntarily on her return to Antigua'. A fellow passenger on the ship which carried them home was George Wyke, the island's Collector of Customs. On arrival at St John's Grace, 'with whose character and situation Mr Wyke was well acquainted, landed with her mistress, without any exception made to her condition, and without formalities at the custom-house observed or required.'

Two years later, having in the meantime resumed her work at the Allans' house, Grace was without any warning seized by a customs officer 'as forfeited to the King, on suggestion of having been illegally imported in 1823'. Wyke gave as his reason that Grace had left the island without endorsement of a certificate which her owner should have had proving she had been registered under the 1817 Act, that no such certificate had been produced on her return to the island, and that she was now a free British subject being held in slavery. Why it took him two years to take this action remains unclear but, as no Collector of Customs ever had many friends and being at odds with businessmen like John Allan must have been a routine part of his existence, it is not difficult to believe it may have been an act of victimisation or part of a vendetta. Whatever the reason, Allan quickly filed an affidavit claiming that he was Grace's sole and legitimate owner, and in August 1826 the case was brought before the vice-admiralty court in St John's. As this was presided over by Nicholas Nugent, who ordinarily was a physician and Speaker of the Assembly, and as such not likely to have looked upon the Collector of Customs with anything but a jaundiced eye, a decision was soon reached 'that the woman GRACE be restored to the claimant, with costs and damages for her detention'. The delay in bringing the case had occurred because – such was the way the plantocracy tried to look after its own – the Attorney-General had at first refused to argue on Wyke's behalf, and proceedings had been suspended while advice was obtained from London. In the end the Attorney-General had been obliged to act, but had do so with no conviction and as briefly as possible.

It is not clear just what would have happened to Grace had the decision gone the other way, but this hardly mattered as Wyke, on behalf of the Crown, immediately appealed and the case was referred to the High Court of Admiralty in London. The appeal was heard in the middle of the following year, when it was argued before the eighty-two-year old Lord Stowell that Grace 'being a free subject of his Majesty, was unlawfully imported as a slave from Great Britain into Antigua, and there illegally held and detained in slavery, contrary to the form of the Statute in such case made and provided.' This was founded on the widely held belief that once a slave set foot on English soil he or she immediately became free; a belief which stemmed from the famous Somerset Case of 1772 which, in fact, did no more than affirm that a slave in England could not be sold abroad by his master, and establish that the courts in England would not view slavery as an enforceable contractual arrangement.

Lord Stowell, after examining 'the well-known case of Sommersett' at some length, decided that temporary residence in England without manumission only suspended the status of a slave who, after he or she had been in the country, returned to a place where slavery was legal. In November therefore he affirmed the sentence of the vice-admiralty court of Antigua with costs, and poor Grace – now enshrined in English law – remained the property of John Allan for another seven years until slavery was abolished.

The decision was of great importance, destroying as it did the myth that no person in England could be a slave, and that no slave could enter the country without becoming free. It caused a considerable stir in the British press; half the newspapers being in favour and the rest outraged. In Antigua, where the original prosecution had created an uproar, the result of the appeal was not received until the middle of December. When it arrived it was greeted with jubilation and relief, except possibly by the Collector of Customs who read in a local news-sheet:

> The long looked for decision of Lord Stowell, relative to the woman Grace, has at last been given; and reason and equity have triumphed over cant and hypocrisy, his Lordship having determined that a slave going back to a colony in which he or she was held in slavery, becomes subject to the laws of that colony, and reverts again to a state of slavery.
>
> This of course is no more than justice entitled us to, but we confess we were very apprehensive as to the result, when we considered the strong prejudices existing against these colonies. This will be bad news for the harpies of office, who were anxiously waiting, ready to pounce upon their prey in the event of a different decision. We should hope prosecutions will be instituted against them immediately, and if requisite, that public subscriptions will be entered into for the purpose of defraying the expences.[19]

What effect the inhumanity of the Stowell decision may have had on Grace Jones is unknown, but this is far from so in the case of another slave who was taken to England less than a year after Stowell's judgement was delivered.

Mary Prince belonged to John Wood, a merchant in St John's who had bought her in Bermuda, her birthplace, in about 1814. Her subsequent life, as a general dogsbody cum nursemaid, was made particularly onerous by the gratuitous cruelty of Mrs Wood, combined with a susceptibility to rheumatism, but relieved from time to time when the Woods were away from the island. During their absences she joined the Moravian Church, learned to read and, by taking in washing and huckstering, gradually accumulated the money needed to buy her freedom. None of this pleased Mrs Wood, any more than did Mary's decision to get married in 1826, when she was thirty-eight years old, to Daniel James, a black carpenter who had already purchased his freedom. As he too was a Moravian they were married in the Moravian chapel at Spring Gardens, in a ceremony which though technically illegal was by this time performed by the Nonconformist ministers with the tacit approval of the Anglican Church and with the Legislature turning a blind eye. Laws remained in existence which forbade marriages between slaves and free persons, and imposed penalties on ministers not belonging to the Anglican Church who performed the marriage ceremony, but these had been ignored for at least twenty years.

The marriage however was not carried out with the approval of Mrs Wood who, as Mary recounted much later, 'was more vexed about my marriage than her husband. She could not forgive me . . . but stirred up Mr Wood to flog me dreadfully with his horsewhip.' In addition she refused to consider letting the new Mrs James buy her freedom:

> She sold five slaves whilst I was with her; but though she was always finding fault with me, she would not part with me. However, Mr Wood afterwards allowed Daniel to have a place to live in our yard, which we were very thankful for.

This move was hardly designed to decrease Mrs Wood's malevolence and at the beginning of 1828, when she and her husband decided to go to England 'to put their son to school, and bring their daughters home', Mary was ordered to go with them. At first both Mary and her husband were reasonably pleased at the prospect:

> I thought that by going there I should probably get cured of my rheumatism, and should return with my master and mistress, quite well, to my husband. My husband was willing for me to come away, for he had heard that my master would free me.

The extent of their delusions became apparent as soon as she reached England, when 'the rheumatism seized all my limbs worse than ever, and my body was dreadfully swelled', and Wood, instead of setting her free, left her in the hands of his wife to wash and clean the house they had rented in London.

After many long months of skivvying when she was well enough to work, and being abused by the Woods when she was not, she managed to make contact with the Moravian Mission and seek help to escape their clutches. Towards the end of the year, after recovering her health with the help of a charitable English family, she found her way to the offices of the Anti-Slavery Society 'to enquire if they could do any thing to get me my freedom, and send me back to the West Indies'. As was soon pointed out to her the ruling in the Grace Jones appeal had made it that 'the laws of England could do nothing to make me free in Antigua', and all the Society could do was to engage a lawyer to approach her owner:

> Mr Ravenscroft, a solicitor . . . called upon Mr Wood, in order to ascertain whether he would consent to Mary's manumission on any reasonable terms, and . . . with some difficulty obtained one or two interviews, but found Mr Wood so full of animosity against the woman, and so firmly bent against any arrangement having her freedom for its object, that the negotiation was soon broken off as hopeless. The angry slaveowner declared 'that he would not move a finger about her in this country, or grant her manumission on any terms whatever; and that if she went back to the West Indies, she must take the consequences.'

A few months later, having managed to stave off an attempt to petition Parliament about the matter, and before any similar moves could be made, the Woods departed for Antigua.

They left behind a free woman, but one irrevocably separated from her husband and the only home she knew. Fortunately she was not left without a means of support as the Secretary of the Anti-Slavery Society, Thomas Pringle, 'being fully convinced, from a twelvemonth's observation of her conduct, that she was really a well-disposed and respectable woman', gave her a job as a domestic servant in his own house at the end of 1829. A year or so later, 'seeing the poor woman's spirits daily sinking under the sickening influence of hope deferred', he decided to make one more effort to get Wood to change his mind. The Moravians in London were asked to get their missionary in Antigua to approach Wood direct, while a letter was sent to the Governor 'soliciting him to use his influence in persuading Mr Wood to consent'. Neither approach met with anything other than a blank refusal, and Mary remained in England, as far as it is known, for the rest of her life.

Her autobiography, from which all the quotations used above are taken, was edited by Pringle and published in 1831.[20] Its appearance created a fresh outbreak of rage among the slaveowners of Antigua and greatly annoyed pro-slavery advocates elsewhere; their combined fury adding to the bellows and thrashings of a beastly system, epitomised by Wood's behaviour, which by this time had been mortally wounded and was in its death throes.

12
Immediate, Entire and Universal Freedom

Gentlemen, my previous sentiments on this subject are well known to you all: be not surprised to learn that they have undergone an entire change. I have not altered my views without mature deliberation. For several days past, I have been making calculations with regard to the probable results of emancipation, and I have ascertained beyond a doubt that I can cultivate my estate at least one-third cheaper by free labour, than by slave labour.

Samuel Otto Baijer, in a speech to fellow planters in Antigua in 1833

Previous to [emancipation] the membership rolls, and the registers of baptism, marriages, funerals, had a column headed '*Civil State*', in which it was recorded whether the person named was 'free' or 'slave'. After long, painful lists, the Register of Baptisms at Freetown, in Antigua, has this thrilling entry inscribed right across the page in flourishing letters:

Here endeth all Registration in which
Distinction of Civil State is specified, August 1st, 1834, being the glorious
Day of Immediate Entire and Universal FREEDOM for every human being in Antigua
F. Deaville Walker
The Call of the West Indies (c. 1927)

The founding of the Anti-Slavery Society in England in January 1823 marked the beginning of the end for the slaveowners. Pressure on the British Government from the abolitionists mounted steadily from then onwards, while in the West Indies change was being urged on all the island legislatures by the missionaries, the free coloureds, and in their own way by the slaves themselves. Among the plantocracy the prospect of losing valuable property, and the fear of the slaves taking matters into their own hands, created an atmosphere of suspicion and distrust, and the adoption of even more reactionary views. In a small island like Antigua, with a relatively tiny white population, this led to the sort of treatment handed out to slaves like Grace Jones and Mary Prince.

In May of the same year Thomas Buxton, who was shortly to take over from Wilberforce as the leading abolitionist in Parliament, introduced a bill in the House of Commons:

That the state of Slavery is repugnant to the principles of the British constitution and of the Christian religion and that it ought to be gradually abolished throughout the British colonies.

Before it could be debated he was persuaded to withdraw it by being told it was the Government's intention to enforce emancipation gradually, beginning with the exertion of pressure on the self-governing colonies to introduce further amelioration laws. Two months later the Secretary of State, Earl Bathurst,[1] sent a circular letter to all governors outlining the measures he wished to see adopted, and ordering these to be put before their legislatures with recommendations for immediate adoption. The copy sent to Governor Sir Benjamin D'Urban[2] in Antigua was received at the end of July.

The changes to the existing slave laws he was required to urge on the Assembly included provision of religious education, the encouragement of marriage and the registration of all Christian unions, the recognition of a slave's testimony in court (provided he possessed a certificate from his religious instructor stating that he understood the nature of an oath), the removal of any taxes or fees associated with manumission, and the establishment of savings banks to enable the accumulation by the slaves of their purchase money. In addition, married women with a certain number of children were to be relieved from field labour, no family was to be split up in order to pay an owner's debts, any flogging over three lashes was to be recorded, and no punishment was to be given on the day of the offence – and only then in the presence of a third person.

Out of all these measures, the one Bathurst considered the 'foundation of any Beneficial Change in the character and future Condition of the Slaves' was the provision of religious education. So important did he believe this to be that government support would be made available for the extra clergymen and teachers the established Anglican Church would need to undertake the work. The Secretary of State made it clear, however, that this support would only be forthcoming if the slaves' weekly market was moved from Sunday to some other day, in order 'that the Sabbath may be appropriated to the purpose of rest from labour, and of moral and religious instruction.'

D'Urban passed on all of this to a Legislature which was composed of men who were past-masters at delay and prevarication when it came to dealing with what they viewed as interference by London, and who knew the value of a committee when needed. The one set up to prepare a new amelioration bill, incorporating the required changes, was still proceeding 'with much caution and circumspection' as the year ended. Nothing had been done by the time D'Urban was transferred to the South American colony of Demerara in 1824, and very little more was achieved even after the arrival of his replacement, Sir Patrick Ross, nearly two years later:

His excellency arrived at Antigua in the year 1826, and during his stay there, ingratiated himself with the *heads of the island*, by his courteous manners, and his humane desire to spare their feelings upon the all-engrossing topic of approaching emancipation.[3]

Such was the extent of his ingratiation that even after he had been on the island for two years Ross was able to inform London that not only was the bill still progressing very slowly, but that 'few of the measures contemplated and recommended from England' were likely to be incorporated. Amongst the few that had been included though, the abolition of the Sunday markets took pride of place. Once Bathurst had indicated the importance he and the rest of the British Government attached to the sanctity of the Sabbath the Legislature realised that by making this the key issue in a new bill, much else that had been specified as being required in the bill could be watered down or ignored. By playing the religious card the plantocracy would not only stem a lot of criticism and assuage some of their opponents in Britain, but would also be able to reimpose the control which had long been lost over the leisure time of their slaves.

In April 1824 a petition had been raised by some of the businessmen in St John's, complaining that Sunday for many years had been 'awfully and presumptuously profaned . . . by the open and unrestrained vending of provisions, liquors, and other articles of merchandise . . . to the opprobrium of the Colony at large, the scandal of all orderly and religiously disposed persons, and in contemptuous violation of the Laws of the Country and of God', and asking for action to be taken to prevent such violation in the future. The Assembly could move quickly enough in a case like this, and within a month an act 'for more effectually preventing the profanation of the Lord's Day' had been passed. By making the sale of spirits illegal and enforcing the closure of shops, it removed much of the pleasure the slaves derived from their traditional day in town, but as 'unrestrained vending' continued in the market itself their enjoyment was not completely ruined. A far more successful effort to do this was made in 1831 with the enactment of a law 'for more effectually enforcing a due observance of the Lord's Day', which prohibited the holding of the Sunday market from 18 March of that year – without substituting any other day in lieu. This omission was intentional. The Legislature by this time were aware that emancipation was in the offing, but were convinced, with the same bloody-mindedness with which John Wood had treated Mary Prince, that the slaves were quite unprepared for freedom:

> With emancipation civilisation will end, the export of the staple commodities of the Colonial terminate, and consequently the import of British Manufactures cease altogether; and a Society, now advancing in improvement, retrograde to original Barbarism.[4]

For the slaves the abolition of the Sunday market meant a serious reduction in the amount of enjoyment they would be able to derive from the one day of the week on which they were not required to work for their owners. Also, as many of them worked for themselves in or around the market on that day, or brought or sent in produce to sell, it meant the end of a major source of income. As a result, publication of the new law in February soon produced many signs of unrest around the island. The main objection was less concerned with the prospect of losing a market on Sunday than with the denial of their right to have a market at all. Agitation grew worse the next month and on 18 March, which was a Friday, hundreds of slaves 'assembled in the Great Market of St John's and in other places' in order to protest, using language which Governor Ross later reported as 'frequently violent and menacing, and accompanied by furious gesticulations and brandished cudgels'. It was too much for the few town police to handle, and troops belonging to the 86th Regiment (which had taken over garrison duties a year earlier) were called in from Fort Shirley. After much confusion and a great deal of commotion, and following the arrest of the more vociferous protesters, the crowd was eventually dispersed; the last few 'obstinate women' not until nearly nightfall.

During the following week, beginning on Sunday, 20 March, many canefields were set on fire: the majority of these were in the parish of St Philip in the easternmost part of the island, but some were on estates uncomfortably close to St John's. Martial law was imposed, the militia called out and the 86th Regiment placed on full alert. For the numerous officers of the militia it provided plenty of opportunity for 'shewing forth their valour, and winning laurels in the field of Mars' as, with tongue firmly in cheek, Mrs Lanaghan recorded:

> Great were the marchings and counter-marchings upon this occasion; mysterious the signs and counter-signs! Then there was such buckling on of spurs, and bracing on of swords – such displays of epaulets and aiguilettes, as would have surprised any one not accustomed to West Indian militia 'turn outs'. Generals galloped here, and colonels there; at one moment a party of gallant dragoons, armed to the teeth, and mounted – some on gaunt steeds of sixteen hands high, and others on diminutive ponies, dashed along the streets; at another, the governor and his brilliant staff might be seen hurrying forward as fresh intelligence arrived of other fires breaking out.[5]

Such activities brought an end to the fires within a few days and eleven suspected arsonists were rounded up. The next month, after they had been tried by court-martial, six were acquitted, four were sentenced to be flogged and one, a slave from a plantation in St Philip's, to be hanged.

Although as a result of all this, nearly all the planters allowed their slaves time off for marketing after martial law had been lifted, mostly on Saturdays, this was not the same as their having a set, fixed time when everyone could be sure a market would be open. Most of the transactions in the Sunday market had taken place through bartering, brought about because some produce grew better in one part of the island than another. Over the years exchanges between producers from widely separated plantations had become the norm, and a lot of pleasure had been derived from all the social interaction which accompanied bartering. In any case, not all that much money circulated among slaves for cash purchases. Because of general dissatisfaction with the new arrangements, and fed by rumours concerning emancipation, the unrest continued with acts of insubordination, the occasional cane-field fire, and even one or two protest marches in St John's.

•

Unrest among the slave population was not all that Governor Ross and the Legislature had to cope with in 1831, as at much the same time the restrictions imposed on the free coloured community came under determined attack. Petitions against the discriminatory laws which hedged in their lives had been presented to the Assembly three times during the previous decade and achieved nothing: 'Instead of the Petitioners being told, in language becoming the character of Gentlemen and the Representatives of the People, that their request could not be granted, they were met in terms of bitter feeling, and reproaches and insults were cast upon them.' In 1830 a petition had been forwarded to the House of Commons without result, and so a year later Henry Loving, the editor of the *Weekly Register*, made it known that he had decided to travel to London in order to represent his and their plight as free coloured members of society in a direct, personal approach to the Colonial Secretary.

The effect this had on the white population was summed up in letters Robert Jarritt, the attorney for the Codrington estates, sent to Sir Christopher Bethell-Codrington (see page 137) in June:

> The Magistracy of St John's is all a farce; the Coloured people commit all sorts of excesses with impunity. It is vain to make any complaint against the coloured people, Mulattoes, there are none now, they are all Coloured Gentlemen and coloured ladies. Our legislature is doing all it can to ruin the country, on stopping the Sunday market.[6]

And a month later:

> I suppose the next step will be abolition of slavery, certainly nothing can be worse than this uncertainty and unsettled state of people's minds, we are living in a society not better than Van Dieman's land. It is almost a misfortune here to have a white complexion. Such a sway have the people of colour.[7]

At the end of July he reported Loving's departure for London:

We have two papers here that are infamous, and have done much mischief. 'Loving' the coloured Editor of one of them, is gone home to England to see what lies he can tell in behalf of those of his caste, having raised subscriptions here and the neighbouring islands. And yet they are under no restrictions any more than the whites, and are equally privileged. Our Negroes never would be dissatisfied or use violence, were they not set on by these privileged gentry.[8]

It was in order to better counteract such views that Loving made his way to London; he and the committee which paid for his passage had decided that the cause of the free coloureds could not be advanced in any other way. Once established in the capital in September he composed a majestic letter to Lord Goderich, the man who had taken over as Colonial Secretary the previous year. In this, on behalf of the 'Free Coloured and Black Inhabitants of Antigua', he elaborated on their condition, detailed their grievances, and flayed the whole of the white ruling elite from the Governor downwards.

He began by complaining that he and his fellow coloureds were 'subjected to many disabilities, restrictions, and exclusions, operating greatly to the prejudice of their industry, subversive of their rights as British subjects, poignant to their feelings as men, and illiberal in this enlightened age.'[9] Of the many discriminatory laws under which they suffered, the 'most illiberal and vexatious' was the White Servants' Act, which by this time served no useful purpose, but was used to prevent coloured men from finding employment as managers or overseers of plantations without first paying a large fee – 'which, in the case of an Overseer, is about £3 more than a moiety of his whole Salary.' If this act were abolished not only would more local men find work, but

> the employment of Free Coloured or Black men upon Plantations would, from the strong fellow feeling which they entertain for, and publicly exhibit towards, the unfortunate slaves, be the means of bringing to light those wanton acts of cruelty which are now altogether concealed, or at best falsely sworn away by a set of drunken, immoral, and subservient White Servants, the outcasts of Europe, British America, and the Antilles.[10]

He turned next to the Militia Act which debarred coloureds from becoming officers, even though by this time 'the military strength of the Island consists of three-fourths of Coloured and Blacks', and voiced what must have been a common complaint:

> It is impossible for men like myself any longer to submit to the galling degradation of being commanded by striplings not possessing the requisite qualifications of property, gentility, or standing in the community, and frequently by needy and unknown adventurers from other countries, many of whom are beneath the countenance or association of my Constituents in private life.[11]

His unfortunate constituents also suffered from not being allowed to exercise 'the invaluable right of serving on Juries of any description, in defiance not only of their Constitutional rights as Englishmen, but also of the Laws of Antigua.' Even though many of them qualified for jury duty by virtue of being freeholders, 'the practice of summoning White Jurors exclusively, operates in every Court and in every case. To have been born of White parents, or to be thought to have been so born, is a sufficient recommendation; and it is a matter of no consequence whether the individual be a resident of one month or one year; or whether his character be good or bad; or whether his ignorance may have made him an object of contempt in society.'[12]

The remainder of the letter dealt with the segregation of coloured people in the Anglican churches, the action taken to prevent coloured elected representatives from sitting in the Assembly, and the constant refusal of the Legislature to take any notice of the petitions submitted in previous years. The Attorney-General and several other 'declared enemies of the claims of the Free Coloured and Black Inhabitants' among the ruling hierarchy were accused of conspiring 'to do the utmost in their power to obstruct and overturn any measure having for its object the advancement of that class of his Majesty's subjects.' As for the Governor: 'When I make allusion to the Servants of the Crown, your Lordship is not to understand that I have reference to Sir Patrick Ross,' Loving continued, tongue in cheek:

> I have not come to England for the purpose of representing the extraordinary intimacy which exists between his Excellency and the Oligarchy of the Island; though my Constituents could, with much justice, complain, that prior to the present year his Excellency never took the trouble to urge upon the other branches of the Legislature the necessity of granting the claims of the Free People.[13]

This missive, which its author hoped would prove 'the means of checking the abuses of the Servants of the Crown in their future conduct towards their less fortunate fellow-subjects', was probably the last thing the Colonial Secretary or anyone else in his department wanted to receive at this time, deep as they were in the middle of drawing up schemes for emancipation. In comparison with what many in the British Government feared might happen once the slaves were set free, the disadvantages under which the relatively small number of free coloureds suffered must have appeared trifling. Loving's letter received the classic bureaucratic treatment. Because it called into question 'the propriety of some of the Governor's measures' a copy had to be sent to Antigua for his comments before Goderich could do anything, and this was despatched at the end of October.

Between then and June 1832 when Loving left England, correspondence passed back and forth between London and St John's, and in Antigua between the Governor and the chairman of the committee which had sent the *Weekly*

Register's editor to London in the first place. Most of it revolved around the remarks he had made about the Governor, to which Ross not unnaturally took exception, and this in the end served to virtually nullify the rest of the original letter's contents. In early April 1832, at the only interview he managed to achieve, Loving was told that the Colonial Secretary intended 'to order that the Free Coloured and Black inhabitants of Antigua be summoned upon Juries', and if it was found necessary he himself would be afforded the Government's 'protection from punishment by the local authorities, on his return to the Island'. It was not much to take back after a year, nor did it give his committee much to rejoice about, but it was a start. In any case, as they all probably discussed, other changes were about to take place. While in London Loving had testified before the House of Commons Select Committee on the Extinction of Slavery, and must have returned with a reasonable idea of when emancipation could be expected. Any antagonism between Government House and himself disappeared when Ross was replaced in 1832, and with the passing of the Emancipation Act a year later the planters had more to exercise their minds than continuing to seek revenge for his outspoken criticism of their past actions.

•

The bill which emancipated all the slaves throughout the British colonies was given the royal assent on 28 August 1833, although it is difficult to say with what grace King William IV, the former Duke of Clarence, put his pen to a document which began 'Whereas divers persons are holden in slavery within divers of His Majesty's colonies . . . it is just and expedient that all such persons be manumitted . . .'. Under one of its clauses those 'persons at present entitled to the services of the slaves' were also entitled to be compensated 'for the loss of such services', and a total of £20 million was to be made available for this purpose. The date fixed for the act to come into effect was 1 August 1834, after which, as 'apprentices', field slaves would still have to work for their masters for another six years, and domestic slaves for four years, while only children under six years old would be immediately free. In order for owners in Antigua, like those in other self-governing colonies, to receive their share of the compensation money, the island had first to pass its own version of the Emancipation Act.

On 11 September a meeting of planters and other slaveowners took place in the courthouse in St John's called to protest against the British Act and to prepare a petition for transmission to London arguing against abolition. Many of the plantation owners were in financial trouble, no longer able to meet their debts, and in some cases not even able to obtain credit to buy enough food for their slaves – of whom it was now generally recognised there were too many. Among those attending, and one of the few planters who still had his head above water, was Samuel Otto Baijer; a man who besides being a member of the Assembly, a judge, and adjutant-general of the militia, was also one of the men Loving had singled out by name for abuse in his London epistle. His address to the meeting, far from endorsing the general attitude towards emancipation, took a totally unexpected and completely different view:

> Gentlemen, my previous sentiments on this subject are well known to you all: be not surprised to learn that they have undergone an entire change. I have not altered my views without mature deliberation. For several days past, I have been making calculations with regard to the probable results of emancipation, and I have ascertained beyond a doubt that I can cultivate my estate at least one-third cheaper by free labour, than by slave labour.[14]

His reasoning was very simple. Because the island was small and virtually all the land was taken up with sugar estates, there would be little that free labourers would be able to do but continue to work for the planters if they wanted to survive. As slaves they were fed, clothed and housed whether they worked or not, and once their working lives were over they remained the responsibility of their owners. On the other hand free labourers – of whom as there were already too many slaves there would be a surplus – would be entirely responsible for themselves, could be paid the lowest wages, and given employment only when work was available. As well as being simple, Baijer's reasoning was also persuasive: all thoughts of protesting emancipation were forgotten, and instead the meeting adopted an entirely different set of resolutions with which to petition the Legislature.

Chief among these resolutions were that apprenticeship would serve no useful purpose, that freedom should not be granted before the owners had been compensated, and that once slavery had ended there should be nothing 'to force upon the Colonists the necessity of employing labourers, over whose conduct they would have no Control.' In addition the owners wanted compensation to be fixed at £30 for each slave, and the much-hated $4\frac{1}{2}$ per cent sugar tax removed. Once suitable petitions had been presented to the Council and the House of Assembly – and some of those who had attended the courthouse meeting were members of one or the other – no time was lost in forming a joint committee to consider the island's own Emancipation Bill.

Not surprisingly, in its report the committee found itself in favour of immediate emancipation in order to 'prevent future agitation', and because of 'apprehension that the apprenticeship system would take away the authority of the master over the slave, without supplying in its place adequate means of controlling him.' It also objected to the introduction 'from abroad' of the stipendiary magistrates who would be needed to supervise an apprenticeship period, and also to the distinction made 'between the praedial and non-praedial classes, as being founded in injustice and bad policy.' In the end, after much waffle about 'The peculiar preparation on the part of both planters and the slaves for immediate emancipation' and 'The comparatively high degree of intelligence and moral principle which existed among the slaves', the report finally stated the real reason why apprenticeship was considered unnecessary; a reason later transmitted by the Legislature to the Governor as:

> The all-important and paramount one of an utter dependence, from peculiarity of climate and the absence of unoccupied lands, except those of absolute sterility, of the labourer or proprietor and capitalist for the means of procuring food; and that a large proportion of the population, whether bond or free, could not hope for the means of subsistence except by some laborious occupation in one of those frequent periods of long drought especially to which we are almost annually subject.[15]

Governor Sir Evan McGregor,[16] who had taken over from the planters' friend Ross the previous year, and was 'a man of the strictest political principles, and of a most enlightened mind', accepted the Legislature's reasoning and immediate emancipation was included in the act passed in February 1834. After some amendment by the Colonial Office it became law on 4 June, and Friday 1 August was ordered to be held as a day of thanksgiving for the 'happy termination' of slavery.

Although the decision to dispense with the apprenticeship period can now be seen for what it was – a cynical move by Antigua's plantocracy to take advantage of the fact that the physical characteristics of the island and its use ruled out peasant farming, and that free labourers would still be bound to the estates but under, as far as the planters were concerned, more advantageous conditions – this was not always so. In the immediate aftermath of emancipation the decision was widely hailed as reflecting 'much honour' on men 'who have ever been distinguished by their desire to mitigate the horrors of slavery';[17] men who 'graciously and generously granted [the slaves] their liberty' and who could pride themselves on knowing that 'nowhere in our West Indian possessions were the negroes treated with more humanity.'[18] If, as the historian Eric Williams recorded: 'The British historians wrote almost as if Britain had introduced Negro slavery for the satisfaction of abolishing it', reading such mid-Victorian encomiums might make one believe Antiguan planters only put up with slavery for the approbation they received for their manner of bringing it to an end.

•

Be that as it may, the months leading up to emancipation day were, in the words of one of these same commentators, 'fraught with hope and bright expectation on one hand, and fear and anxious foreboding on the other.' In October 1833 McGregor had written to the Colonial Secretary about the possible need to increase the size of the garrison:

> Previously to the next First of August it may be advisable in any case to solicit a reinforcement for Antigua, not so much on account of the Free Inhabitants, whom the King's Troops present, and the Militia, are sufficient to protect, as for the sake of the newly liberated slaves themselves, in order to overawe them by a Show of Force, and thereby guard against the consequence of excesses, in which they might otherwise be tempted to indulge, on the first introduction of a great change in the Nature of their social condition.

He followed this up with a request to the General Officer Commanding troops in Barbados for an addition to the garrison, perhaps backed up 'when the period of Emancipation approaches' by a warship in English Harbour 'to guard its Naval Establishment'. This drew a sharp response: the GOC had 'not heard of any appearance of bad Spirit' among the slaves which was beyond the control of 'An Active Magistracy', but:

> If troubles come from any quarter I will endeavour to meet them promptly but I am sure Your Excellency will discourage applications for Troops arising from timidity, or the unreasonable expectations of Planters too indolent to exert themselves in Magisterial or Police arrangements.

Since early 1833 the garrison had been provided by 180 officers and men of the 36th Foot, accommodated in the barracks at Fort Shirley. Such had been the death and sickness rate among them however, that two months before emancipation was due the GOC was obliged to provide around three dozen reinforcements. Their arrival was followed by a re-distribution of troops within the island, with detachments sent to occupy the re-opened old barracks on Monks Hill and in St John's. They then waited with the expectant slaves, the apprehensive whites and the optimistic free coloureds – the last greatly heartened by the Governor's appointment of Henry Loving as Superintendent of Police and another of their number, John Athill, as a magistrate – for the great day to dawn.

The general euphoria felt by the slaves at their approaching deliverance would have been diminished to some extent as they became aware of the laws which had already been put in place 'to hedge them about with such restraints and checks, as would not only prevent them from wanton outrages, but which should confine them to steady industry and economy, in those subordinate situations which they must for a long time occupy.' Under the provisions of the Contract Act the slaves, once they were free, were required to enter into contracts which would oblige them to remain 'in the places which they then occupied', living in the same houses and working for the same masters for a year, but receiving wages instead of food and clothing. At the end of a year they would be at liberty to work where they liked, but any wanting to earn a living as a porter, huckster or pedlar would require a licence. 'Idleness and vagrancy' would not be tolerated, and offenders faced jail sentences with hard labour.

Any feelings of unrestrained joy which may have remained once details of the Contract Act were published were probably quelled by a proclamation addressed to the slaves by McGregor a month before they became free. In this, after reminding them that they would 'henceforth have to depend for the necessaries of life, on the honest and industrious labour of their own hands', he assured them that the full protection of the law would be available 'to those who labour industriously and live soberly and honestly where they are permitted to live.' Any who roamed about idly however would 'be taken up and brought to deserved punishment', as would those found 'guilty of insubordinate, quarrelsome, disorderly, or riotous behaviour, or drunkenness, theft, trespass, or other gross delinquency.' If all this was not enough to keep them in order then perhaps 'fear of offending that Almighty Being, whose power over the stormy wind and tempest, we are taught at that season of the year especially to acknowledge' would serve to 'deter them from every excess displeasing to Him, and endangering their own peace and safety.' Finally, letting his Bible-thumping get the better of him, he exhorted:

> Submit yourselves to every ordinance of man for the Lord's sake: whether it be to the King as supreme, or to governors, as unto them that are sent by him for the punishment of evil doers, and for the praise of them that do well. For so is the will of God, that with well-doing ye may put to silence the ignorance of foolish men: as free, and not using your liberty for a cloak of maliciousness but as servants of God. Honour all men. Love the brotherhood. Fear God. Honour the King.[19]

And so, in a suitably chastened and sombre mood, at one minute past midnight on 1 August 1834, the island's 29 131 slaves became free. Because of the influence the Nonconformist churches exercised over the majority by this time, celebrations were almost entirely religious. Here and there they began immediately. If we are to accept the words of someone who was not actually present, 'In some of the chapels the noble spectacle was seen of the masters attending with their negroes, and, when the clock had struck, shaking hands with them and wishing them joy.'[20] Such improbable episodes apart, the celebrations took place after the sun had risen, with every church and chapel being filled to overflowing from mid-morning until well into the evening. At the end of the day Henry Loving, in his new capacity as the custodian of law and order, considered there had never been 'such universal and unbiased holiness', while a Methodist missionary was able to report:

> I walked through the streets of St John's after ten o'clock at night, and all was as still and tranquil as can possibly be conceived; not a drunkard was

to be found anywhere. We visited the police station and were assured that not a complaint had been heard of the slightest disorder or bad conduct.[21]

The less solemn festivities which took place the next day produced just as little to worry Loving and his police, or any of the white population, and after 'joining in the ordinances of God upon the Sabbath, the greater part of the negroes returned to their agricultural and other employments on the Monday morning with the utmost decorum and good temper.'[22]

The somewhat restrained celebrations of the newly emancipated 29 000 men, women and children were matched later by the mixed reception given by those who had been their owners to the total of £425 549 paid as compensation by the British Government: at an average of under £15 per slave, they received less than half of what they had hoped for. At the same time, for some the money they received was very useful in settling longstanding debts, and for all of them there was consolation in knowing they were no longer responsible for the 4327 children under the age of six (for whom they received about two pounds and eight shillings a head), or for the 1444 'aged and infirm' (who had been judged to be worth less than one penny each in the final reckoning). For one proprietor though, compensation was an incidental matter, as Sir Christopher Bethell-Codrington discovered when he received the letter his manager in Barbuda wrote two weeks before emancipation day:

> I am rather at a loss to know how I am to act on the 1st August the Legislater [sic] of Antigua not having included your Barbuda slaves with those of that Island for emancipation.[23]

13
A Private Governmency

No white man is allowed to settle in Barbuda, but servants to Sir William Codrington; nor is any person permitted to go there without leave first obtained from Sir William's Attorney.

> Governor Sir William Burt (1777)

Antigua have no right to extend her laws to this property – it was a Private Governmency long after the Laws of Antigua were framed.

> John Winter, the Codrington manager in Barbuda, in a letter to Sir Christopher Bethell-Codrington written in 1833

The lease of Barbuda, granted in 1685 to Christopher Codrington, had been renewed in favour of his son by Queen Anne in June 1705 for ninety-nine years: a period during which it remained an important and valuable part of the Codrington family inheritance. In 1710 it passed from the second Christopher Codrington to his nephew, who before his death in 1738 became Sir William Codrington, first baronet of Dodington. His son, the second baronet and also named William, held the lease until 1792, when it passed to his nephew Christopher – a man who later assumed the additional surname of Bethell, and later still also joined the baronetage as Sir Christopher Bethell-Codrington.

They were all absentee proprietors, preferring to reside in comfort and luxury in England while leaving their West Indian estates, including Barbuda, in the hands of attorneys. Various members of the family visited Barbuda on occasion; one in 1746 causing so much trouble among the slaves that one of their number committed suicide, another was murdered, and two ended up being burned alive 'before the Castle Gate' for having carried out the murder. The first Sir William Codrington, who had spent part of his youth in the West Indies, may have lived on the island for a while in the early years of the eighteenth century as he later wrote 'I design to end my days there'. He never did, although it was probably he who began work on a house on The Highlands, about three miles away from the 'castle'. Known thereafter as Highland House, it was too remote and inconvenient ever to be anything other than a country retreat, and had been abandoned by the early 1800s. The 'castle' itself near the lagoon, which was

BARBUDA IN 1848

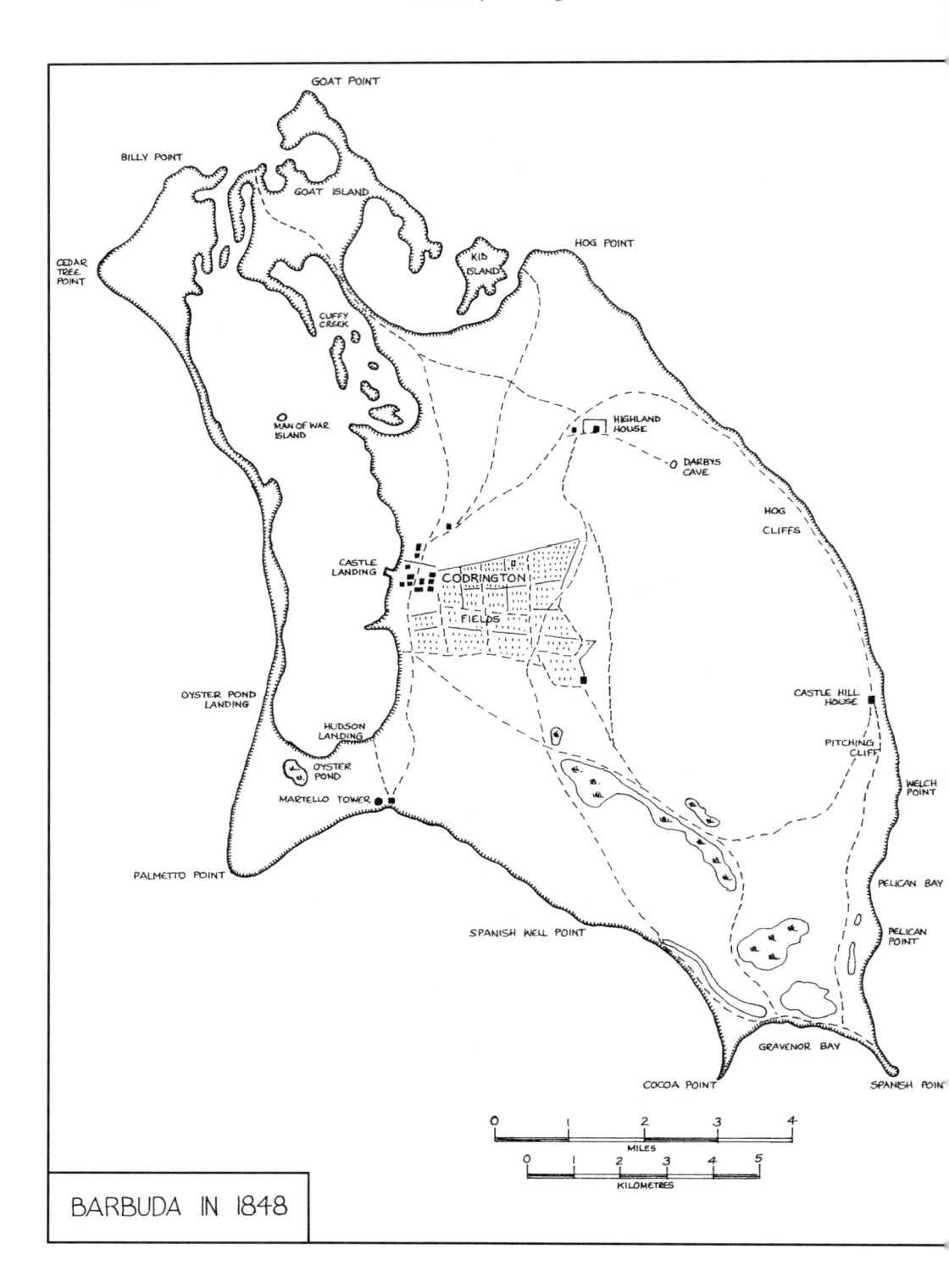

rebuilt and enlarged in the 1720s, consisted of a stone tower 'with several smaller erections attached to it, occupying one corner of an extensive parallelogram, formed by high walls.' Until a separate residence was provided for him it housed the manager or supervisor, and when Highland House was not in use it also provided rough and ready accommodation for any of the Codringtons, their friends or attorneys visiting the island.

The island's slaves also lived close to the castle, where they created the beginnings of the village of Codrington. They were more fortunate than their fellows on the Codrington estates in Antigua, as no attempt was ever made to introduce the plantation system, and their work was not confined to the constant round of planting and reaping sugar-cane. 'I hope and doubt not but that Barbuda will raise Yams Cassada & Peases etc. for breadkind enough to serve all my white Servants in Antigua', wrote the first Sir William Codrington in 1721, 'and Corn yams & Pease enough to serve all my [slaves].' The enclosed provision grounds which were laid out to the east of the settlement were gradually extended to cover several hundred acres, and employed a majority of the slaves. The others were employed in animal farming, hunting the feral livestock, fishing, tanning, burning lime and in all the other occupations needed by a self-sustaining community. Their numbers increased steadily and by largely natural means throughout the eighteenth century, rising from a handful in 1700 to 150 by mid-century, and over 300 by 1804. The island's livestock rose over the same period in an even more impressive fashion. In 1720 Barbuda supported about 300 sheep, 200 cattle, fifty horses, twenty pigs and a dozen goats. Sixty years later it was estimated there were 8000 sheep, 2000 goats, 600 horses and 300 deer, and in 1805 the manager reported there were over 20 000 sheep and so many feral pigs and deer that they were beginning to become a nuisance.[1]

In addition to supplying the Codrington estates in Antigua with all the working animals, fresh meat, fish, ground provisions, leather, lime and firewood they needed, excess produce and working animals were also sold to other proprietors. The naval and military forces also constituted a steady market for cattle and sheep. 'The great Fleet and Army we have in these seas', one of the overseers informed the second Sir William Codrington in July 1780, 'must render your Island of Barbuda a most valuable property exclusive of the Advantage by Wrecks.'[2] His reference to this particular advantage was one that Codrington hardly needed to be reminded of, the ships which ran aground on the island having over the years earned his family a fortune. With the 'right of wreck' written into their lease guaranteeing a major share of the value of anything saved from destruction, salvage operations offered a rich reward – especially if those who actually did the salving, with no option but to risk life and limb, were entitled to no share at all.

This of course had not gone unnoticed in Antigua, where all the salvage claims were dealt with, and where in 1777 the Governor complained 'No white man is allowed to settle in Barbuda, but servants to Sir William Codrington; nor is any person permitted to go there without leave first obtained from Sir William's Attorney.' A year later he was even more upset, informing London that it was impossible to operate the legal system where a 'Wanton Arbitrary Salvage is established', and asking for Barbuda to be brought under the legislative and judicial authority of Antigua.[3] Although the Secretary of State of the day refused to interfere it was enough to alert Codrington to the danger of losing the right when the lease came up for renewal. In January 1790, long before the due date, his nephew and heir Christopher Codrington was sent to Antigua to see if the new Governor, Thomas Shirley, could be persuaded to endorse an application for an early renewal. After a great deal of prevarication Shirley announced in November that 'he did not find himself inclineable to renew, lest it should give offence to Government', and the younger Codrington returned to England empty handed.[4]

It was not until after he had succeeded his uncle as the lessee, and Lord Lavington had taken over as Governor, that any progress was made. After more behind-the-scenes dealings Codrington's attorney was able to report in June 1801 that 'I am . . . informed by Lord Lavington . . . that he has by a late Packet received an order from the King in Council to execute a new Lease of Barbuda to you for Fifty Years from the 5 June 1805 when the old one expires.'[5] Three years later, just to make sure, Codrington petitioned the King for renewal, concentrating on the claim that since 1705 'the said Petitioner's Family had expended very considerable sums in cultivating and improving the said island, and in stocking the same so as to make the same of great use to the said Petitioner's other Estates in the Island of Antigua', but making no reference to wrecks or salvage. The petition was eminently successful and on the due date the lease was renewed for another fifty years, in return for 'one Fat Sheep if demanded' and the right for military or naval forces to enter at any time if the need arose.[6] The 'right to wreck' remained intact, which was just as well as hardly a year passed without at least one ship foundering and a profitable salvage operation taking place.

Wartime brought even more wrecks, and references to salvage operations and awards litter the correspondence sent to England by the various Codrington managers and attorneys throughout the long period of the French Revolutionary and Napoleonic Wars. From a Swedish schooner wrecked in 1799 'the cargo saved did not amount to six hundred pounds', moaned the attorney of the day, 'and you were awarded one-third of the gross sales.' In September 1809 however, another wreck earned Codrington no less than £3369, and four months later he was informed that two more ships were being worked on at the same time, the second 'laden principally with Spanish Red Wine'. And if that were not enough in July 1810 he was informed:

> Sir, On Friday Night the 22nd of last month, the American Sloop 'Uniform', from Rode-Island bound Antigua, with Corn and Provisions,

was wrecked on the North reef of Barbuda, the whole of her deck load consisting of Fish and Wood Hoops, was thrown overboard immediately on her striking; the remainder of the Cargo has been saved with the exception of some Corn which got wet.[7]

It was not only merchant vessels which ran aground: the British frigate HMS *Griffon* ran aground off the south-east coast in 1760, and in 1813 the larger frigate HMS *Woolwich* was 'totally wrecked in a furious hurricane' on the northern reefs. All the crew of the latter were saved, which, though fortunate for them, was unfortunate for Codrington as the sailors carried out most of the salvage work and his share of the eventual award was a mere £243. But even then all was not lost, as the hull remained fast on the reef long after the crew had departed, and this provided plenty of work for the island's manager, John James, and the slaves. So much of the ship's anti-fouling sheathing was recovered that, as a visitor to the island remarked twelve years after she had been wrecked, 'HMS *Woolwich* . . . is now commonly called Sir Bethel Codrington's copper mine.'

Some idea of the scope of the salvage operations, and the amount of labour involved, is provided in letters written by James to Codrington about several ships which were wrecked after the wars ended. In August 1817 a French brig 'from Guadeloupe bound to Bordeaux with Sugar, Cotton, Coffee and Rum' went aground off the south-east coast:

> Immediately on her striking which was about ten or eleven O'Clock at Night the Captain and Crew took to their Boat, without taking in a single Sail supposing themselves to be on the [Anegada] Reefs; she was in sight of the Fort, and a signal was made at day light for a Vessel in distress, but from the distance she was, and having the boats to carry over land three Miles, and then about ten to row against the Wind, it was noon before I could get on board her, by which time in consequence of the Sails having been left standing her bottom was so much injured that she was nearly full of Water, at least as high inside as it was out. I immediately proceeded to unbind her sails, and get down her Yards and topmasts to make her lay more easy.[8]

In spite of her condition salvage operations involving the removal of everything which could conceivably be of value or use were still going on ten days later. For the slaves this sort of work, involving lengthy boat trips followed by the manhandling of rotting cargoes inside broken, moving hulls at the fastest possible speed, would have been both dangerous and totally exhausting – at no time more so than in the middle of 1821 when James reported:

> At the time of writing you last I was about to proceed to the Wreck of the Spanish Schooner in search of Money said to be on board of her, but after every exertion nothing of the kind could be found . . . I was obliged to

return to Barbuda in consequence of another Vessel running on shore on the West side of the island . . . laden with Sugar, Rum and Cotton . . . [which later] went down in about twenty-five feet of water consequently her decks are covered, and all the sugar lost, the Rum is saved, and so I hope will be the Cotton, the latter but a small quantity.[9]

The 'fort' to which he referred in his earlier letter was a three-storey, stone-built tower with an elevated gun platform which had been built in the late eighteenth century to guard the main landing place, known as 'The River', on the south coast. 'The best anchorage', according to the Sailing Directions of the day, 'is off the fort and martello tower, with a flagstaff on it . . . This being the principal export place of the island, the road from thence to the town is very good; should a stranger land here, and hoist a flag on the fort, horses will always be sent down to meet him.'[10] The tower also provided an excellent vantage point from which to keep a lookout for vessels in distress and to summon the salvage team, as was proved with the French brig in 1817. The road between Codrington village and the fort, along which the team had had to haul their boats on that occasion, was described by Henry Nelson Coleridge during a visit he made with his cousin, the first Bishop of Barbados and the Leeward Islands, in 1825:

The vegetation on either side . . . appeared here more like a young forest, the trees and bushes being so high as to preclude the possibility of seeing twenty yards to the right hand or left of the road. The surface of the country is at the same time such a dead level, except an inconsiderable hillock at the other end of the island, that none but the veteran woodsman can traverse it with certainty.[11]

At the time of the episcopal visit the slaves were under the supervision of two white overseers, 'one of them a German', who lived near the castle in 'a more modern formal farm-house looking building.' Fed on an endless supply of fresh meat, fish and poultry, cooked and served by a host of servants, with unlimited access to the more attractive female slaves, they had very little to do except to look busy when the manager was around. John James lived with his family in the castle, where his wife – much to the annoyance of John Osborn, the attorney who looked after all the Codrington estates – felt she required no less than eighteen slaves to act as the family's personal servants. Two overseers on the spot, and a manager who spent a great deal of time off the island, were hardly enough to supervise the work of more than 400 slaves, to regulate their lives in anything but the most titular fashion, or even to impose a strict discipline.

By this time the island 'worked' – that is, produced the salvaged cargoes and the foodstuffs, livestock and other produce for the Codrington estates in Antigua – only because the slaves themselves knew what was wanted, and knew how to do it better than any £80-a-year white drifter who happened to fetch up as an overseer for a year or two. They also knew only too well that, compared with their contemporaries on the Antiguan estates, they were on to a good thing. 'There are but two white men with myself on the Island, and I frequently leave my Wife & Daughters there without a fastening to the House', James informed Bethell-Codrington in September 1824:

> The greater part of the Negroes on Barbuda would lay down their lives to serve me . . . We haul the seine as often as they like; sometimes 3 or 4 days together with fish are plenty. They have occasionally wild hog and goat meat. Many of them have their own Nets, and scarcely does one of your Vessels go to Antigua without a quantity of Fowls, and salt Fish to sell, and in good season an immense quantity of Potatoes. Many of them have 10 to 11 Acres of land in cultivation the produce of which of course is their own Property.[12]

Attempts to change this situation were made after James died in August 1826 and John Winter, who until then had managed one of the Antigua estates, was sent to take his place. By trying as a new broom to impose a stricter discipline and get more work out of the slaves he quickly succeeded in upsetting a community which had led a reasonably contented existence under his predecessor for over twenty years. With only two overseers to back him up he achieved very little other than to provoke widespread recalcitrance, and the correspondence which ensued between him, his superior John Osborn in Antigua, and Bethell-Codrington in England is littered with references to the poor morale and indiscipline of the slaves.

That these troubles were not all-consuming though is borne out in a report Winter sent to England in the middle of 1831, in which Bethell-Codrington was informed that he now had over 500 slaves on the island, an increase of 104 in less than seven years, and that out of the total twenty-eight of them had an average age of seventy-four: 'One man who has seventy children and grandchildren, and who is more healthy than I and takes a great deal of exercise, he is reputed to be ninety years old.'[13] Longevity and procreation on this scale had a lot to do with the placid and stress-free existence which most of the slaves managed to lead in spite of Winter's efforts to ruin it, assisted by the way in which he ordered their non-working hours. 'The reason why your slaves here increase more than almost any other Island is easily accounted for', he told Bethell-Codrington in April 1833:

> They all Live in one Village immediately around my dwelling. They are obliged all to be at home at nights, no *drinking, singing* or *dancing* allowed – only during the Xtmas Holidays. The Women are nearly three to two Men, the latter as soon as they arrive at the stage of Maturity nearly all get Married, the Women being in great Measure prevented from prostituting

themselves and injuring their Constitutions by bad practices, bring forth strong healthy athletic children, which are taken every care of . . . We do not lose one infant in twenty births.[14]

It is possible that such a high birth-rate may also have been in some part inspired by the example set by the Anglican missionaries who had been active on the island from soon after Bishop William Coleridge paid his visit in 1825. The first catechist sent to begin instructing the children in the rudiments of Christianity was a Mr Groot, appointed at a salary 'pretty well adequate for his support in that place' of £50 a year. Whether adequate or not it did not keep him or his immediate successors in Barbuda very long, as Winter told the proprietor in 1831:

> The Bishop . . . placed a catechist here to instruct the children . . . instead of shewing the people a good example he is setting them a very bad one, by forming a connection with one of your slaves. [I] have thought it proper he should be removed immediately [as] this is the third and all disgraced themselves.[15]

It is hardly surprising, given the moral failings of such men, the circulation of rumours connected with emancipation, and his own abrasive supervision, that a year later the general discontent turned into a state of insubordination which Winter termed a mutiny. Although this was prevented from turning into anything very serious by sending to Antigua for troops, the slaves remained so aggrieved and apprehensive that in September 1833 Bethell-Codrington sent them an open letter in which he attempted to explain the effect emancipation would have on their condition. At the end of October Winter acknowledged receipt of this and commented:

> I read [it] to them but I dont think it makes any impression on their minds, they run away with an idea that their usual comforts will be still allowed them when free, as they are now. I requested them to write but they will not – they say they want their freedom but the older ones say they do not, that their master had all their work when they were able and he must feed them now they are old.[16]

He ended this letter by stating his view that 'Antigua have no right to extend her laws to this property – it was a Private Governmency long after the Laws of Antigua were framed.' This was his response to an opinion that the Attorney-General had given to the Governor the previous month, in which he had stated that in connection with emancipation, he thought it would 'be advisable under the projected changes, for the Legislature of Antigua more particularly to include the inhabitants of [Barbuda] in the laws applicable to a state of general freedom.'[17]

Advisable it may have been, but under the existing arrangements between the two islands the Governor, McGregor, could see no way of bringing it about. In order to make the British Abolition Act effective each self-governing colony had to introduce its own abolition bill, but Barbuda not only had no government, no legislature and no judicial establishment, it was considered by the Antiguan Legislature to be an independent settlement which was the private property of the Codrington family. Aware of the trouble being experienced by Winter, and in order to size up the situation of the Barbuda slaves for himself, McGregor visited the island in March 1834. Having listened to the slaves' complaints, which were mostly about the manager's withdrawal of their accustomed rations, and to Winter's accounts of their insubordination, he arranged to provide the island – at the expense of the proprietor – with a magistrate to assist in maintaining law and order. The following month two justices of the peace, accompanied by a small detachment of the 36th Regiment under Lieutenant Burrows and Ensign Mauleverer, were sent from Antigua and everyone on the island settled down to await emancipation day.

In June Bethell-Codrington, who was now paying for the services of the magistrates and their escort, wrote to the Colonial Office asking for an appointment to be made for his London agent to see the Secretary of State in order to discuss what was to happen to the Barbuda slaves after August. As far as he was concerned as lessee of the island, once they became free they would become homeless, landless, provision-less trespassers – unable to do anything without his permission and not even able to leave the island without using his boats – and as such would be in a worse state of slavery than they were at present. In addition, as they were already largely out of the control of his manager, and likely to become more so, he considered his interests in Barbuda were at risk and wished to know what action the Secretary of State intended to take.

Both he and the Colonial Office had left it far too late for any kind of solution to be found before emancipation day. In Barbuda this came and went without anything untoward taking place, and life continued much as it had before. The Colonial Office considered that the Antiguan Legislature should include the island in its laws, as did some members of that Legislature. A joint committee of the Council and Assembly, which had been set up to examine the Attorney-General's opinion delivered the previous year, recommended 'extending our Act of Emancipation to Barbuda' provided it was done in a way which relieved the Antiguan Treasury of any extra expenditure. Unfortunately the majority of the legislators did not agree, and in February 1835 the Assembly, having declared it had no constitutional right to legislate for Barbuda, rejected the recommendation outright.

The state of limbo, neither bonded nor free, in which they found themselves in August 1834 had been accepted without any fuss by the black inhabitants of Barbuda, allowing the magistrates and their military escort to be withdrawn, but when the Assembly in Antigua refused to consider legislating for the island, their situation became intolerable. In March the same detachment of troops returned in response to a request from Winter, in order to quell any disturbance which might arise. The two officers, Burrows and Mauleverer, were sworn in as magistrates, and given orders by McGregor to enquire into any disorder, using 'friendly remonstrance and advice' before taking any legal action, and to attempt to bring about some clear agreement between Winter and the rest of the population. The men and women who less than nine months before had been Bethell-Codrington's slaves were to be told they had no right to remain on his property, any more than they had the right

> to inhabit his houses, and to enjoy the other privileges and advantages they do, without the reciprocal obligation on their parts of giving a portion of their labour to the owner of the soil, and that if they withhold such fair proportion of labour they cannot be allowed to remain a useless burthen on the property.[18]

They were also to be told that refusal to work would be punished by fines or imprisonment, or even removal from the island to one of the Codrington estates in Antigua.

This last sanction was of very dubious legality. The Barbudans may have been the property of Bethell-Codrington up until 1834, but they were now free citizens and residents of an island which was part of a British colony. This was recognised in May when McGregor was ordered by London to revoke any order he had given referring to 'the removal of any Person from the Island of Barbuda'. This instruction arrived too late to prevent the two military magistrates from deciding that a man named Thomas Beazer, by failing to honour an agreement he had made to work for Winter, deserved to be deported. He had been shipped to Antigua in April, ordered to report to the police, and to make himself available for work wherever the attorney for the Codrington estates felt he would be most useful. In the event Beazer refused to work and remained in St John's, where the circumstances of his expulsion from Barbuda quickly appeared in the local newspapers. This led to public criticism of the Governor and his dealings with Barbuda, but produced no reaction from the Legislature which might have assisted him in resolving the situation.

Although McGregor soon rescinded his order about recalcitrant Barbudans being sent off the island, the impasse with regard to how the islanders were to be governed and under what laws they were to live remained. The only solution lay in the Antiguan Assembly agreeing to include the island under its laws and administration, but this its members refused to contemplate – solely because of the cost involved. Under Antiguan administration the Barbudans would require the provision of such things as a law court and a school, and the services of people like clergymen, doctors and policemen. With no freeholders or taxpayers among them, and revenue derived from the island limited to 'one fat sheep a year' and a small share of the occasional salvage claim, the cost of all these would become a charge on the Antiguan Treasury – an institution barely solvent at the best of times. As far as the Colonial Office was concerned, 'If Barbuda is not subject to the laws of Antigua, or included in Antiguan legislation, then the Barbudans are to this day the apprenticed labourers of Sir Bethel Codrington', but if they were to be considered as such, he would have no option but to retain all of them as 'Tenants of his Estate' until the period of apprenticeship as specified in the British Abolition Act ended.

This may have represented the official, legalistic view of their situation, but the Barbudans themselves were more interested in establishing their own security of tenure, in finding out just how they were to live and work, and in discovering to what rights they were now entitled in the only place they had ever considered home. In early May 1835 an acceptable wage scale was agreed with Winter, and hours of work laid down, but restrictions were placed on their freedom of movement within the island, and on what use they could make of its resources. They were also denied the right to leave the island, except once every four months when three of them would be allowed to visit Antigua for up to three days to buy and sell goods on behalf of all the rest.

The legality of this agreement, which was negotiated under the auspices of Burrows and Mauleverer and eventually witnessed by the Superintendent of Police, Henry Loving, remained open to question. McGregor trusted that he would be able to enforce its provisions, and exercise some control over the island, by issuing rules and ordinances, and by sending over a magistrate from time to time. The Colonial Office contradicted this view without being able to offer any alternative. In the end, by the middle of 1835, it was grudgingly accepted that the Governor would issue whatever regulations he thought necessary, but on the understanding that 'the strict legality' of his doing so was 'at least doubtful'.[19] And there, with regard to the governing of the supposedly free citizens of Barbuda, matters rested for the next five years.

Part Three: Neither Planters Nor People Prosper

The West Indian planters for generations had one great crop, cane, an insatiable market, and unlimited labour. This last they still have. In spite of these advantages neither planters nor people prosper.

W.M. Macmillan
Warning From the West Indies (1936)

14

Their Natural Portion

The moral well-being of the Negroes, not less than the prosperity of all Classes, will depend upon their being trained to the exercise of industry in the arts and labours which are their natural portion.

Edward Stanley, fourteenth Earl of Derby (1845)

In the years between emancipation and 1870 the greatest tragedy of all lay in the officially acknowledged abandonment of expectation and promise for the ex-slaves and their descendants. In 1834 to 1838 they had been freed from the tyranny of the estates. After 1846 they were being pressed to return to it of their own accord. By 1870 it was clear that few people in authority would admit that the working-class Negro was equipped to contribute anything but his labour to the society in which he lived and was numerically predominant. Unable to care for himself, as it was assumed, he would have to be cared for; and so the patronage of the British government could readily be substituted for the patronage of the planters.

Douglas Hall
Five of the Leewards, 1834–1870 (1971)

On Monday 4 August 1834 the planters of Antigua waited with some trepidation for the people who up until the previous Thursday had been their slaves to turn up for work as free labourers. Although most did appear disputes began immediately. Dissatisfaction with the rates of pay which had been agreed among the planters – one shilling a day for those employed in the 'great gang' of able-bodied adults, and ninepence a day for the less efficient or useful – was widespread, and there was much arguing about the hours of work and whether they should begin at dawn or sunrise. Within a month or two only about half of all those who might have been expected to be so employed were appearing for work on the plantations on a regular basis. Many men reckoned they could exist quite well on only three or four days' wages, while hundreds more had decided they could do better by becoming porters, fishermen, pedlars, stevedores or bargemen. Many women found that a few days in the fields followed by several more as market-women or hucksters was more rewarding than constant labour on the estates, and there was extensive aversion to allowing children to continue with work associated with slavery. This was not at all what the planters had envisaged and, even though the estate work did get done and there was little disorder, as the harvest season approached they decided more stringent control was needed.

The Labourers' Contract Act was passed by the Assembly in December in an effort to stem the flow of labour from the estates, and to try and prevent casual working through the introduction and strict enforcement of severe contract laws. Under its provisions once a labourer had agreed to work under a contract, which needed to be nothing more than a verbal understanding made in the presence of two witnesses, any absence – unless for a very good reason – would lead to loss of pay. With no such reason any period of absence during the day would mean the loss of the entire day's wages, whole absence on two successive days, or for any two days in a two-week period, could lead to a week in jail with hard labour. Offences such as drunkenness, ill-use of livestock, carelessness with the use of fire or wanton destruction of property all earned up to three months' hard labour. The employer, on the other hand, could for any violation of the contract expect nothing more than a fine of up to £5.

The need for social legislation to accompany the Contract Act was ignored. Before emancipation the owners had been responsible not only for feeding, clothing and housing their slaves, but also for the provision of medical attention and the relief of the old and disabled. Now that slavery had ended the sick, the unfit and the aged were abandoned to find their own salvation with whatever help they could obtain from their relatives, or from the Daily Meal Society, a charity which received no official support until 1855.

Education would have been treated in the same way, had schools of a sort not already been opened by the missionaries, and if the British Government had not specified otherwise. A sum of £30 000 a year for five years, followed by decreasing annual amounts thereafter until 1845, known as the Negro Education Grant, had been included in the British Emancipation Act. From the grant each colony was to be allocated in the first year an amount in proportion to the number of ex-slaves for whom compensation had been paid, with administration of the money 'secured through the agency of the different religious bodies already engaged in promoting Education.' In December 1835, under the first allocation, the Society for the Propagation of the Gospel received £1000 for use in Antigua, and the island's Legislature was called upon to introduce an act to enforce compulsory education. An informed, literate black population was the last thing the plantocracy wanted to see and, with responsibility for education among the ex-slaves safely removed from any charge on the Treasury, another twenty-two years were to go by before any such act was introduced.

Within two years of emancipation nearly 5200 children were receiving some sort of education. The Anglicans, Methodists and Moravians all had day, evening and Sunday schools, with the majority of the day schools teaching their pupils very little other than reading and writing. Arithmetic was taught only in the few 'National' schools, while Bible studies of course dominated those open on Sunday. All the schools were in the main staffed by women, coloured and black, of whom many were considered by one observer to be 'by no means equal to the task'.[1] There were extremely few trained teachers, and even the opening of the non-denominational Mico Charity Normal School in St John's in 1838 did little to improve matters. This institution, which remained in existence until 1899, produced excellent male teachers, but at a rate of only ten to fifteen a year. As many of the trainees came from other colonies as far away as British Guiana the overall benefit to Antiguan education was very limited.

In spite of these shortcomings the number of children attending school increased steadily until around 1847, by which time nearly 6500 were receiving some sort of education. After this the numbers fell dramatically as economic conditions forced children back into becoming wage-earners or made it impossible for their parents to clothe them decently. Those that were forced to abandon schooling at this time did so just as the Moravians opened their own establishment, intended 'to raise up well-qualified native Teachers and Assistants for Missionary Labour', at Cedar Hall a few miles south of St John's. Some years later, after moving to the city, this became the highly respected Spring Gardens Female Teachers' Training College, an institution which continued to produce teachers for all the Leeward Islands until its closure in 1958. A hundred years or so earlier, at about the same time as the first graduates were leaving the Cedar Hall establishment, there were less than 3000 children still attending school; most of them receiving an education judged to be no more than 'elementary and very meagre'.[2]

●

For the authorities in Antigua after 1834 keeping the black inhabitants in their place was of far more importance than the education of their children. In order to maintain law and order on the estates the Police Act of that year authorised the appointment of rural constables, with the right to nominate them being given to the planters. They did not have too far to look to find suitable men, as the Quaker philanthropist Joseph Sturge observed during a visit he made to the island three years later:

> The overlookers, as the *ci devant* [former] drivers are now called, had no sticks of office; except such of them as carried a staff, to denote that they were rural constables. One of the most intelligent negroes on each estate is usually invested with this authority.[3]

The replacement of the whip by a staff may have marked progress of a sort, but in the eyes of the rest of the workers on an estate such a man could never have appeared as an impartial upholder of the law, or indeed as anything but a lackey of the estate owner and an ever-present reminder of their past condition. No change took place until the Police Act was renewed in 1838, when a proper police force was established and the nomination of rural constables passed to the magistrates.

As internal security became the responsibility of the police force from the date of its formation the militia was abolished in July, putting an end 'to all martial glory and deeds of arms among the store-keeper captains and planter colonels of Antigua.' All their arms when called in

> were consigned to a far different purpose from what they were originally intended – being formed into a fence before the arsenal, where they remain [and where they still can be seen today on the south side of the Central Police Station], with their bayonets pointing to the skies, as mementoes of the warlike acts of the island.[4]

From then on the maintenance of law and order in the towns was the responsibility of the regular force, which numbered two dozen by the early 1840s; and in the countryside of the rural constables, of whom initially there were about 250.

Among all the laws and regulations which the police in St John's were enjoined in their early days to enforce was one concerned with keeping the streets free of stray animals. Pigs were a particular nuisance, as Mrs Lanaghan recorded:

> Great has been 'the hue and cry' among the swinish multitude; and day after day has the intelligence arrived that another unfortunate pig has been imprisoned within the walls of the pound, without regard to the feelings of the said quadruped, or its family. Even Sunday . . . was no rest to them, or the parties whose duty it was to capture them; and so far was the disturbance carried . . . that some good people took the trouble to write and disseminate papers, calling upon policemen, magistrates, etc., to observe to keep holy the Sabbath, and not allow pigs to be hunted before the very doors of the churches and chapels, even when service was being performed.[5]

The impounding of stray animals was however only a marginal activity, a diversion from the routine enforcement of all the laws which had been passed to keep the black population in its place, and to protect the property of the plantocracy. Following the English penal code of the time many of what today are no more than minor misdemeanours were treated as felonies and punished accordingly. During slavery the commonest form of punishment, whipping, had been meted out on the spot, with only the more serious offences being heard about and dealt with by officers of the law. As summary corporal punishment had been abolished at emancipation all offences, from breaking off a piece of sugar-cane to murder, were now matters for police investigation, with punishment restricted to fines or imprisonment.

The island's main prison had been moved in 1831 to the old barracks on the eastern edge of St John's, and supplemented with a house of correction for petty offenders, vagrants and those awaiting trial. Committal to either was frequently accompanied by hard labour, with a penal gang employed on road maintenance or other public work projects. 'They do not work in chains', Joseph Sturge was pleased to note during his visit, 'with the exception of five or six whose sentences of death have been commuted, and require only a very slight superintendence.' The use of a treadmill, on which he noted the 'refractory' were punished by being put upon after 'their return at night', was not abolished until 1840. Among the few prisoners not employed on road works, in chains or otherwise, were the island's lunatics (who were kept in jail until the first asylum was opened in 1841) and children such as the eight-year-old boy seen by Sturge 'breaking stones in the court-yard', who had been committed 'for stealing a single cane, whilst passing through the fields' when going to town on an errand:

> For this he was sentenced to pay a fine of seven dollars, and, in default of payment, to imprisonment and hard labour. Not to speak of the impolicy of making a criminal of such a child as this, the fine imposed is equivalent to his earnings for about three months, and is about a hundred and twenty times more than the value of the property stolen.[6]

The prison and house of correction were combined in 1844, bringing about according to the Inspector of Prisons, 'a marked and unquestionable improvement . . . in the mode of carrying out the discipline of the prison' – a discipline which was reinforced three years later by the introduction of 'The punishment of whipping . . . to be applied in extremely aggravated cases only.'[7]

•

The Contract Act, drawn up at the end of 1834, which like all other legislation passed by the Assembly had to go to London for approval, was rejected by the Secretary of State as being unduly harsh and designed to keep the labourers 'below the common level of society'. The members of the Assembly recorded their 'great surprise and chagrin' at this disallowance, as they did to rejection of yet another attempt they had made to be exempted from payment of the detested $4\frac{1}{2}$ per cent export duty. They could do nothing about the latter except to suck their teeth until it was abolished in 1838, but an amended version of the Contract Act was sent to England in August 1835 and became law later the same year. With its supporting regulations – vagrancy laws to punish those who would not work, and licensing laws to try to restrict those who wanted to be self-employed – the new act still ordered the lives of the bulk of the black population in ways which were unacceptable to many and unsatisfying to all. It provided for written or verbal contracts which would run for a year and be terminable only at one month's notice, and which contained the unique provision that a yearly contract could be implied from a labourer's occupation of accommodation on an estate, with no other form of understanding. Any absence from work still led to loss of pay, but could now also lead to homelessness from being given one month's notice to quit an estate. Those not prepared to put up with these conditions had an extremely limited choice of escape: either they had to find somewhere to live which was not on an estate, or they had to leave the island altogether.

The latter was hardly an option while the apprenticeship system remained in force in all the other island colonies in the Caribbean, ensuring there were no labour shortages, but even so there were opportunities further afield. 'We are still in want of young labourers . . . the Planters of Demerara are doing all they can to entice our People', wrote Samuel Auchinlech, the manager of the Codrington estates, to his proprietor in January 1837; 'A sort of kidnapping practice has been going on, to induce the labourers to break their Contracts and steal off in open boats to Montserrat where a Vessel lay ready to receive them.'[8] He was referring to agents sent on behalf of the planters in British Guiana, where there was a shortage of labour and where government bounties were paid to employers who brought in workers. These had some success, as Joseph Sturge was able to determine when he came across one of them later in the same year:

> In Antigua he had induced thirty-two negroes of both sexes, carpenters, sailors, house-servants, and a few field-labourers, to indent themselves for various periods of one to four years, at a rate of wages of three to seven dollars per month, and generally on higher terms after the first year.[9]

It must have taken a lot of smooth talking to persuade people that sweating away in a South American cane-field could be in any way preferable to bending their backs in an Antiguan one, and it is doubtful if more than a hundred were enticed in this way. When agents working on behalf of the Trinidadian planters began recruiting a couple of years later they met with a similar reluctance among Antiguans to accept that a devil that they did not know was, or could be, much better than the one they already knew only too well: between 1839 and 1846 only 200 of them moved to Trinidad, compared with over 2000 from Montserrat and more than 2600 from St Kitts. The main reason why so few were persuaded to leave was, however, because those unwilling to remain tied to a particular estate were able, within a year or two of emancipation, to exercise their only other option and make a home elsewhere in Antigua.

The move away from the estates got under way in 1836, with the help of the Moravian missionaries. Part of the church property at Newfield in the east of the island was divided into small lots and leased for houses, and a few months later the same happened at Grace Hill, the United Brethren church to the west of Monks Hill. The labourers who moved to Grace Hill joined with others who had already begun to build on an adjoining estate which had been sold off in small lots by its female proprietor, and so laid the foundation of what became the first 'free village', appropriately named Liberta. The planters, as was to be expected, opposed such developments, considering 'unattached labourers and their petty settlements' harmful to 'the connexion of tenancy and labour' which they thought essential to maintain order in society and to ensure the profitability of their estates.

Their cause was not helped by the arrival of a new governor, Sir William Colebrook,[10] who took over from McGregor in 1837 and quickly became convinced that communities such as Newfield and Liberta 'if judiciously encouraged and carefully watched over would inevitably become nurseries of labour for the whole island.'[11] With the backing of the Colonial Office Colebrook brought pressure to bear on the planters to assist, and by the middle of 1840 a number had broken ranks and were selling off the less fertile parts of their estates, including areas which subsequently became the villages of Swetes and Buckleys. Within another two years, as more planters realised there was money to be made from selling off bits of land with little agricultural potential, there were twenty-seven free villages housing some 3600 people. Many of the thousand or so houses were built of stone with shingle roofs, and compared very favourably with the estate housing which Joseph Sturge had observed a few years before:

> The houses are now very comfortable; consisting of one, and sometimes two rooms, of from ten to fourteen feet square, and kept very clean, a few of which are furnished with a four-post bed, and other household goods. Each kitchen is a little detached shed, thatched . . . The huts are also thatched with cane-trash, thrown on in a very slovenly manner, but the interior roof is constructed of strips of palm leaves neatly plaited.[12]

•

On 8 February 1843 any labourer's house built of stone, whether on an estate or in one of the villages, was probably reduced to rubble by an extraordinarily powerful earthquake – 'the most awful convulsion of nature ever recorded in the history of this portion of the West Indies' – which shook the entire island in the middle of the morning. It was so strong 'that on board a ship at sea, at a distance of one hundred and sixty miles from any of the islands, the shock was so severely felt that the shipmaster imagined the vessel had struck on a rock.' Because it happened during daylight hours only about twenty people in Antigua were killed, but the damage to property was immense, even if not quite as bad as recorded by a young army officer who wrote that 'there was not a single stone or brick building which had not been levelled with the ground.'[13] In the countryside nearly every parish church was ruined, and out of 172 windmills thirty-five were completely destroyed, eighty-two 'split from top to bottom' and the remainder rendered in need of repair of some sort. St John's was very badly affected: 'About one-third of the stores and dwellings were levelled with the ground; and the remainder (with the exception of those buildings erected of wood) so shattered and torn, that they were rendered intenantable.'[14] The courthouse, police station and other public buildings were 'rendered unsafe', but the worst affected was St John's Cathedral, the building which until only a few months earlier – up until the appointment of the first Bishop of Antigua – had been merely the parish church.

Much of the re-building and repair work that followed was carried out with the aid of a loan from the British Government, some £100 000 being made available for the restoration of public buildings and to provide a fund from which private individuals could borrow. Using this, what was now the city of St John's was soon returned to something approaching its former condition; not that this was particularly outstanding according to a carping visitor in 1851. Charles Day found little that was good to say about either the buildings of St John's or the animals which had replaced the 'swinish multitude' by this time:

> St John's has the anomalous character of all West Indian towns – long, low, unpainted wooden houses, weather stained and dilapidated, interspersed with compact wooden mansions, neatly painted white with green *jalousies*. The general effect is extremely disagreeable, the good houses not being sufficiently near each other to redeem the other . . . There is one nuisance . . . which makes St John's resemble one of the worst Turkish towns – this is the plague of dogs. Each negro-hut contains at least one long-eared, mangy, half-starved cur, which at night is driven into the streets or roads, where numbers congregate – yelling, barking, and fighting amongst themselves, besides baying in packs [at] every unfortunate wayfarer.[15]

The one building which did meet with Day's approval was the new parish church, now 'the cathedral, an extremely imposing and handsome structure of very white freestone . . . adapted to withstand an earthquake.' This had been consecrated in 1848, its construction having exercised the minds of the clergy, discomposed the Legislature, exasperated the Governor and provided a massive drain on the Treasury for the whole of the preceding five years. By itself it had taken over a third of the British loan, causing Governor Sir James Higginson[16] to complain before it was completed that the island's resources 'were incommensurate with so large an outlay, and that a less costly edifice would have better suited the state of the public finances.' In 1848, some months after it had been consecrated, his lament was even stronger: 'The cost of erecting this building, which has exceeded £35 000 sterling, has proved a heavy drain on the public resources; and the effects of this extravagance will, I fear, be sensibly felt for some time to come.' Two years later John Candler, an agent of the Anti-

Slavery Society sent out to examine the results of emancipation, and as a Quaker a man with no great love of the established church, was even more critical:

> The Cathedral of St John's has cost the enormous sum of £40 000, and has been paid for by taxes laid on the people. A member of the Legislature told me that this enormous outlay had crippled the colony. Such is the mercy of the Church of England; such the blessings of a Bishop![17]

•

Daniel Davis,[18] the first Bishop of Antigua, was by all accounts a reasonably enlightened man who had in his youth been connected with the anti-slavery movement, but the church of which he became a prelate in 1842 was – as far as the West Indies were concerned – by and large a compassionless institution grounded in intolerance. During the forty or fifty years before emancipation any interest it might have taken in the general wellbeing, religious or otherwise, of the slaves had been surrendered to the dissenting churches. In Antigua, while Robert Holberton (who became Archdeacon at Davis's elevation) had through his work with the Daily Meal Society demonstrated a praiseworthy concern for the welfare of at least some of the black population, his views and activities had not been copied by the rest of the Anglican clergy. After 1834, when they were obliged to begin to show some regard for a host of new parishioners, their activities were devoted solely to the promotion of religious and moral education of prospective church members. Unfortunately, under the influence of the evangelical movement in Britain – which considered conversion of the heathen as a prime imperial duty, but eradication of licentiousness as being no less important – the clergy sought their role in concentrating on the latter. In doing so they caused unnecessary distress to many of the newly emancipated blacks, destroyed many of the aspirations of the by now sizeable coloured community, reinforced the existing sharp divisions in society, and rendered Anglicanism synonymous with narrow-minded hypocrisy.

In the years before emancipation when the Moravians and Methodists had been busy among the slaves, both churches had been keen 'to extirpate the degrading custom of concubinage'. Their missionaries had welcomed the 1797 Amelioration Act, which had sanctioned the form of union whereby, as they themselves had no legal right to solemnise marriages, 'such as wished to be united in matrimony appeared before them, and after declaring themselves man and wife . . . were so registered in the records of the church, to which they [were] afterwards held amenable for their conduct in that relation.' This form of ceremony then became the accepted substitute for an orthodox Church of England marriage and by 1812 both the Moravians and Methodists had made it a firm rule 'to exclude from their communion all persons, who were living in a state of concubinage.'[19] All of this met with the full approval of the Anglican clergy until 1 August 1834.

After that date the only form of marriage recognised and permitted was that conducted for a fee in an Anglican church by a Church of England clergyman. Dissenting ministers were no longer allowed to carry out the ceremony, and all unions previously registered by them – and until then universally recognised as marriages – became overnight no more than examples of sectarian condonation of concubinage. This abrupt change not only discouraged marriage from then on among the many who had no connection with the Anglican Church, or who could not afford the fee, but affected existing relationships, as Sturge observed: 'The parents of numerous families have taken advantage of the law, to dissolve their unions of many years' duration.' It also had the far more profound effect of making the children of couples who had not been married in the Anglican Church illegitimate; and this in the climate of the day – with the growing emphasis on respectability and public morality – was a barrier to any sort of social advancement. For the vast majority of the black population in the years immediately after emancipation, this probably meant very little as few could aspire to any elevation in status, but this was to change. For the coloured community it was however devastating.

Following the abolition of slavery the majority of the coloureds, understandably wanting to believe that their best hopes for the future lay in assimilation into, or at least complete acceptance as equals by, the white community, sided wholeheartedly with the whites in their attempts to keep the newly emancipated black Antiguans firmly in their place. They were assisted in thinking that this was in their best interests by men like Loving and Athill, who were active servants of the law from the beginning, and others such as Daniel Hill, who became the Governor's secretary in 1837, and Joseph Shervington, who rose to become Deputy Treasurer by 1840, both very much part of an otherwise all-white administration.

These appointments had only been made at the insistence of either Governor McGregor or his successor Colebrook – in the face of opposition from the Legislature and most of the white population – and were resented accordingly. The plantocracy may not have been able to prevent such appointments, but any general aspiration to equality on the part of the coloureds could be dealt with in other ways. Once respectability had become the watchword, the mere fact of possessing a non-white complexion marked out the owner for condemnation, as such a colour could only have resulted from an illicit liaison sometime in the past. Worse still, if the person concerned, as was the case with the majority, came from a non-Anglican family, the implications were obvious. As two American visitors observed at the end of 1836:

> There was a strong aversion among the higher classes of the whites, and
> especially among *females*, to associating in parties with colored people; but it
> was not on account of their *color*, but chiefly because of their *illegitimacy*.[20]

This preoccupation with illegitimacy, led by the Anglican clergy and the white female members of their flocks, which made respectability the *sine qua non* for entry into island society, served a number of purposes. The white men, 'the authors of that *illegitimacy*' which their wives found so distasteful, were forced to distance themselves as much as possible from coloured men in any public or business dealings, in order to avoid taint by association. Socialising between whites and coloureds, where both men and women were present, was made as difficult as possible: 'seeing [the men] might not unfrequently be subjected to the embarrassment of introducing to their white wives a colored mistress or an *illegitimate* daughter.'[21] But, perhaps best of all as far as the female members of the plantocracy were concerned, it put the blame for the transgressions of their menfolk firmly where it belonged – among the 'colored females, who are considered as having no character to gain or to lose; and who, consequently, became the ready instruments of vice.'[22] Within twenty years or so of emancipation this social exclusion combined with worsening economic conditions to produce a marginalised, frustrated and shrinking section of the population, distanced from whites and blacks alike.

•

The destruction of the workers' houses on the estates caused by the 1843 earthquake represented only a fraction of the total damage but, because the planters refused by and large to go to any great expense to rebuild them their loss only hastened the growth of the free villages. Within three years the number had increased to seventy, containing 3300 houses (now regrettably of much less substantial construction) and sheltering well over 9000 people, from among whom Governor Higginson was sanguine enough to record 'may spring the germ of a middle class, which must exercise considerable influence over the future destinies of the colony.'[23] He was going to be proved right in the very long term, but at the time not if the plantocracy could do anything to prevent it. Although they did not make any great effort to rebuild estate housing, the owners for the most part remained unwilling to part with the land needed if their workers were to be housed in reasonable dignity and comfort elsewhere. There was a constant demand for land, and as soon as it was known that part of an estate was going to be released for sale in small lots 'numbers flock forward as candidates for preference'. The result was inevitable, as a less charitable administrator than Higginson reported in 1855:

> A further enhancement of the general rate of mortality may safely be asserted
> to have been the result of the predilection which of late years the peasantry

have manifested for the crowded and ill-ventilated 'free villages' as residences in preference to the cottages scattered at large [sic] over the several estates which had previously been their homes. However sound may have been the principles which, in connexion with the then existing state of public sentiment, presided over the original establishment of these 'free villages', – the number of which has now risen to 86, – their increase has been probably detrimental to the general health at least of the island.[24]

The acute shortage of land for housing, caused by unhelpful planters, and the lack of means to buy proper building materials among the majority of labourers, stemming from the miserable wages most of them were paid, combined during the first couple of decades after emancipation to set the pattern for village life for another hundred years or more.

During the formative years, at a time when the conditions under which they lived were changing, the labourers found that the conditions under which they worked could also be changed. Once a man was not tied to an estate he could bargain for his labour, and earn more money by being paid to complete a particular job than by drawing a daily wage. By engaging in task work he enjoyed more freedom, not only to choose who to work for, but when to work in order to leave more time for money-making activities away from the estates. This in turn brought about an increase in the daily wage rates in an effort by the planters to prevent more of their resident estate workers from leaving. It also resulted, as Sir Robert Horsford noted in 1845, in 'a marked diminution of the deference which [the labourers] have hitherto been accustomed to pay those in authority over them.' Horsford, who had been appointed as a stipendiary magistrate in Antigua in order to provide impartial adjudication in any dispute which arose between the planters and their workers, deprecated the shift towards task work, fearing it gave the workers 'a false impression that the temporary independence which they have latterly been able to obtain, has placed them much more upon a footing of equality with their employers', something which was 'a mistaken notion, much to be deplored.'[25]

Such biased remarks, coming from a man who even if he was very much part of the plantocracy was being paid to exercise some sort of neutrality, echoed the main complaint of the planters – that any independence shown by the labourers was a threat to society and detrimental to the ordered running of their estates. Bemoaning the loss of the complete control which they had enjoyed before 1834, and had hoped to retain with the disallowed Contract Act, they began to wonder if another source of labour might not be found. Immigrant workers would serve two purposes: by remaining under their complete control while presenting the presumptuous inhabitants of places like Liberta and Freetown with enough competition to force them back into subservience.

In 1845, in complete disregard of all that had gone on in the past in connection with white servants, a few dozen English and Irish agricultural labourers were induced to undertake plantation work. 'The experiment must, I fear, be pronounced on the whole a failure', Higginson reported to the Colonial Office the following year, 'a large proportion of the people thus introduced into the Colony have either died or have left the island for America; others are obtaining casual employment, and several are inmates of the Daily Meal Society's infirmary.'[26]

These poor yokels had been brought to the island under the authority of an act passed by the Assembly which was subsequently disallowed, but another bill introduced a year later had more success – as did the planters in finding another source of workers. 'Between 600 and 700 Portuguese immigrants, including men, women and children, have been within the last few months imported from Madeira, and more are expected', wrote Higginson in May 1847. 'I have visited the estates on which these people are principally located, and found them comfortably accommodated, and well satisfied with their condition.' Going on to praise them for being 'sober, willing, and industrious', and to suggest that they would 'greatly benefit their own condition of life, and at the same time prove a valuable acquisition to the colony', he ended with the comment: 'The rates of wages have not been affected, but it is said that native labour is more readily obtained since the introduction of foreign aid.'[27]

Just over 2500 Madeirans went to Antigua between 1846 and 1870, more than to any one of the other islands between Trinidad and Jamaica, but even so they represented only a fraction of the total of all who left their homeland for the West Indies.[28] They emigrated in such large numbers because after 400 years of occupation Madeira had become overcrowded, and erosion, soil exhaustion and a steep fall in the demand for the island's main product – the fortified wine called Madeira – had by the 1840s produced a state of famine. The conditions they left behind made them highly susceptible to illnesses and, regardless of what the Governor may have thought to begin with, they were mostly unfit for heavy manual labour. Three years after the scheme began, by which time over a thousand Madeirans had arrived, Higginson was forced to admit that 'on the whole, the experiment has not proved successful, and will not, I think, be persevered in', the reason for this being that:

> During their first year's residence, the extent of sickness prevailing amongst the Portuguese did not indicate the mortality which . . . has subsequently occurred, and which appears sufficiently conclusive of their inability to cope with the severe toil and constant exposure inseparable from field labour on a sugar plantation.[29]

For the unskilled black labourers at this time, and especially for those still living on the estates, life took a definite turn for the worse. Wages had risen steadily to reach two shillings a day for a first-class field-worker by 1845, but three years later had fallen to the immediate post-emancipation rate of only half this amount. This sudden reduction came about through a combination of factors: a hurricane followed by a severe drought had destroyed food crops and forced more people to turn to estate work in order to survive; the declining market in Britain for West Indian sugar had compelled planters to cut production costs in order to remain competitive; and it was undoubtedly encouraged by the advent of immigrant labour. By the late 1850s wages generally were stuck at a level which could barely sustain life. Labourers working on the estates and those supporting themselves in the villages, where church influence was strongest, remained for the most part subdued and fatalistic. In St John's, where there was more money and greater opportunities, there was less resignation among the unskilled, but also less tolerance. This was especially true of the port workers, then as later a rougher, more vocal and less submissive lot, who were in 1858 the instigators of a riot.

The stevedores employed by one of the merchants became so incensed when he took on an immigrant labourer – in this case a man from Barbuda – that they burnt down the house in which the new employee was living and forced him to take refuge in the police station. This too was then attacked by an even bigger crowd, which only dispersed after the police opened fire on them. The killing of eight of the rioters and the injuring of another fourteen, instead of quelling the fury of the mob, only served to channel it to the homes of other Barbudan residents and those of the policemen themselves – all of which were destroyed after nightfall. Martial law was declared, extra constables sworn in, help summoned from among the planters, and requests for troops sent to Guadeloupe and Barbados. In the event the assistance of troops was not needed, as before any had even been mustered the riot had been put down with the aid of the many estate owners, managers and overseers who had ridden into the city and acted as a troop of cavalry.

In his report of the affair to the Colonial Office, Governor Hamilton[30] complained of being forced to appeal to the French in Guadeloupe for troops as he had no military forces of his own to call upon. The militia had been abolished soon after emancipation, the dockyard was now rarely used by the Navy, and the garrison had been withdrawn four years earlier. The police force, he wrote, 'although efficient for ordinary purposes, is numerically insufficient, in time of tumult, to uphold the Civil Power'.[31] He had a solution, however, as the men who had been largely instrumental in ending the riot were not prepared to remain passive in the face of the possibility of similar threats to public order, and had decided to form a volunteer mounted security force. Three years later it was given official standing when, under a new Militia Act, 'persons having certain property qualifications became liable to service' in the infantry, artillery or cavalry. The qualifications ensured that few, if any, blacks could join, even if they had wanted to, and the 400-strong force which mustered in 1861 can only have been seen by them as yet another move by the plantocracy to keep them subjugated. This view would have been reinforced by the knowledge that each estate was obliged to provide one cavalryman, with the proprietor being paid £25 a year for his services. While the enthusiasm of those who joined the infantry and artillery soon waned, just as it always had in the past – causing the Militia Act to be reported as 'almost a dead letter' within three years – the cavalry was still in existence under a different name fifty years later.

Re-introduction of the militia did nothing to improve the economic condition of the island, any more than it had to improve relations between whites and blacks, and many of the latter, deciding they now had few prospects remaining in Antigua, left to find better-paid work elsewhere in the region, primarily in Trinidad and British Guiana where there were acute labour shortages.

Their departure only aggravated the situation they left behind, and produced a renewed demand for immigrants to undertake estate work. As the Madeiran source had almost dried up (an average of only about thirty people a year arrived between 1856 and 1870) it was necessary for the planters to look elsewhere. 'The desire expressed for continuous agricultural labour in addition to that furnished by the local labouring population', Hamilton sighed in his official report for 1861, 'induced the Legislature to pass an Immigration Act providing for the introduction of African, Indian, or other agricultural labourers.' It did not meet with his approval:

> Notwithstanding the urgent sentiments expressed in the House of Assembly for the reception of immigrants, I am of [the] opinion that immigration to this Island cannot be carried out to any large extent . . .
> The improved economic management of plantations, and the skilful application of labour, with the employment of modern implements of husbandry, are likely to do more for this Colony, already supplied with a sufficient population, and where labour is cheap, than the costly experiment of introducing foreign labourers, who are not likely to do more work or demand less wages than the native peasantry.[32]

His views were sound, but not what the planters wanted to hear. They felt aggrieved by the refusal of the native peasant to work for a pittance at something which a contemporary observer thought had 'been made so distasteful . . . that the possession of half an acre, or the most meagre subsistence and independence, seem to him, in comparison with estate service, the very acme of luxurious enjoyment.'[33] Some idea of just how distasteful field-work remained is perhaps best summed up in the knowledge that as late as 1868, because carts were not permitted in the cane-fields, the labourers were still required to tote baskets of manure on their heads.

No African or Indian workers were found as a result of the Assembly's Immigration Act, but two years after it was passed they paid a large bounty to 937 labourers from – of all places – Barbados, where at the time wage rates were between 10 and 25 per cent higher than in Antigua. In May of the year in which the Barbadians arrived, a French ship, the *Perseverance*, on passage from Macau to Cuba with Chinese immigrants, was wrecked on Barbuda. The crew and all 115 passengers were saved, and once they had been transferred to Antigua the master found another vessel he could charter to complete the voyage. Deciding they had had enough of the sea, or that they had got close enough to their destination, all the Chinese refused to accompany him, preferring instead to be set to work 'on some of the sugar plantations as agricultural labourers' alongside the Barbadians in Antigua. Two years later, in August 1865, 'the immigrants from Barbados' were reported as having

> done good service; they fraternise with our people and a generous emulation prevails, which, with the proximity of Barbados and the readiness with which her people come among us, leads us to hope that our own people will exert themselves more than heretofore, rather than force our agricultural body to import fresh labour.[34]

The other immigrants did not earn quite the same praise: 'The Chinese in many instances prove steady labourers; but a large number were tailors and bakers and quite unfit for agricultural service.' What happened to this little group in the end is, regrettably, unknown. The Barbadians, on the other hand, when their three-year contracts expired, 'with few exceptions' returned home.

Portuguese immigrants continued to arrive until 1870, but in ever-decreasing numbers, with each year's arrivals being outnumbered by those who had either succumbed to illness or left to join larger communities in British Guiana, St Kitts or Trinidad. Those that survived and stayed on in Antigua left the sugar estates as soon as they were able to do so, and moved into more congenial occupations such as retailing and shopkeeping. Those who ended up in the city found themselves in competition with members of another small, close-knit community of retailers who had established themselves there some years earlier. 'There is one street in St John's known as Scotch Row, from its being inhabited chiefly by Scotch shop-keepers', it was noted in 1850 by the curmudgeonly Charles Day, who found them 'mighty *nonchalant* in manner, whilst their shopboys, mostly from some high flat in the Gallogate, are often absolutely rude.' In addition to employing 'terms of offensive familiarity' several of them were 'confirmed drunkards', and in his opinion all were lazy:

> One, for a week at a time, is never sober; another rarely quits his bed, and lies drinking rum and porter from morn 'till dewy eve, and eve 'till morn

again. Canny Scotland indeed seldom shews itself to advantage in the West Indies.[35]

The Portuguese had little to worry about. Because they were naturally thrifty and had migrated in families, making them socially self-assured, they were generally successful in business. Their origin gained them preferential treatment over any black competitors from the merchants and wholesalers with whom they had to deal, and reasonable prosperity followed sooner or later. By the early 1870s those who remained were firmly part of Antiguan society: none still worked as a field-hand, and one, A.J. Camacho, already owned a 500-acre sugar plantation of his own.

15
The Fortunes of the Planter

With the fortunes of the planter are linked those of all other classes, for the produce of the soil constitutes the only source of wealth. Let it be abandoned, and the progress of moral and social regeneration is at an end. Civilization itself stands still, and the emancipated negro relapses into his original state of ignorance and barbarism.

Governor Sir James Higginson (1850)

The Legislature is composed entirely of planters, or of those whom the planters choose to put there. In some districts of Antigua the influence of one large proprietor is sufficient to elect two members of Assembly. The application of the vast machinery of the British Constitution, and its inseparable Church Establishment, to each of the lesser West India colonies, is susceptible of the *reductio ad absurdum*. The machinery is so imposing, and occupies so much space, that popular liberty in a small community is squeezed into the narrowest possible compass.

W.G. Sewell
The Ordeal of Free Labour in the British West Indies (1861)

After the abolition of slavery the money received by the planters in compensation gave some of them the means to settle their debts and sell up, and others with a windfall which enabled them to take advantage of this and increase the size or number of their estates; but it allowed far more to put their plantations into the hands of agents or attorneys, and return to Britain. By 1838 about two-thirds of the estate acreage belonged to some fifty-five absentee owners, with the remaining third belonging to another fifty-seven resident proprietors. A few of the latter were also attorneys for some of those abroad. Among all of them, absentees, attorneys and residents alike, there were very few with the interest and ability to give serious thought to the modernisation of the sugar industry which, it soon became obvious, was badly needed. By this time sugar had been produced on the island for well over 150 years, and was grown on land that was by now much over-worked, using methods which were badly outdated. While the cost of labour had been met by the savings made from not having to maintain an over-large slave workforce, and by the introduction of labour-saving equipment such as ploughs, harrows and wheelbarrows, productivity had not improved and any profit to be made depended almost entirely on the inflated price for the island's output obtained through a protected market in Britain.

All was reasonably well until the aims of the Free Trade movement, which had been gathering support since the early years of the nineteenth century, came to fulfilment in the 1840s, and the duties on a large number of raw materials and manufactured goods entering Britain were changed or removed. The Sugar Duties Act of 1846 ruled that the preference given to sugar produced in the British colonies would gradually be phased out and end completely within six years. This raised a storm of protest among West Indian planters but, apart from getting the elimination date put back for two years, proved unavailing. In Antigua, which was still recovering from the great earthquake and would be hit by a damaging hurricane in 1848, the results were predictable. The only costs which could be cut were those of labour, and if halving the daily wage rates did not help to maintain profitability the estate went under. More transfers took place and yet more estates became the property of absentee proprietors not interested in anything but a return on their investments. 'Antigua is distinguished pre-eminently among her neighbours', the Colonial Office was informed in 1851, 'for the extent to which its landed proprietors are absent from it. Of its whole surface, entirely appropriated as this is, at least three fourths is thus abandoned.'[1]

Regardless of what their owners sitting in the British Isles may have hoped for, many of these estates were so burdened by debts, annuities and the costs of settlements made in the past when conditions had been more favourable, that they could never be truly profitable. Any consideration of acquiring more debts by investing in new production machinery such as steam engines, vacuum-pan boilers to replace the old coppers, or centrifugal driers – all of which were in use or being tried out by the wealthier planters – was out of the question. As a result the labourers on these estates were the worst off of all. Being paid as little as possible to work for 'indiscreet unrelenting managers', under conditions which had barely changed since the days of slavery, it was mostly their children who were forced to leave school because they could no longer be clothed respectably, or because their earning capacity could not be forgone. By the early 1850s there were perhaps 6000 black Antiguans working on the estates, with a much greater number managing to survive around the fringes, mostly by subsistence farming on minute plots of land in or around the villages. This ought to have encouraged the failing planters to consider other agricultural ventures, but with the affairs of many in the hands of local agents, and in considerable debt to local merchants – with the role of attorney and creditor often combined – any such incentive was stifled.

There was an equal lack of interest on the part of either central or local government in considering new possibilities. In the era of free trade the British

Government was not prepared to offer financial aid which might have encouraged economic development: a colony like Antigua which had resisted any interference in its affairs by London throughout its history was not going to be bailed out at this late date. As for the local government, not only was it already saddled with the 1843 earthquake loan – a debt which it would take nearly a quarter of a century to settle – but the Legislature was hardly filled with men of vision, as the Governor indicated to the Colonial Secretary in 1855:

> Up to the present time, owing to the large proportion of property which is still in the hands of the old island families resident within the United Kingdom, but exercising through their agents preponderating influence in our local councils, Antigua had probably undergone less change in her social and economical circumstances than any other island of the Caribbean group.[2]

Rather than putting their minds to considering how to use the island's limited financial resources to encourage new agricultural initiatives, or to motivating the mass of the black population by providing them with more than just the barest means of subsistence, the Assembly preferred to assist the governments of Portugal and Barbados in dealing with similar problems by paying for their surplus labour.

The money which had to be offered to attract such labour came from a Treasury which was not far from empty at the best of times. Most of the revenue was collected through import duties, which affected all, black and white, rich and poor, alike, because the Legislature refused to consider any other form of taxation, as the Governor recorded in 1850:

> The proposal to enact an effective land-tax, whereby the absent proprietors might – I conceive with evident justice – be made to contribute to the revenue would at present be unpalatable to both Houses.[3]

As many of the men who sat on the Council or in the Assembly represented the very people such a tax would have fallen upon, it was to remain unpalatable for many years. In 1856, Governor Hamilton went even further in his denunciation of the situation, making a point which would be equally valid in a non-colonial Antigua, in connection with a different sort of 'absent proprietor' at the end of the twentieth century:

> It is seen that by the existing fiscal arrangements a large proportion of the finest properties in the colony, whose owners are non-resident, bear little or no portion of the public burdens. So large a proportion of the land being owned by the absent proprietor, whose wealth is spent in other climes, and does not tend to enrich the public Treasury, the revenue of the colony is obtained from those less wealthy proprietors whose circumstances constrain them to a residence in the tropics.[4]

•

The reason why so little was done to raise the revenue needed to bring about any economic revival, or to improve the wellbeing of the black population, was because the affairs of the island were in the hands of men far more interested in preserving the status quo. In 1851 twenty-two whites and six coloured men sat as members of the House of Assembly, the latter much to the displeasure of the former, who had fought a long battle since the 1830s to preserve their hegemony. Among the white members too many represented the interests of absentee proprietors to want to interfere with the tax system, nearly all of them had too much tied up in one aspect or another of the sugar industry to be able to consider alternatives, and none of them was interested in the welfare of the blacks. While the coloured members may have possessed rather more active social consciences – at least when it came to matters affecting their own community – they were too few in number to have any effect on the Assembly's decisions and, in most cases were at one with the white members in a determination to keep the blacks just where they were.

The Assemblymen were elected under the terms of an act passed in 1842 which, for the first time, had laid down the qualifications needed by both those standing for election and those who wished to have a vote. They represented St John's (which returned four members), Parham and Falmouth (one member each) and eleven rural districts (each, with one exception, returning two members). To be eligible for election, a candidate needed an annual income derived from property in Antigua of at least £66, or £200 if derived from a business or profession. Voters fell into two categories: those in the towns had to possess, or be the tenant of, land with an annual value of £26; those elsewhere needed to own ten acres of land, or five acres with buildings, or land with a value of £111, or one acre with buildings valued at £222, or be a tenant paying £88 or more a year in rent. Although at least half a dozen coloured men qualified to stand for election by 1850, and a reasonable number of their fellows must have been able to register as voters, these requirements ruled out – as they were intended to – any possible participation in the running of the island by blacks. In fact the whole electoral process was little more than a farce. The total number of registered voters failed to reach 500 until the beginning of the 1860s, and when it did it only needed 200 of them to elect all twenty-one of the country members. In the worst case, the two members for the Dickenson's Bay Division, in the north, were returned by just three voters.

If many of the men who sat in the House of Assembly were more or less assigned their seats, those who sat on the Council, the other arm of the Legislature, were purely nominees. Made up of men from among whom any one could have served as a model for Gilbert and Sullivan's Lord High Everything Else, Pooh Bah (when he was created later in the century) the Council was even more unwilling than the Assembly to consider any change which might threaten the established order. For over a quarter of a century after emancipation the entrenched attitudes of the two bodies, and the way in which they acted alone or jointly to foil or delay legislation which might have improved social or economic conditions proved an endless source of frustration to successive inhabitants of Government House.

This was relieved to some extent for Governor Hamilton in 1860 when he was able to report 'the inauguration in this Colony of a new form of Government by which the Governor has been brought into closer alliance with the Legislative Houses.' The change, similar to that which had been introduced in Jamaica six years earlier, was brought about by the setting up of an Executive Council, 'composed of influential persons chosen from the Legislative Council and the Assembly'. Out of this body, which was intended to function as the governor's Privy Council, a three-man Administrative Committee was selected and paid to assist him in performing 'the duties which hitherto devolved upon joint committees of the Legislative Houses.' Such joint committees, according to Hamilton, 'were irresponsible, and omitted to perform, or imperfectly performed, at pleasure, the administrative work of the Government', and he found it 'surprising how the work of the local Government came through with the practical result with which it was sometimes distinguished.' Under the new system, as the three members of the Administrative Committee were 'chosen from and [possessed] the confidence of the Legislative Houses', and were 'being adequately remunerated for their services', he expected a considerable improvement in the way the administration functioned.[5] The new executive committee assumed responsibility for preparing the budget and for administering the public finances. The power to propose expenditure at will which individual members of the Assembly had enjoyed was withdrawn, and from now on government consent was needed before any such proposal could be put to the vote.

The new arrangement worked reasonably well and in no time at all, in true Pooh Bah-ish style, the committee's chairman was soon nodding gracefully as the more sycophantic members of society took to addressing him as 'Mr Prime Minister', while his two colleagues jostled to be called 'Mr Chancellor of the Exchequer'. Administrative procedures continued to improve as long as the Governor and the Legislature remained in agreement over basic issues, but once a disagreement arose it was a different story. It was then not clear whether the committee was to be considered part of the executive, committed to supporting the Governor in the face of opposition from the Executive Council which had elected it, or as a part of the legislative apparatus which could be dismissed if it failed to support the views of the rest of the Legislature. The issue was resolved two years after the committee had been formed, when Hamilton and the Assembly disagreed about the need for immigrant labour and the committee members, who had supported the Governor's opposition to further immigration, were forced to resign. The formation of a replacement was delayed until after the arrival of a new Governor, Colonel Stephen Hill,[6] the following year. After that the committee was never seen as anything but a part of the Legislature, nor did membership of it ever mean as much.

In its business of administering public works, in granting contracts, and in regulating the island's finances, the committee was obliged to deal with men who, among other positions they held, also occupied seats in the Assembly. The frequent clashes of interest which resulted, and the level of antagonism which could be aroused, meant that no member of the committee could ever feel totally secure or not be aware that someone else in the Council or Assembly was keen to take his place. That the new system was little better than the one it replaced, and that there was far too much self-interest among members of the Legislature, was borne out in 1865 when the government became insolvent. Ten per cent of the 1843 earthquake loan remained outstanding, a new large loan had been taken out to build a much-needed waterworks for St John's, and because of a long drought sugar production was 50 per cent lower than it had been three years earlier.

The British Government seized on this situation, with fiscal solvency shattered and a Legislature which was little more than a discontented self-seeking oligarchy, to press for a major constitutional change. It was recognised that the Assembly was completely unrepresentative because of the narrowness of the franchise, but equally that any extension would result in the blacks acquiring the vote – an eventuality not to be contemplated if the Colonial Office was not to end up having to protect the white community from the oppression of a black oligarchy. On the other hand, if things continued as they were sooner or later Britain might well find herself having to protect the blacks from total white domination. The answer lay in making the vote worthless by replacing the Assembly with a Crown Colony form of government. Although Governor Hill had been instrumental in convincing the executive committee of the need for the waterworks, as someone who married into the Antiguan plantocracy and was to become an estate owner, he was not the man to persuade the Legislature that, under the circumstances, such a radical change to the constitution was required. It was left instead to his exact contemporary, Sir Benjamin Pine,[7] the man who had been the Lieutenant-Governor of St Kitts since 1859.

Pine, who was an astute administrator with a legal background, had recommended a move towards Crown Colony government in St Kitts as early as 1861, but it was not until after the Morant Bay uprising in Jamaica four years later that the Legislature was prepared to take any action. Tales of a 'negro rebellion' in Jamaica intended to destroy the whites provided, in April 1866, the incentive needed for the Council and Assembly of St Kitts to be replaced by a single-chamber Legislature with ten elected and ten nominated members, sitting under the presidency of the Lieutenant-Governor vested with an original and casting vote. Shortly afterwards Pine temporarily assumed the administration of the Leeward Islands while Hill was absent on leave, and on 10 October in St John's, in an address to both Houses, he called upon the Council and Assembly of Antigua to adopt a similar system.

The island's financial embarrassment, he argued, was undoubtedly the result in some measure of the severe drought, 'but it also seemed in part owing, and other defects seemed entirely owing, to imperfections in your administrative machinery.' In his view the present Constitution was the creation of other times and of 'circumstances which have long passed away', and although 'unsuited to a small Colony at any time, was not quite so incongruous at the time it was established . . . as it is at present.' He then ran through the weaknesses of the existing administrative machinery before coming to his proposed measures 'to remedy the evils and defects which I have tried to point out'. Two courses of action presented themselves:

> One of these was to substitute for the existing Legislature a Chamber composed exclusively of nominees of the Crown, making the Island what is called a Crown Colony; the other course was to establish a single Legislative Chamber consisting one half of officers and nominees of the Crown, and the other half of persons elected by the people, giving a casting vote to the Crown.

Naturally, it was the latter course he had chosen as 'it gives us one compact Chamber, in which all interests are fairly represented, in place of our present cumbrous machinery', and would put 'the duty of preparing and submitting bills upon responsible and properly paid officers of the Crown, instead of upon unpaid and therefore really irresponsible members of committees.'[8]

Well aware of the previous year's events in Jamaica, and of the action already taken in St Kitts, his listeners had little option but to accept Pine's arguments and the necessary act was passed in 1867. Under its provisions the Assembly was abolished and a new Legislative Council established. Presided over by the Governor, this consisted of four ex-officio members (the Colonial Secretary, Treasurer, Attorney-General and Solicitor-General), eight members nominated by the Governor, and only twelve elected members. A much-reduced Executive Council remained as the Governor's advisory body. The qualifications for members and voters remained as they had been, but the number of electoral divisions was reduced from fourteen to eleven, with the city of St John's returning two members. Acknowledging the subsidiary role to which the elected element had been reduced, the number of voters who bothered to register fell to 426, with over half of them in St John's. Three of the other divisions each ended up with less than ten, among them Popeshead Division with just one.

The main reason why so little interest in voting was shown outside St John's was probably because the majority of those involved with the plantations, whether as owners, attorneys or managers, were beset by problems which it was thought unlikely any form of local government could solve. Plantations had been failing and owners going bankrupt since the middle of the 1840s, and by this time a majority of all the estates on the island were encumbered by charges which in some cases had been accruing for forty or fifty years, or even longer. These charges were so intricate and involved so many people – many in Great Britain with no other connection with, or interest in, Antigua or the West Indies – that it was often impossible for an estate to be sold because of the amount of time and money it would take to go through the legal proceedings required to produce a clear title.

It was by no means a situation unique to Antigua, and had been recognised as a problem affecting all the West Indian colonies since 1848, when a Parliamentary Commission had investigated it on behalf of the British Government. As a result, a bill was passed six years later to effect a means whereby such estates could be bought quickly, and cheaply, by new owners who it was hoped could then run them profitably. The object of the West Indies Encumbered Estates Act of 1854 was to make the sale and transfer of land held by insolvent proprietors easier by means of proceedings brought before a central court in London, and in the colonies' own courts. In the latter, commissioners drawn from among judges of the local supreme courts would enquire into the ramifications of ownership of any encumbered estate offered for sale, and establish the priority with which the purchase money was to be distributed. To bring its benefits to each of the colonies concerned a local version of the act was all that was required. In Antigua, as always where it was felt Britain was interfering in local affairs, the Legislature delayed for as long as possible, and its own Encumbered Estates Act was not passed until 1864.

As well as delaying the act out of sheer cussedness, the planters in the Assembly were only too well aware of who stood to benefit most from its passing, and they had no wish to see such men acquiring more land and property than they had already. While any number of retired parsons, maiden aunts and impoverished second sons dotted around the British Isles may have had some sort of lien on one or another of the estates, it was the merchants in Antigua and Britain who had by far the greatest claims, and it was these who, once the act was in place, would be its main beneficiaries. If a merchant had been supplying an estate on credit for years, as many had, once it came up for sale he could purchase it for an absurdly small sum as his substantial lien would have priority; and this is precisely what happened. Between 1865 and 1892 a total of seventy-three estate transactions were handled by the court in Antigua, more than in any other colony except Jamaica, with merchants forming a majority of the buyers. Within thirteen years of the act coming into effect only a handful of estates remained in the hands of the families which had owned them at the time of emancipation, and the structure of land ownership had changed entirely.

•

Long before this agrarian transformation was complete yet another change to the way in which the island was governed was brought about. In 1869 Sir Benjamin Pine was transferred to Antigua, to take over from Hill as Governor of the Leeward Islands. He had spent ten years as Lieutenant-Governor of St Kitts, and was one of the very few administrators ever honest enough to admit that such a position was not much more than a sinecure, declaring as much to the Colonial Secretary:

> Few persons contend that for administrative purposes a Lieutenant-Governor is at all necessary. During the whole period of my administration I was strongly of [the] opinion that I was unnecessary. The mere ordinary work of the Government did not occupy me, on average, for more than half an hour a day – scarcely so much. Had I not had some hobbies, such as studying languages and making codes of law, I should not have known what to do with myself.[9]

The whiling away of his time in this way was not wasted. Having successfully induced the Legislature of Montserrat to adopt full Crown Colony rule, and those of Antigua, St Kitts and Nevis to accept a modified form of it, he was now instructed to carry out further reform by uniting all four islands with Dominica and the Virgin Islands under a single government. Although this was a scheme he had proposed shortly after being appointed to St Kitts, only now did the Colonial Office decide that he was

> expected to devote his whole energies to this great object of uniting these islands as closely together as the Orkneys and Shetland islands, which are much more numerous, and which have a much more tempestuous sea rolling between them, are united.[10]

In canvassing support for such a federation Pine found that there was some opposition in all the islands, but only of any great intensity in St Kitts, which at the time was in a better economic condition than any of the others. He persevered regardless, fully aware that he could count on the support of the ex-officio and nominated members of the Legislature there, as in all the other islands, and in December 1870 all six legislative bodies voted overwhelmingly in favour of a federation. The two elected members in Antigua who could not bring themselves to support such a move lacked the courage to oppose it, and made themselves absent when the vote was taken.

Under the terms of the Leeward Islands Act passed as a result in London in August of the following year, Antigua became one of six presidencies making up the new federation, but retained its premier position as the seat of government. The island was also given more elected seats than the others in the General Legislative Council, and made liable for a larger share of the federal expenses. This Council, which had no independent source of revenue and could exercise no control over the fiscal affairs of the presidencies, assumed responsibility for matters such as education, policing, prisons, immigration, and the administration of justice (a supreme court being established, with three judges having jurisdiction in all the islands). Council membership consisted of a President (the Governor) and nine other nominated members drawn from among the official members of the Island Councils, and ten 'elective members' chosen from among the Island Councils' elected membership. As the Governor resided in St John's, and the General Council met there at least once a year, Antigua was more fortunate than the other five presidencies – all of which soon had cause to complain about the inefficiency, dilatoriness and expense of the federal form of government.

For the Antiguan plantocracy any changes brought about by the Leeward Islands Act probably meant very little compared with those which took place as a result of the Encumbered Estates Act. For the great mass of the population, however, this change in the method of government was, if anything, a retrogressive move which placed their welfare in the hands of increasingly uncaring and unresponsive officials for whom, it often appeared, the future of the sugar industry was more important than the future of the people.

16

Great Misery and Distress

The increased death-rate for the years 1862 and 1863 may to some extent be attributed to mortality from small-pox . . . The disease left no estate or negro village unvisited, and ran through nearly the whole of the black population . . . In addition to this visitation the Colony suffered during [1863] from one of the severest droughts on record . . . The labourer was in consequence of these disastrous circumstances brought to a state of great misery and distress.

Report of Colonial Secretary of Antigua for 1863

The death-rate of Antigua is higher than that of any other country from which I have received statistical returns.

In England and Wales in 1876 the death-rate was 21.0 per 1000 of the population, which is but little more than half the number per 1000 that we have in this Island.

Report of the Registrar-General of Antigua for 1878

By the beginning of 1864 more than 15 000 people, well over half the black population, were living in what were still being referred to as 'free villages'. In all of them there were a few 'neat and well-ordered cottages, belonging to tradesmen, small shopkeepers, and head workmen', but these were vastly outnumbered by cramped, unfloored, unventilated dwellings built of the poorest materials. Crammed together on hillsides and ridges, in remote and otherwise valueless corners, or grouped around one or other of the Nonconformist chapels, few of them consisted of more than a single room. In such a 'wretched hovel' the Colonial Secretary, Edwin Baynes, informed Governor Hill in his annual report for 1863, 'not unfrequently five or six persons, adults and children of both sexes, sleep together at night.'[1]

Whatever evil resulted from these conditions was made all the worse by the complete absence of any form of sanitation or running water, or indeed of any water other than 'the ponds in the neighbourhood, the water from which in a dry season is generally muddy, foul, and stagnant.' While Baynes deplored the conditions under which the villagers lived, in true Victorian manner he not only considered they themselves largely to blame, but that any improvement was something which rested equally largely in their own hands. The Government, he proudly recorded, knew 'of the Spiritual wants of the people', and had made provision 'for the maintenance of six rectors and seven curates of the Established Church, besides which grants are occasionally made for the support of the other religious denominations'; but in spite of this there had 'been a positive retrogression [in] the moral and sanitary condition of the people', as well as a failure on their behalf to do anything to help themselves:

> The labourer seems insensible of the advantages which would accrue to himself and family from free ventilation, cleanliness, and an adequate supply of pure water, and would not willingly contribute his labour or his money for either of such purposes. It has been found impossible to induce those residing in the villages to give even a couple of days' work in cleaning the ponds in the immediate vicinity of their dwellings, hence the ponds have either to be cleaned at the expense of the general revenue, or from the want of cleaning get filled and become useless.[2]

Why it was thought that a man already living in poverty, unable even to clothe his children properly or spare the few shillings a year charged for schooling, could afford to sacrifice even one day to do unpaid work of this sort is difficult to understand. That Baynes apparently believed that the villagers willingly lived in utter squalor, and were unable to appreciate what a supply of 'pure water' would have meant to their lives, is almost beyond comprehension. In the end of course public money did have to be spent in trying to keep the ponds in order, but no amount of cash or labour over the years could ensure that rain would then fall to fill them.

The living conditions of the black inhabitants of St John's were almost as bad. The largest numbers were to be found to the south in an area close to where the old Sunday market used to be held, now called August Town. There the residents were reasonably close to two ponds, one of which, called the 'Country Pond', was stone-lined, but those who lived elsewhere – particularly in the less salubrious areas along the waterfront – were as pressed for fresh water as any village dweller. The white and coloured residents, except in times of severe drought, could normally depend on supplies from cisterns under or alongside their houses. When the Assembly passed the act in 1864 which authorised the raising of a loan to construct a waterworks for the city, the members may have had the plight of the more unfortunate blacks in mind, but if so it was very much a secondary consideration:

> This Act will confer one of the greatest boons on our people, in a sanitary point of view, at the same time affording a double protection to the owners of property in the city and vicinity by giving them an available means for the extinction of fire; and by thus causing a reaction on the charges of the

insurance companies, whose rates are now almost prohibitory, but perhaps not too high for the risk they run in a town almost entirely built of wood.[3]

Completion of the waterworks scheme in 1867 enabled water to be pumped, from springs and gathering grounds near Sawcolts estate on the north-east side of the Shekerley Mountains, about five miles to a reservoir on top of a low hill a mile south of St John's. From there it fed standpipes in the city, 'from which water is taken without any restriction both by day and night', and others in the villages around the reservoir. It also supplied fire hydrants, shipping at the public wharf, public buildings such as the hospital, prison and police station, and any houseowner who asked to be connected. It was a brave attempt to deal with providing the city with a regular water supply, but one doomed never to be entirely successful. The demand soon outstripped the maximum of 75 000 gallons a day which could be supplied, and the ever-increasing population of the city and its adjoining villages always nullified subsequent increases made in the capacity of the reservoir. No attempt was made to provide a better water supply for the inhabitants of the other villages. The ponds were cleaned more frequently, but with limited rainfall and no sanitation arrangements for those who had to use them, the water they held was neither plentiful nor pure.

Some attention to the health of the villagers began to be paid in 1861, when an act was passed 'to provide Medical Attention for the Infant Children of the Labouring Population and for the Poor and Destitute, and to render such Medical Attendance accessible to the Labouring Population at large.' This provided for children under the age of ten and adults over sixty to receive free medical treatment, and for all the rest to be treated according to a scale of fees set within what was hoped were their means. The original intention was to have a resident doctor in each parish outside that of the city of St John's, each on a salary of £150 a year, 'but the medical men in the Colony, acting together, refused without concession as to some particular rates of remuneration, to accept the appointments.' Governor Hamilton found that no doctor was prepared to forsake his city practice in order to go and live in the country if he could not expect to make a comfortable living, and as a result was 'obliged to content myself for the present with the largest amount of benefit which I could obtain, rather than leave the Act altogether inoperative.'[4]

The district medical officers were supported by a Board of Health which had been established seven years earlier. When they eventually got down to work they could send patients as circumstances dictated to the hospital, poor house or lazaretto (lepers' hospital) established by the Daily Meal Society, which had been taken over as public institutions in 1856 and were now known jointly as the Holberton Institution; or to the lunatic asylum which had been opened in 1850 in the old barracks on Rat Island. Considering the amount and quality of the healthcare available to the poor in Britain at this time, the Antiguan authorities did not have too much to be ashamed of in 1861. Unfortunately, while things only improved in Britain during the remainder of the nineteenth century, in Antigua they merely stagnated or, in the material state of the various institutions, slowly deteriorated. As a result the general health of the black population, the infant mortality rate, and the prevention of epidemics were all no better in 1901 than they had been forty or fifty years earlier.

The improvement in the general mortality rate which took place in the late 1860s was in some part a result of the passing of the Medical Attendance Act, and to inspections of the villages carried out by the Board of Health, but equally to better rainfall figures, the completion of the city's waterworks, and to more jobs becoming available.

The start of the American Civil War had created a shortage of cotton in England, and several planters had taken the opportunity to revive moribund estates by planting a crop which had been grown in the past, but never to any great extent nor to meet a specific demand. By 1865 'A considerable extent of waste land had been reclaimed, and planted in cotton, and a comparatively large quantity of that article exported.'[5] It continued to be exported for the next seven or eight years, peaking at 650 000 pounds in 1868. Like anything else dependent on wartime conditions, however, this little boom soon ended and when production ceased a few years later – aided by a severe hurricane in 1871 which killed thirty-five people and caused much damage, and a succession of droughts lasting until 1874 – no more cotton was planted until the early years of the twentieth century.

The noticeable improvement which had taken place in the lives of the labourers came to an end and once again many decided the time had come to emigrate, this time by heading for Puerto Rico and Guadeloupe as well as Trinidad. The great majority of those who remained continued to live in the insalubrious villages, or in estate housing which by this time, with little attention being paid to it by the owners, was equally unwholesome. The annual report on the population compiled by the Registrar-General, which can never have done anything but depress the occupant of Government House at the best of times, made particularly painful reading in 1878. A large percentage of the deaths that year had resulted from 'dysentery and other diseases of the digestive organs', with 'fatal cases of dysentery and fever' occurring 'in every month during the year', and the report's compiler was appalled at the death-rate of over thirty-nine per 1000:

> higher than that of any other country from which I have received statistical returns . . .
> In England and Wales in 1876 the death-rate was 21.0 per 1000 of the population, which is but little more than half the number per 1000 that we have in this Island.[6]

That the rate was so high, the report pointed out, was mainly the result of 'excessive mortality among infants', with nearly one-third of all deaths recorded being of children under one year of age.

From his straitlaced mid-Victorian viewpoint, where respectability ruled, the Registrar-General could only put this down as 'the natural outcome of uncontrolled illegitimacy'. The children knew 'nothing of the care and attention received . . . in properly organised families' because their parents 'seldom live together for any length of time' and it was 'too often the case that the father coldly abandons his children'. After that, 'The mother possessing but little natural affection for her children feels this an intolerable burden of which she desires above all things to be relieved'; this led to 'the studied neglect of the children' and the destruction of their lives 'as effectively . . . as could be done by the most cruel violence'. And if all this was not enough, 'the children of parents whose lives are so dissolute and irregular are often born with such an enfeebled condition of system that they succumb to the slightest attack of disease under the best care that can be bestowed upon them.' He ended his jeremiad with the suggestion that the solution lay in curbing illegitimacy. Although, as Mrs Grundy would undoubtedly have agreed, 'the task of legislating upon it would not be an easy or pleasant one, yet this is no reason why it should not be fearlessly undertaken.'[7]

This simplistic view of poor black men and women as being in the main little more than uncaring infanticides, by concentrating on what was perceived as their moral laxity, completely ignored the circumstances under which they were forced to live and try to raise their offspring. Edwin Baynes, who under the federal structure was by now called the President of Antigua, showed only a little more understanding in his comments on the Registrar-General's report:

> Illegitimacy . . . is no doubt one of the causes leading to the high rate of mortality among infants, but perhaps the principal cause of this sad state of things is to be found in the circumstances that the mothers of the infants are in most cases employed in agricultural work and make no provision, whilst employed away from their houses, for the care of their children.[8]

What he failed to add was that these unfortunate women had little option. Both men and women had to work to eat, and just as many women worked in the fields in the 1870s as in the 1770s. The mothers who gave birth under the most primitive and squalid conditions – living with a perpetual shortage of clean fresh water – were, if they were to survive and be able to nurse their babies, obliged to return to the fields as soon as possible after delivery. This brought distress all round, as Dr Freeland, one of the district medical officers, recorded at this time:

> The faint and famishing cries of those dependent solely for actual support upon the actual presence of their mothers, as well as the hungry and louder

lamentations of the older children, are being heard daily throughout our estates and villages.[9]

Instead of attempting to legislate illegitimacy out of existence it would have been much more compassionate to do something about setting up a crèche in each village and on each estate; and this to his credit one governor had tried to do:

> Governor [Sir Henry] Irving, during his administration of the Leeward Islands in 1873 and 1874, proposed to the Legislature, with the view of remedying the evils pointed out by Dr Freeland the establishment of village nurseries, to which the children in the villages should be sent whilst their parents are in the field, and where a daily meal should be provided for them.[10]

It is hardly necessary to record what happened to this sensible and humane proposal. Because it would assist the blacks to raise themselves an extra inch out of the mire, but worse yet, involve public money:

> The proposal was . . . strongly opposed by the planting body and by a majority of the Local Legislature, owing no doubt to the suggestion that the cost of establishing and maintaining the nurseries should be met by *a tax upon the land, or by a small increase in the export duty* [author's italics]. The scheme was consequently allowed to drop.[11]

Just as nothing was done to provide the villages with nurseries, so nothing was done to improve their water supply, and the death-rate climbed even higher. At the beginning of the next decade Antigua was in the position of being 'unhappily distinguished from the other Presidencies constituting the Colony of the Leeward Islands, and, it may be . . . from all the other West India possessions of the Crown, by the stationary, if not declining, number of her people.' The mortality rate was 'greater during the last quarter of 1882 than it had been for any corresponding quarter' during which records had been kept. The reason, as given in the Registrar-General's report for that year arose 'from a variety of causes, the principal of which are the want of proper sanitary regulations, defects in the water supply, the want of proper care, and nourishment, of the children, but particularly the gross neglect of the sick of all ages by their friends which often renders fruitless all efforts on the part of the medical man to afford relief to the suffering.'[12] The situation was alleviated slightly the following year, when an 'Act to provide public nurseries for infants and young children' was eventually passed by the island Legislature, but that was all. 'The great and pressing need of the people throughout this island', the Colonial Secretary of the Leeward Islands complained in 1883, 'is a supply of good water, [as] what they are now compelled to drink they get principally from polluted ponds'; but still nothing was done – except to continue condemning the number of illegitimate births.

'The report of the Registrar General repeats the old story of the moral degradation of the masses', the Colonial Secretary moaned in 1886. 'It appears that of the children born last year, 65.1 per cent were illegitimate, a rate exceeding that of any other West India island.' Pausing only to note that this was a slightly lower figure than that of three years earlier, and to decree that such a rate 'operates fatally on the rearing of infants and young children', he launched into a prime piece of cant:

> In 1885, 132 marriages were registered, being fifty-three less than the number registered in 1884. The blacks will have no wedding unless they can spend on it much money in dress and revelry. Hence a decline in prices and wages means a falling off in marriages, and in a general way the long waiting until sufficient money has been accumulated to pay for ridiculous ostentation and vulgar orgies ends in the cohabitation being never sanctioned by the marriage ceremony.[13]

By concentrating on what were seen as the moral failings of the black population attention was diverted away from the failure of the administration to take the only sensible action which could reduce the death-rate, or allow village infants a better than one-in-three chance of surviving past their first year. As a result the first steps towards providing the villages with running water were not taken until 1890, and many of them still entered the twentieth century without a clean source of this most basic of life's necessities.

•

If black Antiguans suffered during the long decades after slavery was abolished from the apparent inability of the Legislature to recognise its responsibilities for their health and welfare, they suffered equally from its lack of interest in their education. This was a subject which the legislators in the years immediately after emancipation considered of little importance, as was recorded in 1852:

> No system of common education is maintained here; the Council and Assembly having declined to entertain a proposal lately submitted to them . . . to that effect. The maintenance and superintendence of schools is consequently left with the ministers of each denomination.[14]

The first Education Act was passed in 1857, after a great deal of dispute between the Council and Assembly, and all this did was provide £1000 a year from which grants were made to approved schools of any denomination, and levy a charge on each pupil of just under four shillings a year. Six years later there were fifty approved schools, with a total enrolment of 4400, but only thirty-two trained teachers. 'Much of the class work in these schools', the Board of Education reported, 'is carried on by monitors, whose services . . . cannot be depended upon, and unless more effective aid can be obtained the standard of efficiency cannot be greatly raised.' The number enrolled in any particular school bore little resemblance to the number who actually attended, which usually averaged between 50 and 60 per cent. The reasons for this were well summarised in 1864, when the average total attendance of less than 2100 was reported as being 'in consequence generally of the want of clothing, and, in the Windward districts, to destitution and the presence of small-pox.' The sort of education received by those who did manage to attend was basic in the extreme. That in the 'Infant and Dame Schools' was limited to reading, spelling, writing on slates and learning hymns; while in the 'Juvenile and Mixed' establishments 'arithmetic, writing on paper, [and] the elements of grammar and geography' were also taught.[15]

Nothing had changed for the better by the time education became a responsibility of the federal government of the Leeward Islands in 1874. A year later, of the forty-six schools which were then on the approved list, the newly appointed Inspector of Schools commented:

> Out of these eight were classed as infant schools; and in respect of attainments, at least eight more might have been so classed; of the remainder, about two-thirds appear to have been doing really useful work as mixed schools.[16]

With regard to the curriculum, which it is not unreasonable to think might profitably have been overhauled and expanded by this time, his views would not have been taken amiss in the staffroom at Dotheboys Hall:

> The advisability of making grammar a compulsory subject is much questioned. If it is thought desirable to extend the compulsory range beyond reading, writing, and arithmetic, with the addition, for female pupils, of sewing, then, in the opinion of the writer . . . geography would be found a more satisfactory and not less useful subject . . . In the communities with which we are dealing, singing might with advantage have been left to take care of itself . . . The popular instincts would suffice to ensure singing of some sort as part of school routine, and congregational wants would go to produce satisfactory singing wherever the ministers in charge interested themselves in the matter.[17]

Regardless of what was taught or not, the village schools remained poorly attended, and the number of children receiving full-time education remained in the minority – even after the employment of those under the age of nine was prohibited in 1890, and education made compulsory two years later.

A school offering more than an elementary education was founded by the Archdeacon of Antigua in St John's in 1884. While not the first such institution to be opened, it was the first to succeed. The Moravians, as always with anything to do with education in Antigua, had led the way and had run a school which afforded some degree of secondary education for about fifteen years before running out of funds and pupils in 1870. The Antigua Classical School which had been opened as a rival establishment by the Bishop of Antigua in 1861 – charging its pupils £12 a year for tuition – had lasted less than five years.

In 1884, Antigua Grammar School not only charged fees but refused to accept boys born out of wedlock, a restriction which, even if it disappeared in time, initially – as was intended – ensured that only white and 'respectable' coloured boys became its pupils. The Antigua Girls' High School (which like the Grammar School still exists) was founded two years later by an English couple who were both teachers, and operated on the same principles, effectively barring black pupils by charging high fees and discriminating against illegitimacy. Coke College, a high school which was opened by the Methodists in 1888, also refused admittance to the children of unmarried parents, but lasted no more than four or five years. The first successful secondary school which did not discriminate in this way, founded by an eighteen-year old black female teacher named Nellie Robinson, did not open its doors until 1898.

•

The black workforce, trying to survive in the face of low wages, lack of fresh water, rudimentary healthcare, and few educational opportunities, was not the only section of Antiguan society in distress as the island floundered through the 1880s; the entire population was facing some form of adversity.

The estate owners, managers and overseers, who with their families formed the bulk of the 1800 or so whites, were struggling to keep the sugar industry alive, in the face of fierce competition from European beet sugar. After the great turnover in ownership of land brought about by the Encumbered Estates Act, some 10 000 acres had gone, or were about to go, out of commercial cultivation. Cotton-growing had long since ended, and there seemed to be no alternative but to press for a return to a protected market for West Indian cane sugar – something hardly likely to be considered favourably by a British Government still largely committed to free trade.

Their cause was not helped by the succession of particularly supine administrators who came after Sir Benjamin Pine had brought about his constitutional changes, none of whom did anything while in office, for good or ill, for which they might now be remembered. Sir John Glover,[18] in a letter to his wife written shortly after taking up the post in August 1881, outlined a daily routine with which several of his predecessors, and even more of those who succeeded him, would have been only too familiar:

> Coffee and bread in my bedroom until I dress, and drop in, for a second time, into the marble bath. For breakfast, bread, fruit, claret and water, at ten o'clock. The Colonial Secretary comes at eleven o'clock with papers to sign, which lasts till twelve, and other people come till two. Then

luncheon, and, for the first month, visitors from three to five on Tuesdays and Fridays.[19]

Jenico Preston, the fourteenth Viscount Gormanston,[20] who took up the burden in 1885, was an Irish peer who spent most of his three years in office worrying more about his estates in Ireland – under attack from members of the Irish Revolutionary Brotherhood – than he did about the condition of the estates of Antigua. If we are to believe a story recounted in a local resident's book about the island's governors compiled in 1962, at one time Gormanston became so convinced the Fenians would pursue him across the Atlantic that he decamped to Clarence House, to be 'guarded day and night'; when a suspicious-looking vessel hove in sight he hid himself under a bed.[21] Whether the tale is true or not, neither he nor men like Glover were likely to cause the Colonial Office staff to work overtime in dealing with proposals to ease the planters' plight.

The distress felt by the more affluent and better-educated members of the coloured community was of a different nature. Up until the 1850s it had seemed that some of the social barriers erected in earlier times were likely to fall, especially as by mid-century there were six non-white members of the House of Assembly. 'Many highly respectable men, who were [once] slaves now fill the office of Legislators', John Candler had enthused during his visit in 1850, or are otherwise employed in civil office, owing to their talents and qualifications for public business.'[22] Among the latter were John Smith, who had then just left the island to take up the post of Colonial Secretary in Sierra Leone; Henry Loving, who had gone on from being Superintendent of Police to a magistrate's position in Barbados and was now Colonial Secretary of Montserrat; and Joseph Shervington, who had been Deputy Treasurer of Antigua since 1840 and would end up as Colonial Treasurer before his death in 1864. Others were or had been justices of the peace and members of the various boards and commissions which supervised matters connected with health, markets, water supplies and the prison.

The entry of such men into what had been the exclusive preserve of the white population had only been possible because of the support of a couple of more enlightened governors, and had been restricted to members of a fairly small group of families. It was resented and resisted by the whites, particularly the white women who as time went by devoted more and more effort to making respectability and legitimacy the criteria for acceptance in society and suitability for public office. The economic depression which had set in during the late 1840s had made the whites even more determined to preserve their hegemony and during the second half of the century – supported by a succession of governors who were fully prepared to go along with the elevation of respectability into the premier requirement for appointment to any public position – many of the earlier barriers were re-erected.

The Legislature's ready acceptance of the new Executive Council and Executive Committee system in 1860, and of quasi-Crown Colony rule seven years later, was largely a result of this determination to keep government out of the hands of any but white men. Those who voted for these changes were so blinkered that, not only were they prepared to be ruled from London rather than let the coloureds have a say commensurate with their numbers in how the island was to be run, but were unable to accept that a man's views were not necessarily conditioned by the colour of his skin. Their perception that coloured representation in the Legislature or in the administration was only a step on the way to black rule could not have been more erroneous: for those in the upper levels of coloured society and, it has to be admitted, among the majority of the less well-off, most wanted nothing better than to be accepted by the whites as partners in a system ordered in such a way as to keep the black population just where it was.

The despair of the coloureds from being denied more than a nominal political role in the second half of the nineteenth century was made worse by their gradually worsening economic circumstances. The few who had managed to move into planting were soon forced out as it became more and more difficult for small estate owners to make a profit, and those who were shopkeepers and merchants came under increasing pressure from competitors. White men, mostly from Scotland, arrived in the 1850s and 1860s to open retail businesses; the established white merchants became even more powerful after the passing of the Encumbered Estates Act; and a new group of Portuguese retailers appeared in the 1870s. The response of the coloureds took several forms. Some left the island to see if they could make better lives elsewhere, while others made sure their children went to where they might have a brighter future. Others gradually lost their identity through a much freer mingling with the black community with regard to jobs and marriage partners. Those that did not leave, and who refused to compromise their exclusivity, condemned themselves in the main to a marginalised and sterile existence. Because far fewer women than men left the island, the marriage prospects of those who remained were limited. With a place in society so firmly bound up with legitimacy, a successful marriage depended on finding a partner whose respectability was beyond question, and few out of the limited number of men who were left enjoyed all the necessary qualifications. Rather than choose a possibly suspect partner, let alone one from among the plentiful supply of black men, many remained unmarried. As a result, by the end of the century what remained of the old coloured community was, as the historian of its decline so sadly writes, 'a number of elderly men and a host of elderly never-married women of modest means, without political or economic power, and socially isolated from both those below and those above.'[23]

Yet another group of people were suffering in Antigua in the 1880s. The Chinese labourers who had landed on the island from the wrecked *Perseverance* in 1863 were only a tiny fraction of the 135 000 who were brought to the Caribbean during the nineteenth century, the great majority going to Cuba, British Guiana, Jamaica and Trinidad. In 1881 the Antigua planters, having had mixed success with imported workers from the British Isles, Madeira and Barbados, and perhaps encouraged by those *Perseverance* survivors who had taken to the work in the cane-fields, decided that they too ought to have Chinese labourers. Of the 385 whom an agent in Hong Kong was paid to obtain, seventy-eight managed to abscond before the ship which was to take them to Antigua left harbour. Thirty of the remainder died during the voyage, and two more succumbed as soon as the vessel arrived in St John's Harbour. Of the 275 who made it ashore – less than three-quarters of the number the Government had paid for – it was soon discovered that 'A large proportion were not agricultural labourers', and were far from happy about the conditions they found waiting for them on the estates. 'The importation of Chinese labourers into Antigua did not promise well', recorded Lady Glover, who by the time they landed was busy assisting her husband cope with his onerous gubernatorial duties.

> For soon after [their] arrival . . . from Hong Kong, they murdered one of the overseers in a barbarous manner. A black woman was witness of the crime, which led to their conviction, and death sentence was passed on two of them. On the day of execution hundreds of negroes swarmed all around the gaol, but no hangman could be found among them. A Chinaman at last volunteered to execute his brothers. This did not apparently increase the popularity of the race among the Creoles.[24]

Even though, in addition, another fifteen were given long prison sentences with hard labour, the decision to employ indentured Chinese labour was not a total disaster. Glover's successor, Sir Charles Lees,[25] was able to report in 1884 that 'Of the number imported a large proportion have settled down on various estates to which they were allotted and are proving to be steady and satisfactory labourers.'[26]

Whether the Chinese ever gained any popularity with their fellow workers or not they were responsible for a marked improvement in the latter's health and living conditions. Appalled by the standard of sanitation they found on the estates they set about digging their own pit latrines, something which had never been done before in Antigua but which, once it was copied in the villages, brought about a great reduction in insect and rodent infestations, offensive odours and, in due course, many of the diseases associated with untreated human waste.[27] It was not the noblest thing to be remembered for after the indenture period expired and all but a few of the Chinese had left the island, but it was enough. Of men like Sir John Glover and Lord Gormanston, or indeed most of those who administered the island during the fifty or sixty years after emancipation, it could be said that once they left Antigua it was as if they had never been.

17

Deemed to be a Dependency

> The cash wages of Barbuda are very low . . . but each adult has a house, with ample grounds, rent free, and pays no taxes of any sort. He rears pigs and poultry, turkeys, geese, etc., and raises a profusion of yams and eddoes, most of which he sells. He has also the privilege of shooting the wild guinea-birds, ground pigeons, and other minor game. Venison is only killed for the magnates, although the huntsman comes in for his share of the spoil. Altogether the negro population of Barbuda has nothing like real cares.
>
> C.W. Day
> *Five Years Residence in the West Indies* (1852)

> Now therefore be it ordered and declared by the Queen's Most Excellent Majesty with the advice and consent of Her Privy Council that the said island of Barbuda shall be and is hereby annexed to and made and shall be deemed to be a Dependency of the said Island of Antigua.
>
> Order in Council (1860)

If during the long decades after emancipation the development of Antigua progressed only slowly and in fits and starts, that of Barbuda stagnated or even regressed; and if life for black Antiguans improved only very gradually as the nineteenth century wore on, that of the Barbudans became if anything worse. The state in which the inhabitants of the island were left after 1834 – nominally free but still very much bound to their former master for the necessities of life because of the Antiguan Legislature's refusal to extend its rule to Barbuda – continued long after Sir Christopher Bethell-Codrington had died and his son, Christopher William, had succeeded to both his West Indian estates and his baronetcy.

The situation pleased no one: the Barbudans were resentful of the restrictions placed on their freedom; the new baronet (who preferred to be known as Sir William Bethell-Codrington) was complaining, within a year of taking over the lease in 1839, that 'Negro emancipation seems to have made the Proprietor the Slave. The former *will* reside on my Property and have daily Wages whether I have work for them or not';[1] and the Colonial Office and the Governor of Antigua remained very conscious of its dubious legality.

In June 1840 two magistrates who had been sent from Antigua the previous month reported to the Governor on the state of the island and its population. Their report confirmed his views, and subsequently those of the Colonial Office, that the conditions under which the Barbudans lived were completely unsatisfactory, and added to their joint fears that the unclear and unresolved constitutional status of the island could only lead to increasing embarrassment. The magistrates found that the workers had long arrears of pay, many of the old and infirm were utterly destitute, numerous restrictions had been placed on attempts made by the islanders to support themselves independently, and there was no building in which produce or goods could be stored while awaiting shipment to Antigua. Also, the Barbudans felt keenly the lack of a resident clergyman, a resident medical man, a resident magistrate to supervise the five rural constables who had been appointed, and someone other than a disabled local lay-reader who could not write as a resident schoolmaster.

None of these failings or shortages could be resolved without the agreement and assistance of the lessee or, in the case of a resident magistrate, without a change to the constitution. This led to a long-drawn-out correspondence between the Colonial Office, the Governor, the Bishop of Antigua and Sir William Codrington, during which life for the Barbudans remained as restrictive as ever, and which eventually resulted in nothing more than the appointment of a deacon, the Reverend Arnold Culpepper, as the resident clergyman towards the end of 1846. It required an incident the following year, connected with the salvaging of a wreck – that aspect of their lease about which the Codrington family remained ever reticent – to bring about some more temporal improvement to life on the island.

Although the number of vessels wrecked on Barbuda grew steadily fewer during the nineteenth century, as navigation methods improved and steam propulsion gradually took over from sail, the island remained a serious hazard to shipping. The Codringtons were happy enough to continue profiting from this, paying the men who made up the salvage team a few pence a day each 'according to the risk in saving such Vessel, her Cargo, or Materials'. At no time was any effort made to provide the island with a navigational light or daymark which might have warned of danger and lessened the risk of stranding, and by the 1840s both the manager and the salvage crew had become very blasé about any wreck. 'I was fortunate in being about the First on board and saving nearly half the cargo with my own vessel', wrote the manager, John Winter, to Codrington after the brig *Borealis* had run aground in April 1845, 'the salvage awarded is [one-third] on the gross sales [and] it will pay me very well . . .'. A little over two years later Winter's successor was in charge of a similar operation in connection with a French ship, *Le Nouveau Justin*, which was just as profitable, but which was to have considerable repercussions.

The master of the ship was, as frequently happened, reluctant to accept the reality of the situation: that the grounding of his vessel certainly meant it was doomed, or that speed was of the essence if anything was to be saved, and he attempted to prevent any salvage work from taking place. The Barbudan salvors, acting with knowledge born of long experience, not untinged with an element of rapacity, ignored him, and carried ashore all they could while the going was good. As a result the master afterwards protested that the salvage operation had been carried out without his consent, and by men who had behaved dishonestly and violently. The Governor of Guadeloupe, from where the ship had sailed on its last voyage, took up the matter and lodged an official complaint with the Governor Sir James Higginson in Antigua.

This elevated the affair into a minor international incident which, as well as providing a diversion for the Foreign Office and the Quai d'Orsay, raised once again the question of the constitutional status of Barbuda. At the same time it caused the Colonial Office to examine the terms of the Codrington lease to see just what benefits the lessee derived from the 'Right of Wreck'. An investigation ordered by Higginson found that the French accusations could not be substantiated, but in order to try and prevent anything similar from recurring he was told by London to appoint someone in Barbuda as a justice of the peace, and to ensure that person understood 'what must be held to be law there'. As the Codrington manager could hardly be expected to hold this office with any impartiality, and a Barbudan was out of the question, the Governor had no alternative but to instruct the Reverend Mr Culpepper and give him the appointment in August 1848.

The examination of Codrington's rights to all the 'Flotsam and Jetsam, and Wrecks which shall be found within the low water mark' of Barbuda then got under way, initiating another long round of correspondence between the Colonial Office, the Governor and Codrington himself; something which had still not been concluded by the time the lease was due to expire in the middle of 1854. Some months earlier Codrington had applied to the Secretary of State for renewal, presenting himself as a benefactor, and an enlightened proprietor with everyone's interests but his own at heart. He recorded with great embellishment and some economy of the truth all that he had done for the island and its inhabitants, but carefully avoided any mention of the wrecks or salvage work which made possession of the lease so profitable. The Secretary of State was not so easily persuaded and, in order to give time for 'the legal condition of the island and its inhabitants' to be settled, and for 'the right of wreck . . . to be placed on a new footing', the lease was renewed in June, but only for a further six months.

Another exchange of letters now took place between the Colonial Office and Sir Robert Mackintosh, who had taken over as Governor in 1850, concerning the current views of the Legislature about the extension of Antigua's laws to Barbuda, the provision of medical care for the island's inhabitants, and the whole question of salvage. This resulted in a decision to offer Codrington a new long-term lease, provided he agreed to pay for both a resident clergyman and a resident medical attendant, and accept that all future salvage work would be carried out under the supervision of a 'Receiver of Wreck' appointed by the Governor. Codrington accepted these conditions and a new lease was granted under Letters Patent in May 1855 for a term of fifty years from the previous June, in return for the inevitable annual payment of 'one fat sheep, if demanded'. The lease ignored the anomalous constitutional status of the island, and even if Barbuda now had a resident magistrate in addition to several unpaid special constables, there remained no law and no court, and hence no proper way of settling disputes or of keeping order.

The increasing antagonism between Barbudans and Antiguans, fuelled by discontent on both sides about the lack of law and order in Barbuda, which resulted in the riot which took place in St John's in March 1858 (see Chapter 14), eventually brought about a resolution. Alarmed by what had taken place, mostly as a result of its refusal to act earlier, the Legislature at last agreed to extend its authority to Barbuda. This made no difference for another two years, as when the necessary act was sent to London for approval, doubts about its constitutional validity held up the issuing of an Order in Council until well into 1860. Only after this reached St John's in the middle of that year did Barbuda, at long last, legally become 'a Dependency of the said Island of Antigua'.

This gave the Barbudans the security they had previously lacked (and eased Antiguan fears about lawless neighbours at the same time), but it did nothing to improve their way of life, or to provide them with more liberty in their homeland. The manager appointed and instructed by Codrington still ruled their lives by denying them access to a large part of the island, depriving them of natural materials such as lime and timber, prohibiting their use of firearms, and ceasing to employ them if they stepped out of line. Matters were made worse after Sir William Codrington died in 1864; because his heir was still a minor, administration of his estate passed to the Court of Chancery. From then on, in order to try and make sure the island paid its way and was not a drain on the estate, even more stringent measures were introduced.

In 1867, at much the same time as the distressed Barbudans petitioned the Governor about their plight, the Court of Chancery decided that the lease had become a liability and proposed its surrender. During the three years it then took before the Codrington connection with Barbuda could be ended, life for the inhabitants became almost unbearable as the manager was pressed to achieve even greater economies and less and less work became available. Another petition sent in desperation to the Governor in 1869 caused Sir Benjamin Pine, in forwarding it to the Colonial Office, to record that 'The Object of the Agents seems to be to compel the people to leave Barbuda', and to lend his support to the view that the lease should be terminated.

After protracted negotiations with the Codrington family's solicitors it was eventually surrendered in the middle of 1870. This brought to an end a connection which had lasted for nearly 200 years, during which time successive members of the family – without any of them ever deigning to spend more than a few weeks on the island – had exploited its natural resources through the men and women whose only home it was, to ensure that year after year, in times of peace and war, drought or deluge, and whether before or after emancipation, their estates in Antigua returned a profit. At no time during those two centuries were the Barbudans of any consequence to the Codringtons, other than as they appeared on a balance sheet: assets as slaves and liabilities as wage-earners. On 18 July 1870, the day the deed poll which ended the association was executed, most of the island was covered by thick, virtually impenetrable bush – just as it had been when the original lease was granted in 1685. Elsewhere there was no harbour, no roads other than rough dirt tracks, and no buildings of masonry other than a small church, houses for the parson and manager, the crumbling ruins of a 'castle', the overgrown remains of a house in The Highlands, and a decaying fort at The River. The 500 or so inhabitants lived in wattle-and-daub huts thatched with leaves, of no bigger or better construction than those their ancestors in West Africa had lived in two or three hundred years earlier, all huddled together around a well near the eastern side of the lagoon. Their community possessed no running water, no school, no infirmary, no police station, no courthouse, and no meeting place or public building of any sort other than the church. With the unexpired portion of the lease about to be advertised the Barbudans were left a legacy of utter neglect, produced by avarice, inhumanity and the absence of even a hint of *noblesse oblige*.

The only offer for the remainder of the lease was made jointly by two men already resident on the island, George Hopkins and the Reverend William Cowley: the former because he had now lost his job as the Codringtons' manager, and the latter – it would be comforting to believe – because he did not wish to abandon his flock at such a crucial time. In return for an annual rent of £375 they were granted a twenty-one year lease from July 1870 which relieved them of any responsibility for providing social services, but stipulated the rights to be enjoyed by the inhabitants. As well as being allowed 'full and free liberty' of their houses, areas of common land, the lagoon, the main landing place, and the roads which connected them, the Barbudans also received the sole right to 'render and perform independent salvage services' on behalf of the lessees 'to any vessel in distress wrecked or stranded' on the island. One-tenth of the value of any salvage claim submitted by the lessees to the Antiguan court would then be retained by the Crown, while the salvors could expect to receive 'fair and reasonable remuneration' for their services.

The appointment of a resident magistrate early in 1871, followed by the posting to the island of a dispenser and several policemen – all to be paid for out of the lessees' rent – were welcome enough signs that Barbudans were at last to be given the same rights and services as Antiguans, but any sense of wellbeing these engendered did not last for very long. If the island could not be made to pay its way during its final years under the Codringtons, when it was rent free, it was hardly likely that Hopkins and Cowley, with £375 to pay into the Antiguan Treasury every year, could find the means to make it profitable. For over 150 years the value of Barbuda had lain in its direct connection with sugar estates in Antigua and on the profits derived from salvage work. The reduction in the number and size of salvage claims as the century progressed had undoubtedly played a large, if unspoken and unwritten, part in the decision by those administering the Codrington estate to surrender the lease. As the new lessees had no connection with any estate in Antigua, and as they could do nothing which was not criminal to increase the number of wrecks, it took less than seven years for them to admit defeat and look around for someone else to whom the lease could be assigned. This led, between 1877 and 1898, to four more attempts being made to make a profit out of the island, including one by the Reverend Mr Cowley acting alone. In one way or another, all such attempts managed to upset or alienate the Barbudans, all eventually led to some form of dispute with the authorities in Antigua, and all failed.

In November 1898 the Governor Sir Francis Fleming[2] was obliged to repossess the island once again, after the last lessee, Robert Dougall and his Barbuda Island Company, defaulted on the rent. Enough was now enough, and the Antiguan Legislature was at long last forced to agree to make proper financial provision for the island. In 1901 Barbuda was brought under the complete control of the Governor and a manager appointed to run it as a Crown estate. Three years later, having been placed firmly under the laws of Antigua and under the authority of a Warden appointed by the Governor to replace the manager, the Barbudans became tenants of the Crown.

•

During the last twenty years of the attempts to govern and administer Barbuda through the conditions of a lease, each of the lessees was involved in some way with an unproductive scheme to mine phosphate of lime. This was a substance then much in demand in the United States and Europe as a fertiliser, and which in the 1860s had been found in sizeable quantities in various Caribbean islands, including two of the minor members of the Leeward Island group. By the beginning of the 1880s the knowledge that profitable mining operations were taking place both on Sombrero, a small island in the Anegada Passage between Anguilla and Anegada, and on Redonda, an even smaller island between Montserrat and Nevis, raised hopes that in a limestone island like Barbuda there ought to exist similar and even more profitable opportunities.

Perhaps fortunately for the islanders, who would have ended up doing all the hard work and enjoying none of the profits, this proved not to be the case. Some exploratory work was carried out in the north-eastern part of The

Deemed to be a Dependency

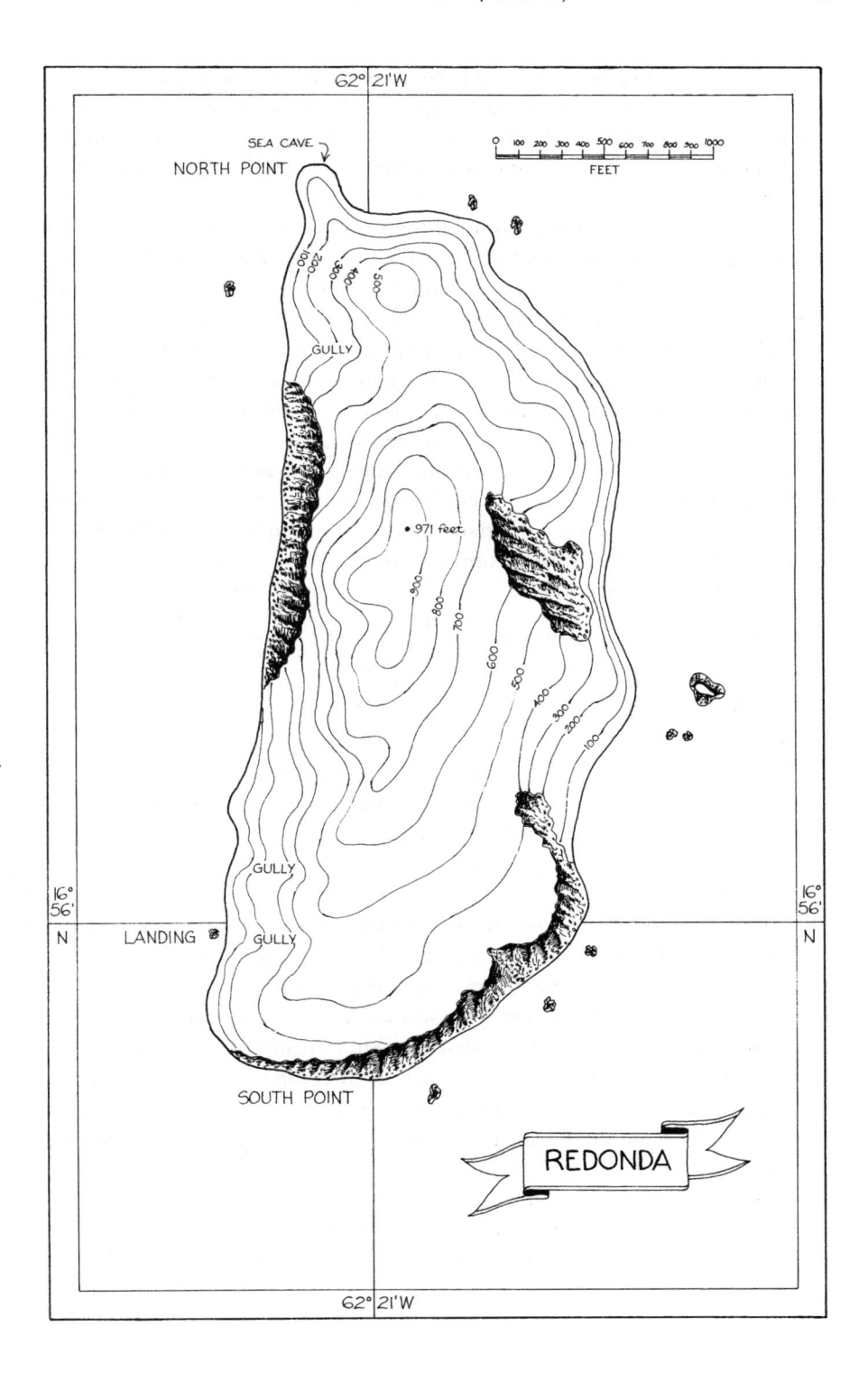

Highlands, and a few tons of phosphatic ore were extracted in the early 1890s, but that was all. The deposits were too small, too difficult to extract, and impossible to remove from the island without a large capital outlay in infrastructure – and a large amount of capital was something none of the later lessees possessed.

The lack of capital was not something that worried the phosphate mining operation which, having leased the island through its parent company in the United States, had been busy on Redonda since the 1860s. Although mining there was carried out almost exclusively by men and boys from Montserrat, making their experiences very much part of the history of that island, what took place there is equally relevant to the history of Antigua, as it was the discovery of Redonda's substantial deposits of phosphate of alumina which ensured that, like Barbuda, it too became an Antiguan dependency.

It was the surface layers of accumulated dried bird excrement, guano, which first brought the operation to the island, but it was quickly discovered that below these there were larger quantities of an equally useful phosphatic material called variscite. This was found everywhere on Redonda but, because of geological action, only

> in the form of a cement filling the crevices among the masses of volcanic rock of which the island consists. In places it would be in sheets of the thickness of one's finger between the boulders, and in others pockets would be filled with several tons.[3]

Up until the discovery of these deposits the island – which is less than a mile long and no more than about a quarter of a square mile in area, surrounded on all sides by steep cliffs – was of little interest to anyone. Treeless, waterless, and possessed of no safe landing place or any completely level ground, it had never been inhabited, and had been visited only very occasionally by fishermen and egg-collectors from Montserrat: to which island it was, insofar as anyone ever gave the matter any thought, considered to belong. Not until mining was well under way, and the island supported a sizeable population, were measures taken to clarify its constitutional status. This was done through an act passed in 1872 by the recently created Federal Legislature of the Leeward Islands. In view of Antigua's dominant position as the seat of government, and the fact that Redonda – through a royalty levied on each ton of phosphate exported – now produced a revenue, any claim which Montserrat may have had was ignored, and in March:

> From and after the date of the Governor's Proclamation transferring and annexing the said Island of Redonda to the said Island of Antigua the said Island of Redonda shall be deemed and taken to be within the parish of Saint John in the said Island of Antigua.

MINING OPERATIONS

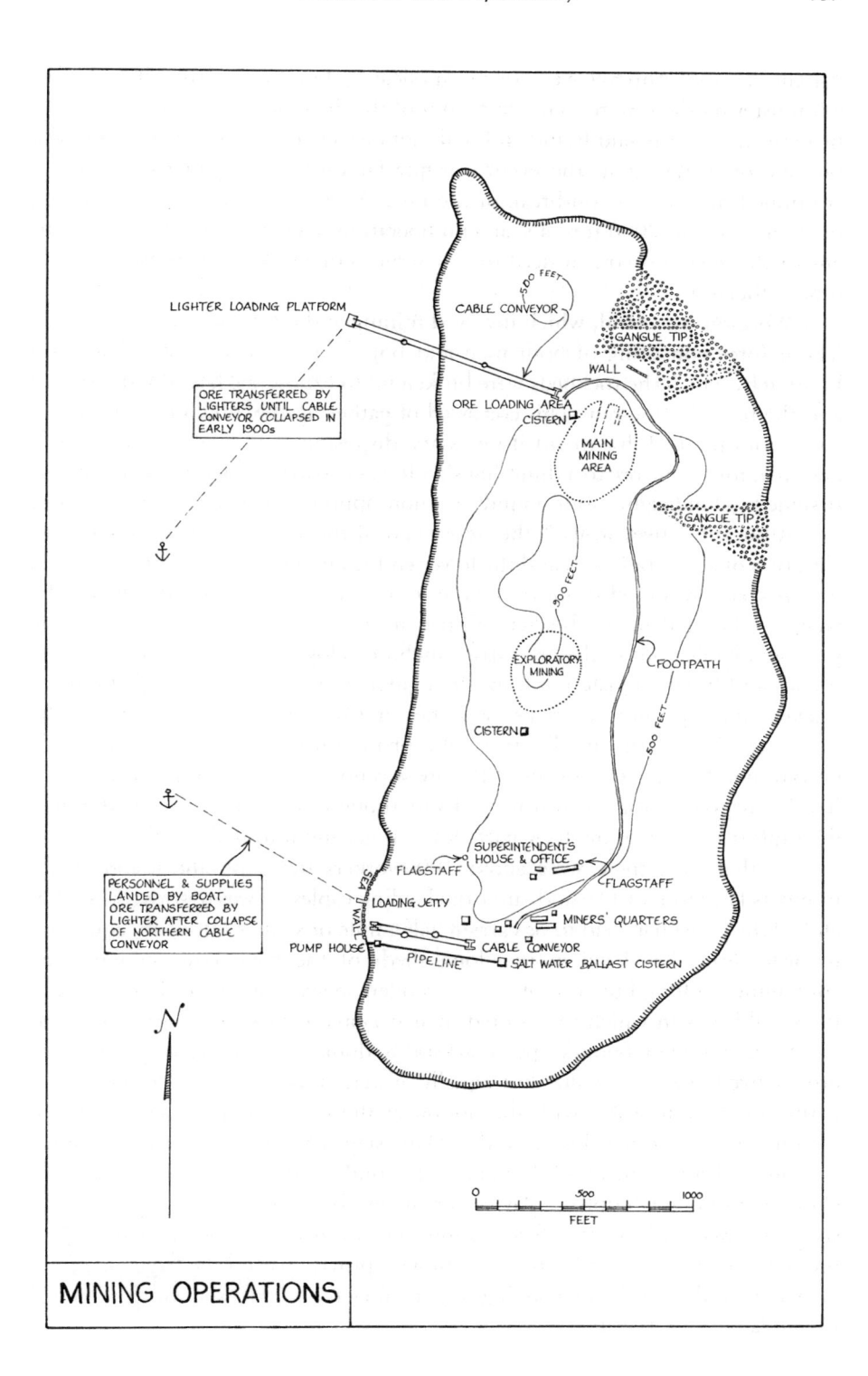

All the laws of Antigua were to be applicable, but all expenses incurred in administering them were to be found out of the 'income or revenue which may be derived from the said Island and shall not be a charge on or payable from the revenue of Antigua.' In the event revenue far exceeded expenditure: mining continued up until the outbreak of the First World War, with exports ranging between 700 and 7000 tons a year, and operations were run in such a way as to ensure there was infrequent need for the services of a coroner, magistrate or any other official.

Work on the island, which involved mining and quarrying, required a large labour force consisting of both men and boys. The men did the drilling and blasting by which the rockbeds were broken up to expose the layers of phosphate and the boys did the rest. This consisted of gathering the loose ore, chipping it away from the rock fragments if necessary, disposing of the tailings over a cliff, and then toting the ore to a dumping site. It was carried on their heads in baskets designed to hold eighty-four pounds, or more appropriately, six stones in weight.

A bucket conveyor, with the upper end of the system of wire cables at an elevation of about 600 feet, and the lower end secured to a pontoon moored just off the coast, was used to move the ore to sea level. To be shipped it had to be weighed, lowered in the buckets, tipped into a lighter moored alongside the pontoon, hauled out to the ore-carrier anchored close off the leeward side of the island, and finally transferred from the lighter into the ship's holds using more buckets and the ship's derricks. Whether at the mine or quarry-face, at the dumping site or in the lighters, phosphate dust covered everybody and everything. As over 40 per cent of the ore was nothing but phosphoric acid it is hardly surprising that a visitor in 1890 thought its removal 'caused much discomfort to the workmen by particles of it getting into their eyes'.

At that time there were about 100 workers living on the island. Their numbers later rose to 130 and, after the loading cableway was destroyed in 1899 and all the phosphate had to be carried half a mile or so to a subsidiary conveyor, to over 180. They lived in two long sheds of the most basic design, each containing nothing but tiers of rough wooden shelves on which they slept and the small boxes in which they stored their personal possessions. The few skilled hands, the foremen, book-keeper, blacksmith, donkeyman, cook and one or two others, lived apart in smaller but equally austere huts. Each was engaged for a period of three months, with the option at the end of either going home or 'signing on' for another three months. Many stayed for several consecutive stints and one at least spent two full years on Redonda without a break. To earn the equivalent of one US dollar a day each man and boy worked ten hours a day for six days a week. Most came from Montserrat, from where a sloop chartered by the company made several trips a month with provisions and the large quantities of wood needed both for cooking and to fuel the condenser which supplied Redonda with fresh water.

The small amounts of fresh meat and vegetables delivered by the sloop were not intended for the workers, who existed on rations not much better than those their forefathers had received in the days of slavery, but for the mining superintendent and his family. Throughout the years when production was at its height the company was in British hands, with much of the ore being shipped to Germany, and from 1882 until his death twenty-two years later the superintendent was a British merchant marine officer named Harding. He was appointed at a critical time in the history of the mining operations and chosen, because of his background, to impose naval-style discipline over a community he arrived to find 'seething with rebellion and civil war (the two most fertile causes of trouble being native rum and "destructive, damnable, deceitful woman").'[4]

While it is not difficult to understand why the miners of Redonda, living like unwilling anchorites of a tropical Mount Athos, might have started the odd brawl at the sight of a couple of floozies clutching bottles of Montserrat mountain dew being brought ashore with the rations, it is equally easy to understand why Captain Harding – with among other things the sensibilities of his wife and daughter to consider – was having none of it. In no time at all native rum, along with native women, were a thing of the past, and Redonda was turned into a cross between Simon Legree's plantation and an English public school. Two American visitors in 1890 were greeted on arrival by 'the workmen drawn up in two lines, bowing and murmuring, "Good ebenin, massa", past whom we were conducted.'[5] The following day, from the verandah of the superintendent's house, they watched the same men file past on their way to work. Each man was obliged to report and give his name, otherwise he lost that day's wages. The same procedure was repeated every day of the week, as Harding:

> had devised the arrangement of dividing a man's weekly wages into seven portions instead of six, and obliging him to report at roll call on Sunday or forfeit his weekly earnings. This method put them on their good behaviour during this day as well as the others, whereas they had previously claimed Sunday as their own in which to do as they pleased.[6]

The damage caused by a hurricane in 1899 could well have brought about the end of the mining, as most of the buildings were destroyed along with the main cableway, but too much had already been invested in the operation for it to be abandoned. After the necessary repairs had been made and new and enlarged barracks built, ore continued to be shipped to Germany until the outbreak of the First World War brought the trade to an end. The company continued mining, at a greatly reduced rate, throughout the war and a large stockpile of ore was created. No ship ever returned to collect it after the war ended, as by this time artificial fertilisers could be produced more cheaply and the market for

Redonda's phosphate no longer existed. The ore remained where it had been dumped near the only landing place, and over the next decade it gradually disappeared into the sea – along with the little wharf and the various small buildings at the landing. A couple of men were employed during the same period to maintain the rest of the buildings and equipment, but within a short time of their being withdrawn and the lease being relinquished in 1930 everything fell into total disrepair.

After that the island assumed the appearance, condition and status it has borne ever since. Its rugged and faintly sinister appearance from a distance is complemented by the forlorn, unwelcoming, rat-infested landscape seen by the very infrequent visitor, just as its tiny size is matched by the all-but-forgotten minor episode of colonial history which brought about its incorporation into 'the parish of Saint John in the said Island of Antigua'.

18

Always Incapable and Frequently Corrupt

> Local Government (falsely so-called) is the curse of the West Indies. In many islands it means only the rule of a local oligarchy of whites and half-breeds – always incapable and frequently corrupt.
>
> Joseph Chamberlain, Secretary of State for the Colonies (1896)

> The antiquated machinery and the obsolete methods now employed in the manufacture of sugar in these islands should years ago have been replaced by modern factories, but year after year no improvement takes place, the crops become shorter, and hundreds of some of what were formerly valuable cane lands are now thrown out of cultivation. A very large proportion of the best artisans and labourers has left, and still continue to leave, Antigua in search of employment elsewhere as now there is no inducement for them to remain owing to the small wages which they receive.
>
> Governor Sir Francis Fleming (1900)

'It must not be lost sight of', Governor Sir George Berkeley[1] complained to the Admiralty in July 1879, 'that the abandonment of the dockyard at English Harbour must be looked on as the severance of the last visible link existing directly between the colony of the Leeward Islands and the mother country.' In responding this way to a proposal by the Admiralty to close down its last remaining facilities in Antigua, Berkeley was appealing more to sentiment than common sense. The dockyard had been little more than a storage yard and coaling station, manned by a boatswain and a small gang of labourers, for the previous thirty years or more; defenceless ever since the garrison had been withdrawn in 1854 and now rapidly falling into dereliction. From 1840 onwards English Harbour had been used as a port of call by ships operated by the Royal Mail Steam Packet Company, which plied regularly throughout the Caribbean from the Packet Station in St Thomas, the company having been given special privileges for carrying mail, cash and passengers between the islands. In conjunction with the deep-sea passenger vessels which also operated to and from St Thomas, the company provided Antigua and all the other colonies with a safe and reliable connection with the rest of the world. If the Governor required more rapid communication with the 'mother country', then Antigua had been in telegraphic contact with London for the previous seven years, the British Government having subsidised the laying of the necessary undersea cables during the late 1860s. The line laid by the West India and Panama Telegraph Company between Antigua and London – via St Kitts, the Virgin Islands, Puerto Rico, Cuba and the USA – had been opened in March 1872.

Regardless of all this, sentimentality and inertia continued to prevail as far as the dockyard was concerned for another ten years. It was eventually closed in the middle of 1889, after all that remained of any value had been packed up and removed by the crew of the corvette HMS *Canada*. Subsequent proposals to use the deserted base as a prison, a sanatorium or a lunatic asylum all came to nothing and the buildings were left to decay. In 1906 the land on which they stood was returned to the Antigua Government, by whom it had been given to the Admiralty in the first place. Fourteen years later an American visitor noted that 'the great naval base is so far forgotten that there are imposing ruins of buildings whose very names and functions are unknown even to local officials' – a statement which would remain true for at least another thirty years.

The closure of the dockyard brought an end to the use of English Harbour as a port of call, not only for the Navy but for shipping in general. In so doing it re-focused attention on the major drawback of St John's Harbour: the bar across its entrance which prevented ships drawing more than ten or eleven feet of water from approaching closer than about two miles from the city. While this was excellent for the numerous boatmen and bargemen needed to operate the craft which ferried cargoes and passengers to and from ships lying in the roadstead outside the bar, it was entirely unsatisfactory for everyone else; adding time and cost to every transaction between ship and shore.

In 1891 a dredger, the *Pholas*, was bought largely at the instigation of Sir William Smith,[2] the more go-ahead Governor who had taken over from the Fenian-haunted Gormanston a year earlier, and set to work cutting a passage 150 feet wide through the bar. When the work was halted two years later ships drawing up to seventeen feet were able to use it, but still, on account of the inner harbour's shallow water, not get closer to the city than about one mile. Although this improved port operations, the fact that the dredging had been more expensive than was first estimated was considered even more important, and such was the penny-pinching attitude of the Colonial Office that the Governor was summoned to London to give an account. As a member of the Middle Temple, having become a barrister before joining the Colonial Service, this he was well able to do before returning to Antigua to see out, as far as the Antiguans were concerned, a very rewarding seven-year term of office. Among the other improvements to the island with which his name can be associated were the establishment of a Botanical Station and Industrial School, the removal and destruction of the remains of the gallows which had been visible on the knoll just to the south of the prison, the introduction of compulsory education for all children between five and twelve years of age, and the provision of piped water to the villages.

The only area where enough water to provide this supply could be obtained was in the Shekerley Mountains, close to the Sawcolts gathering grounds which supplied St John's, and even closer to the spring on which the original settlers had depended 250 years earlier. Without interfering with either of these two sources, work began in 1890 on the creation of a large reservoir by building a dam across the mouth of a combe, and on the construction of a pumping station. These were both completed in 1893 but funds ran out three years later before all the required pipes had been run, or more than a few holding tanks put up. As Smith had been relieved by this time the impetus behind the scheme ran out, with only a small number of villages connected, and no further work took place until 1900 and then only slowly.

•

The reason why funds ran out before the village water project could be completed was that the economy was once again on the verge of collapse. The market for sugar in the USA, to where up to three-quarters of the island's entire output was being shipped in the 1880s, was now falling to competition from Brazil, soon to be followed by Cuba and Puerto Rico; while that in Britain continued to be supplied more easily and cheaply by beet sugar. By 1895 sugar production in Antigua was only 60 per cent of what it had been ten years earlier. The number of estates on which cane was still grown had fallen to seventy-eight, each still producing sugar much as it always had done, using antiquated methods and obsolescent machinery; only about fifty having replaced their windmills with steam engines. All the estates of any size belonged to overseas proprietors, in most cases companies with interests in Britain and other countries, and the entire industry was in dire need of a complete overhaul and modernisation.

The same was also true of the island's Legislative Council, a body held in contempt both by the Colonial Office and those who controlled the sugar industry. The size and general standard of integrity of the white population had decreased so far that the Governor had difficulty in finding enough competent and reputable men to fill the nominated seats, while the franchise was so ridiculous that the twelve elected seats were filled at the will of a mere one or two hundred voters, some of whom had more than one vote. For ever arguing against any Colonial Office proposal to improve conditions which might involve an increase in taxes, while at the same time always begging for grants or relief from existing taxes, the elected members represented little other than their own narrow, biased interests. The businessmen who might have been willing to put much-needed capital into the sugar industry found them equally worthless, supporting the view of one of the estate managers that they would be unwise 'to invest their money in this Island as long as such a body as constitutes the elective side of the Legislative Council have any voice in the administration of the Colony's affairs.'[3]

Fortunately for prospective investors, and most unfortunately for even the suggestion of democracy in the island, things began to change shortly after Joseph Chamberlain became Secretary of State for the Colonies in 1895. He probably entered office already holding the view he expressed the following April that 'Local Government (falsely so-called) is the curse of the West Indies', and it did not take him long to see that, if there was to be any economic improvement among them, the less representative government there was the sooner it would take place. As a minister in a Conservative Government allied to capitalism, he was fully aware that not too many investors were likely to pay much attention to any island where popular representation might at some stage pose a threat to their interests. In Antigua the one or two coloured members of the Council were already trying to get the franchise extended and to increase the number of elected members – sure indications for the whites that black rule was on its way.

Towards the end of 1896 a royal commission, under General Sir Henry Norman, was appointed 'to enquire into the conditions and prospects of the colonies in the West Indies and of the sugar industry in those colonies, and of the labouring classes there, and especially whether the sugar industry is in danger of extinction.' Norman and his four fellow commissioners were also asked to determine the causes of the existing depression, whether by removing these causes the depression could be ended, and what other industries, if any, might take the place of sugar production. Leaving England in December they visited every colony during the next four months, and reported their findings the following September. In their opinion the sugar industry was in danger of extinction and could only be saved by the British Government's intervention. Their main recommendations were that the colonies should be helped with grants and loans, that their public debts should be cleared, that immigration from the smaller islands should be aided, and that communications between the islands, and between the West Indies and Great Britain and North America, needed to be improved. Other recommendations were that labourers should be given the opportunity to settle on land suitable for growing alternative crops, and that other agricultural industries deserved to be encouraged. With regard to Antigua, the commissioners considered a central factory was needed, but that it would be impossible for this to be constructed without a government subsidy, or before a proper water supply was available.

Chamberlain was unable to persuade his Cabinet colleagues to consider imposing extra duties on imported beet sugar to counter the bounties paid to its producers, needed if cane-sugar was to be made competitive, but did manage to extract £500 000 from Parliament to be used for the benefit of the West Indian colonies. This, however, came with strings attached, as the Treasury would only agree to assistance being given to those colonies which were 'subject to the absolute financial control of Her Majesty's Government in regard to both taxation and expenditure.' Antigua was singled out as one of the islands where 'full and positive control of legislation' was required before any grant would be made. Governor Sir Francis Fleming was informed of this in January 1898, and advised to persuade the Legislative Council to vote for Crown Colony rule. Two months later the Council met in closed session, and by a large majority voted for a new body comprised of the Governor, eight official members, and eight nominated unofficial members. Somewhere along the way, either at this time or shortly before, a tacit agreement was reached that only one non-white man would be nominated among the unofficials: an unwritten law which was applied until 1925, when the number was doubled.

●

Changing the constitution immediately opened the way for the island to gain access to the general fund set up by the British Government, and enquiries began into the possibility of establishing a central sugar factory, without which Fleming considered the island could 'not hope for much improvement in the future'. A year later, after the conclusion of the Spanish–American War had given the USA access to the sugar of Cuba and Puerto Rico, he believed such a factory was then 'the sole hope' for the island, but:

> It is said . . . that capitalists are not disposed to embark their money in the sugar enterprise so long as the uncertainties connected with the bounty system continue. This may be, and probably is, true, and it is therefore to be hoped that every discouragement will be given to a system which is generally considered to be unfair to the British producer.[4]

It took until 1903 for the beet producers of Europe to meet and agree in a convention drawn up in Brussels 'to suppress the direct and indirect bounties by which the production or exportation of sugar may profit', and only then were the plans which had been drawn up for a central factory in Antigua put into effect. In the interim funds were made available to promote a return to the growing of cotton as an alternative to sugar, and also to enable work on the village water supply scheme to be resumed.

The cultivation of cotton was revived with the help of the Imperial Department of Agriculture for the West Indies, which had been set up as a result of the Norman Commission's report, and the encouragement of the British Cotton Growing Association. About 5000 acres of fallow land were considered suitable for its growth, and by making this available to black labourers 'on easy terms', it was hoped a sizeable increase in the number of small-scale peasant farmers would take place. Growing began in 1903 but progressed very slowly for the first few years. 'The cultivation of cotton has improved the prospects of the island', the acting administrator of the colony reported in 1906, 'but it is abundantly clear that very few peasants can undertake this cultivation with any prospect of success. Cotton requires a very thorough cultivation, and unremitting care and the exercise of rather more than a little intelligence is necessary for its success.'[5] As well as much ignorance – which a more impartial observer might well have thought had much to do with the island's educational system – the crop also suffered from insect pests and, inevitably, the erratic rainfall. However, the growers persisted and, although the number of acres under cotton varied enormously from year to year, were shipping well over one million pounds of lint annually by 1914.

The work necessary to complete the village water supply project – which had resumed in 1900 – continued on and off for another nine years. By the time it was finished the 13 000 000-gallon Wallings reservoir, as it was now called, was connected to fifteen villages and a number of public buildings. In the same period another eight villages had been provided with catchment tanks or reservoirs of their own. All this improved country life greatly, but only as long as the main reservoir, which was not fed by any perennial streams, was regularly replenished by rainfall. This failed to happen for three years running as soon as the scheme was completed, and by September 1912 there was 'considerable distress in the country districts' once more as the reservoir at Wallings was 'practically empty'.

The prolonged drought also brought about 'an almost complete failure of the supply in St John's, and for some days an acute water famine prevailed.' The situation was saved by heavy showers during the rest of the year, but it was obvious that the existing supply for the city was once again totally inadequate. Fortunately the man who had taken over that year as Governor, Sir Hesketh Bell,[6] was one of the more dynamic of the island's administrators, and under his prompting funds for yet another water scheme were obtained. This involved damming the course of a stream which, when rain was falling in the mountains, flowed north-west from a source not too far from Wallings reservoir, through a series of ponds (the 'Body Ponds'), past the village of Bendals (from which it took its name), before emptying into Five Islands Harbour. Although the scheme failed to result in the formation of the large reservoir which had been hoped for, it did provide St John's with a supplementary water source which was found capable of being improved later to meet the constantly increasing demand. Nothing was done about improving the Wallings scheme, either then or for another thirty years, and it must have been very galling during this period for the inhabitants of many of the villages it supplied to know they were having to share its increasingly insufficient capacity with people who, by and large, they disliked and distrusted – the owners of the sugar factory.

The factory, a large group of buildings erected in 1904 at Gunthorpes estate, about three miles to the east of St John's, represented the largest construction project carried out on the island since the Cathedral had been put up sixty years earlier, and at £45 358 cost almost exactly the same amount. That was the only thing the two had in common: after all those years, the Cathedral still meant nothing to the majority of black Antiguans, whereas for many the factory – even within a year or two of its opening – was central to their existence. It was largely prefabricated, having been ordered from a manufacturer in Scotland by the London firm of Henckell DuBuisson and Company, who had been given the contract for its establishment, together with a British Government grant of £15 000 towards the cost. Complete with a narrow-gauge railway connecting it to the most seaward wharf in St John's and to some of the estates which surrounded it, the factory was originally designed to produce 3000 tons of sugar a year. At the same time another British firm, the proprietors of Bendals estate, were given a grant of £3500 towards modernising their sugar factory, on the understanding that they would invest a further £15 000 and agree to buy at least 1500 tons of cane each year from peasant farmers.

When completed, both factories used the vacuum-pan method of producing grey crystallised sugar, and between them could easily process all the cane then being grown on the island. As soon as they went into production in 1905 all the other estate factories, still only able to produce unrefined, brown muscovado sugar, were rendered redundant, and after the 1920s only one, at Montpelier in the most eastern part of the island, managed to remain in production, finally closing down in 1955. Within less then ten years the factories at Gunthorpes and Bendals both had to increase their capacity, the former to 10 000 tons a year, and the latter to 4000 tons. To cope with the demand for cane the railway network was constantly extended, and by 1918 nearly fifty miles of track had been laid, linking the factories with each other and with estates in all parts of the island.

To operate efficiently each factory needed a large force of skilled and semi-skilled mechanics and tradesmen, as well as general labourers, and all of these were found from among estate workers. In bringing men together in such numbers, giving them proper training where needed, and in introducing them to working conditions never before seen on the island, the factories – in particular the factory at Gunthorpes – were responsible for the start of the greatest social change since emancipation. Outside the factories, life for the unskilled field labourers remained as arduous and as unfulfilling as ever, but with one or two signs of improvement.

The owners of Gunthorpes were under no obligation to grind cane grown by peasant farmers, but dealt primarily with that grown on their own estates and on those whose owners were contracted to supply in quantity. Any small farmer who happened to rent land on an estate within the factory's sphere of operations was more or less obliged to sell his cane through the estate at a price below the factory rate. If he tried to sell direct he risked getting even less, as small quantities did not readily fit into the delivery system, and if delayed in processing lost much of their value. At Bendals, on the other hand, it was reported in 1906 that: 'Advantage has been taken by peasants of the obligation on the part of the owners of the factory to grind their canes to such an extent that the labour market in that particular quarter of the island has become affected, to the detriment . . . of the owners.'

For unskilled workers who did not farm on their own behalf the choice remained as it always had, between continuing to labour in the fields or finding work outside Antigua, and since 1904 the second option had become increasingly attractive. 'There has been a good deal of emigration during the year, especially to the Isthmus of Panama, and complaints are being made locally as to the scarcity of labour', Governor Sir Bickham Sweet-Escott[7] stated in his 1907 report to the Colonial Office, before adding:

> This emigration has, however, resulted in increased wages, and there can be no doubt that the condition of the peasantry has been materially improved by the competition for labour which has taken place between the local planters, the sugar planters of St Croix, and the Isthmian Canal agents . . . The fact is, that the Presidency has, in some directions, materially benefited, for the present at any rate, by the emigration. The labourers left behind have been able to press with success for higher wages, and those who have left, in the majority of cases, sent generous support to their dependants.

The Governor could also have mentioned the Dominican Republic, which was another place during the opening decades of the twentieth century that attracted seasonal workers from Antigua and the rest of the Leeward Islands. There the regular work, higher wages and opportunities to save more than compensated for the appalling living conditions and the dislike of the native workforce they had to endure.

In addition to the introduction of the central factory method of sugar production, and the completion of the Wallings and Bendals water supply schemes, other changes took place before the First World War which helped social development, especially in or around St John's. In 1902, in preparation for use by the British troops then expected in the island along with the Boer prisoners of war they were to guard (none of whom in the end ever appeared), a building was put up on a low hill to the south-east of the city. By 1912 this had been transformed into the central part of a reasonably modern hospital, replacing the long outdated forerunner established by the Reverend Robert Holberton, but justifiably retaining his name. Five years before this opened the leper asylum had been removed from the old Holberton Institution to the former barracks on Rat Island, after the hapless insane had been transferred to a purpose-built asylum at Skerretts on the other side of the city. The poor house, which had also been part of the Holberton Institution, had been renovated in 1910 and now housed the Antigua Grammar School. For the less privileged children not able to attend any of the city's three secondary schools, schooling elsewhere had only improved slightly since the introduction of compulsory education. The all-age primary schools attended by the majority continued to be run by the various churches until 1914, when they were taken over by the Government. Only after that did any great improvement in education take place, and even then at a painfully slow rate.

In 1913 the first attempts were made to improve both the environs of St John's and the general standard of housing for the poor. In that year 'Hyndman's Village', a 'dilapidated and insanitary collection of huts', was removed from where it had grown up on the northern side of the city. At the same time a model village was laid out to the east at Clare Hall, on land previously acquired for use by the Botanic Station but left vacant after this had been moved closer to the city ten years earlier. A year later the first seven dwellings which were built there, each with 'ample yard accommodation, and each having a neat enclosed garden in front', were cited as providing 'valuable object lessons to such villagers as appear to be contented with their squalid and overcrowded huts.'

In the country three years later still Sawcolts estate, which had been bought by the Government in connection with the first water scheme, was 'set aside for land development' and offered for sale in small plots each of a few acres. Although initially treated with some 'suspicion by the peasants', particularly as only about a third of the plots were made up of 'good arable land', they were soon all sold. This encouraged a similar, privately run scheme to be started in 1918 on an estate near the Antigua Sugar Factory (to give the Gunthorpes concern its official designation), but for slightly less altruistic reasons:

> The plots within easy distance of the Antigua Sugar Factory were planted in cane and the produce was sold to the factory. It is more than probable, if the small owners are given opportunities of acquiring plots of land on reasonable terms, that the solution of the problem how to stem the ever increasing flow of emigration of the more intelligent labouring population, which is a serious menace to the agricultural future of the Presidency, will be found.[8]

Even if this might have appeared to be an attempt to bind the labourers to the land by making them buy it in the first place, it did not mean that sugar-cane was all that could be grown, or that the land could not be used in other ways.

While the encouragement of peasant farming was a step in the right direction, there were at the same time many other matters affecting the lives of ordinary people in which no progress seemed likely to be made. For nine years after it had been established in 1898, a twelve-man Board was responsible for the running of St John's, with powers to levy rates and taxes for improvements, sanitation and maintaining the water supply. As half the members were elected the Board retained a degree of independence which had been lost to the island government and which, once its decisions brought it into conflict with the legislative Council, could not be allowed to continue. In 1907 the Board was replaced by five commissioners and made a department of government. When the original Board was discharged those who had been elected must have wondered how they ever came to be allowed membership in the first place, as even the trustees of the public library, which had been founded as a private institution in 1830 and taken over by the Government in 1854, were all appointed by the Governor. Few aspects of life were beyond official control, supervision or interference, and none more so – as was demonstrated soon after central factory operations began – than anything which even hinted at workers' rights or trade unionism.

In 1907, at a time when skilled tradesmen were still very much in demand at the Antigua Sugar Factory, one of the mechanics at Betty's Hope very sensibly decided that if the Codrington's manager wanted him not to seek the opportunities offered at Gunthorpes, then he deserved to be rewarded accordingly. His mistake was in offering to represent the rest of the estate's artisans, and to ask for higher wages not only for himself, but for all who worked as tradesmen – an unheard-of and, as far as the estate management was concerned, an unacceptable procedure. The man concerned, known as Kenny Joe, was not only sacked and thrown off the estate but soon afterwards, under an act of 1875, charged with conspiracy. His subsequent trial, conviction and two-year jail sentence effectively stifled any further moves in the direction of united action on the part of any group of workers for another decade.[9]

Any thoughts which may have been surfacing about worker representation by 1914 were suppressed by the effect that the First World War had on the island and its economy. Two days after its outbreak martial law was declared, and the Defence Force assembled for training. The Defence Force was but the current title for what until 1897 had always been known as the militia or the yeomanry cavalry. It consisted on paper of one company of infantry and another of mounted infantry, in one or another of which all males between the ages of eighteen and forty-five, with an income of £50 a year or more, were required to serve. As a horse and tack were something not too many black Antiguans owned, even if they earned £50 a year, it goes without saying that – just as with the yeomanry cavalry when it was formed in 1864 – service in the Antigua Mounted Infantry was very much the prerogative of the white community.

Presumably acting on the assumption that Antigua was bound to figure prominently in any invasion plans drawn up by the German High Command, the whole force, together with the armed division of the police and members of a Reserve Corps, when not training to repel a landing, were sent to man lookout posts all around the island or to dig trenches. Such posturing was soon seen to be quite pointless and, as dreams of martial glory faded, the administration gave their attention to more relevant matters such as fixing food prices and encouraging the growing of crops other than sugar or cotton – crops such as onions, maize and fruit.

After the initial alarms and burst of enthusiasm Antiguans on the whole, in comparison with the inhabitants of some of the neighbouring islands, showed not much more than a token interest in the progress of the war, or in assisting the Imperial war effort. This had much to do with the fact that after Governor Bell left at the end of 1915 the island was without proper leadership for the remainder of the war years. The man named as his successor, Sir Edward Merewether,[10] was returning to England from his previous post in Sierra Leone in 1915 when the ship in which he was travelling was captured by a German raider. Chivalry not having completely disappeared from warfare at this time, he and all the other passengers were despatched to the United States and subsequently paroled. This precluded him from military service for the remainder of the war, and as governorship of the Leeward Islands included the title of Commander-in-Chief he was then unable to proceed to Antigua until the beginning of 1919. The administration was left in the hands of the Colonial Secretary; the official who, even in peacetime, was usually overworked.

While several dozen white Antiguans took part in the war, having very patriotically made their own way to England in order to volunteer for one or other of the services, no avenue existed for black or coloured men to follow their example before late in 1915, after the formation of the British West Indies Regiment. The raising of this regiment was the result of a campaign centred in Jamaica, begun in order to satisfy the desire of many ordinary West Indians to take an active part in the war in Europe. Once this had been recognised in London, and a reluctant War Office forced to countenance the use of black troops against a white enemy, all the islands were asked to raise specific numbers of volunteers to be ferried across the Atlantic at irregular intervals. Of the 347 officers and men raised from the Leeward Islands just under a third came from Antigua. Although this figure compared very unfavourably with those of islands such as Grenada, which raised 441, or Dominica, where some 700 men volunteered, black Antiguans had reason enough not to respond with any marked enthusiasm in view of the lukewarm support being given to the war effort by the rest of the population. It also, surely, cannot have escaped their notice that while they were now being asked to don a uniform in order to help defend Great Britain, they were still considered unworthy of assisting in the defence of their homeland. The contribution made to the prosecution of the war by the island as a whole, other than that of the young men, white and black, who volunteered to fight, was modest to say the least. The total of £4788 which was raised for relief funds opened by institutions like the Red Cross was only half the amount given in St Kitts, and about a quarter of that raised in Dominica. Government grants were equally unbalanced: St Kitts finding £7000 of public money to contribute, compared with Antigua's £1000 – an amount which even poverty stricken Montserrat could match. If this then was the extent to which the administration and upper levels of society were prepared to go, it is perhaps not surprising that in 1916 most black Antiguans were not prepared to forsake the small improvements in the general quality of life which were then apparent, for a cause which was not their own.

The outbreak of war had immediately produced more favourable market conditions for the sugar industry, and production had increased accordingly. 'The island had the best growing season since 1891', the Colonial Secretary was able to report in 1916; adding: 'The crops on the original contracting estates were 50 per cent heavier than their average throughout the previous eleven years . . . and this fairly represents the position throughout Antigua.'[11] Things were just as rosy the following year, giving the island a revenue 'which is the largest on record for at least thirty years'. Part of the increase came from duties on imports and was attributed 'to the improved purchasing power of the labouring population owing to the higher rate of wages.'[12] The cotton industry also benefited from the war, but only after an initial setback caused by the loss of the principal markets in Belgium and northern France when the fighting began. By 1917 though, 'owing to difficulties in obtaining sufficient supplies of Sea Island cotton for aeronautical purposes', the British Government undertook not only to purchase all that could be grown at a fixed price, but to arrange for its shipment, and so relieve the growers 'of all difficulties as to the provision of tonnage and of the heavy war rates of insurance.'[13]

It was all too good to last. In 1918 the inevitable drought produced a sugar crop 'at least 33 per cent below normal'; the cotton crop suffered 'severe . . . attacks of caterpillars and cotton stainers' at a time when insecticide stocks had all but run out; and the sugar-estate owners decided on a course of action with regard to the labourers they employed to reap the crop which was to lead to a bloody riot and herald a major change in labour relations.

Part Four:
The Struggle and the Conquest

The whole history of political struggle in the British West Indies has been a struggle to achieve the parliamentary institutions and practices which were limited on purely racial grounds to white people.

Eric Williams, in a speech at the University of Dakar in 1964

19
Bound to Succeed

There is no private institution or person of any standing engaged in trade and industry in this island who is not in financial difficulties. There is no market for real estate of the most moderate value. All the plantations are suffering from the strict cutting down of expenses policy that has to be exercised in their operation if the plantations are to be kept alive. Labourers' wages and numbers employed have continually diminished, as well as the number of days of employment. The diminished distribution of wages is reflected in trade depression in the City and decline in support given to weakened social institutions. The labouring classes are being cut off from the most ordinary necessaries of life, and attacked by any critical disease they die. These are conditions prevailing today in Antigua.

Petition signed by the unofficial members of the
Legislative Council of Antigua and others, presented
to the Council in December 1934

Despite the obstacles that are placed in our way by those who feel themselves rulers of our country by their financial positions, and are trying all they can to debar our progress, we are bound to succeed.

Reginald St Clair Stevens, first President of the Antigua Trades and
Labour Union, in a letter to Sir Walter Citrine, 1939

Preparations were being made at the beginning of 1918 to harvest a sugar-cane crop which, because of the previous year's drought, was expected to be of poor quality. Faced with the prospect of a much-reduced tonnage of sugar as a result, and in order to reduce production costs as much as possible, the estate owners announced that a new method of payment for cane-cutters was intended. Up until then they had been paid 'by the row', a time-honoured method to which the way cane was grown lent itself, enabling each cutter to determine exactly how much he had earned each day, but one which paid no attention to the size and quality of the cane or to what happened to it between field and factory. Under the new method payment would be based solely on the weight of cane received by the factory – something over which the cutters had no control, and which provided them with no means of knowing how much they were likely to be paid for a day's work. The change was greatly resented by the majority of workers, particularly by the peasant farmers who cut and delivered their own cane, but there existed no legal means for disputing their employers' decision.

Workers were still very much bound by the terms of the original post-emancipation Contract Act. Although this had been amended and made less restrictive over the years, it still denied them any right to march, picket or strike in protest, or even to set up any form of representative organisation. Any such action, as the mechanic Kenny Joe had found out a decade earlier, could lead to a charge of conspiracy of sedition. The only associations which were tolerated were a few friendly societies, and the branches of various orders which had originated in Britain or the United States as offsprings of freemasonry. The former were encouraged because they had a respectable history in the island of encouraging thrift and self-help, and the latter because their ceremonial, fraternal aspirations and convivial meetings were considered harmless and amusing – especially among those merchants and planters sweating in their dark suits and regalia in the Freemasons' Lodge, busily blackballing any coloured aspirant to their mysteries.

As benign and entertaining as institutions like the Independent Order of Odd Fellows or the Ulotrichan Universal Lodge may have appeared to outsiders, they did enable their members to meet under reasonably secure conditions to discuss their social and economic conditions, and to argue about their rights as citizens and workers. Amid such exchanges of views about how work and pay conditions might be improved and changes in society brought about, the more forceful and eloquent members were also given a grounding in public speaking and the elements of leadership. One such group of embryo politicians, belonging to a lodge adventurously calling itself the Antigua Progressive Union, held an open meeting in 1917 to which they invited the leading estate owners, along with the Bishop and the President of the Legislative Council, to discuss with them the abolition of the Contract Act and the subject of workers' rights. It was a bold move but one which achieved nothing. The establishment figures who attended rejected any suggestion of workers requiring more consideration or better treatment, or that any relaxation of the law was needed. This in turn must have reinforced the views of the politically minded members of all the lodges and societies that such things were not going to be achieved without a long, hard struggle.

The contest began sooner than anyone from Bishop to Odd Fellow probably expected, and entirely as a result of the decision taken to pay cane-cutters 'by the ton' instead of 'by the row'. The grumbling about this which accompanied the start of the 1918 harvest remained nothing more until the workers on one or two estates found their wages being delayed as a result of the new system, and the peasant farmers who had previously been paid at the factory were told future payments would come through the estate owners whose land they leased. The grumbling now turned to action, and by late February the workers on several estates had reduced either their output or the hours they were prepared to remain in the fields, and on others work had stopped altogether. In the village of All Saints a lodge member named Charles Martin, in contravention of a law prohibiting such gatherings, urged a meeting of peasant farmers to demand direct, higher payments for their cane. In doing so he laid himself open to a charge of sedition, particularly when a day or two later fires were started in the fields of several estates, including two, the Villa and Gambles, on the outskirts of St John's.

On 1 March 1918 the acting Governor, Thomas Best,[1] alarmed at all that was taking place, declared martial law and called out the Defence Force, which had had nothing to do since early August 1914. The police force was ordered to set about restoring order, by finding those responsible for firing the cane-fields and arresting those, like Charles Martin, who were perceived as troublemakers. Over a week later, at much the same time as Martin very sensibly left the island together with several other men for whom the police were searching, George Weston and Williams Collins were named as prime suspects in connection with the cane fires.

By midday on Saturday 9 March, when it was generally known that the police were searching for Weston and Collins, a large number of people accompanied the two men to the police station in St John's. These were mainly from the poorer, western part of the city where Weston lived, and where he had already begun to acquire something of his later reputation as a spokesman for the underdog with a passionate interest in the education and welfare of black people. All might have been well, but before the two suspects reached the police station they were picked out for abuse by an irate and overbearing estate overseer and accused of fire-raising. At this the crowd became increasingly noisy and unruly, the accuser was manhandled and the police were prevented from carrying out the arrests. Within an hour or so the crowd had become a mob, and by early afternoon the authorities considered they had a riot on their hands.

The Riot Act was read only after attempts by the Chief of Police, the acting Governor and the Bishop to persuade the people to disperse had all proved futile. A warning was then given that the police, now armed, would use force to clear the streets if this still remained necessary after another hour had elapsed. Amid all the noise and confusion it is doubtful if more than a tiny fraction of the mob heard this warning, or that the stick-wielding and missile-throwing troublemakers in the middle or on the fringes had any idea of just how seriously their actions were being regarded; no sign of a dispersal took place. Accordingly, the period of grace expired, and without further warning the order was given for the police to fire one volley into the mass of people before them. This had the required effect and, amid even greater noise and confusion, with screaming men and women running blindly in all directions, the street emptied. Eighteen people were left behind – three who had been killed outright and fifteen with wounds of varying seriousness – and the riot was over.

Surprisingly, in view of the bloodshed and loss of life, the event was soon largely forgotten. The three men whose names remain connected with the affair did not become martyrs or folk heroes. Collins was given a three-year jail sentence; Martin never returned from exile; and Weston, after being cleared of all charges, soon left for the United States where he eventually became the vice-president of the Universal Negro Improvement Association established by Marcus Garvey. To the authorities it was no more than a period of 'misunderstanding and unrest [that] terminated in a riot which had to be quelled by force of arms and which caused much expense and anxiety to the Government.' The 9 March never became a day of remembrance, even after a political party representing Antiguan workers came into being, any more than it did after the island became independent under a Government formed by the same party. Only in 1984, somewhat inappropriately as part of the celebrations held to mark the 150th anniversary of the abolition of slavery, was a commemorative marker erected near the site of the fatal shootings.

The deaths, maimings, burnings and all the other 'misunderstanding and unrest' in the end achieved nothing. Even before the riot took place a commission had been appointed 'to enquire what would be a fair wage to labourers employed in cutting canes in Antigua during the 1918 crop'. This came to the conclusion that, provided the labourers' interests 'were adequately safeguarded' by ensuring that the receiving and weighing procedure was seen to be completely open and above board, 'the only fair and equitable way of computing wages . . . was by weight'. As the riot intervened before this could be made public it was judged prudent that the remainder of that year's crop should be paid for in the old manner, and payment by weight delayed until the following season, after which it was the method used for the next thirty years or more.

•

Even though the change may well have been 'fair and equitable' in the eyes of the authorities, as well as to anyone else who gave the matter any serious thought, it was the way in which it was introduced that was offensive, and which led to the violence. For a whole section of the population already living in or very close to poverty, and in a great deal of ignorance because of the lack of proper schooling, anything which appeared to threaten their meagre wages heralded disaster. Piped water, pit latrines, public health inspectors and compulsory education may all have helped to improve the life of black workers, but for many the slightest fluctuation in income made all the difference between eating once or twice a day, or whether a child could be sent to school or not. 'Women in rather graceless turbans are more numerous than men in the canefields, where wages average $4\frac{1}{2}$ pence per hundred holes of cane, whether for planting, hoeing, or cutting, making the daily wage of the majority about fifteen

[US] cents', a bigoted and insensitive American visitor wrote in 1920 before commenting on the sort of houses in which they had to live:

> Shacks covered with shingles from mudsill to roof-tree, interspersed with fewer thatched and once whitewashed huts . . . house the country people in scattered formation or occasional clusters bearing such misnomers as All Saints' Village.[2]

His observations were made at much the same time as another imperceptive American, quite unconnected with the first, noted near Liberta the 'hamlets of grass-thatched huts snuggled under cocoanut palms with a goat or two and innumerable pickaninnies naked and unashamed.'[3] How much of their fifteen cents a day the gracelessly turbanned women the one had seen could spare for clothing children of the age the other had observed was something which they were not alone in failing to understand.

Insensitivity of this sort was not confined to citizens of the United States, nor indeed just to visitors. With no leadership, no representation at work or in public life, and no decent education, the people on whom the economy of the island depended received little respect from anyone – including on occasion even those who ought to have known better. In late August 1924, during a short period when the Colonial Secretary Reginald St Johnston[4] was acting as Governor, the island in his words was 'smitten by certainly the worst hurricane it had experienced for twenty-five years, and on subsequent comparison of the numbers of fatalities, by probably the worst hurricane since the year 1817.' The entire island was badly affected but the south-western part was devastated, as St Johnson discovered on his tour of inspection the next day:

> The villages were indeed scenes of desolation. Hardly a house still standing, litter and confusion everywhere, and the men and women sitting about mournfully surveying the scattered and broken odds and ends of what had once been their treasured possessions.

His immediate concern was genuine enough, but the overseeing of the distribution of 'some sacks of bread and rice, and some carpenter's tools' marked the limit of his compassion, just as in his description of what followed his cynicism, and the use of the words italicised by the present author, betrayed his true feelings about a large section of the society he had been appointed to assist in governing:

> I cheered them up as much as possible, but did not dare to promise too much by way of assistance from the Government, as there is always too great a tendency among *these people* to rely upon 'the Government' putting food into their mouths, probably a relic of the days of slavery when all initiative on their behalf was invariably taken by others.[5]

St Johnston, for all of this, was a conscientious and more than competent colonial official who later became Administrator of Dominica and then of St Kitts–Nevis, before returning to Antigua in June 1929 to take over as Governor of the Leeward Islands from the man for whom he acted at the time of the hurricane, Sir Eustace Fiennes.[6] Fiennes by then had had the job since 1921, and St Johnston was to retain it until 1936. Between them, during this fifteen-year period, they introduced a number of much-needed improvements and brought Antigua firmly if belatedly into the twentieth century.

Governor Fiennes, who had been created a baronet in 1916, was fifty-seven years old when he arrived in Antigua, having previously served for three years in the same capacity in the Seychelles. Before that he had had a distinguished Army career and spent twelve years as a Liberal Member of Parliament. He was far from the stereotypical colonial governor of the day, and a marked contrast to his predecessor, Merewether, who 'was one of the old school, stiff as a ramrod and said to be unapproachable'[7] (and who, of course, had only been able to take up his appointment after the Armistice in November 1918). With an eagerness and dynamism which belied his age, the true politician's ability to move easily among all sections of society, and ably supported by St Johnston as the Colonial Secretary for the first three years, Fiennes set about trying to improve the island and to introduce the changes he saw were necessary. Some of these would have taken place eventually, regardless of who administered the island, but it was his drive and enthusiasm which ensured that developments such as an electricity supply for St John's, a wireless service with other West Indian islands, and further improvements to the city's water supply took place as soon as they did.

At his instigation, and in order to attract more visitors, efforts were made to clean and tidy up some of the old fortifications, a tree-planting exercise was carried out in and around St John's, the jetty which provided the main landing place at the lower end of High Street was re-built, and another jetty was constructed at Fort James, on the northern side of the harbour entrance, to facilitate landing near a premier bathing beach.

Before Fiennes left office the Canadian National Steamship Company had begun to operate a fortnightly service to all the islands of the eastern Caribbean from Halifax, Nova Scotia, using three ships which carried both passengers and cargo. It was largely through the efforts of Fiennes to make the city and the island more attractive that from then on many of the passengers on the *Lady Nelson*, *Lady Hawkins* and *Lady Drake* landed and spent time in Antigua, helping to lay the foundations of the modern tourist industry. Another indication of what the future held, even if it would not have been recognised as such at the time, occurred in the year Fiennes left. After an advance publicity flight by the famous aviator Charles Lindbergh along the route, an air service between Miami and Buenos Aires was inaugurated by Pan American Airways in 1929, with Antigua as one of the many eastern Caribbean ports of call. The aircraft used were seaplanes, and these landed regularly in St John's Harbour from then on until the service was brought to a halt by the entry of the United States into the Second World War.

The interest and enthusiasm shown by Fiennes also brought about improvements in the lives of many ordinary people. At his insistence health certificates were made compulsory for bakers and anyone else handling foodstuffs for a living; the first city bus service was started; and an improved water supply was obtained by digging another well near the village of St Lukes, and constructing yet another dam in the Body Ponds area. Both the well and the dam still bear his name, as does his major memorial, a home he had built near the hospital to accommodate at least some of the many indigent he came across as he went around the island. When finished the Fiennes Institute proved to be so popular that it was soon grossly overcrowded. In order to deal with this the Governor and Lady Fiennes, who were both keen dancers, arranged for a dance to be held there, during which those who were seen to be dancing in too sprightly a manner were later told to leave and find work. It was a method of weeding out the unworthy which annoyed no one, greatly appealed to the population at large, and only enhanced the Governor's reputation as a man of the people. His impact on ordinary black Antiguans was summed up by one of them, a man named Samuel Smith, whose colourful and often moving memoirs provide a unique record of estate life in the first half of the twentieth century:

> He was a melle [well-informed] man. He love nega [black people's] business and he got to know what was happening in the island. I think he very well understood the feelings of the negas. He took pride in his work and he wanted that his term of office would mean something to the people. For me, he was entirely different to all the governors that reach the island before and I believe he will remain the best ever.[8]

Smith was not so enamoured of St Johnston, whom he compared very unfavourably with Fiennes, and criticised quite unjustly for attempting to destroy much of what his predecessor had achieved. St Johnston may well have been much less approachable than Fiennes, a snob and – if his memoirs are anything to go by – a world-ranking name-dropper, but he did what he could for the island and its inhabitants while operating under the most stringent financial restraints imposed by the Colonial office. And even though he probably left at the end of his term of office still referring to the perceived demerits of 'these people', it was for the poor black section of society that his most enduring memorial was begun. His name is today attached to a large village a mile or so to the east of St John's, which had its origins in a model housing scheme he inaugurated after having fought a long, hard battle with the Colonial Office for the necessary funding.

A further change took place during the 1920s which, although it had nothing to do with the Governor or the administration, represented the first appearance among the population of another group of immigrants, this time from Lebanon, then part of Syria. As Syrian communities had by this time been established elsewhere in and around the Caribbean for many years, following a terrible massacre of Christians carried out in their homeland by the Turks in 1860, the arrival of a few itinerant traders in Antigua a few years after the end of the First World War caused no great surprise. Their acute business sense and trading skills, combined with a willingness to seek customers among even the poorest members of the population, soon earned them a secure place in society. This in turn encouraged further immigration and laid the foundation of a community which, within one generation, would be found playing a major role in the island's retail trade, and within another would be in command of the larger part of its commercial activity.

•

If the main source of discontent among most of the black population in the years immediately after 1918 was all to do with wage levels and working conditions, that of the majority of the coloured middle class was in connection with constitutional matters. In Antigua, as in all the other islands, there was a growing demand for reform of the constitution, for the addition of elected members to the Legislature, and for some degree of coloured participation in government. In response to such a widespread call for reform, the Parliamentary Under-Secretary of State for the Colonies Edward Wood (later Lord Halifax), was sent on a tour of all the British West Indies towards the end of 1921 in order to carry out an investigation and to formulate policy recommendations. His visit to Antigua took place during the first four days of the new year, and his discussions were entirely confined to officials, members of the Legislative Council, and some of the more prominent white and coloured businessmen – the great majority of whom were strongly opposed to any change whatsoever.

In his report, published in June 1922, Wood ruled out responsible government for any of the colonies, as he had found no widespread demand for it, and believed that because large sections of society everywhere were 'backward and politically undeveloped' its introduction would be hazardous. He also considered that they all lacked leadership of sufficient 'impartiality or integrity' to which responsibility for government could safely be passed by the Crown. At the same time, while recommending that a certain degree of representative government might be introduced in Trinidad and the Windward Islands – provided elected members remained in a minority – he ruled this out for the Leeward Islands. In Antigua, as in St Kitts–Nevis and in Montserrat, he considered the social foundations for the healthy growth of such government were lacking; plus, he was careful to point out, there was strong opposition to the introduction of the elective principle among all those who now ran the island.

As well as those concerned with constitutional matters the recommendations of the report also included several connected with the sugar industry, which Wood had everywhere been informed was in need of support, but these were all ignored. During the rest of the decade, as the average world price for sugar fell from well over £30 a ton to less than £10, conditions in Antigua deteriorated for everyone from the grandest estate owner to the poorest field-hand. The workers remained cowed, unorganised and leaderless, the predominantly coloured middle class remained unrepresented and increasingly frustrated, and all the planters and wealthier merchants could do was to complain and petition the British Government for relief.

In June 1929, within a few days of his taking over as Governor, St Johnston 'was asked to receive a deputation from the Agricultural and Commercial Society, who requested me to forward a petition from them to the Secretary of State for the Colonies asking for some sort of assistance from the Imperial Government to save the sugar industry from threatened collapse.' This was forwarded with the Governor's endorsement, but the Labour Government which had assumed power at the end of the previous month was committed to a policy of cheap food and more interested in removing import duties than in imposing new ones. 'This was indeed a bombshell', St Johnston recorded later, 'and immediately the sugar market fell still further', presaging a situation where most of the estates would have to be put out of cultivation and where 'practically the whole population would be out of work and starving.'[9]

Neither eventuality was fortunately realised, as the petition, along with all the other pleas for assistance he received from other islands, prompted the Secretary of State Lord Passfield to appoint a two-man non-parliamentary commission to carry out an investigation into the crisis affecting the West Indian sugar industry. This was undertaken in November 1929, and in their report of the following February the commissioners recommended that, if the industry was to survive, West Indian sugar had to be given an increased preference on the British market and, as far as Antigua was concerned, the island needed a loan of £55 000 at a low rate of interest 'in order to meet the direct loss on the 1929 crop'. The main recommendation was accepted and acted on, but no loan for Antigua was forthcoming and the island's producers 'by dint of heroic and drastic reductions in factory and field costs, and with loans from the Company that owned the factories' had to struggle on as best they could.[10]

One possible solution to Antigua's problems, which were also very much those of the rest of the Leeward Islands, was thought by some to lie in bringing the islands into closer union with one or more of the other West Indian colonies. Notions of some kind of federation had exercised the minds of one or two men in other islands for many years, but had been raised in 1922 only to be met with a response in the Wood Report that it was 'inopportune and impracticable to attempt any amalgamation of the existing units of government into anything approaching a general federal system.' No one in Antigua at the time had shown much interest but now, seven years later and faced with the possible collapse of the economy, anything was worth trying. The unofficial members of the Legislative Council petitioned the Secretary of State at the end of 1929 with a proposal that the Leeward Islands be united with the Windward Islands and Trinidad and Tobago, all to be administered by a single governor and one legislature, with each member island handling internal affairs through a commissioner and local council. Where matters of finance were concerned, these would be handled locally, but only with the approval of the central government. This was sent to London without the endorsement of St Johnston, as he considered that 'an amalgamation of colonies' was not going to reduce the cost of administration and 'was not really tackling the major problem of the islands, which was that of the sugar situation.'[11]

This was not a view shared by Lord Passfield, particularly when soon after it reached him he received the report of the commissioners he had asked to study the sugar industry and read:

> It appears to us not only that the simplification of the system of government of the Leeward Islands and St Lucia is necessary, unless the existing system is to be maintained continuously at the cost of the Imperial Exchequer, but that an administrative association of all these islands with St Vincent and Grenada would be more conducive to their agricultural progress and prosperity . . . We think that a conjunction of all these islands could not fail to be advantageous, and we strongly recommend the consideration of these possibilities to your Lordship.[12]

He was fully prepared to consider the possibilities, but as he was replaced as Secretary of State in 1931 it was his successor who in the autumn of the following year announced that another Commission was about to be sent to the Caribbean – much to the disapproval of St Johnston in Antigua – 'to investigate, purely from an economic point of view, the possibilities of the suggested amalgamation, or "Closer Union", of the colonies.'

This provided an opportunity for the region's committed federalists, and members of the Representative Government Associations (drawn almost exclusively from among the coloured middle classes) which had been formed in some of the islands, to meet and discuss issues to do with the franchise, self-government and federation in advance of the Commission's arrival. A conference was convened at Roseau in Dominica on 28 October 1932, and among the seventeen delegates who attended, drawn from Trinidad, Barbados, the Windward Islands and the Leeward Islands, was one from Antigua: Harold

Wilson, the editor of *The Magnet* newspaper. Unlike the British Government, which viewed a possible federation as little more than a means of cutting administration costs, all who attended saw the closer association of their various colonies as a necessary step towards the achievement of self-government, and their discussions were concentrated on this aspect. A draft federal constitution was drawn up during the six-day conference, but disagreement about the need for adult suffrage and whether or not each colony needed to attain self-government in advance of federation, only showed up how far all the islands had to go before any kind of political association could be more than a pipedream.

This was recognised by the Closer Union Commission in its report submitted after a tour of the Caribbean which began in November and lasted four months. In trying to ascertain local opinion about closer association its members, General Sir Charles Fergusson and Sir Charles Orr, had found everywhere that the majority of people interviewed only wanted to discuss reform of their own island's constitution, and were forced to the conclusion that the colonies were no more ready for federation than Wood had found them to be ten years earlier. As a result the report's main recommendation was that:

> The Colonies of the Leeward Islands and the Windward Islands should be united into one colony under a Governor with headquarters at St Lucia. The present federation of the Leeward Islands should be dissolved and each Presidency should be given in general the same independence as is at present possessed by the three islands of the Windward group each retaining as now its own Executive and Legislative Council under the Presidency of the Administrator or Commissioner enacting its own laws and regulating in general its own finance and local affairs.[13]

At the same time it was considered that a legislature in each island consisting of a mixture of nominated and elected members was the system 'best suited to present conditions', and the report recommended that their constitutions be amended accordingly.

Following receipt of the report the governments of the islands concerned were asked to provide estimates of the cost which would be involved in forming the proposed association: an exercise which led to the conclusion that, rather than bringing about any reduction, it would result in an increase in the cost of administration. The report also occasioned 'violent protests from the islands as to which should become the headquarters of the proposed new colony', something that St Johnston in Antigua considered 'will always happen, for the islands have been intensely jealous of each other for 300 years, and are hardly likely to change this attitude now.' Not surprisingly the Secretary of State and the officials of the Colonial Office were soon convinced that the amalgamation scheme was quite impracticable, and the only change made, as far as Antigua was concerned, was one which the Governor, a few months before it took place, still viewed with a jaundiced eye:

> The electoral principle was conceded in all the islands (except the little Presidency of the Virgin Islands), and an official majority on the Legislative Councils was also conceded, subject to certain reserve powers for the Governor. At the time of writing [June 1935] legislation is being drafted to bring the new form of constitution into operation. Time alone can show what the result of it all will be.[14]

By the time the required Order in Council had been published to bring these concessions into effect, the increasingly desperate plight of Antigua, as the price of sugar remained firmly under £10 a ton, had at last brought about the beginnings of some sort of co-operation between the middle and working classes. While those who ran the island and the sugar industry were seemingly unable to envisage any solution to their problems, other than constant, unavailing appeals for subsidies or relief, a few coloured men began to recognise that they had more to gain by assisting black Antiguans to win their rightful place in society, than in supporting an increasingly embittered white minority in holding on to the position to which they assumed they alone were entitled.

•

Battle lines began to be drawn in 1931 when the estate owners formed the Antigua Sugar Planters' Association, in order to better organise a campaign to eradicate a serious sugar-cane pest, the borer moth *Diatraea saccharalis*. Having been brought into existence in order to enable successful united action to be taken in this way, it was then seen that the Association could play an equally useful part not only in enforcing uniform wages and working practices, but also in preventing any repeat of the 1918 episode through divisions among estate owners. A land settlement programme had begun the previous year, to encourage an increase in peasant farming, and this also made it imperative that the owners from whom land was being leased for this purpose were able to speak with one voice. From 1936, after the factory at Bendals had been taken over by the owners of Gunthorpes, such peasant farmers, along with all the rest of the workers in the industry, were very much at the mercy of the Association.

A body to give the peasant farmers a voice of sorts had been established in the late 1920s at the instigation of Charles Franklin, a Moravian minister, but it was not until after their numbers had greatly increased as a result of the land settlement scheme that the Antigua Agricultural Association could make itself heard. Even then it could only bargain with the factory owners for slightly higher rates for cane in return for greatly increased delivery quotas; and this on behalf of only a fraction of the industry's total workforce. In 1932 several of the men involved in running it, including the newspaperman Harold Wilson, left to form an association to which workers other than self-employed small farmers could belong. They made little effort to attract those who most needed their help, the estate workers, and membership of the Antigua Working Men's Association was in the main confined to better-paid men on the waterfront or in the construction industry. Like the Agricultural Association it lacked any legal status, other than that of being registered as a limited company and, as any industrial action taken by either could have resulted in an employer's claim for damages, neither achieved very much, and both faded out of existence before the end of the 1930s.

At the end of 1934 yet another petition was forwarded to the Governor, complaining about the state of the island and the difficulties being felt by everyone from those 'of any standing engaged in trade and industry' to those of 'the labouring classes . . . cut off from the most ordinary necessaries of life', and calling upon the Secretary of State for the Colonies 'to take such steps . . . as will secure reasonably the welfare, progress and happiness of the people of this island as a whole.' Among the signatories, besides the white unofficial members of the Legislative Council and the Dean of Antigua, were several merchants of Portuguese origin and half a dozen coloured men following various professions; among them Harold Wilson and Charles Barrow, president and vice-president respectively of the Antigua Working Men's Association. One of the changes called for was a revision of the constitution to restore the elective principle to the Legislature, as had been recommended by the Closer Union Commission over eighteen months earlier.

Another two years were to pass before this came about, and it was not until 1937 that a new constitution was introduced. This reduced the size of the Council but maintained the imbalance between the official and unofficial elements, with six seats to be held by the Administrator, the Attorney-General, the Treasurer and three nominated members, and only five by elected members. For the latter there were no constituencies; anyone with the necessary qualifications could stand as a candidate, and the five who received the most votes would be returned. The franchise was limited to men owning property worth at least £100 or who earned £30 a year, or who paid at least £12 a year in rent: all sums which ruled out participation by the vast majority of the ordinary working population. The qualifications needed by a candidate – property valued at £500 or earnings of £200 a year – ensured that no wage earner could stand, but failed to prevent a coloured shopkeeper from St John's from contesting and winning a seat in the elections held soon after the constitution was amended.

As a man who not only carried on a trade as a jeweller, but was also the head – The Most Noble Patriarch – of the Odd Fellows Lodge in St John's, Reginald Stevens's appeal to those who voted for him was as great as the disdain shown for him by most of his fellow legislators after he had taken his seat. This was of no great consequence but, once he showed that he was not prepared to act as a token and began to call on behalf of the common man for improvements in housing, the health services, education and other aspects of island life, their contempt turned to anger. At the time, as his appeals would have reminded them, the infant mortality rate was three times higher than that in England, large numbers of people were still living in wattle-and-daub houses, less money per capita was being spent on education than in any other island of the British West Indies, and rates of pay for unskilled workers were the same or even less than they had been a century earlier. All these facts may have been well known, but it was too much to be forcefully reminded of them by some jumped-up tradesman, and the anger felt by the rest of the Council turned to vindictiveness. An enquiry was called into Stevens's financial affairs, in an effort to prove he had not possessed the required qualifications to stand as a candidate. At the end of October, after only a few months in the Legislature, and on the most specious grounds, he was forced to resign his seat. All was not lost however as, having taken care to clarify his qualifications, he fought a by-election the following January and regained the seat he was to hold until his death in 1945.

Seven months after Stevens had been re-elected word reached the island that, because of the distress which was by then only too apparent through the British possessions, and which had led to strikes, disorder and riots in some of them, a royal commission had been appointed 'to investigate social and economic conditions in all the West Indian territories, and to make recommendations'. The Commission, under the Conservative politician Lord Moyne, left England in October 1938 and spent over six months in the Caribbean, where it took formal evidence from 370 individuals or organisations in twenty-six places, collected nearly 800 memoranda, and was presented with written details of some 300 cases of individual grievances. Hearings in Antigua were held during the last three days of the year and concluded on 2 January 1939. Among the other nine members of the Commission was Sir Walter Citrine, the general secretary of the British Trades Union Congress, and it was his presence that gave Stevens, Wilson and one or two other men interested in workers' rights the opportunity to seek advice and take action which was to have a profound affect on the whole of the subsequent history of the island.

While the hearings were adjourned on New Year's Day, Citrine was invited to look around the city and to visit the prison, Holberton Hospital and the adjacent Fiennes Institute. Duly shocked by what he saw, the same evening he addressed a meeting, chaired by Wilson, which had been arranged in a large schoolroom close to the Cathedral. Speaking before a large audience he outlined the history of the trade union movement in Britain, and gave as his opinion that the only hope of change in the condition of the mass of working-class Antiguans that he could see lay in a direction similar to that which had been taken by working-class Britons, with the formation of a trade union. This was a message he conveyed with such clarity and vigour that by 5 January a meeting to discuss the possibility had been held in Stevens's jewellery store, and eleven days later a union had been formed and named.

With Stevens as president and a man named Berkley Richards as general secretary, the Antigua Trades and Labour Union (ATLU) came into being on 16 January; it had no constitution, no funds and no members other than the twelve men who had volunteered or been pressed into service as its executive committee. It also had no legal status, there being no way of registering it under the existing laws other than as a limited company liable to tort. None of this deterred Stevens and his confederates, who by the end of April headed an organisation of about 3000 members. Not all had joined entirely of their own free will, but all had paid one shilling each to join, and undertaken to pay dues of six pence (or four pence if a woman) each week. A constitution had been drawn up, based on material supplied by Sir Walter Citrine, who was kept informed of progress, and a member of the executive who was also a lawyer worked on getting the law changed. After April, at the same time as the union's green organisers and officials were groping their way around the island trying to sell trade unionism as a means of improving the lot of Antiguans, the members of the West India Royal Commission were equally hard at work in London, preparing a report which it was hoped would improve the future of all West Indians. Both the ATLU and the Commission were to achieve their aims eventually, but not as rapidly as either probably believed possible in the middle of 1939.

To employers in Antigua the formation of the union, after the initial surprise caused by its sudden birth had worn off, was of no great concern. The inexperienced and naive negotiators they found themselves dealing with were by and large treated with condescension or amused contempt; threats of strikes or other disruptive action all came to little or nothing; and any progress made in bringing about improvements in wages and working conditions all ceased with the start of the Second World War. The outbreak of war also had a baneful effect on the reception given to the findings of the Royal Commission, which were delivered to the British Government in December.

In a massive and eloquent document, ever afterwards known as the Moyne Report, the Commission presented a complete indictment of the way the colonies were administered, and revealed in startling detail all the inadequacies which had been found in almost every aspect of West Indian life. The recommendations made to improve the situation were equally detailed and extensive, and were centred on the creation of a special fund from which a comptroller living in the region would be able to spend up to £1 million a year for the next twenty years on education, housing, health services, labour departments and social welfare. Such a report was enough to embarrass a government at the best of times; in the winter of 1939–40, when its contents would have made excellent German propaganda, its publication was

15 Weighing phosphate on the Redonda in 1912

16 Work on the Body Ponds water scheme in 1913 (FCO Library)

17 The abandoned dockyard in a deserted English Harbour in 1913
(Cambridge University Library)

18 High Street in St John's decorated for the visit of Princess Marie Louise in 1913
(Cambridge University Library)

19 Governor Henry Hesketh Bell with a police guard of honour at the lower end of High Street in 1913 (Cambridge University Library)

20 Governor Bell with members of the Antigua Cricket Club in 1913 (Cambridge University Library)

21 High Street in St John's in 1928
(Cable and Wireless Archive, Porthcurno)

22 Sir Eustace Fiennes Bt in retirement in England in 1931
(Topham Picturepoint)

23 Barclays Bank and the Court House in St John's in 1928
(Cable and Wireless Archive, Porthcurno)

24 Governor Reginald St Johnston's model housing scheme at Clare Hall
(Cambridge University Library)

25 Lord Baldwin in the process of upsetting the *Herrenvolk* by socialising with the workers in 1949 (Popperfoto)

26 The swearing-in of Reginald St Johnston as Governor of the Leeward Islands in 1929 (José Anjo)

27 The Antigua Legislative Council pose with Princess Margaret in 1955 (FCO Library)

28 Vere Cornwall Bird, Prime Minister of Antigua and Barbuda in 1981
(Hulton Getty)

unthinkable. A much abbreviated version containing the recommendations only was made public in February, and later in 1940 a Colonial Development and Welfare Act was passed to provide funds for the relief of all the British colonies. When the full report was published after the war, because of all that had happened elsewhere in the world in the interim, it would be found that its findings had lost much of their power to shock. In Antigua by that time, after five years of having to vie with all the other West Indian colonies for assistance from the Development and Welfare Fund, many aspects of life would be no better than they had been before the war began.

The news which reached Antigua on 3 September 1939, that Britain and Germany were again at war, produced alarm among those who administered the island and concern among those responsible for its business and commercial life, but was only of passing interest to the majority of people. While the Governor and his officials began worrying about what the consequences would be on matters such as defence, shipping and food supplies, and the businessmen, estate owners and merchants considered the effect war was likely to have on trade, sales and profits, there was little else for the rest of the population to do but carry on as usual earning a living. Wartime certainly made no difference to the ATLU activists, who continued to recruit new members wherever they could be found, in the fields, in the sugar factory, on a building site, or on the dockside.

They were helped in early December when, mostly at the urging of the Governor, Sir Gordon Lethem,[15] the Federal Legislature passed a Trades Union Act, and their activities were legitimised. Efforts were then concentrated on the Antigua Sugar Factory, and by January 1940 nearly 90 per cent of its employees had joined the union. Two months later the ATLU was officially registered; an event which took place in the middle of its first proper wage negotiations, undertaken with the factory management. These followed a period during which there had been some brief unauthorised strikes at the factory, as well as among waterfront workers, resulting in a modest rise in wage rates for field-workers.

This success not only enhanced the image of the union, bringing it yet more members, but also boosted Stevens's popularity as a member of the Legislative Council with his constituents. This was shown later in the year when, in the triennial elections for the Council, he was returned with a much larger share of the vote. Elected with him were Harold Wilson, a lawyer named Sydney Christian, and a merchant named John Jeffrey. The only white man – and the last such ever to be elected to the Council or any subsequent body in Antigua – was Alexander Moody-Stuart, the son of one of the founders of the Antigua Sugar Factory and the son-in-law of the other, who also happened to be the attorney for all the estates owned by the factory and secretary of the Antigua Sugar Planters' Association. With such credentials Moody-Stuart had more influence, and more in common, with the official and nominated members of the Council than with the other four unofficial members, and the latter were almost invariably denied his support when trying to bring in measures to improve the lives of ordinary people. Not that this mattered a great deal a year after the war had begun, in the light of events then taking place in Europe. The 'Phoney War' had ended in April; by late summer the Battle of Britain was well under way, and the Battle of the Atlantic was about to begin in earnest. With Britain teetering on the edge of disaster the welfare of everyone in Antigua was at stake.

On 2 September an Exchange of Notes took place between London and Washington DC concerning the leasing to the United States of bases in selected Caribbean territories, in exchange for fifty badly needed destroyers, an act which was the prelude to the formal United States–United Kingdom Leased Bases Agreement signed six months later. Antigua was among the colonies listed in the Notes and on 19 October a Board of Experts, headed by a rear admiral of the United States Navy, arrived on the island to confer with the Governor and to select suitable sites for a naval base and an air station. Both were found in the northern part of the island: the whole of a long peninsula (unnamed at the time but subsequently known as Crabbs, after the estate at its root) to the north of Parham for a naval seaplane station; and a much larger area to the west of this, embracing most of the land to the north of Piggotts and to seaward of Barnes Hill, for an airfield.

Once the sites had been selected, their owners had no other option but to agree to sell them to the Government; the Legislature then transferred them to the US authorities, and a grant of both for a period of ninety-nine years was approved by the Council in December. Fifty officers and men of the US Marine Corps arrived three months later, to form the first American military presence on the island, and construction work at both sites began soon afterwards.

The creation of these bases, together with the creation of the ATLU two years earlier, were – as far as the black working population was concerned – without a doubt the two most important events to take place on the island since emancipation. Although at the time no one, black or white, could have foreseen it, the union and the American presence between them were to be responsible for bringing about more changes in the structure of society during the next forty years than had taken place over the previous three centuries.

20
Unrest in the Graveyard

The tradition of slavery still hangs heavy over Antigua and imbues the attitude of the European employers towards the coloured workers. [Their] arrogant superiority is bolstered by the predominant position their race, particularly the British section of it, has held in the world . . . as well as the fact that the island is a Colony, a 'possession' of the Mother Country. This attitude, which it is not too much to describe as *Herrenvolk*, is manifested in a number of different ways calculated to make the coloured man feel that he is an inferior being ineligible to be treated on a basis of equality. The Europeans in Antigua have their own club to which men of colour, however eminent in their professions, are not admitted . . . There is a separate white people's tennis club just across the road from the coloured upper class tennis club. The whites live in one section of a district, the coloured in another. With the racial line so sharply drawn when it comes to coloured people of ability, it can easily be imagined what sort of relationship existed between the workers and their masters. Some aver that things were peaceful before the Union came to the island. That is possible to concede, for circumstances did not permit otherwise. After all, there is peace in a graveyard.

Vere Cornwall Bird (1949)

Early in 1941 Governor Lethem called upon the ATLU, through its president, to renounce strike action for the duration of the war. As a member of a Legislature which was fully committed to assisting in the war effort, Stevens had little option but to carry this request to his executive and persuade them to adopt the necessary resolution. Although the reasons were understood and accepted by the union's leadership and its more thinking members, it was regarded by many of the rank and file as a breach of faith, and one which over the next two years led to a decline in membership. It also brought about a sharp decrease in Stevens's popularity, and the beginnings of a movement to replace him, and some other members of the executive, with younger and more militant men.

The fall in membership was not helped by the start of the construction work in February at the sites of the two US bases, which produced an instant demand for labour. The American contractors involved refused to enter into any agreement with the union, or to allow union activity to take place on either site but, as the wages offered were much better than those paid to workers in the sugar industry, few of those who found work with them were much interested in joining the union anyway, or in continuing with their weekly dues if they were already members. The magnitude of this requirement for labour and the extent of the response were such that at the end of May there were not enough workers available to reap the cane harvest – a situation the union was asked to rectify, but which Stevens brushed aside when the Sugar Planters' Association refused to consider a wage increase.

The amount of work undertaken in connection with the construction of the two bases was, in Antiguan terms, enormous, and was carried out with a speed and urgency never before seen on the island. Dredging operations for seaplane runways, a turning basin and a ship channel in the approaches to the naval base were progressed while 'some 1000 native labourers' were set to work on Crabbs peninsula building a pier, a concrete apron and seaplane ramps, a power station, hangars, houses, offices and barrack accommodation for over 350 naval personnel, the US Marine Corps detachment and members of the US Coast Guard. The first seaplane landed on 25 June 1941, the marines moved into permanent quarters on 29 August, and the entire base was complete by February of the following year. Even more workers were employed in constructing what was soon to be known as Coolidge Air Field.[1] The facilities at the air station included two 5000-foot runways, hangars, fuel and water tanks, ammunition stores, warehouses, officers' housing, and barrack accommodation for up to 2000 men. The first aircraft landed on a temporary runway on 6 June, and enough progress had been made by October to allow part of the 35th Bomber Squadron to be stationed on the island. By May 1942 the entire air station was complete, with a complement of over 600 officers and men manning a permanent base for at least twelve aircraft. Among those who had helped in its construction was Berkley Richards who, perhaps not quite demonstrating the solidarity that Sir Walter Citrine might have expected, had resigned as the ATLU's general secretary the previous December in order to find work with the contractor.

That both the Navy and the Air Force bases became fully operational within a few weeks of the United States entering the war in December 1941, following the Japanese bombing of Pearl Harbor, made the speed with which they had been built all the more praiseworthy. Antigua made an ideal place from which air surveillance of the whole of the north-eastern Caribbean could be mounted, and regular anti-submarine patrols out to about 350 miles from the island were carried out by both services from March onwards. German submarine activity in the Caribbean was greatly intensified during 1942, with a consequent increase in the loss of shipping. Along with all the other British colonies, Antigua suffered some serious shortages, especially of foodstuffs, as a result; but without the protection afforded by the American patrols the number of ships lost would have been much higher, and the shortages far more severe.

The need for local labour did not end once the bases were complete and operational, but was reduced with the emphasis moved from construction and heavy manual work to the provision of maintenance and domestic services. Those who were no longer required, and had to return to a more usual occupation at a more usual pace, found that wages in the sugar industry had been increased while they had been away – an extra sixpence a day for both field and factory workers having been extracted from the employers in February. Although welcome the increase did not make a great deal of difference to anyone, as neither this nor any subsequent wage hike enabled ordinary workers to catch up with a cost of living which continued to rise as long as the war lasted.

Some of the men laid off by the Americans found alternative employment with the Defence Force; after the bases had been built, this body was given some responsibility for their protection, as happened with the local forces in all the other territories where US military facilities were to be found. It was immediately apparent that none of these units would be able to meet their new responsibilities without proper training and a more professional administration: something which – its provision having long been resisted by the War Office – the British Army was now called on to undertake. In October, in order to produce a more professional and useful organisation capable of meeting its new commitments, the Antigua Defence Force became part of the Leeward Islands Battalion under a cadre of regular officers and senior NCOs. This encouraged recruitment to the extent that, by the end of 1943, under pressure from the Colonial Office, the War Office reluctantly agreed to a West Indian contingent being allowed to take part in the war in Europe. The Caribbean Regiment, formed for this purpose, came into being the following May, and two months later several dozen Antiguans found themselves among the 1000 men of the 1st Battalion of the new regiment transported via the USA to Italy. Soon after arrival it became apparent that further training was needed before the unit could be sent into action, and in October the battalion was sent for this purpose to Egypt. Largely because the War Office and senior Army authorities had a quite unjustifiable lack of faith in West Indians as front-line troops it remained there for the rest of the war, and was shipped home and disbanded in December 1945; through no fault of their own, its officers and men had achieved nothing.

●

While the men of the Caribbean Regiment were doing their best to get into the fighting in Europe, and the American Navy and Air Force personnel were doing all they could to rid the Caribbean of German U-boats, other struggles – along with one or two far-reaching changes – were taking place in Antigua. Early in 1943 a split had developed in the ATLU executive over the action to be taken in trying to get a pay rise for the non-established government workers which had undermined Stevens's authority and further reduced his popularity. Although he retained his seat in the elections for the Legislative Council held in September, he was returned with far fewer votes than three years earlier, and lost the position of 'First Elected Member' to Harold Wilson. Moody-Stuart failed to retain his seat, being too busy consolidating his position as the island's biggest employer. Antigua Syndicate Estates, a company which had been formed shortly before the elections were held, combined nearly all the major sugar estates under a single ownership with Moody-Stuart as the Managing Director. As he was already a major shareholder in the company which owned the sugar factory, this left him in an unrivalled position with regard not only to the sugar industry, but to the economic future of the island. His status was now such that his participation in the running of the colony could not be left to the whims of a few hundred voters every third year, and he soon found himself as one of the three nominated members of the Council, answerable to no one but the Governor.

At the annual conference of the ATLU held on 30 January 1944 dissension over Stevens's leadership dominated the proceedings. By this time the make-up of the executive had changed considerably and among the new members were younger men who could see that through trade unionism lay the way to political power, and they were not prepared to creep towards it at a pace determined by men like the president, who were of a different generation and a more deferential temperament. The attack on Stevens – for being too soft, too dependent on outside advice, and too ready to concede to the demands of the administration – was led by a man named Vere Cornwall Bird. Dominating the conference with his physical size as much as with his belligerence, Bird eventually reduced Stevens to such a state of distress that he not only resigned as president, but quit altogether the organisation he had been so instrumental in bringing into existence only five years earlier. A little over a year later he was dead. Following his abrupt departure from the conference Bird was elected by acclamation to take his place, and in April 1945, in the by-election which followed the death of Stevens, the new president of the union also found himself a member of the Legislative Council.

When he became leader of the ATLU Bird was already thirty-four years old, and until joining the union he had earned his living in various clerical jobs – something he took pains to gloss over, preferring to have his past associated purely with his earlier activities as an officer of the Salvation Army. Blessed with a commanding presence, a fluent tongue, plenty of common sense, a natural talent for flattery, persuasion and compromise, an ability never to let the right hand know what the left was doing, and the talent to lie convincingly when necessary, Bird had all the makings of a politician. Once he had a power-base as head of the union, and the forum of the Legislative Council in which to make his voice heard, he was made. The articulate and charismatic working-class leader – the black demagogue that those in authority in Antigua since 1834 had always feared might one day appear – had arrived at last.

Labour relations deteriorated as the end of the war approached. Under its new leadership, the ATLU adopted new policies and took up a more militant stance over anything to do with wage demands, conditions of employment and workers' rights. Peace was ushered in by a strike on the waterfront, followed by others among construction workers, the employees of one of the larger wholesale merchants and, inevitably, among those toiling in the cane-fields and at the sugar factory. The sugar industry, now to all intents and purposes under the control of one man, Moody-Stuart, had done quite well out of the war – its entire output having been bought by the British Government – and appeared to have a reasonably prosperous future, given the same Government's announced intention to keep on buying West Indian sugar. Bird's main concern now was to make sure the workers shared in this prosperity; Moody-Stuart's was to make the industry as efficient and as profitable as possible for his shareholders. At other times and in other places these aims might not have been incompatible, but in Antigua in 1946 they could only lead to a long and rancorous battle of wills, and produced a situation in which each improvement gained by the workers assisted in the eventual demise of the industry.

When this conflict began the overall state of the island (outside the confines of those areas leased to the United States) and the general conditions under which the majority of the population lived were not much better than they had been before the start of the Second World War. The Colonial Development and Welfare Act of 1940 had so far produced little other than 'ambitious and far-reaching programmes . . . with the dual objects of overtaking arrears in the standard of social services and ensuring the better utilisation of the natural resources – primarily agricultural'. The island retained a poverty-stricken appearance, as a report prepared in 1946 made all too obvious:

> Houses in St John [sic] occupied by the poorer sections are for the greatest part wooden buildings constructed with imported lumber. They are in the majority of cases in poor condition.
>
> In the country districts, a timber-framed house is the chief type of dwelling owned and occupied by the greater number of the poorer section. Approximately 32 per cent are of sound construction and 58 per cent are unsound but capable of repair within economic limits . . . at present no plan of slum clearance has yet been initiated nor are there any schemes to assist owners to improve their dwellings.[2]

The condition of the schools and hospital was little better. There were twenty-five primary schools and nearly 8000 enrolled pupils, but only four of the schools were of modern construction, and less than two-thirds of the children attended regularly. Of the total of 233 teachers only twenty-seven were fully qualified, and 116 were no more than pupil teachers. Less than 700 children were receiving secondary education at one or other of five privately run secondary schools, with only fifty in receipt of a Government scholarship. Holberton Hospital, which dated from the early years of the century, consisted of no less than twenty-seven separate buildings, yet afforded only ninety-one beds for a population of 42 000. 'It has been condemned as unhygienic and unsuitable by every medical authority who has visited it during the past thirty years', a Government report would declare in 1950, 'but action has still to be taken.'

Other services were equally worthy of condemnation. The telephone system was 'of ancient vintage', having been installed in 1888. 'It is at present unable to cope with the growing demand for telephonic communication locally, especially in the city or central area', the author of the annual report to the Colonial Office complained in 1948. The electric light service in St John's was also 'totally inadequate for the needs of the present community', continued the same writer, 'like the telephone system, the demands upon it are greater than it can meet, with the result that only some parts of the city area are lit electrically.' Needless to say the supply of fresh water remained a perennial problem. In spite of all the efforts of pre-war governors to improve matters there was rarely enough to meet the demand. A severe drought in 1948 produced 'a period of extreme distress' throughout the island:

> There were no vegetables or other local produce on which the peasants usually subsist in hard times. All the reservoirs and ponds were dry. The people of St John's had about three gallons per head per day, and in the country the Government delivered tanks of water to various villages as often as possible and villagers would spend a day to collect one or two tins of it from some well or spring. It might take nearly an hour to collect one tin of water which was always partly salt and usually muddy. About the same time the pasture failed and many animals died of starvation. Money was short, work scarce, and in many places even building had to stop for lack of water.[3]

In 1946 there was only one major, readily apparent difference to life on the island from pre-war days, and that was in the access – among those who could afford it – to air travel. The use of St John's Harbour by the seaplanes of Pan American Airways had come to a halt at the beginning of the war, but by then it had been recognised in the region just how useful air transport could be to inter-island communication. In 1940 a small company calling itself British West Indian Airways had been set up in Trinidad, operating regular services to Barbados and Tobago, and in the following year it began pioneering routes to other islands. In March 1943 the first landing by a civilian aircraft on Antigua took place a mile or so to the north of St John's, on a 3000-foot grass strip called Villa Field after the owner of the land on which it was situated. This marked the true beginning of air travel between Antigua and the outside world. Flights in and out of Villa Field did not interfere with any military aviation activities, and the regular, if sparse, service which was soon in operation between Antigua and any other island with an airfield continued from then on. The importance of this air strip declined rapidly after Coolidge Field was opened to commercial traffic in February 1946, and disappeared altogether when the latter was transferred by the United States to the Antiguan administration three years later.

•

Soon after Vere Bird had taken his seat on the Legislative Council the ATLU formed a political committee and began to agitate for constitutional reform, calling for either all, or a majority, of the Council members to be elected. As the date for the 1946 elections approached it was decided that the union would field five candidates, all pledged to work for a slate of reforms including full adult suffrage, improvements to all public services, loans to small farmers, housing grants and the encouragement of secondary industries. As a result Antiguan voters witnessed their first true election campaign, and one which was so successful that on 26 July 1946 each of the five union candidates, with Bird well in the lead, trounced his opponent by an enormous margin. Even if this shocked the losers and the few who had voted for them, it pleased the entire working population, whether they belonged to the union or not.

It also allowed the Governor, Sir Brian Freeston,[4] to show when the new Council met for the first time that he at least recognised which way the wind had now begun to blow:

> I now have the satisfaction of knowing that the Council which sits before me today is more fully representative on its unofficial side, and can claim to speak for a larger proportion of the people of the Colony, than I think any of its predecessors. Probably as a consequence of a wider basis on which the elected side of the Council now rests. The order paper for today includes an unprecedented number of questions and resolutions emanating from the unofficial members. Here again we have welcome evidence of a quickening of active and intelligent interest in the affairs of Government which of course are the affairs of the people.[5]

Freeston also recognised that other changes were needed, and appointed the coloured lawyer Sydney Christian (who had not stood as a candidate for election) to the Council, where he joined Moody-Stuart and a man named Cadman, the managing director of a firm of wholesale merchants, as the nominated unofficial members. Bird himself was appointed a member of the Executive Council where, even if he was forced to rub shoulders with Moody-Stuart – who was appointed at the same time – and few of his proposals were ever acted upon, he at least gained valuable experience and a deeper insight into the workings of government.

If relations between Bird and Moody-Stuart on the Executive Council were prevented from becoming too inimical by the adroitness of the Governor – a man who in addition to 'an acute and tidy mind and a keen, sardonic sense of humour' possessed a presence all of his own, being 'preternaturally tall and thin, so that it seemed to take an interminable time for him to rise and uncurl from his chair' – the same could not be said for the two organisations they represented. Labour relations grew steadily worse during 1947 and in February of the following year the sugar workers came out on strike. The cause of the dispute, with many of those involved apparently looking thirty years into the past instead of to the future, centred on a demand by the cane-cutters for a return to the system of payment 'by the row' and not 'by the ton'. Leading to real distress among many of those involved, it began just as Freeston reached the end of his term of office and was still in progress at the end of March when his successor arrived.

Oliver Baldwin,[6] who had recently succeeded his father as the second Earl Baldwin of Bewdley, was by no means a conventional aristocrat, any more than he was – as might have been expected of the son of a Conservative Prime Minister – of a conventional, conservative frame of mind. Both before and after the Second World War he had sat in the House of Commons as a Labour Member of Parliament, and his appointment as Governor of the Leeward Islands was given to him by the Labour Government in some measure as compensation for his having had to resign as an MP on succeeding to his title. Although a capable enough man – a socialist who detested distinctions based on race or class, genuinely concerned for the social and economic progress of black people – he had no experience of colonial affairs and had been given no clear guidance by the Colonial Office on what was expected of him. 'I find the owners [of the sugar industry] thinking I have a bomb in each pocket', he wrote home a day or two after his arrival, 'and the black workers expect me to bring them a new world. All very difficult.' By dint of much arm-twisting he and the Administrator eventually brought about a settlement of the strike in the middle of April, persuading Moody-Stuart to agree to the demand for payment 'by the line', in return for the appointment of a Commission to look once again into all aspects of the sugar industry, in the hope that its findings might prevent any similar disputes from arising in the future.

The Commission under Lord Soulbury (the Chairman of the National Assistance Board and previously a long-serving Conservative Member of Parliament), with Bird as one of its members, met in Antigua in July 1948 to gather evidence about sugar production, wages, working conditions and land ownership. At the end of two weeks, leaving the island wilting under that year's drought, the members retired to London in order to prepare their report. This took an unconscionable time to complete, and when it was eventually delivered in March 1949 its findings pleased no one.

The ATLU had argued, following the lead of the Labour Government in Britain, for nationalisation of the industry and for agrarian reform by 'splitting up the Syndicate's property into a number of relatively small units', but the report firmly rejected this:

> In the absence of any evidence to support the view that greater efficiency would be secured under public ownership, we are bound to conclude that the adoption of the Union's proposal . . . would expose the industry and the livelihood of the majority of the inhabitants of Antigua to hazards unjustified by the evidence and unwarranted by experience . . . the cost of the compulsory acquisition of the Factory would be about £875 000. It is very doubtful whether [the] Government possesses or could borrow sufficient funds to carry out a transaction of this size.[6]

As far as the workers were concerned 'the only prospect of any material increase in wages over existing rates rests on the ability of the Factory and the Syndicate to maintain and improve their standards of productive efficiency.' All the Commission could therefore suggest was that a cost of living index be 'reconstructed', that the wholesale and retail profit margins be 'reviewed', and that the various bonuses paid to workers be 'consolidated' and adjusted for those who had had 'no basic wage increase since 1939'. The employers were called upon to supply the Government with employment statistics, to have the wages they paid made subject to review by a 'Wages Board or Council', and to appoint a welfare officer at the factory.

With regard to the land, the Government was urged to 'exercise its powers to acquire, for the purpose of land settlement, agricultural land which has been allowed by the mismanagement or neglect of its owners to degenerate', and to raise the annual tax on 'under-cultivated, neglected and misused agricultural land' to ten shillings an acre. It was considered that those who then wished to settle on Government land 'should receive leases for a period of twenty-five years, with the option to renew for a further twenty-five years.'

All of this pleased Bird least of all, and while the report was being finalised he withdrew from the Commission, informing Lord Soulbury that he was 'satisfied that the meetings serve no useful purpose to me and my people, as what has been drafted is already agreed to by you and the other members of the Commission, and except for minor points you are not prepared to deviate.' He then prepared a detailed 10 000-word minority report in which he described the state of the island, the condition of the majority of its population, and made his own case for land re-distribution, proper land utilisation, nationalisation of the factory, relief for the unemployed, and 'a new approach in industrial relations' in words which were probably too near the knuckle for many of his readers:

> But this means a change of heart, and the white capitalists must come to regard the indigent workers not merely as their employees to whom scant attention need be given, because they are in any event easily replaceable, but

as human beings and fellow citizens, in a common political entity – the British Commonwealth. The people of Antigua, through their organisation, have accepted the proposed Caribbean Federation [see Chapter 21], which will compass people of many races, and any suggestion of a *Herrenvolk* attitude by any one section is to be deplored. All the races – Indian, Chinese, European, Negro – must grow to live and work in mutual respect.[8]

However much his comments may have upset some of the recipients of the Soulbury Report, their wrath was tempered by the knowledge that his proposals stood little chance of being implemented; as he himself must have been aware when he penned his final sentences:

With the present very limited financial resources of the island, it will not be possible for the Antigua Government to finance a programme of this kind. It will, therefore, be necessary to get the assistance of the Imperial Government.[9]

By this time he had been part of the Government of Antigua for long enough to realise that, although there had been a Labour Government in Britain for the past four years, no member of it was yet prepared to consider the introduction of socialism into Antigua or any other colony.

Governor Baldwin probably found the conclusions of the main Soulbury Report disappointing, offering little hope either for the sugar industry or its employees. At the same time he quite likely found much in Bird's long addendum which matched his own views on how life on the island could be improved. From the time he assumed the administration he had made every effort to break down the existing race and class barriers, mixing easily with all with whom he came into contact, and in his dealings with ordinary black Antiguans reminded many of the days of Governor Fiennes. The comparison was valid in that both men had come to the job after experience as politicians and not as colonial administrators, and both were 'colour-blind' to a large extent, with a genuine sympathy for the plight of the less fortunate. In Baldwin, however, there was a degree of naivety which had not been found in his older and more experienced predecessor.

His invitations to a complete cross-section of society to functions at Government House were accepted resentfully by those who had previously considered such things their sole prerogative, but some of his other actions were considered intolerable. It was all very well to hold the annual King's Birthday reception in the grounds of his residence, but a party for the inmates of the Fiennes Institute held under the same trees was a disgrace. A yearly visit to the prison was all part of a governor's duties, but to interview each inmate and grant the odd pardon or remission of sentence most definitely was not. For the Governor to receive and entertain any freeloader passing through the island who stopped to 'sign the book' at the gate of Government House was all part of what he was paid for; for him to see each convict on his release from jail in order to hand the man a pound note and a word of encouragement was a waste of time and money – even if the latter was out of his own pocket. Such behaviour was not only thought eccentric by those Bird in his minority report had abused as Antigua's *Herrenvolk*, but worse, was considered to lower the dignity of the office of Governor. Baldwin's support of the island's first steel-band musicians was the last straw. Playing instruments copied from those which had originated a few years earlier in Trinidad, these noisy, disreputable, potential troublemakers needed to be outlawed – not encouraged to learn to read music and practice under the Governor's patronage. Combined with the suspicion that he had been sent from England to introduce such evils as adult suffrage and an all-elected Legislature this was all too much, and a concerted, behind-the-scenes campaign to have him removed was mounted even before Baldwin had completed his first year in office.

A summons to London 'for discussions' followed in January 1949, a move seen by both the Governor and his detractors as a prelude to his replacement. It was also recognised as such by all those who appreciated what he was trying to do, and the ATLU took the lead in organising a counter-campaign to try to prevent his removal. With the help of labour leaders in St Kitts and Montserrat – Baldwin was after all Governor of all the Leeward Islands – petitions were got up in all three islands and forwarded to London the following month. These undoubtedly helped, but Baldwin was more than capable of arguing on his own behalf to save his job after he arrived in London in the middle of February. Instead of being sacked, he was now given the instructions and guidance which he ought to have received a year earlier, and returned to the island by sea on 23 March.

On landing at the pier in St John's he received a tumultuous reception, with several thousand ordinary black Antiguans anxious to demonstrate their delight in his return by pushing him in his official motor car to Government House. Among the small official welcoming party which was quite lost in the melée was Moody-Stuart, the man popularly suspected of having been the instigator of the campaign to have the Governor recalled. It cannot have been the happiest day of his life, especially when he was physically assaulted by one of the multitude, but he did not have to wait too long to see Baldwin's popularity disappear, and he could smile again.

The reprieved administrator now had to attempt the impossible in order not to lose his job. The Colonial Secretary, Arthur Creech Jones, whose interest in colonial reform dated back to the 1920s, was keen enough to introduce changes which would eventually lead to self-government, but only through constitutional amendments made at a measured pace: a pace Baldwin knew from the start was too fast for Moody-Stuart and the minority of the population he could be said to epitomise; and too slow for Bird and the majority of his constituents. At the same time he was required to oversee the development of the economy, by supporting the sugar industry without upsetting its employees; and to improve the general welfare of the workforce without offending their employers. Whatever he did was bound to upset someone, and not surprisingly, within a few months of his return from London, he had lost the confidence of Bird and all those he represented.

The proposals for modest reform of the constitution which the Governor had been authorised to make fell far short of the abolition of Crown Colony rule that Bird and his colleagues on the Legislative Council demanded, and attacks on him began to be made in *The Workers' Voice*, a newspaper which had been founded in 1944 as the mouthpiece of the ATLU. Such criticism might well have been less telling had Baldwin been able to bring about any significant improvement in the area of social welfare, but access to the funds which had been made available by the second Colonial Development and Welfare Act, passed in 1945, was dependent on the preparation of a ten-year development plan for the entire Leewards Islands colony – an exercise which showed no signs of ever being completed. Even after this had been abandoned in the middle of 1949 none of the nearly half a million pounds allocated to Antigua could begin to be used until the island's own plan had been finalised and approved. By the end of the year, under sufferance by the Colonial Office, heartily disliked by those who passed as the upper classes in Antiguan society, under increasing attack from the ATLU leadership, and stymied by bureaucratic wrangling from overseeing any improvement in the lot of the great majority of the island's inhabitants, another strike was the last thing Baldwin needed to add to his woes.

The absence of any marked improvement in the lives of most Antiguans was not matched by a total lack of improvement to the face of the island, as one area was then being developed and transformed at a rate similar to that used by the US Army and Navy contractors at the beginning of the decade. In 1948 some 1300 acres of the large peninsula between Nonsuch and Half Moon bays on the east coast had been sold to a company set up by an American architect, for the creation of an exclusive resort for any of the rich and famous among his countrymen who wished to make sure they vacationed only among their own kind. The contractor brought in the following year to build the necessary clubhouse and the individual villas most of the members required followed the example set in wartime, and in all his dealings with local labour refused to recognise that the ATLU existed. This was a mistake. Wartime conditions no longer applied, the union leadership had by now ten years' worth of experience, and too many of the workers at what was to become the Mill Reef Club had too many complaints about the conditions under which they were forced to work. The strike, which was called towards the end of 1949, was observed by the majority, but failed in its objective of forcing recognition of the ATLU and settlement of grievances. There were too many other non-union tradesmen and labourers only too anxious to find work, and the contractor had little difficulty in recruiting strike-breakers. Eventually, after several months and a failed attempt to blow up the transport carrying the blackleg labour to work, the strike ended with no clear gain for the ATLU. Construction continued and the Club was soon established as a very exclusive province of the seriously rich. Racial exclusivity was never an issue: black people were welcome from the beginning, provided they knew how to cook, wield a mop, drive, trim a lawn or clean a swimming pool; token non-residential membership was extended to a select few of the more influential non-white citizens as and when changes in the political structure of the island in later years rendered such a move essential.

Long before this happened Lord Baldwin, greatly frustrated and presumably not a little sick of being made the whipping boy of, among others, the Colonial Office and the ATLU, resigned on grounds of ill-health and departed for England in June 1950. He left behind an island which was backward and rundown in appearance, and a people for whom he genuinely cared generally little better off than they had been ten or twenty years earlier. Following his death in England in 1958 his ashes were returned to Antigua, in accordance with his wish that they be interred on the summit of Green Castle Hill, between the villages of Jennings and Emanuel, where they now remain beneath a plaque inscribed *He loved the people of these islands*.

His successor arrived after a gap of three months to find Antigua in a worse physical condition than ever, with many of the inhabitants suffering acute distress. On 18 August a serious fire, caused by the explosion of a kerosine-operated refrigerator, had destroyed a hotel and various other buildings in the middle of St John's, and the following day the Federal Secretariat and its entire contents had been similarly destroyed. An enquiry into the cause of the second conflagration, as well as 'six other fires which occurred about the same time' found they were all 'due to electrical causes resulting from faulty electricity and telephone systems' – both still awaiting their long overdue overhaul or replacement. Although over 90 per cent of all the buildings in the city at the time were still of wooden construction neither of the two main fires had, providentially, resulted in a major disaster. Catastrophe was postponed until later the same month when, within ten days of each other, two powerful hurricanes destroyed between them over 1300 houses around the island, seriously damaged another 2300, and rendered more than 6500 people homeless.

As the hurricanes also affected all the other Leeward Islands to some extent, and occurred shortly before Kenneth Blackburne left England to take over as Governor, a contemporary newspaper report concerning his appointment may have been condescending but was hardly unfair in commenting that:

> In his new post he will be responsible for half-a-dozen scattered, backward, and poverty-stricken islands where the greatest need is capable, practical administration of the kind required to manage a not too prosperous country estate.[10]

Blackburne was the ideal man for the job. Between 1943 and 1947 he had served as administrative secretary to the Comptroller for Development and Welfare in the West Indies, before spending three years in Whitehall as the Colonial Office's Director of Information Services. He was not only fully aware of the practical needs of his impoverished 'country estate', and how best to acquire and use the funds available to meet them, but was also unusually well-briefed on the British Government's attitude towards colonial reform. In addition, as a professional colonial administrator, he had a clear understanding of his role, and experience enough to be able to deal firmly and equally with all those he had been sent to govern without any of his predecessor's unworldliness.

From the time of his arrival all interest centred on recovery from the effects of the hurricanes. Money, food, clothing and medical supplies were received from Britain as well as from other Caribbean territories for the immediate relief of the distressed, and by the end of the year most of the damaged housing had been repaired. Much of that which had been destroyed had been rebuilt after a fashion, providing their owners with some form of accommodation until funds became available for the large-scale slum clearance and 'self-help' housing project being planned. Industrial squabbles and disputes which had been suppressed as a result of the disaster remained dormant until the beginning of 1951, when labour relations were given a new twist by the establishment of an organisation to represent all the island's employers.

The creation of the Antigua Employers' Federation was seen by Bird and the ATLU as little less than a 'declaration of war against Antiguan workers'[11]: that Moody-Stuart became its chairman was no more than they expected, but its registration under the terms of the 1939 Trades Union Act they found very galling. Wildcat strikes among stevedores, peasant farmers, factory workers, cane-cutters and cotton-pickers,[12] which began in January, culminated four months later in a general strike, called by the ATLU as the result of a dispute with the Federation over holding the first day of May – May Day – as a workers' holiday. Urged on by the union the sugar workers in particular had taken the day off despite the employers' objections, and this had led a week later to an announcement by Moody-Stuart that the Federation would no longer recognise the ATLU as the sole bargaining agent for the employees of the sugar industry.

The general strike call which followed immediately did not meet with universal approval or acceptance, and a not inconsiderable amount of harassment took place in the middle of the month against those workers known, or thought to be, strike-breakers. Blackburne's attempts at mediation were constantly frustrated by the intransigence shown by both Bird and Moody-Stuart, but eventually he obtained their agreement to the holding of a Board of Inquiry, and the strike was called off two weeks after it had begun. Even so, by the time the man appointed to preside over the inquiry, the eminent West Indian jurist Sir Clement Malone, had arrived a great deal of tension still persisted, especially in St John's. The arrest of several union activists on charges of assault had led to a judge being threatened in the street; Malone considered that the police would be unable to cope with any serious trouble, and he suggested to the Governor that he 'bring in a few troops'.[13] Blackburne, perhaps unwisely, accepted his advice and sent a request for aid to Jamaica, the nearest place where British troops were stationed.

The Malone Inquiry into the 'causes of the dispute which have disrupted industrial relations in the island' began hearings on 11 June 1951, only to be suspended three days later when the ATLU representatives walked out in protest at the arrival of a company of the 1st Battalion Royal Welch Fusiliers, and the declaration of a state of emergency. This may well have allowed some of the more timorous residents of St John's to sleep more peacefully, but otherwise it served little purpose other than to allow Bird to make capital out of what he saw as the shame the Governor had brought on the island. Certainly nothing occurred which warranted the state of emergency, and the soldiers left after a month having been called upon for nothing. The Inquiry hearings were resumed on 21 July and concluded twelve days later.

Among the Inquiry's findings was nothing that could upset anyone of average intelligence possessed of an ordinary amount of common sense, just as among its recommendations there was none that could not be made to work by anyone not totally blinded by self-interest. The Board's report pressed for the removal of fear and suspicion by both the ATLU and the Federation. It rejected the latter's call for a ban on wildcat strikes as 'inadvisable and impracticable', and its demand that the union divorce itself from politics as unrealistic; while criticising the former for its 'nonchalance' and 'irresponsibility' in trying to introduce the May Day holiday in the way it had. At the same time it urged both to agree with the Government on the creation of a new public holiday to mark Labour Day. Other recommendations dealt with the settlement of outstanding industrial disputes, including the long-running battle between the union and the Mill Reef Club contractor, but the most important concerned the ownership of land – a subject the Board felt lay behind much of the trouble afflicting the island – and it was considered that improved labour relations would result from the acquisition by the Government of all the tenantry areas of the Antigua Syndicate Estates.

All the Inquiry's findings were accepted, and without too much lamentation on the part of either the ATLU or the Employers' Federation. Before the Board had issued its report Moody-Stuart had already informed Blackburne:

> My federation shares Your Excellency's view that improved relations among all sections of the community are much to be desired, and that, so far from seeking the destruction of Trades Unionism in Antigua, it is our desire to see

the day when agreement can be made and kept between the Federation and the Union . . . and . . . we shall encourage our members at all times to abstain from any avoidable step which may tend to injure good relations.[14]

In 1964 the ATLU's first historian and earliest apologist was able to write:

> The period between 1951 to the present has been one of comparative industrial peace in the island. The settlement of the tenancy lands of the Syndicate Estates and the application of the roster system on the waterfront removed the basic causes of the former grievances and the way was made clear for free negotiations on specific industrial matters without extraneous matters being introduced.[15]

Even if Blackburne may have been too hasty in sending for British troops, and in so doing had interrupted the Inquiry's hearings, the results obtained from his appointment of the Board more than justified the rest of his handling of the situation which had arisen after May Day. The increased prestige he acquired as a result now helped smooth the way for the introduction of major constitutional reform.

•

Before Blackburne had left London the previous year a decision had been taken in the Colonial Office to introduce full adult suffrage throughout the Leeward Islands, and to alter the composition of the Legislature in each island in order to give the elected members a majority over all the others. 'This presented no problem in peaceful Montserrat', he recorded later,

> but there were obvious difficulties in Antigua and St Kitts with their labour leaders thirsting for political power. In both places the labour members would dominate the legislatures and could bring government work to a grinding halt unless they were also made to accept responsibility for their votes and actions.[16]

By the middle of 1951, however, having had direct experience of working with Bird on the Executive Council, and with his four colleagues on the Legislative Council, the Governor decided his initial concerns about government work 'grinding to a halt' had been misplaced. On 23 August legislation was introduced which created eight electoral districts and, by removing all restrictions on the registration of voters, entitled all men and women over twenty-one years of age to take part in an election to be held at the end of the year. Bird felt obliged to argue for ten electoral districts and an all-elected Legislature, but well before the elections took place he was happy enough to settle for eight constituencies, provided the elected members would then form a majority on the Council: exactly what had been intended all along.

The first elections under full adult suffrage took place on 20 December 1951. Bird, together with two men, Ernest Williams and Edmund Lake, who had been in the Legislature with him since 1946, were joined by five other ATLU candidates in order to contest all eight seats. By this time very few of those connected with the formation of the union remained among its leaders, some having left altogether, and the selection of the other five had taken place only after a good deal of in-fighting. As no one on the island realistically expected that all eight would not be elected, it proved difficult to find anyone to stand against them. In the end four men came forward, all stood as independent candidates, and all four were soundly beaten; among them the stalwart Harold Wilson, who received a derisory seventeen votes to finish his political career. The other four union candidates, including Bird, were returned unopposed, and in all the ATLU received 87 per cent of the total vote.

The new Legislature was not what Bird had been agitating for earlier but, safe in the knowledge that a full ministerial form of government would be introduced before the next election, he and his seven colleagues took their seats in the Legislative Council at the beginning of 1952. They were joined by the Administrator, who acted as President, the Financial Secretary, the Attorney-General, and by three members nominated by the Governor. The Executive Council also had a radically different composition, with three of the elected members, Bird, Lake and Williams, chosen by the others to sit on it under the Governor, together with the Administrator, the Attorney-General and one of the nominated members. It was inevitable that Moody-Stuart should be one of the nominated members of the Legislative Council, and equally inevitable that he should be the one then appointed to the Executive Council. Under the system devised by Blackburne, as what he saw as a necessary stage before the introduction of ministerial government, the three elected members of the Executive Council were then made chairmen of committees, formed from among the members of the Legislative Council, to 'watch over' as Blackburne would have it, three main aspects of government, and to advise accordingly. Bird now began his true introduction into the business of governing by becoming, to use Blackburne's preferred terminology, the Member for Trade and Production, with Lake looking after Social Services, and Williams responsible for Public Works and Communications.

With these three quasi-ministers in positions of power and responsibility giving the lie to Blackburne's earlier fears, and access to the long-awaited Colonial Development funds, improvements were soon taking place all over the island. Early in 1955 it was reported that during the previous two years there had been 'many major developments in public works, water supplies, education, housing, fisheries, land settlement, health, communications and electricity', although, as always in Antiguan history, these had been 'over-shadowed by the severe drought conditions experienced during 1953 and the first half of 1954.'[17] The tenantry areas of the Syndicate Estates, about 3000 acres, had been acquired and incorporated into 'a land settlement reorganisation plan for the island as a whole . . . By the end of 1955, there were twenty-seven settlements covering a total area of 17 650 acres of which about 8500 acres of developed arable land were operated by 4800 allottees.'[18] In St John's by this time the water supply had been increased, the electricity supply replaced, and the telephone system completely renewed. The first Government secondary school had been opened, and Holberton Hospital had been modernised at long last.

During the same period steps were taken to create the institutional arrangements needed to improve the economy. Ordinances were passed to aid the creation of new industries and the development of tourism, and an Industrial Development Board, under Bird's chairmanship, was set up with the main aim of 'investigation of the island's industrial possibilities'. The Board also engaged in more practical activities. In 1952 it took over the running of a cornmeal factory which had been established before the Second World War, but had never managed to produce cornmeal suitable for human consumption. At the same time it opened a cotton gin in which the lint was separated from the cotton seeds, later adding an oil factory in order to extract and refine the oil obtained from the seeds.[19]

As a result of all this, and well before the next elections were due, Blackburne's 'membership system' – the close association of elected members of the Legislature with the day to day running of the island – was considered 'an outstanding success'; to 'have given a marked impetus to Government activities'; and to 'have admirably paved the way for the introduction of a ministerial system.'[20] Approval for its introduction at the end of the following year was given by the Secretary of State for the Colonies in December 1954. At the same time he informed the British Parliament that it was proposed to abolish the Leeward Islands Federation, which was something the colony's General Legislative Council had called for in a resolution passed four years earlier.

Both announcements stirred up a new and increased concern about the future of Antigua, as the prospect of a Government under ministers who were also trade union leaders – seemingly committed to the interests of one section of society before all others – was not to everybody's liking. When Bird, Lake and Williams became ministers a year later they were advised by Blackburne, acting on instructions from London, to resign their positions on the ATLU executive, in order to conduct themselves under the 'rules of obligation' that the holders of public office in Britain were required to observe, and to be free of any possibility of a conflict of interest. That all three rejected his advice was not without some justification, considering that for most of the previous 300 years the Legislature had been the preserve of men who represented little more than their own personal interests, but in retrospect was a short-sighted and unwise response. There was nothing the Governor or the Colonial Office could do about it, but with the next elections due at the end of 1956, the unease felt among the middle classes led a lawyer, Rowan Henry, to form the island's first political party with a view to opposing the ATLU at the poll.

The Antigua National Party (the ANP) stood no chance of success, even with the support of a few former members of the union's executive, including a past assistant general secretary, who had all either fallen foul of Bird or been repelled by what they saw as his leanings towards autocracy. Too many of the population had waited too long to see men from humble backgrounds similar to their own in positions of authority to want any change at this stage. The ANP campaign, conducted at public meetings and through the pages of a newspaper started by Henry, concentrated on the dangers seen in the close connection between the Government and the ATLU. It met with little response other than organised heckling and stone-throwing at the meetings, and abusive denigration in the pages of *The Workers' Voice*. None of the candidates the party put up for election on 20 November got more than a handful of votes compared with those received by the ATLU candidates, who were the same eight men who had won the seats five years earlier. The only change made in the make-up of the Legislature was among the nominated members: two being replaced, while Moody-Stuart remained.

Bird, Lake and Williams, now in charge of their respective departments as ministers but with Bird very much *primus inter pares*, returned to their desks to be greeted almost immediately with the contents of a letter from the Secretary of State. In this he spelt out the duties the new ministers owed to the public, and called upon them to avoid any action which could 'give colour or substance to the belief that they are doing anything which the "rules of obligation" forbid.' His particular concern was with their positions in a trade union:

> While I readily understand that the close identification of trade unions with political parties in some of the West Indian territories makes it difficult for politicians to divorce themselves from direct association with trade unions immediately on their assumption of Ministerial office, the objections to this association are very strong. Even if Ministers with trade union associations are able to avoid their dual interests coming into conflict, there must always be some doubt in the mind of the public as to the true position. I hope, therefore, that Ministers will take steps to dissociate themselves from active participation in trade union affairs as soon as possible.[21]

While the contents of this long missive were on the whole unobjectionable, even if one or two phrases might lead one to believe its author, Allan Lennox Boyd, had held his nose while dictating them, the manner in which they were communicated not only to ministers in Antigua, but to those in all the other Leeward Islands – by means of publication in the official gazette – was graceless and insensitive: a perfect illustration of the contempt which from then on the majority of British politicians were to show towards those of the West Indies. As far as the new ministers in Antigua were concerned, it made little difference how widely the Secretary of State's doubts about their propriety were circulated. Bird remained president of the ATLU, Williams the senior vice-president, and Lake a member of the executive, knowing that few of those who had voted them into office would wish it otherwise.

21

In No Mood to be Dictated to

> 10 Lovely islands all in a line,
>   One sought independence, then there were Nine;
> 9 Lovely islands trying to federate,
>   One goes independent, thus leaving Eight;
> 8 Lovely islands hoping for a Heaven,
>   One joins Trinidad, then there were Seven;
> 7 Lovely islands now in a fix,
>   Wondering if Barbados will drop them to Six;
> 6 Lovely islands could hardly survive,
>   If another pulled, leaving only Five;
> 5 Lovely islands – small and very poor –
>   Better stick to BRITAIN LADS, and be
>   COLONIES ONCE MORE
>
> Anonymous contribution to the Antigua–Barbuda Democratic Movement's pamphlet S1 no. 13, 6 October 1962

Mr Bird intensely dislikes interference from London.

He has worked an economic miracle in Antigua, developing the tourist trade to the point where the island's budget has been able to dispense (defiantly) with grant-in-aid. An oil refinery is being built in the island, and a deep water harbour is not far off.

He is rightly proud of his achievements; sees Antigua as on the verge of self-sufficiency, and is in no mood to be dictated to.

Professor Sir Arthur Lewis
The Agony of the Eight (1965)

The full text of the Moyne Report, containing the findings of the West India Royal Commission which had toured the West Indies immediately prior to the Second World War, was published soon after the war ended. One of its many recommendations was that, subject to local agreement and improvement in communications between them, the Leeward and Windward Islands should be federated, with a strong central legislature possessing wide powers, and each island under a Commissioner and Council dealing with purely local affairs. It was a proposal that was generally welcomed in 1945, so closely by this time were federation and self-government tied together in the minds of all the newly risen West Indian leaders – including those of Antigua. A conference convened in Barbados the same year to re-launch the Caribbean Labour Congress, was attended by both Harold Wilson, who had been in on the drafting of a federal constitution at Roseau in 1932, and Vere Bird, the newly elected president of the ATLU. The delegates considered 'the Conference as having laid the foundation for a unified West Indies based upon the desire of the people of the various units for closer union', and pledged themselves 'to work towards a Federation' of all the islands.

In February 1947, as there had been no progress towards an all-embracing federation by this time, representatives from all the Leeward and Windward Island legislatures, Bird among them, met in St Kitts where they passed a resolution in support of their own federation 'with a strong government'. They followed this up with draft proposals for a unicameral legislature with elected representatives from each island, and the establishment of a federal government with exclusive taxation powers and sole authority over everything but purely parochial matters. Before very much discussion of these proposals had taken place in each of the islands concerned the Secretary of State, Creech Jones, who was greatly in favour of West Indian progress towards self-government, called for a conference to be held at which the formation of a much larger federation could be debated.

Montego Bay in Jamaica was chosen as the venue and representatives of all the British West Indian legislatures, other than that of the Bahamas, gathered there in September, with Bird as a member of the Antiguan delegation. The main outcome of their discussions was the setting up of a Standing Closer Association Committee in order to study what federation would involve, and to draft a suitable constitution. As one of the conference resolutions had accepted 'the principle of a federation in which each constituent unit retains complete control over all matters except those specifically assigned to the federal government', the delegates on this committee from Antigua and the other islands of the Leeward and Windward groups were aware from the beginning that the federation now envisaged was quite different from the one they had agreed to in St Kitts. A suggestion that the smaller association they hoped to form be allowed to enter the wider federation as a single entity had been made, but quickly rejected.

A draft constitution was presented the following March and after much debate accepted by all the territories except British Guiana, British Honduras and the British Virgin Islands. It was endorsed by the Antiguan Legislature in 1951, the same year in which a Regional Economic Committee was established with Bird as one of its members. Formed to study basic matters such as shipping services, trade possibilities and the setting up of a customs union, it met regularly in different island capitals, providing Bird with valuable experience in working with the region's senior civil servants and leading politicians, and introducing him to the art of statesmanship. The work carried out by the committee, and that of the Standing Closer Association Committee, resulted in a series of conferences in London which led to the signing of the British Caribbean Federation Act in February 1956. This was followed two months later by the establishment of a Standing Federation Committee in Barbados, to work on details connected with the organisation of government departments, the appointment of officials, and the drawing up of rules and regulations. The Leeward Islands Federation, which had been in existence since 1871, was dissolved on 1 July, unmourned by anyone from Governor Blackburne down.

Eighteen months later, on 3 January 1958, Antigua, along with Barbados, Dominica, Grenada, Jamaica, Montserrat, St Kitts–Nevis–Anguilla, St Lucia, St Vincent and The Grenadines, and Trinidad and Tobago, became part of the Federation of the West Indies; exchanging one form of colonial rule for another. Through the appointment of a British Governor-General, the Crown still retained ultimate power and could legislate by Order in Council not only on matters of defence and foreign affairs, but also to maintain financial stability. The Federal Legislature in Trinidad (chosen as the site for the Federation's capital after much wrangling), once it was formed, was to consist of a nominated nineteen-member Senate and an elected forty-five-member House of Representatives. Antigua was to have two seats in each.

During the final London conference two years earlier, Bird had joined with labour leaders from Jamaica, Barbados, St Kitts, St Lucia and Grenada in forming the West Indies Federal Labour Party, and it was this party that won the federal elections which took place in March, narrowly defeating the opposition Democratic Labour Party. Bird himself, seeing rightly that his future lay in remaining a big fish in the Antigua pond, rather than in becoming a small one in the federal lake, refused to stand. The two ATLU stalwarts he chose to offer themselves instead, Novelle Richards and Bradley Carrott, were duly elected and the former was made Minister without portfolio in the Government formed by Sir Grantley Adams, the former Premier of Barbados who now became the Federation's Prime Minister. A retired civil servant, Carlton Moore, and a well-respected retired teacher named Bertha Higgins, were nominated to represent Antigua in the Senate.

The Government which Novelle Richards joined in Trinidad in May was extremely weak, having no power to levy taxes, dependent on scaled contributions from all the units for finance, and responsible only for matters which were relatively unimportant: the West Indies Supreme Court, the federal civil service, the University College of the West Indies, control of immigration from outside the Federation, creation of a West India Regiment, control of federal shipping, and administration of the Colonial Development and Welfare funds. After more than ten years of conferences, committee meetings, arguments and discussions, no one was at all sure just what purpose the Federal Government was intended to serve. The constitution under which it worked was out of date; Jamaica, Trinidad and Tobago and Barbados had already achieved partial self-government, and all the other units were reasonably close to it; but it had been agreed that no change would take place for five years. This restriction soon proved impossible for either Jamaica or Trinidad and Tobago – as the units carrying most of the cost – to accept, and in September 1959 they demanded additional representation in the Federal Parliament together with self-government for the Federation. The extra seats were granted after much opposition from among the smaller units, and early in 1960 full internal self-government was granted by a British Government already only too keen to begin bowing to the 'Wind of Change' observed by its Prime Minister.

•

Very little of what was taking place in connection with the Federation had much effect in Antigua, where the Government, as with those of all the member units, retained complete control over key issues such as taxation, education and the development of the economy, and where in 1959 the constitution was amended once again. The post of Governor of the Leeward Islands was abolished at the end of December, the last man to hold it being Sir Alexander Williams,[1] who had taken over from Blackburne two years earlier. Before leaving he announced that at the next elections, due in a year's time, the position of Chief Minister would be introduced and the number of elected seats in the Legislative Council increased to ten. In the interim the ministerial team was to be strengthened by the addition of a Minister of Labour, but only on the understanding what whoever was appointed was not an executive member of the ATLU.

Bird's selection of Lionel Hurst as the man to fill this position, when combined with his earlier choice of Novelle Richards as one of the men to run for a seat in the Federal Parliament, was to have profound and far-reaching consequences. Richards had been forced to relinquish his position as union treasurer in order to stand in the federal elections, and in 1958 the vacated treasurership had been taken over by a man named George Walter. Now, in order to become Minister of Labour, Hurst had to resign as general secretary of the ATLU, and Walter fought a vigorous campaign to beat off rival candidates and take his place. At the time no one could have even begun to suspect that the assumption of this post by a young, energetic and fully committed union activist marked the beginning of the end of the ATLU's monopoly in labour representation; or that it would lead to the introduction in Antigua of genuine two-party politics.

In 1960 this was all very much in the future, and in the run-up to the elections to be held the following January there were no signs of any loss of popularity by Bird or the ATLU. Rowan Henry had left the Antigua National Party and ceased to publish his newspaper by this time, leaving the opposition fragmented and without any clear policy or aims. At the few public meetings held to promote non-ATLU candidates the opponents of the union 'received rough treatment',[2] and one had his house set on fire. This unnerved some of the candidates so much that they withdrew from the race, and on election day only five of the ten seats were contested. With Bird holding by far the greatest claim to become the island's first Chief Minister, and with a clear prospect of more constitutional changes to come, none of the five ATLU candidates who were opposed had any trouble in winning. Among these was McChesney George, the man returned by the voters of Barbuda, who had been given their own representative in the Antiguan Legislature for the first time. With another sweeping victory behind him, Bird combined the work of the Finance Ministry with that of Chief Minister; Lake, Williams and Hurst resumed where they had left off in their respective ministries; and McChesney George found himself on the Executive Council as Minister without Portfolio, required to do little more than to act as a locum in the absence abroad of any one of his colleagues. The Legislative Council still retained its three nominated members, but this time Moody-Stuart was not one of them. Preferring to dissociate himself from any further constitutional developments, or perhaps unable to come to terms with his main adversary's new title, he refused the nomination, turned over his business interests to his son, and retired to England. In this he was doing no more than Englishmen who came to Antigua to make their fortunes had been doing for the previous 300 years, except in his case he was helped on his way by the award of a knighthood for all he was considered to have done for the community.

Bird had been so confident of victory that he had left the island in the middle of the election campaign in order to hold talks in the United States with agents of Natomas, an oil industry holding company with interests in the Caribbean region. At the time a number of American oil companies were making plans to exploit the West Indian islands for oil trans-shipment, re-fuelling or refining purposes, and Natomas had expressed an interest in establishing a refinery and associated bunkering facility in Antigua. Although the Industrial Development Board had by this time overseen the setting up of several new ventures such as an edible oil factory, an arrowroot starch factory, and one or two garment factories, not all had been successful or, in total, added very much to the economy. Bird now intended to make sure the chance was not lost to bring a far more substantial industrial project to the island, and his brief abandonment of the election campaign was made in order to ensure that the executives of Natomas realised their interest was fully reciprocated. In this he was entirely successful and, although work did not begin for another three years, an agreement for the construction of a refinery signed in March 1961 between the Government and the newly formed West Indies Oil Company was one of the first documents signed by the new Chief Minister. His co-signatory was the Administrator, the British official who retained the ultimate authority now that there was no governor, but who from now on was to have less and less influence on the way the island was governed.

•

In May 1961 Bird left the island again, this time for London where he attended a Lancaster House conference on the future of the Federation, which was threatening to fall apart only three years after it had been established. The disagreements between Jamaica and Trinidad that had been apparent from the beginning were by now seemingly irreconcilable. Eric Williams, the Premier of Trinidad, wanted a much more centralised federation with wide-ranging powers, in which the larger units would subsidise the smaller ones as necessary; something which was anathema to Norman Manley, the Premier of Jamaica, who thought the smaller islands were getting too much out of the Federation as it as, and who had no desire to surrender any more power to an institution on the opposite side of the Caribbean. The previous year the two men had been invited to Antigua by Bird, and after two days of face-to-face talks in early August had still failed to reach a compromise.

The agenda of the London conference reflected this deep division, causing Bird to remark at one of its sessions that much of the trouble stemmed from the fact that both Williams and Manley had spent so much time and energy convincing their supporters at home that their views were the only ones which were correct, that neither was now prepared to go back on anything he had said, or admit that he might have been mistaken. Both needed to rise to the occasion, he scolded: 'Shorn of all that they were told, the people of the West Indies want Federation . . . and are expecting their leaders to reach agreement.'

Williams may have been prepared to listen, but Manley was in a much less secure position at home, where an opposition politician was leading a campaign for Jamaica's withdrawal from the Federation. Even though the conference had been called to discuss independence for the West Indies, and before it ended a new plan for the Federation had been drawn up, this was not enough to save the day. Manley returned home, held and lost a referendum on whether Jamaica should remain in the Federation or not, and as a direct consequence – after vain last-minute attempts to keep it going – the Federation was dissolved in May 1962. Attempts to form a smaller Eastern Caribbean Federation, which were made during the next three years, all came to nothing. Bird was closely involved throughout, but eventually gave up in disgust when it became obvious that, without massive British aid to carry out a capital development programme in all the islands to provide a firm economic base for a new federation, Antigua was likely to end up worse off by having to subsidise some of the other members. The British Government's refusal even to discuss aid on the scale required was the main cause of the failure and not, as has often been stated since, the parochialism of the politicians involved, or an inability on their part to work together for the greater good; a point well made by one of the region's most astute historians in 1968:

It has become fashionable to label the history of the West Indies Federation a failure of the West Indian political spirit. But it was as much a failure of the British political spirit. That one abortive conference followed another was due, not to West Indian political childishness, but, frankly, to the fact that Great Britain was anxious to use Federation as a means of discarding its now unwanted responsibilities as a colonial power and to the fact, further, that she sought withdrawal from the Caribbean area without providing the sort of economic aid to which, on any showing, the colonies were entitled.[3]

•

This abrogation of responsibility was all too clear in Antigua in the 1960s, a period during which the sugar industry was in terminal decline and, under Bird's leadership, every effort was being made by his Government to establish a broader-based economy. The closure of the deal to build an oil refinery was brought about mainly through the Chief Minister's personal initiative, and nearly every other advance was made in the face of British indifference, disapproval or outright opposition.

Tourism had been encouraged since the early 1950s, with incentives given to individuals investing in hotels and 'resort development', and by 1965 the island had more than two dozen hotels and guest houses catering to around 50 000 visitors a year. Well before then it had become obvious that if the industry was to progress the airport – many of its facilities still not that much different from those turned over by the Americans in 1949 – needed modernising and enlarging. In 1962, as no aid from Britain was forthcoming for this, Bird had authorised the use of funds provided for other purposes to be diverted to airport improvements; an action which had infuriated the Administrator and, when reported to London, produced a threat to suspend the constitution. This came to nothing, unlike Bird's bold move a couple of years later which assisted in ensuring that funds for a much-needed runway extension were made available.

One of the main attractions of the island for visitors, other than its beaches, was the old naval dockyard at English Harbour; something which had been recognised even during Governor St Johnston's time in the 1930s. In 1948 an architect from the Ancient Monuments department of the Ministry of Works had reported that the more important buildings were well worth restoring, and that this could be done at a cost of about £48 000. As no one at the time could sensibly believe Britain would fund such a project nothing was done until, on Governor Blackburne's initiative, a restoration appeal was launched in 1951. This led to the dockyard being re-opened as a tourist attraction ten years later, after £40 000 had been raised. Although it must have been obvious by then that, even with the limited amount of restoration which had been carried out, the place had enormous potential for the new industry, none of the British princes, parliamentarians and other dignitaries who visited and extolled the 'romance' of English Harbour ever suggested that even a modest amount of official aid might replace private donations, and enable the dockyard to achieve that potential.

It was one thing for the British Government not to want to spend money on restoration work in a harbour which had long ceased to be of much practical use, but it was quite another to refuse to make funds available to develop the port facilities in St John's Harbour. The attempt to improve the access to the port by dredging undertaken in the early 1890s had landed the governor of the day in trouble with the Colonial office, and nothing of a similar nature had ever been tried since. Long before the outbreak of the Second World War the port of St John's had become a byword for delays and inefficiency for the masters of the large, deep-draught ships trading with the Caribbean from Europe and North America. By the early 1960s, with Caribbean cruising already well-established (even if only for the well-to-do with plenty of time to spare), a deep-water port with berthing alongside for ocean-going vessels had, in Bird's opinion, become essential if Antigua was to have a viable future. For the British Government, on the other hand, this was an expensive luxury that the island could do without, and one for which they had no intention of paying. If Antigua wanted such a port, then Antigua would have to find the money to pay for it; and the only assistance forthcoming would be in helping the Chief Minister to secure a loan. This was done in 1965, when US$7 million was obtained on easy terms from the Import Export Bank of the United States to pay for the design and construction of the required facilities. When work began on the project the following year, construction of the oil refinery about one mile north of the city limits was already well advanced, and an offshore bunkering station a couple of miles north of the harbour mouth, fed by an underwater pipeline, was about to go into use. At the same time, the signs of progress which all this activity brought with it were unfortunately not evident elsewhere on the island.

By 1965 the sugar industry had ceased to be the mainstay of the economy and was no longer the island's largest employer. With the advent of tourism and the introduction of an industrialisation programme all those who could find work away from the cane-fields had done so, leaving in some years a shortage of labour at harvest-time which had to be filled by importing temporary workers from other islands. Sugar-cane was grown on just over 15 000 acres, less than half the figure of a century earlier, with peasant farmers either owning or leasing one-third of the total. Early in the year the Government was informed by the board of Antigua Syndicate Estates that both the factory's water supply and the company's remaining financial resources were insufficient to guarantee their being able to process the new harvest. If the industry was not to collapse then and there Bird had no option but to arrange for an additional water supply, at the expense of other consumers, and to invest in the industry by purchasing 41 per cent of the issued shares, putting the Government another Eastern Caribbean (EC)$1 million in debt to do so. At the same time he asked the British Government to appoint one more in the long line of commissions to examine the industry and its prospects, and to study 'the means by which diversified agricultural production could be introduced with or without irrigation in order to reduce the Island's economic dependence on sugar production.'

In December, a month before the Commission's report was due to be delivered, Bird and his team once again faced a general election. The ATLU candidates this time were opposed by a new party, formed three years earlier by an estate owner and former civil servant named Robert Hall, which included some of the men who had contested the previous election. The Antigua–Barbuda Democratic Movement, the ABDM, which based its platform on the necessity in a democratic society of an elected opposition in the Legislature, campaigned boldly in spite of much intimidation, and contested all ten seats. Although none in the end was successful their victorious opponents were not given such an easy ride to victory as in the past.[4]

Bird's campaign was based on the need for further constitutional reform and the promise of independence, but many of his supporters had more immediate and down-to-earth concerns. Those in the sugar industry were worried about the industry's decline and the accompanying long-delayed wage rises; those in the burgeoning tourist industry about their exploitation by foreign hotel owners and airline operators; and those in the construction industry about the lack of union backing in wage negotiations. Since the introduction of the ministerial system the ATLU members in Government, not unnaturally given the new responsibilities they had acquired, had grown ever more detached from union affairs, and these were now almost entirely in the hands of the general secretary, George Walter, and his lieutenants. Before the election this had led to a number of disagreements between Walter and the Government about pay increases for certain groups of workers – including non-established Government employees – which the ABDM had been able to exploit to some extent. The result of the election did nothing to lessen the wrangling between the Government and the ATLU, or to reduce the size of the rift which had developed between the union's president and its general secretary. Nor were relations improved by the contents of the Sugar Industry Commission's report, received a few weeks after the elections had taken place.

In dealing with the possibilities of agricultural diversification, the report made various generalised recommendations about research programmes, reviews of existing legislation, marketing practices, distribution systems, and land tenure reform – all in connection with cotton, livestock and food crops – but came up with no specific proposals. The island was too dry, the soils too poor and the arable land too over-worked for the introduction of any new crop of economic significance. Along with the 15 000 acres under sugar-cane, 600 under cotton, and 1100 growing food crops, the Commission calculated there were no less than 34 000 acres of mixed scrub and grazing land. Of the last only about 1000 acres were of a quality capable of supporting a reasonably sized cattle population, while as far as agriculture was concerned all the rest was 'virtually worthless. The mixed scrub and rough grazing lies idle, and some of the scrub is quite impenetrable. Rough pastures comprise bahia and beard grasses which are unproductive and cannot support much livestock.'[5]

With regard to the sugar industry the Commission's views made even more depressing reading:

> We discovered . . . an industry which, in research and agricultural practices, has largely stood still over the past decade; an industry in which field, transport and factory are sadly in need of much new equipment, an attitude of reluctance to agriculture, and particularly sugar, by those who work in the field, and competition for water resources which may well result in an inadequate supply for cane cultivation as a whole.[6]

Rehabilitation of the industry would take five to six years 'in the most favourable circumstances', and between £2–3 million sterling 'would be required to finance the losses forecast for that period, the new equipment required for field, factory and transport and the cost of irrigation facilities.' But that was not all:

> Such a programme would call for ability and management of high order, and complete co-operation and identity of views between the Company and the people and Government of Antigua, not only in the short, but also the long, term. We regret to report that we could not see any chance of such a programme succeeding in the present and foreseeable circumstances of Antigua.[7]

Because of this the Commission's principal conclusion had to be that 'there is not, in our opinion, a long term future for the sugar industry in Antigua, with or without irrigation.'[8]

This forthright document was received just as the sugar-workers were urging the union to enter into negotiations with the Employers' Federation about an increase in daily wage rates in advance of the start of work on the 1966 harvest. As it was obvious to the Government that any increase in the wages bill could only put the industry into even more debt than it was already, the general secretary was told to inform the union's membership that no increase should be demanded, and to explain why this was necessary. Had relations between Bird and Walter not already been strained by this time, it is possible that this might have been done without stirring up too much of a fuss, but hardly likely. Not only had non-established government workers just been granted a substantial increase in pay, but every last cane-cutter was aware that the Government had for some reason recently given a million dollars to the factory owners. Walter knew only too well the base on which his constituency was founded, and greatly to the annoyance of the union's executive and the Government launched into protracted negotiations with the Employers' Federation over the wage issue. One result was that much of the crop was lost and only 7000 tons of sugar were produced. The other was that in August, soon after the management had thrown in their hand and given the labour force a 25 per cent pay increase all round, Antigua Syndicate Estates and the Antigua Sugar Factory went into receivership.

One of the main reasons why this came about, and the situation had been allowed to deteriorate as it did, was the fact that from the previous December the Chief Minister's mind had been on more elevated matters; and between the last week of February and the end of March he, the Administrator, and most of the Government were absent from the island in London.

•

The attempt to form some sort of federation among the smaller islands of the eastern Caribbean, which began when the Federation of the West Indies broke up and Jamaica and Trinidad and Tobago became independent, continued until August 1965, when the Government of Barbados announced its intention of seeking independence. After that, with no prospect of any viable association being formed by the remaining islands, Bird had directed his efforts towards following the example of Barbados. The early years of the 1960s had seen a transformation of both Antigua and the Chief Minister: the island acquiring the beginnings of a new economic base, largely as a result of its leader's intransigence in the face of British apathy or resistance, and Bird's reputation as an astute politician and a statesman-in-the-making increasing as a result. 'Mr Bird intensely dislikes interference from London', wrote the noted West Indian economist Sir Arthur Lewis in 1965, following the breakdown of the attempts to form an Eastern Caribbean Federation:

> He has worked an economic miracle in Antigua, developing the tourist trade to the point where the island's budget has been able to dispense (defiantly) with grant-in-aid. An oil refinery is being built in the island, and a deep water harbour is not far off.
>
> He is rightly proud of his achievements; sees Antigua as on the verge of self-sufficiency, and is in no mood to be dictated to.[9]

The election campaign which followed had reflected this mood, with the ATLU political committee's manifesto stating that one of their aims was independence for the island. 'The size and population of the territory should be no obstruction to independence', it asserted:

> We have been watching the attainment of independence by several states that have far less viable economies than Antigua and are of less strategic importance and we are determined that what they have secured, we also can win.[10]

This message had been registered in London, and a Memorandum with an outline of a suggested new constitution, giving the island 'self-government in a new relationship of association with Britain' arrived shortly after Bird's election victory in December.

As the Government was then asked to prepare detailed proposals for the constitutional arrangements required by this new relationship, prior to attending a conference in London in the spring of 1966, it is hardly surprising that before this conference opened on 28 February no one in the administration had much time for the travails of the sugar industry, or the contents of the Sugar Industry Commission report. By the time it had ended on 25 March and Bird, the Administrator, and their officials and advisors had returned to the island it was too late: the industry, being squeezed by its bankers on one hand and its workers on the other, and with most of the crop still standing unreaped, had lost all financial credibility and was beyond redemption.

The new constitution had been agreed after a great deal of argument and, although a Government mouthpiece was later to decry it as having been accepted reluctantly and unhappily, was more than the Chief Minister or anyone else on the island could ever have hoped for when the delegation had set off to attend the conference. Under a novel scheme, quickly termed 'independence in association', Antigua was to be given full internal self-government within a year, with Britain retaining responsibility for defence and certain aspects of external relations only and losing any further right to amend the constitution, while at the same time Antiguans would retain British citizenship. Government was to be totally transformed with the creation of the office of Premier, the introduction of Cabinet rule with collective responsibility, and the establishment of both a Senate and a House of Representatives. The latter initially would comprise ten elected members, with the number to be increased as required, while the ten members of the Senate would be appointed by the Governor on the advice of the Premier – the office of Governor having first been filled by someone nominated by the Premier for the approval of the Crown. In everything but a declaration of war, or the ability to appoint any cronies or financial backers he may have had to ambassadorial posts, the Premier of Antigua would exercise just as much power and authority as the Prime Minister of Great Britain. To many outside observers, as well as to the great majority of Antiguans, the new constitution was seen as offering the best of both worlds, the legislative equivalent of having one's cake and eating it.

Preparations for the introduction of the new form of government now took precedence over everything else, including the disaster which overtook the sugar industry in August and the increasing discord between members of the Government and the general secretary of the union to which they all belonged. A Statehood Committee was appointed to organise the appropriate celebrations, and the enthusiasm with which ordinary Antiguans looked forward to 'Statehood Day', set by Britain for the following February, was demonstrated in the 600 designs for a national flag, 517 variations of a new coat-of-arms and national motto, and 405 prospective national anthems submitted as entries in competitions run by the Committee. The winning entries – all of which remain in use today – were displayed or, in the case of the anthem, sung, for the first time on 1 November 1966, a date chosen by the Government for no very good reason to celebrate as 'State Day'. This drew a mixed welcome and was not widely observed, as the ABDM weekly newsletter reported afterwards:

> Apart from the display of State symbols . . . there was no evidence of the grand celebrations promised by Government – no street jump-up, no music; no assemblage of school children in their respective schools where patriotic addresses could be delivered . . . The children of the nation were told nothing; all they knew was that their schools were closed on that day.[11]

There were however several incidents which may have been seen by the more prescient Antiguans as omens, indicating that life after the official Statehood Day a few months hence was going to hold far more than the steady advance towards universal brotherhood and prosperity being promised by the Government. 'The only official State Day function . . . was a party at the Chief Minister's residence. 1700 guests were invited to the feast and preparation was made for that number of people', a somewhat jaundiced observer noted:

> Around the Chief Minister were his grandees, his henchmen, his bootlickers, his sycophants and others who were invited because of their standing in the community. It was noticeable, however, that not a single member of the Antigua–Barbuda Democratic Movement attended . . . Mr Bird treated his official State Day party as a private affair and would not invite the unofficial opposition to it.[12]

Towards the end of the function the same Jeremiah reported that 'the three-tier cake in the banquet hall apparently without cause toppled to the ground and broke in several pieces. The attendants feverishly picked up the bits and carried them away, but managed to make the necessary repairs [before bringing] back the cake to be cut by the Premier as a mark of the birth of the nation.'[13] Conspicuous among the 'grandees' who then received a slice was the Minister without Portfolio, dressed in 'a tall grey topper, cut-away tailed coat, white bow tie, striped morning pants [who] so stole the show that all the guests wondered if he was the governor-designate.'[14] Few of them, as they later watched the elegantly clad McChesney George dancing (albeit 'with his topper on'), could have suspected that within less than a year he and Bird would have become the bitterest of political enemies.

A great deal of genuine speculation took place between then and the official Statehood Day about who would become Governor, and who would be nominated to the Senate and to sit on bodies like the Public Service, Police Service and Constituency Commissions. Bird's choice – of a jurist born in Grenada of Antiguan parents, and until his acceptance of the nomination a puisne judge in Barbados – to be the Governor was inspired, and Sir Wilfred Jacobs was to serve Antigua well until his retirement in 1993. His other nominations were more expedient, the Senate being packed with a large majority of ATLU members, and a host of union sympathisers appointed to the various commissions. Novelle Richards, who after having been nominated to the Senate was elected its president, later recorded that 'many people were annoyed that they were left out, and criticisms were levelled at Bird for omitting persons who, it was thought, could make a better contribution to the Senate and Commissions than some who were selected. Even he, a full-time union official and ex-Federal Minister, 'felt that a less partisan approach could have been made to these appointments.'[15] Among the many who had hoped, but to whom nothing was given, was George Walter, whose failure to be appointed to the Senate only fuelled his bitterness and hastened a confrontation between Bird and himself.

The flag-raising ceremony which took place on Monday 27 February 1967 was attended by Arthur Bottomley, the Minister of Overseas Development and one of the lesser luminaries of the Labour Government in power in Britain at the time, who handed over the constitutional instruments which brought the new State of Antigua into being. More or less forgotten at the time, very much as they had been before, during and since the constitutional conference in London, were the twelve or thirteen hundred inhabitants of Barbuda – an island which received little more mention in the new constitution than deserted Redonda. That McChesney George had taken part in the London talks, and had been retained as Minister without Portfolio but with responsibility for Barbuda affairs in the Cabinet, was thought to offer his constituents more than enough to keep them happy. It was going to take only a matter of months to reveal that this view was very much mistaken.

22

Removing the Pillars

As far as I see the Antigua Trades and Labour Union is dead. Government has extracted all its teeth . . . Government has removed the pillars on which the union stands. The union cannot negotiate with any government department on behalf of the workers . . . If the president and all members of parliament do not resign from the executive of the ATLU I will form a new union in Antigua.

George Walter, addressing a public meeting 17 May 1967

Apart from the fact that they [Barbudans] are British citizens, the people of Barbuda are in extreme doubt as to their present status now that Antigua has been granted Independence in Association with Britain.

Antigua Star, 6 March 1968

With the Statehood Day celebrations safely out of the way, the problems connected with the bankrupt sugar industry and the growing row between the union's executive and its general secretary returned to exercise the minds of the newly created Premier and Cabinet. In April the Government raised another huge loan, this time of nearly EC$6 million and bought the entire assets of the Antigua Syndicate Estates and the Antigua Sugar Factory. 'At one bold stroke', their apologist recorded a few years later, 'the Government became the proud owner of almost all the arable land in the State without the bitterness and confrontations usually associated with Government's acquisition.'[1] In fact there was nothing to be proud of: unless several thousand men and women were to be thrown out of work the Government had no option but to acquire the industry; and the directors and creditors of both companies were more than delighted with the deal – knowing full well that the huge increase in pay for the workers they had agreed with Walter the previous year had effectively ruined any chance of the industry being run at a profit.

Trouble broke out immediately. One member of the statutory board appointed to run the newly nationalised concern was McChesney George who, on orders from Bird 'told the board's chief accountant to cut wages by 30 per cent across the industry.' This was done, much to the chagrin of the rest of the board, who were not consulted; greatly to the distress of the workers, many of whom then left the industry for ever; and to the fury of Walter, who at the beginning of May was accused by Bird of disloyalty at an emergency meeting of the union's executive and dismissed as general secretary. His main supporter, a union field officer named Donald Halstead, was fired at the same time, and another field officer a day or so later. Their dismissals caused more consternation among the union's rank and file than Bird, as its president, or any of the other members of the executive could possibly have imagined, and all three made the most of the opportunities this presented. On 9 May, four days after their expulsion, they gave their version of events at a public meeting, laying much stress on the conflict of interest which resulted from the fact that the Premier and his ministers all belonged to the ATLU. Eight days later, at an even bigger outdoor meeting, Walter dwelt on this at length, finally ending his discourse by stating that if Bird 'and all the members of parliament do not resign from the executive of the ATLU, I will form a new union in Antigua.' Safe in the knowledge that such resignations were not going to take place he lost no time in putting his promise into effect, and the Antigua Workers' Union (AWU) was formed a few days later with Walter as its general secretary.

Within the space of two months the AWU was claiming a membership of 3–4000 and, even if such figures were an exaggeration, this gave both the ATLU and the Government cause for concern. The majority of the non-established government workers and the employees of the sugar industry, who together formed the largest section of the island's workforce, knew on which side their bread was buttered, and remained loyal to the ATLU. This left the AWU to concentrate on recruiting from among hotel, construction and waterfront workers. In no time at all, with one union battling to retain its supremacy by victimising workers who showed signs of disloyalty, and the other endeavouring to poach from its rival or to unionise workers previously ignored, a deep and lasting division had been made in the entire Antiguan labour force. Matters were made worse by the positions adopted by the Government, the Employers' Federation, and by Bird himself. While the Government, the Federation, and other employers who did not belong to the latter all refused to recognise that the AWU now had the right to represent some or all of their workers, and so added to the discord, Bird's supine attitude and seeming inability to appreciate the harm being done to the new state puzzled both his enemies and his supporters. 'Bird withdrew into himself', one of the latter recorded.

> He was inwardly hurt, and saw before him workers for whom he had spent all his life to help and a country whose economic development and social uplift came about through his efforts and the efforts of his colleagues turn ungrateful and were won over by deceit.[2]

Whether ingratitude and deception were involved or not, Walter's efforts to increase the AWU membership led to a series of disputes, strikes and marches lasting until March 1968, when they culminated in a call for a general strike.

The strike began on Saturday 16 March, and involved all those who had joined the AWU – hotel employees, shop assistants, airline staff, and the core of the union's support, the waterfront workers. Nothing particularly untoward happened until the following Monday when members of the Defence Force, who had been called out over the weekend, were discovered attempting to discharge the cargo of a schooner. This was soon brought to a halt by Walter and a gang of strikers who afterwards, in order to protest the use of such 'government-backed scabs', organised a march on the Premier's official residence. Beating up a member of the Defence Force they came across on the way, the marchers arrived at the residence to find it under armed guard, and access denied to all but a small delegation with a petition demanding full recognition for the AWU. Having delivered this and received the Premier's assurance that the situation would be resolved, the demonstrators dispersed, returning to their homes by early evening just in time to hear that a state of emergency had been declared.

Although this specifically banned 'all assemblies and gatherings of five or more persons in any public place', as well as picketing and the carrying of placards, it had little effect, and by nightfall the streets of St John's were crowded with AWU supporters refusing to disperse until they had been addressed by Walter and his immediate associates. After lengthy negotiations with a harassed police chief, who had far too few men at his disposal to prevent it, a short public meeting took place – much of it occupied with 'praying and singing' – before the streets were emptied.

The following morning, totally ignoring the provisions of the state of emergency, and with even more support from workers who had now joined them in sympathy, the AWU strikers again gathered in the city. This time the police and Defence Force were better prepared, and in scenes which must have been reminiscent of those which had taken place in March 1918, fighting broke out between large groups of angry men and women who considered they were being denied their basic rights, and small units of armed men hardly trained in crowd control and scared of being overwhelmed. The police countered bottles and stones with tear gas and baton charges in, for the most part, disciplined attempts to keep the peace, but the badly trained and poorly led part-time soldiers, once they had been given permission to use their firearms, acted in a much less orderly manner. During the day, as they cleared the streets, often firing at random, they managed to wound no fewer than fifty-eight people, one of them a young boy. In retaliation a fire was started in the magistrates' court, and during the night a number of other public buildings were set ablaze.

The situation was prevented from deteriorating even further by the arrival from Barbados the next day of Desmond Kerr, the Deputy British Government Representative for the Associated States, who swiftly and skilfully arranged a formal meeting between Bird and Walter under the chairmanship of the Governor, Sir Wilfred Jacobs. As a result, Bird agreed to give full recognition to the AWU and to make it known that workers had complete freedom to join whichever union they chose. At the same time he also agreed to increase the number of seats in the House of Representatives from ten to twelve, in order to provide a better chance of a parliamentary opposition being elected; something for which opposition groups like the ABDM who were represented at the meeting, had been calling since the state came into being. Afterwards both Bird and Walter made placatory radio broadcasts, the strike was called off, and the state of emergency was lifted; bringing to an end an unpleasant and largely unnecessary series of events which had further undermined the Premier's standing. One reason why the agreement had been reached so quickly and Bird had been, and remained, so ready to compromise (he soon increased the additional seats in the House of Representatives to four), was because he probably felt that the state had already been showing sufficient sign of falling apart before the whole ugly episode had begun.

•

Among the Associated States in which Desmond Kerr represented the interests of Great Britain was the one known by the cumbersome name of St Kitts–Nevis–Anguilla, which like Antigua had come into being in February 1967. Soon afterwards the people of Anguilla, incensed at being lumped together with St Kitts under an antipathetic Government, had rebelled, burnt down Government House, expelled the Warden and the police force (all from St Kitts), and begun a constitutional crisis which was not to be resolved until Anguilla became a British colony again fifteen years later. All that had transpired there had been observed with the keenest interest in Barbuda, which was perceived by its inhabitants as now being nothing more than a colony of Antigua, and soon many were agitating for action of a similar nature. Whether their parliamentary representative felt the same way to begin with is doubtful (a ministerial salary and slices of cake from the hands of the Premier being as attractive as they were), but well before the end of 1967 McChesney George had more than sensed which way the wind was blowing. He met with Bird on several occasions, pressing him either to make the development of the island a priority or to 'release Barbuda from your administration, return it to Britain as an associated state, and give her a chance to plan her own financial future.'[3] As such appeals only served to irritate and then annoy the Premier, at the beginning of December he relieved George of any further responsibility for Barbudan affairs, much to the latter's mortification.

A day or two later, still in a state of shock but, as he later informed Bird, clinging 'desperately to the last vestiges of my admiration and respect for you which has been built up by close and friendly relations for a quarter of a century',[4] he returned to his homeland and called a public meeting. At this he told his assembled constituents that he was now all in favour of secession and needed the support of a delegation to represent this to the Government of Antigua. In throwing his hat into the ring in this way he went back on all he had agreed to at the London conference in March 1966, and put an end once and for all to the 'close and friendly relations' he had once enjoyed with Bird who, when a report of the meeting reached him, ordered an extra twenty-five policemen to be sent to Barbuda and imposed a ban on further public assemblies. The arrival of the police contingent did nothing to improve Barbudan views of their relationship with Antigua, any more than did the reception given to the delegation George led to see the Premier. As their talks failed to produce anything other than a promise by Bird of an investigation into Barbuda's potential for development George resigned from the Government, offering as his reason that he no longer felt 'able to continue in the service of a government whose policy is to suppress the free expression of the thoughts and views of people because they happen to be a minority group.'

The next few weeks passed without incident, but on 5 March George, now the 'former Minister without portfolio' and an independent member of the House of Representatives, led a demonstration march through Codrington involving, according to a report in the following day's edition of the *Antigua Star*, 'every Barbudan except the very young, the old and feeble and the few civil servants', to present a petition to the Warden. Addressed to the Queen, this charged that the islanders had 'been neglected socially and economically by the Government of Antigua both before and after a measure of internal self-government [had] been granted to them', and that

> Antigua, itself an underdeveloped territory which requires substantial outside finance to assist in its own development, is unable to supply the finance required to meet Barbuda's basic needs, and certainly cannot finance its . . . development.[5]

As Barbudans remained British citizens, the British Government was asked to instruct the Antiguan Government to withdraw the police contingent, to draw up a constitution for Barbuda, and 'to secure the disassociation of the island from the State of Antigua.' The petition would not have been welcomed by the British Government at the best of times, but in the spring of 1968, with the Anguillan imbroglio on their hands, it was the last thing anyone in Whitehall wanted to read. All that was taking place in Barbuda was judged to be an internal problem and the petition was returned to Antigua, where it landed on the Premier's desk at much the same time as Walter and the AWU called their general strike.

At the time the petition was drawn up the general appearance of Barbuda had barely changed since the beginning of the twentieth century. The quality of most of the housing in Codrington had been improved (although concrete block construction was not to begin for another decade and there were still one or two wattle-and-daub huts to be seen), an airstrip had been laid just outside the village in 1958, and a hotel had been built in the far south-eastern corner, but otherwise the island looked very much as it had when the first Warden had

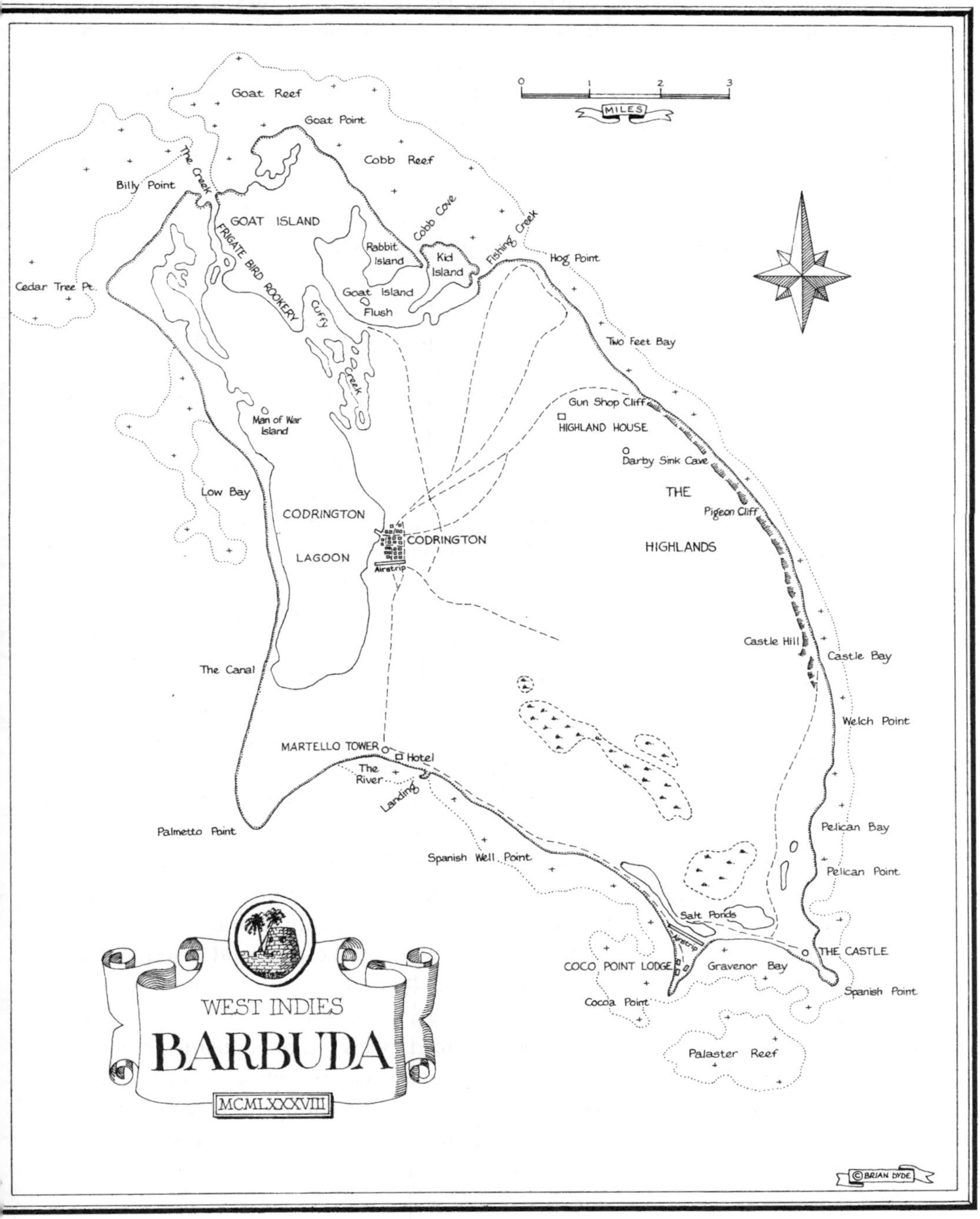

MILES
0 1 2 3
Goat Reef
Goat Point
Cobb Reef
Billy Point
The Creek
GOAT ISLAND
FRIGATE BIRD ROOKERY
Rabbit Island
Cobb Cove
Kid Island
Fishing Creek
Hog Point
Cedar Tree Pt.
Goat Island
Flush
Cuffy Creek
Two Feet Bay
Gun Shop Cliff
HIGHLAND HOUSE
Darby Sink Cave
Man of War Island
Low Bay
THE HIGHLANDS
Pigeon Cliff
CODRINGTON LAGOON
CODRINGTON
Airstrip
Castle Hill
Castle Bay
The Canal
Welch Point
MARTELLO TOWER
Hotel
The River
Landing
Palmetto Point
Pelican Bay
Spanish Well Point
Pelican Point
Salt Ponds
Airstrip
THE CASTLE
COCO POINT LODGE
Gravenor Bay
Cocoa Point
Spanish Point
Palaster Reef
WEST INDIES
BARBUDA
MCMLXXXVIII
©BRIAN DYDE

been appointed in 1904. The various agricultural projects – schemes to grow cotton, coconuts, peanuts or vegetables in commercial quantities – had all come to nothing; not all as a result of poor soil and low rainfall, but just as much because the Barbudans had no wish to perpetuate the sort of lives lived by their forebears. Much of their income derived from remittances sent home by men and women who had emigrated to Britain or the United States, but those who benefited from this lived in conditions which, even in comparison with Antigua, still bordered on the primitive.

All the islanders lived in Codrington, where under the communal system of land distribution no one possessed clear title to a dwelling, and sites for new houses were allocated by the Warden. Any house left unoccupied at death, if there was no immediate family member to take it over, reverted to the community and could be allocated by the Warden in lieu of a fresh building site. Plots of land outside the village which had been cleared and fenced by individuals with the Warden's permission were used for subsistence farming. Running water was unheard of, and all the inhabitants depended on what they could obtain from the village well for drinking, cooking and hygiene purposes. A walled catchment area known as the Duck Pond provided water for washing clothes. An electricity supply, begun as a private venture in 1962, provided an erratic source of artificial light for a few hours each night. The children attended a school built in the previous century, where they could obtain no more than a primary education. There was no hospital, no clinic and no resident doctor. A medical officer from Antigua was supposed to pay quarterly visits, but rarely appeared more than once or twice a year, and then never remained on the island for more than one day at a time. Outside the village communication remained, if not on foot, then on donkey or horseback along tracks which over a period of nearly 300 years had become deeply rutted and potholed. Motorised transport consisted of no more than the Warden's Landrover and a couple of tractors.

To visit the island from Antigua was an experience very similar to stepping back fifty years in time, as George and his delegation had tried to bring home to Bird at their meeting in December 1967 by informing him that to provide Barbudans with even the basics of modern life – running water, a proper electricity supply, one or two paved roads, a cottage hospital and a secondary school – would probably cost around EC$10 million. Unfortunately it was something that the Premier, already alarmed by all that had transpired since Walter's dismissal from the ATLU, and disturbed by his loss of popularity, did not want to know. As a result the Barbudans, far too small in number to make their plight of any interest to the world at large, were left to struggle on as best they could; with only modest and reluctant help from Antigua and no improvement in the way they were governed for another eight years.

•

Bird's self-esteem took another knock in August 1968 when the promised by-elections for four new seats in the House of Representatives were held. Four months earlier another political party, the Progressive Labour Movement (PLM) had been formed which had attracted enough support from among disenchanted members of the ABDM to replace the latter as the main opposition party. As it had also become affiliated to the AWU this had given a vice-president of the union, Donald Halstead, a chance to ignore Walter's protestations about keeping the union out of politics and to offer himself as a candidate for one of the new seats. He was elected easily enough, as were the other three PLM candidates, including Robert Hall, one of those who had switched his allegiance from the ABDM. Having taken their seats, and having been recognised in the House as the official opposition, they demanded – as was provided for in the constitution – opposition representation in the Senate. To avoid a crisis the three sitting senators who were not directly connected with the ATLU were persuaded by Bird to give up their seats, and were replaced by three PLM nominees.

Throughout the late 1960s, while such changes were taking place on the political stage, equally important events were happening elsewhere, not least in attempts to broaden the economy and to improve the quality of life. The oil refinery, which had been under construction for the previous three years, began refining operations early in 1967, and a year later was at its maximum capacity of 10 000 barrels a day, producing gasoline, diesel oil, jet fuels and liquefied petroleum gas. Three years later its capacity was increased to 16 000 barrels a day. Besides supplying all Antigua's needs for these products, the West Indies Oil Company (WIOC) also sold to other islands, to other Natomas companies in North America, and on the open market. The refinery also supplied its profitable bunkering operation to the north of the entrance to St John's Harbour, inside which by October 1968 the new deep-water port facilities had been completed.

The construction of the port brought about a complete break with the past; the need for gangs of unskilled lightermen, boatmen and stevedores faded at the same rate as the requirement arose for skilled mechanics, fork-lift truck drivers, crane operators and tug crews. It was a situation which could have been resolved easily enough with foresight and plenty of information bulletins, a re-training programme and a redundancy plan – all the things a trade union is supposed to obtain from an employer for its members. In this case, however, as the employer was the Government and the waterfront workers belonged to the AWU, none of these was achieved, and the Premier attended a dedication ceremony at the new facilities on 31 October 'under an atmosphere of tension'.[6] Instead of being opened to shipping at that time the new port remained inoperative until the following July; none of the dockers were prepared to work until properly trained and their redundant colleagues had been given severance pay. After that St John's

Harbour never looked back. It now took a freighter one or two days to discharge its cargo instead of a week, and with the cruise-liner traffic constantly increasing berths at the new wharf were soon at a premium. Within a decade of being opened all the port's facilities were under severe strain from the amount of shipping being handled.

One commodity which was not much in evidence once the deep-water harbour was in full operation was sugar, as there was nothing much anyone could do to revive the ailing industry which produced it. The 1965 Report had spelled out what was needed in terms of money, management skills and worker commitment, and none of these was forthcoming. Before being taken over by the Government production had rarely fallen below 20 000 tons a year, and on occasion had been over 30 000 tons. From 1967 until the industry collapsed five years later production averaged less than 5000 tons a year.

Tourism had now replaced sugar as the mainstay of the economy. The number of beds available for visitors in hotels and guest houses tripled between 1961 and 1968, as did the receipts from the industry, reaching EC$21 million in the latter year when nearly 56 000 tourist arrivals were recorded – over four times the figure for 1958. The establishment of the industry had not taken place without its fair share of problems, nearly all to do with the fact that the majority of the hotels were under foreign ownership and operated, in the main, by managements only too eager to exploit cheap black labour while trying to keep the island's best beaches as all-white preserves. This sort of attitude had led to a number of clashes between the Government, the ATLU and some of the more bigoted and obstreperous hoteliers, before acceptance of the unionisation of hotel employees and unlimited access to all beaches (a freedom on which Bird, much to his credit, took an uncompromising stand) was achieved.

Another problem associated with the growth of the tourist industry was that, while it was good for the economy, it exacerbated the effects of the island's perennial water shortage: each additional hotel room and tourist arrival increased the demand for something which could often only be supplied to the detriment of the population at large. In 1967, in an attempt to deal with this once and for all, a contract was placed with an engineering concern in the United States for the construction of a large desalination plant on Crabbs peninsula. When completed it was hoped this would produce 1 200 000 gallons of fresh water a day, and that the associated generating station would provide a sizeable proportion of the island's demand for electricity. At much the same time, after a study carried out by British engineers, work began on the creation of a large reservoir in the lowest part of the island lying between the villages of All Saints and Newfield. With the construction of two small dams about a mile apart, water from the Shekerley Mountains which had previously flowed in times of heavy rain into the sea at Nonsuch Bay and Willoughby Bay, was trapped and over a period of time formed a shallow lake covering parts of the Yeamans, Little Duers and Delaps estates. With an area of about 320 acres Potworks Reservoir, as it soon became known, had a capacity calculated at around 1 billion gallons – a figure which, given the erratic rainfall and a vast evaporation rate, was largely theoretical. Although officially 'opened' in May 1970, little of the water could be used for another five years until a water treatment plant, designed to handle 2 million gallons a day, had been built and the necessary distribution system installed. This was done just in time, as by 1975 the desalination plant – like the sugar factory – had been closed down because the Government did not have the skilled manpower and financial resources to operate and maintain it properly.

That not enough money was available to keep the desalination plant running was not surprising, given the state of the economy in the middle of the 1970s, but the lack of sufficient numbers of suitably qualified personnel had more to do with the state of the educational system during previous decades. Although the number of primary schools had been increased substantially between the end of the Second World War and the achievement of statehood, more or less keeping pace with the number of children entering school age, secondary education had been greatly neglected and higher education all but ignored. Only one public secondary school existed until 1964 when the Antigua Girls' High School and the Antigua Grammar School were acquired by the Government, and only two more were opened before 1971. Until 1972, post-secondary education or training was limited to attendance at the Leeward Islands Teachers' Training College at Golden Grove a mile or so south of St John's, which had replaced the old college at Spring Gardens in 1959, or to the pursuit of basic courses in a few trade occupations at a training centre established in 1961 by the US International Co-operation Administration. In 1972 a new college at Golden Grove was opened, offering both teacher and technical training courses. Any higher education, or more specialist training, was only obtainable abroad, limited to those who could afford to pay for it, or the fortunate very few given Government scholarships – the selection for one of which, regrettably, depended more on the political persuasion of the applicant's parents than on any academic ability. To a cynical outside observer at the start of the 1970s, the education system would have appeared to be designed to produce a huge, barely literate, unskilled and compliant workforce, leavened by a sizeable contingent of trained but equally compliant hotel-workers, plumbers, motor-mechanics and electricians, together with the necessary number of teachers trained to perpetuate the system; the whole topped off by a small elite of lawyers, doctors and other graduate professionals all under some obligation to the Government and equally willing to support the status quo. To one such observer, supplied by the British Overseas Development Administration in 1972 to report on the educational development of the island, it was a system which had 'produced less satisfactory results than any of its neighbours in the Eastern

Caribbean', and one in which even 'The level of attainment in literacy and numeracy at the end of the primary course is a cause for concern.'[7]

The deficiencies of the educational system became ever more apparent after 1967 when Antigua became more dependent on its own resources. Together with the effects of all the turmoil which had accompanied the creation of the AWU, and the inspiration offered by the PLM's by-election successes, this brought about a marked shift in public opinion. Before the end of the decade the ATLU and its leaders in Government could no longer count on the wholehearted uncritical support of the mass of the island's workers; and for many the Premier had ceased to be 'Papa Bird', the man lauded on Statehood Day as the 'kind and benevolent leader to whom they could take their problems and who would fight for them through thick and thin.'[8] Instead he was seen as an increasingly remote and sometimes vindictive politician whose hegemony had lasted too long.

In October 1969, after twenty-five years in the position – and thirteen years after being advised by the British Government to do so – Bird finally resigned as president of the ATLU, but he did so only in order to become leader of the political party then founded by the union, the Antigua Labour Party. Prior to this, although reference had been made at election times to such a party, the ALP had had no formal existence, being merely a shorthand for the political committee of the ATLU. A month later George Walter, in contradiction of his frequently stated dictum that a trade union had no business being directly involved with a political party, packed the annual conference of the PLM with supporters of his union and got himself elected leader of that party in place of Robert Hall. It then required considerable pressure to be brought upon him by the rest of the party before, with great reluctance, he resigned his post as the AWU's general secretary at the end of January 1970. Afterwards both parties, each under a leader who had very good reason to detest the other, set about preparing for the next general election, due before the end of the year and at which the number of seats to be contested would be increased to seventeen.

The following months saw a renewal of clashes between the Government and the AWU, mainly over the insistence of the union's leaders that they had a right to represent civil servants, which had a widespread effect on the community as a whole and brought about further polarisation in society. Even though the AWU was now under a new general secretary, and largely freed from the machinations of men like Walter and Halstead, there was no doubt in anyone's mind that it was tied to the PLM, and that to be a member of one organisation involved automatic support of the other. The union may not have had things go all its own way during the year, but its dynamism and willingness to take on the Government gained it plenty of approbation from among the non-unionised, the unemployed, and disaffected ATLU members, approval which was then re-directed in support of the PLM. At the same time the feeling arose among those mainly middle-class people who had previously given their support to the ABDM or the ANP that – just possibly – an opposition party now existed which could bring an end to what they considered an excessive period of one-party rule. This was not a view shared by the entire middle class by any means, as was shown by the support given to the Antigua People's Party (APP), which had been formed the previous year in one more attempt by Rowan Henry to found a viable political party with no connection with trade unionism. In the event it turned out to be his last attempt. The APP was to fare no better than the ABDM or ANP had in previous elections, and in 1974 'after prolonged negotiation and much soul searching' Henry agreed to merge his party with the ALP. A year later both he and his wife were murdered in a senseless attack carried out by their deranged gardener.

As the 1970 election approached the break with the leadership of the ATLU, which had been brought about by the creation of the ALP, worked against the Government's best interests. The union, under a weaker leadership, and with a general feeling among the rank and file that they had somehow been deserted, was no longer able, or indeed all that willing, to give an election campaign the level of support it had provided in the past. As a senior party figure was to record later, well before the due date for the election:

> The ALP seemed to be suffering from old age, or inertia. The Government was wobbling along, and it was clear that unless some spectacular development in the party came about that the party was doomed to defeat.[9]

In fact the Government was wobbling so much that Bird allowed its five-year term, the maximum permitted under the constitution, to expire without setting an election date. Apart from any constitutional issue involved this merely added to the general impression that he was no longer fit to lead the State, and that his Government deserved to be thrown out of office.

When the election eventually took place in February 1971 not only did Walter and the PLM sweep into power with thirteen seats, but Bird was not even among the ALP members who won the remaining four. Such an unceremonious dismissal from a position of power gradually and legitimately acquired over a period of more than a quarter of a century would probably have ended the career of most men of his age – he was sixty-one at the time – but he had not come this far from his days as 'a Salvation Army drummer boy'[10] without also acquiring a formidable strength of character. Knowing full well that there was little chance of a return to power before 1975 but also, as the British Prime Minister Harold Wilson had said a few years earlier, that a week was a long time in politics, he soon came to terms with his loss, turned over chairmanship of the ALP to one of his sons, Lester Bird, and settled into the position of a watchful recluse.

23
For Good, or Come What May

> The time has arrived when we should part company. We must of necessity continue to hold on to our mother country: Great Britain. As unlike Antigua, we are not nearly ready to take such a giant step; nor do we think it is fair to Antigua that we should be saddling a new struggling nation with our own problems which are many.
>
> Eric Burton, Parliamentary Representative for Barbuda (1979)

> *Arise all Antiguans;*
> *Salute the fateful day*
> *Of our independence*
> *For good, or come what may.*
> *Antiguans march onward*
> *United, strong and free.*
> *From eastward and westward*
> *God bless our liberty.*
>
> Novelle H. Richards
> *Arise All Antiguans* (1981)

The twelve men from among whom Walter was able to choose to form his Government included three lawyers, Gerald Watt, Sydney Christian and Claude Francis; two other university graduates, Geoffrey Scotland and Selvyn Walter (George's half-brother); an ex-secondary school headmaster, Basil Peters; a licensed land surveyor, Sydney Prince; and the former senior civil servant Robert Hall: a fact which caused the new Premier, after he had handed them their ministerial appointments, to boast that he had the most educated Cabinet in the region.

This may or may not have been true, but by the time the new session of Parliament opened on 25 February 1971 he certainly had – for the size of the State and the number of its inhabitants – one of the largest. Either from having to fulfil promises made before the election took place, or more likely in a perverse attempt to show the world that his Government was twice as good as that of Bird, Walter found a ministerial post or its equivalent for all but two of the twelve; including one for Scotland who 'by a very strange move was appointed Cabinet Secretary, the only known unofficial appointment of this kind in the Commonwealth and under a parliamentary system of Government.'[1] Among his other appointments, around all of which much was to transpire later, were that of his half-brother to Trade and Tourism, the less academically endowed Donald Halstead to Home Affairs, Prince to Public Works, and Francis – the Barbudan who had defeated McChesney George – to Barbudan Affairs. Walter himself retained the Finance Ministry. In the Senate, that resting place for worthy placemen or unelectable party faithfuls, seven seats were given to PLM supporters, including the president of the AWU and one made Minister without Portfolio. Two had to be given to the ALP (one of which was filled by Lester Bird), and the last to another Barbudan.

The new Government, led by a Premier who had no parliamentary experience whatsoever and who, up until he assumed power, had spent his life mostly in confrontation with the forces of law and order, the business community and the majority of the foreign investors who had been attracted to the island, ran into trouble almost immediately. It had assumed office with no clear alternative policies to those of its predecessor, having been elected in the main by people interested only in the removal of Bird and an end to the ATLU's influence on the running of the State, and it quickly adopted a policy of widespread victimisation of one sort or another. Known ATLU members among public service workers were laid off or threatened; Bird appointees to public service boards were replaced; the many policemen who had been recruited from other islands were summarily dismissed and deported; the Defence Force – considered to be very much Bird's private army – was disbanded; institutions which had been set up by the deposed Premier such as the Industrial Development Board, the Industrial Court and the Central Housing Authority were either abolished or deprived of funds; outside investors with any connection with the previous Government were obstructed or forced into abandoning projected developments; and a determined effort was made to suppress the freedom of the press through acts imposing licensing fees and the deposition of sureties to meet defamation awards which became law on 1 January 1972.

Time was found amidst all these shenanigans to commission yet one more report on the prospects for the sugar industry – as it turned out, the last that would ever be needed. Nothing to do with the industry had changed since the 1965 inquiry, except that by now it was nearly EC $6 million in debt, and the report prepared by a firm of accountants found that it 'could not be revived as a commercially viable proposition', before going on to state:

> That while under certain favourable circumstances the social benefits of rehabilitating the Sugar Industry could exceed the social cost, on account of the vagaries of the weather and declining productivity of the land, as well as

the constantly rising cost of production together with other factors, it was highly unlikely that the social benefits would ever exceed the social cost.[2]

To make matters worse the authors of the report were 'unable to suggest an alternative agro-industry capable of providing year-round employment for 900 workers (the average number employed by the sugar industry), which would make a positive contribution to the economy and which could be developed in the foreseeable future.' Some agricultural development could take place in livestock, cotton and vegetable production, it was thought, but only if the Government was prepared to enter further into debt and invest some EC$2 million over a nine-year period. As this was unacceptable the decision to abandon the 1972 cane crop, close the factory, and finish with sugar once and for all – while both sensible and long overdue – was reached without offering anything to take its place. Very soon, as a result of this, distrust of and dissatisfaction with the Walter Government had risen to a level matched only by the bedraggled appearance given to much of the island by the uncut and overgrown fields of cane.

In April, following earlier ATLU-inspired marches made in protest against the abandonment of the sugar industry, a number of these fields were set on fire, adding areas of scorched earth to the growing scene of dereliction. Arson was then succeeded by bomb threats at the airport and in St John's, by the sabotage of power lines and, in June, by the theft of arms and explosives from the main police magazine on Crabbs Peninsula. Responsibility for all of this was claimed by a group calling themselves, in a scurrilous news-sheet which appeared on the streets from time to time, the Antigua Freedom Fighters. The distress caused by subsequent small explosions at a communications relay station and the income tax office, and by death threats issued to one or two public figures and some foreign investors, was not eased by the seeming inability of the undermanned and demoralised police force to track down, or even unearth, any reliable information about the perpetrators. Nor were members of the general public reassured by the Home Affairs Minister Halstead's decision to employ his own 'special constables' to look for the stolen arms and explosives – any more than they were by the introduction of a new Public Order Act giving the uniformed police powers to regulate public meetings and marches and, when they considered it necessary, to conduct searches without warrants. The recruitment and arming of the so-called 'special Police', among them 'some persons of known criminal record and others of doubtful character',[3] was particularly resented, smacking as it did of events in Haiti, where the notorious Tonton Macoutes had operated for many years in league with the regular and wholly partisan police force. Law-abiding citizens felt increasingly intimidated; prospective tourists and other overseas visitors were deterred; and potential foreign investors were alarmed by what they saw as the beginnings of a police state.

Even after the revised Public Order Act became law at the end of November, and with Halstead's ruffians to assist in the search, another eight months passed before the Antigua Freedom Fighters' terror campaign was brought to a halt. It ended, as the result of an anonymous tip-off, with the discovery of printing equipment and a quantity of newly printed Freedom Fighter news-sheets in the home of a man named Clarence Pilgrim, identified as 'a leading figure in the ALP and AT&LU.'[4] Like Dorothy and her travelling companions killing the Wicked Witch of the West and revealing the true identity of the Wizard of Oz, in arresting Pilgrim the police released the island from the spell of the Antigua Freedom Fighters. Although Pilgrim was in all probability the originator – and more than likely its only member, as all threats, sabotage attempts and explosions ended with his arrest – this will never be known for sure. Represented by two lawyers, Lester Bird and Vere Bird Jr, who used every delaying tactic known to the West Indian legal profession, a date for Pilgrim's trial was successfully delayed throughout the remaining years of the PLM Government, and all charges were dropped after the ALP returned to power in 1976.

With such matters exercising the collective mind of the Cabinet during the PLM's first two years in office it was hardly surprising that the Government was in no condition to deal effectively with the economic crisis which overtook the island, as it did the rest of the world, in 1973, following the Arab–Israeli War and the huge resulting increase in oil prices. Already adversely affected by internal events the island's tourist industry suffered immediately: the cost of air travel increased, air routes were abandoned, the amount of time and money available for vacations was reduced, hotels laid off staff or closed down altogether, and any remaining interest in investment ceased. The region's only inter-island airline, Leeward Islands Air Transport (LIAT) which had been founded in Antigua in 1956 and based there ever since, was forced into receivership, an event which involved the Government in protracted negotiations with many of the other islands, Great Britain and eventually Venezuela in order to find a means of keeping it in existence. The oil crisis was only partially responsible for its collapse, as at the time LIAT was a subsidiary of a British travel firm whose grandiose ideas and high-spending profile sat uneasily with mediocre management skills and a lack of airline operating experience. The re-organised LIAT (1974) company was jointly owned by the governments of Antigua and ten other of the Commonwealth Caribbean countries between Jamaica and Guyana.

The assistance which the British Government had undertaken to provide in 1971, to finance a five-year economic and social development programme covering everything from freshwater distribution through road and agricultural improvements to school extensions, at a total cost of £3 750 000, began to look increasingly paltry long before the five-year period had ended. That such aid did not come entirely without strings was demonstrated in December 1973 when, much to everyone's surprise and the relief of many, the Minister of Home Affairs and the Minister of Trade and Tourism were dismissed: their removal universally understood, although never openly admitted, as having been made a stipulation for continuance of the aid programme. Both men had shown they were quite unfit to hold public office. Halstead's private police force had been disbanded shortly before 'when the men became disgruntled due to the inability of the Government to meet the cost of its upkeep' and it was discovered their 'loyalty to the Minister did not go beyond the receipt of the pay envelope'.[5] He was now sacked because he 'had brought Antigua to the verge of becoming a totalitarian State' and because his ministry was thought 'responsible for setting up alleged pockets of vice and prostitution in the State by the granting of permits to adventuresses from Santo Domingo to carry out their illicit trade.'[6] Selvyn Walter had to go because his ministry had become 'a ministry of no trade and merely served as a launching pad for the Minister's peregrinations abroad and at considerable expense to a depleted treasury.'[7]

Although the Premier's action in taking a broom to the Augean Stables in this way delighted the population at large, it did nothing to improve the economy. This received another blow in 1974 when the price of crude oil rose to a height which made it no longer profitable to continue refining operations in Antigua. A year later the refinery closed down and WIOC became little more than an internal supplier and distributor of petroleum products. The disused refinery then added one more major eyesore to a landscape already disfigured both by unharvested sugar-cane and the results of a very severe earthquake which had struck the island, fortunately causing no deaths or any serious injuries, early one morning in October 1973. St John's had been particularly badly hit, with damage occurring to many of the older and more substantial buildings, including the Cathedral, the courthouse, the public library and the Treasury. Elsewhere churches and other large buildings were badly affected, as were installations at the port and at the oil refinery.

Perhaps the only part of the island showing any signs of rejuvenation in 1975 was to be found between the village of Bethesda and the Potworks reservoir, where a United States firm, American Agricultural Industries, had been granted a fifteen-year lease of 10 000 acres of a former sugar estate, on which a subsidiary company was to grow corn and sorghum for animal feed and operate a battery farm. Walter's lauding of the establishment of Antigua Agricultural Industries as a replacement for the sugar industry marked a complete reversal of his party's agricultural policy, which up to then had been to deter outside investment and concentrate on the development of peasant farming. Regrettably, as with so many other projects hailed by Antigua's politicians both before and since, as holding the key to future prosperity, the will – and perhaps even more importantly, the water – were not there to ensure success. After only three years, during which time very little was grown or exported, AAI collapsed in great debt, with the lands it had leased soon reverting to the unkempt and overgrown condition the countryside had generally assumed by that time.

Even as Antigua Agricultural Industries began its brief existence, with the rest of the economy in ruins and the remainder of the island exuding an air of melancholia, the Premier's mind had turned to thinking that the way to salvation, both for Antigua and his Government, lay in an end to associated statehood and the achievement of full independence. The next general election was due at the beginning of 1976, and considering all that had happened since 1971 it was one which the PLM had little hope of winning, without a major campaign issue of this sort.

Under the existing agreement with Britain independence could not be obtained without the support of two-thirds of the members of the House of Representatives and, more importantly, a two-thirds majority in a general referendum. As the latter was out of the question under the opprobrium in which his Government was now held Walter led a delegation to London to ask for this requirement to be waived. It was a request the British Government – anxious to be rid of any further responsibility for the remaining Associated States (the people of Grenada had already been delivered without benefit of a referendum into the hands of a crackpot bully of a Prime Minister in 1974), and ready as always to insult the intelligence of ordinary West Indians – was only too willing to grant. The delegation returned home and, having introduced a new registration act in order to scrap the existing electoral roll and reduce the voting age from twenty-one to eighteen, prepared to make independence the key issue in an election set for 18 February 1976.

In response the ALP campaign, now firmly under the control of 'Papa' Bird – fully revitalised at the age of sixty-six after five years of kicking his heels in the wilderness – concentrated on arguing that the 'sacredness and seriousness' of independence made it far too important a matter to be considered without a referendum, and that the PLM candidates were consumed by 'political lust and greed for absolute and arbitrary power'.[8] This was something with which by now a majority of Antiguans wholeheartedly agreed, as the election results soon showed. Combined with promises to abolish personal income tax, to revive the sugar industry, and to carry out a massive re-employment programme, the party's high-falutin comments about a circumspect approach to independence carried the day, and the ALP was returned with an overwhelming majority. Bird returned to Parliament with ten other members of the party, including two of his sons, to face an opposition consisting of Walter and four of his PLM colleagues. The Barbuda seat was retained by Claude Francis, who quickly announced he belonged to neither party.

When formed, the new Government was bigger than ever. Not content with creating the position of Deputy Premier for his son Lester (who also became

Minister of Trade, Industry and Economic Development) Bird also made another eleven ministerial appointments; three of them going to unelected members of the Senate, and one, Barbudan Affairs, being given 'after certain negotiations' to Claude Francis. Only two of the elected ALP members failed to end up with a ministerial position, one surprisingly being the Premier's other son, Vere Bird Jr. In the Senate the PLM were allowed two seats, one of which Walter gave to his half-brother Selvyn as compensation for having failed to be elected to the lower house, and a third was left to be filled by a Barbudan.

In fulfilment of another promise made in the ALP manifesto one of the new Government's first acts was to abolish the post of Warden in Barbuda, and create a Local Government Council with wide powers to administer the internal affairs of the island. Together with their own minister and senator, this went some way towards satisfying Barbudan aspirations, although any hope that it would stabilise the relationship between the two islands soon proved to be illusory.

The Premier's attempt to deal with the long-running Barbuda problem was quickly followed by his decision to order an enquiry into some of the activities of the previous Government. This followed an independent audit of public accounts, but was perhaps not wholly uninfluenced by a desire to seek recompense for the five long years he had spent as an impotent spectator of what he could only have seen as the gross mishandling of the affairs of state. A three-man commission appointed under the chairmanship of Karl de la Bastide, a retired judge from Trinidad, began to collect evidence into 'the irregularities involving certain former ministers and civil servants' at the beginning of September. None of the previous Government attended the hearings, all contesting that the commission had no legal foundation, but based on the evidence collected elsewhere the former Premier and two of his ministers were arrested in February 1977. Walter and Prince, the former Minister of Public Works, were charged with misbehaviour in public office and conspiracy to defraud, and the disgraced Minister of Home Affairs, Halstead, with corruption.

As the legal system of the state, in common with that of the rest of the West Indies, was renowned more for the loquacity of its practitioners than the speed with which it dispensed justice, preliminary hearings occupied most of the next two years. This allowed plenty of time for Halstead to jump bail and depart for the United States, where he was to remain a fugitive until 1986.[9] The three-week trial of the other two, which began at the end of January 1979, ended with Prince being acquitted, and Walter sentenced to eight years' imprisonment. An appeal was lodged immediately, but such was the urgency with which this was treated that he spent more than four months in jail before being released to await its outcome. This was long enough as, even though the following April the verdict was overturned as being 'unsafe and unsatisfactory', the disgrace of imprisonment and the hounding he had received were more than enough to ruin any hope Walter may have had of continuing a worthwhile political career.[10] Robert Hall, who had already assumed the role of leader of the opposition in Parliament, now became leader of the PLM.

While the setting up of the Commission of Inquiry in 1976 gave the ALP supporters the dubious satisfaction of seeing Walter and his administration dishonoured (the eventual outcome was to cause one member of Bird's Cabinet to rejoice that he could now die a happy man having helped to make 'George Walter a jailbird and Donald Halstead a fugitive')[11] it did nothing but antagonise the followers of the PLM and members of the AWU, and to wrench an already divided society even further apart. With little or nothing to choose between their policies, party rivalry was raised to an emotional level which threatened to beggar belief, becoming centred on little more than the colour each party adopted: red for the ALP and blue for the PLM. This was something which had been gathering momentum since 1971 but now, and for the next four years, love or hatred of one or other of these colours became an issue of ridiculous proportions. A man's job could be in jeopardy if he turned up to work in a shirt of the 'wrong' colour, just as a girl could lose a boyfriend if she wore *that* dress. A shopkeeper could go broke if his store happened to be painted in a shade which did not suit the majority of his customers, and in certain areas a house owner needed to think twice before he re-painted his front door or picket fence. For the keen party member colour was of prime importance even in the choice of a motor car, as was demonstrated to the present author in 1974 when his wife sold one which was almost new but which just happened to be one of these talismanic colours, to someone who was then not prepared to take it on to the road before paying for it to be completely re-sprayed in another.

•

The clash of colours did nothing to help the state recover from the depression of the first half of the decade, any more than did the investigation carried out by the De la Bastide Commission, but within a year or so of Bird's return to power – and aided by the abolition of personal income tax – the economy was already showing remarkable signs of improvement. By 1978 the tourist industry was directly responsible for some 40 per cent of the gross domestic product (compared with 30 per cent ten years earlier) and indirectly for perhaps as much again. Although the sugar factory remained closed and the oil refinery inoperative, progress was being made in industrial development by attracting small manufacturing concerns to a business park sited close to the airport.

A less successful attempt to attract modern technology to the island, and one which was to have an extremely embarrassing outcome, took place at the end of 1976, when approval was given for the Canada-based Space Research Corporation to establish a 'long-range test facility' for high altitude research purposes, using the outer half of Crabbs Peninsula and land in the extreme north-east of the island. Equipment for these two sites, which arrived from Canada the following year, was soon under suspicion as being little other than cover for an operation intended to break the United Nations embargo then in existence on the provision of arms and ammunition to South Africa. The accusations voiced locally led to the issue being taken up in the foreign press, and the whole sorry business – which revealed the Antigua Government as having been the innocent dupes of a Mephistophelean arms manufacturer (who was subsequently murdered in Europe) – was exposed worldwide towards the end of 1978.

Earlier the same year, after the Space Research Corporation had packed its bags, but while the sorry farce it had initiated still had some months to run, the Government became involved in another equally absurd project – the re-establishment of the sugar industry. A massive loan of some EC$30 million was obtained from the Caribbean Development Bank in order to refurbish the factory, while the few farmers in possession of suitable areas of land who were also sufficiently committed to the ALP cause were persuaded to start planting sugar-cane. Three years later, in March 1981, after enormous effort and expenditure had gone into its restoration and modernisation, the factory was re-opened by the Premier. The ceremony took place before some 3600 invited guests and about a similar number of gatecrashers – their combined total being probably twenty times greater than the number of Antiguans who remained willing to work in the sugar industry. During the next four years the factory produced a total of just over 500 tons of sugar; unrefined, unclean in appearance, and largely unsold as few locals would buy it and there was no market elsewhere. In 1985, having spent something in the region of EC$60 000 for each ton of sugar produced, the factory ceased operations and closed its gates for the last time.

As if one attempt to revive a white elephant was not enough, and five years before admitting in this way that sugar had no future in Antigua, in 1980 the Government entered into an agreement to re-activate the oil refinery. This was signed with a firm calling itself National Petroleum, an organisation which was subsequently found to have considerably more interest in international banking ventures than anything to do with oil or refining operations. The figure of US$15 million was announced as having been committed to the project at the time: the results were still awaited as this book was being written nineteen years later.

•

In September 1978, leaving the Space Research headache behind him, and less than three years after an election campaign during which he had argued vigorously against rushing into ending the State's link with Britain, the Premier went to London to raise the issue of independence with the British Government. The reasons he gave for his change of mind – the burgeoning economy, increased tourism, rising employment, expanding industrialisation, higher exports, more stability – were all unnecessary. By this time the Labour Government in Britain was even less interested in the future of the Associated States than it had been during Walter's visit in 1975. The Under-Secretary of State in the Foreign and Commonwealth Office, Edward Rowlands, was only too pleased to see Bird, whom he had pressed to ask for complete independence during a visit he had made to Antigua two years earlier, and to give his approval for a quick transfer of power. No mention was made of any need for a referendum. Walter had been told this could be dispensed with and, although Bird had objected at the time, it now suited his purposes to agree with Rowlands that the only mandate needed was for the Government to win a general election in which independence had been made a key issue. However, before such an election was held, and in order perhaps to ease the Under-Secretary of State's conscience, it would be necessary to produce some sort of corroboration that independence would be welcomed by the population at large. The Premier returned home and a few weeks later set up an Independence Committee under Lester Bird which, aided by various sub-committees, was given the task of gathering enough evidence from around the island to persuade the British Parliament that the Government's plans for independence did, in fact, enjoy widespread support.

The committee's efforts met with a very mixed response, other from among the stalwarts of the ALP who voted in favour of independence at a special party convention, and from members of a dissentient coterie known as the Antigua Caribbean Liberation Movement, who had their own agenda for wanting a completely independent state. The ACLM had been formed five years earlier, following the merger of the Afro-Caribbean Movement, a small group of middle-class men and women much influenced by the Black Power Movement in the United States and revolutionary activities in southern Africa, with Youth Forces for Liberation, a working-class Black Power organisation from that poor and crowded suburb of St John's known as The Point; afterwards it concerned itself less with Pan-African affairs than with the post-colonial ills of Antiguan society.[12] Supporters of the PLM were on the whole opposed to the pursuit of independence, mainly because it was no longer their party's leadership leading the chase, while the rest of the population had views ranging from apathy to antagonism, with the majority feeling only apprehension.

Six months elapsed before it was considered that the views collected at various public meetings, or found among written submissions, proved there was a consensus in favour of independence. An outline constitution was cobbled together, and at the end of March 1979 Lester Bird travelled to London to initiate the next step. The timing of his visit could not have been worse. Shortly before leaving Antigua he had been made aware that the people of Barbuda, whose views on the subject had gone uncanvassed, strongly opposed independence; two weeks earlier the legitimate Government of Grenada, the first of the Associated States to have been given its independence, had been overthrown by a paramilitary coup; and just before he arrived in London the Labour Government had lost a vote of confidence and called a general election. It was hardly a propitious time to talk to anyone about independence, and the Deputy Premier was obliged to return home to await the outcome of the British elections, and to confront the Barbuda problem.

•

After the Barbudans had been given their own Local Government Council in 1976, and particularly after all nine of the elected seats on it had been won by ALP-backed candidates, it had been hoped in Antigua that little more would be heard of the secessionist movement. It was a forlorn expectation, as the defeated candidates soon began working on another petition to be sent to Britain, in which they asked that the island be released from its association with Antigua and returned to British rule. Otherwise they feared that independence would allow members of the Government in Antigua to claim 'sovereign rights over the lands and beaches of [Barbuda] and in the name of "Development" make land deals with enterprising foreigners'; instead of the money obtained being used to assist Barbuda, it would then go

> to swell their bank balances in overseas secret accounts, reduce or pay off the huge debts that Antigua has incurred over the years, as well as assist in the numerous ambitious programmes they have for the development of Antigua.[13]

This fear was well founded, as Barbuda's remote situation, tiny population and anomalous constitutional status had begun to attract foreign interest well before the end of the colonial period. A ninety-nine year lease of the Cocoa Point peninsula in the south-east had been granted to an American businessman in 1959, and an exclusive tourist resort with its own airstrip had been in operation there since the middle of 1961. As this had been constructed with the developer paying the greatest attention to Barbudan sensibilities, and with the intention of employing an all-Barbudan staff, this had only been of benefit to the island. The finished resort was also of a size commensurate with the area of Barbuda and the number of its inhabitants; something which could not be said of any of the other schemes which were dreamt up later by something calling itself the Barbuda Tourist Development Corporation, and which were given consideration by the Antiguan Government. These involved the leasing of hundreds of acres in the north for the construction, in one form or another, of a large resort complex consisting of a hotel, casino, golf course, marina, offices and condominiums. Fortunately nothing came of any of them, but early in 1979 approval was given for a Canadian contractor to build a resort on the south coast, and for two

American speculators to start a large-scale sand-mining operation in the southwest. Both these projects were allowed to proceed without proper consultation with, or the wholehearted approval of, the Barbuda Council. Although outside the scope of this book it is not inappropriate to record that even more preposterous schemes followed. A year after sand began to be shipped from the island, a proposal was made to build an oil refinery and offshore trans-shipment terminal on the west coast. Two years later an extremely shady organisation – the ludicrous Sovereign Order of Aragon – wanted to turn a large slice of Barbuda into an independent, self-governing 'Principality' in order to market diplomatic passports. Three years after that a Chinese businessman resident in Montserrat proposed the leasing of 40 square miles of the island in order for him to establish the 'New Hong Kong Economic Territory', with full autonomy and membership of the United Nations. Two years later still, in 1987, an American salvage expert wanted to lease a large part of the east coast for the construction of a huge hotel, an underwater restaurant, a cruise-ship dock, an office and banking complex, together with a treasure museum to display the artefacts he hoped to recover from the island's numerous wrecks.

With such grandiose, megalomanic proposals in the offing those who drew up and subscribed to the petition which was sent off to London in 1978 did well to be wary. It was despatched shortly after the death of Claude Francis, the island's parliamentary representative who, *faute de mieux*, had been made the Minister for Barbudan Affairs. He was replaced at the subsequent by-election as the representative, but not as the minister, by a businessman named Eric Burton, who owned the only store of any size, ran Codrington's only hotel, had extensive fishing and agricultural interests, and as such was the wealthiest man on the island. He was also someone who could envisage an even more important place in society for himself in a Barbuda free of any connection with Antigua, and once elected he began to belabour the secessionist drum.

In January of the following year he provided a damning indictment of both the current Government and its PLM predecessor in a speech in the House of Representatives, in which he listed some of his constituents' grievances:

> No proper medical services. A doctor for eight hours a week. A hospital with no ambulance, [and] without proper electricity; no road worth mentioning . . . No running water . . . no reliable electricity supply . . . no proper airport facilities, not even a proper runway. We have absolutely no connection with the outside world. There is no telephone and we don't anticipate getting any before 1980 or later. We are only now struggling to get our secondary school to reach secondary standards.[14]

Not surprisingly, when four seats on the Barbuda Council were contested two months later, all were won by members of the Barbuda People's Movement committed, as were most of the islanders by now, to a policy of 'no independence with Antigua'. After their election, and with Burton at their head ready to demand self-rule, the scene was all set for confrontation with the Government, and major disruption of the Premier's plans for a swift end to the connection with Britain.

•

After Lester Bird's visit to London in March all further talks about independence were suspended during the British election campaign, and not resumed until early in August when a minister in the Foreign and Commonwealth Office, Nicholas Ridley, found it expedient to visit Antigua. The Conservative administration of which he was a member remained just as anxious as its Labour predecessor to be rid of the state but, obviously alarmed by the growing secessionist demands coming from Barbuda, as well as by events in Grenada where Maurice Bishop and his cabal had established an oligarchy, not at any price. Both issues were also exercising the minds of the Antigua Government, and on his arrival Ridley was presented with a memorandum in which problems with Barbuda were ignored but events in Grenada used to claim that:

> Any delay in independence might well frustrate economic growth and lead to economic and social upheaval opening the door for a departure from Antigua's traditional adherence to Western democratic principles. It is this real possibility of a change in Antigua's ideological direction, apparent in other Caribbean countries, that the ALP wishes to avoid.[15]

Such sophistry might well have appealed to Caiaphas, but Ridley was not deceived. It was obvious to him that Barbuda was the main stumbling block, but equally apparent that many Antiguans remained to be convinced of the benefits which might accrue from independence. At the conclusion of his visit, during which he made it patently transparent that the British Government would not entertain any suggestion of Barbuda being separated from Antigua, he put off any further negotiations until after such time as he had received 'a clear manifestation of the wish of the majority of people for independence'.

Any suggestion of a referendum being the only true means of producing such a 'manifestation' was ignored. Instead, for the next seven months the Government concentrated on a programme 'of education about independence in which the principal activist was Lester Bird'. This consisted of haranguing the public at large in outdoor meetings, in trying to persuade the business community of the ALP's commitment to democracy and human rights, and in assuring church leaders that 'freedom of worship will be sacrosanct in our new Constitution'; and ended with a general election being called for 24 April 1980, at which the return of the Bird Government would be taken as the required 'demonstration of the people's desire to advance to independence'.[16]

As it transpired the people were given no opportunity to demonstrate one way or the other, as the manifesto issued by each of the three parties which contested the election made clear. That of the ruling party stated openly that if returned, 'immediately after the General Elections, the ALP will seek independence for Antigua'. The PLM, also ignoring Barbuda and its inhabitants, announced that it had both 'the personnel and expertise to lead Antigua into independence' as well as 'the will to work for a united front to develop an independent Antigua'. The third party, the ACLM, which for the first time had decided to engage in electoral politics, at least had the grace to recognise the full extent of the state by offering unreserved support for 'national independence for Antigua and Barbuda'.

Not that this did the ACLM any good whatsoever. When the election took place, with a turn-out of some 78 per cent, their candidates received just over 1 per cent of the popular vote, compared with the ALP's 58 per cent, which produced a total of thirteen seats in the new Parliament. Three seats were retained by the PLM, and Burton – remaining aloof from any party – was returned for Barbuda. All the ALP members, with one exception, were given ministerial appointments, as well as one of the party's senators who was made Minister without Portfolio. Vere Bird Jr, once again denied a ministerial salary, had to be content with being made Deputy Speaker. Responsibility for Barbuda Affairs was tacked on to the remit of the Minister of Labour.

Confident now that the people – of Antigua at least – had expressed a firm desire for independence, the Government re-opened negotiations with British officials in London in July 1980. Burton refused to take part, and a few months later informed the Foreign and Commonwealth Office that his constituents 'would prefer death to a union of any sort with Antigua'. At much the same time, in preparation for the independence conference which had been scheduled for December, a campaign was launched in England to draw as much outside attention as possible to the wish of Barbudans to secede: an eminent London QC was retained, and two highly respected academics with a longstanding interest in the history of the island began to provide support and encouragement through letters and articles in the British press.

•

The conference which opened at Lancaster House on 4 December 1980 was convened in order to agree on a new constitution for a fully independent state, its discussions centring on a draft prepared in advance by the Antiguan Government. Because of the criticism which had been levelled at some of the draft's provisions, or lack of them, and even more because of the Barbudan secessionist stance, when the proceedings opened Ridley and his small team of officials found themselves outnumbered nearly four to one. The enormous delegation which faced them was made up not just of representatives of the

Antigua Government, but also those of the main opposition party and the Barbuda separatists; each faction containing many people whose function and purpose in attending was, and remained, far from clear.

The seventeen-strong Government delegation, under the Premier, consisted not only of the Deputy Premier, the Attorney-General, the Minister with responsibility for Barbudan Affairs, the state's most experienced senior civil servant and the two lawyers mainly responsible for the draft constitution, but also the Minister of Education, the Premier's personal bodyguard and gofer, Novelle Richards, one of the Premier's non-politician sons, plus seven other hangers-on (including a dentist) whose presence can only have been needed to make sure the official delegation was not outnumbered by the other two. The PLM deputation headed by Robert Hall was of a more reasonable size, but still larger than was warranted by the combined input to the proceedings made by its seven members. The Barbuda delegation was twice as big, being made up under Burton's leadership of McChesney George, the chairman of the Barbuda Council and eleven others – including the high-powered triumvirate of J.R. MacDonald QC, Professor David Lowenthal of University College London and Dr Colin Clarke of Liverpool University, several members of the Barbuda Council and, last but not least, Mrs Eric Burton.

The conference lasted until 16 December and was dominated by the Barbuda question. In his opening statement Burton adopted an uncompromising position, stating that if Britain refused to allow the island to separate from Antigua and return to being a British colony, he and the 1200 or so people he represented were 'prepared to go into full independence on our own'.[17] A few days later another member of his delegation, when interviewed by the BBC, raised the stakes even higher by claiming that his fellow Barbudans were prepared to commit mass suicide on the island's beaches, rather than consider independence in conjunction with Antigua. Neither statement went down well with either the chairman of the conference or Antigua's Premier. Ridley had no intention of allowing the two islands to be separated and insisted that there had to be 'a way which will be satisfactory to all to integrate the state of Antigua with the island of Barbuda', while Bird was equally insistent that 'territorial integrity must be paramount to self-determination'.[18] Nine of the conference's twenty-two plenary sessions were devoted to trying to get each side to make some concession, with Ridley and his officials working overtime to get Burton to renounce secession, and Bird to agree to greater devolution of authority to the Barbuda Council. In the end a compromise of sorts was reached, and the gory prospect of mass self-immolation on Barbuda's beaches receded when Burton, with bad grace, dropped his demand for separation, and Bird, equally reluctantly, agreed to an increase in the powers of the island's Council.

The remaining conference sessions, involving long and tedious arguments over what the PLM delegation considered missing or unacceptable clauses in the draft constitution, were perhaps equally tiring to all concerned, but at least such disputation did not presage, as the Barbuda impasse had, a failure of the conference to achieve its objective. At its close, disappointed and perhaps suffering from an undefinable feeling that they had somehow been railroaded by Ridley and his FCO minions into something they might have cause to regret, both Burton and Hall refused to sign the conference report: the former, in view of his volte-face, in order to to retain some dignity; the latter in order to show solidarity because of 'the failure satisfactorily to resolve the Barbuda situation'.

Endorsement of the report presented no such problem for Bird; having celebrated his seventy-first birthday nine days before the conference ended British approval of the new constitution made a splendid, if slightly belated, birthday present. He and the rest of his delegation travelled home to start planning for independence day, leaving Ridley and his officials to begin preparing the necessary legislation to lay before the House of Commons. Hall and his team also returned to Antigua, to begin trying to explain away to their supporters their failure to introduce any significant amendment into the new constitution; while Burton and his party headed for Barbuda to face the music.

In the middle of the following April, with independence preparations well advanced, the 1976 Barbuda Act was amended in accordance with the understanding reached at Lancaster House, and after the new act had been signed into law Burton's bailiwick became virtually self-governing. The island's Council assumed responsibility for the administration of agriculture and fisheries, social services and public utilities, for the construction and maintenance of roads, for promotion of the island's tourist potential, and for raising and collecting the revenue needed to meet the cost of such administration. All of this was very acceptable to the inhabitants, who by this time had more or less come to terms with the fact that their future was going to be bound up with that of the Antiguans whether they liked it or not, but what was not acceptable was that they were not given control over the land, nor made responsible for their own security.

A belief that all the land outside the limits of Codrington was owned in common by all Barbudans – even though this had no legal foundation whatsoever – was at the centre of island life and formed the heart of Barbudan identity. As far as the Council and the rest of the population were concerned, no land could be alienated by outsiders or used without permission. No carpetbaggers from Antigua, or anywhere else, would be tolerated, and any legal status concerning land devised by Antigua would not be recognised. As far as security was concerned, for members of the Antiguan police force to continue to be stationed on the island was tantamount to placing Barbudans under the control of an occupying army and was unacceptable.

Such was the furore caused by the new Barbuda Act that in June the Deputy Premier took a small delegation to the island in an attempt to resolve the situation. In a meeting with the Council he made the case for proper policing – something which was a responsibility of the state – and for recognition of the state's claim to former Crown property – which was what Barbuda had been until 1967. He offered to convey freehold rights to lands traditionally occupied for housing, and to introduce a joint consultation procedure with the Council before the disposal of any other part of the island, but nothing he had to say made any impression. The Council remained obdurate in its insistence that Barbudans alone owned and controlled Barbuda, refused to enter into any discussion of Bird's proposals, and the entire exercise had to be written off as a waste of time. As a result the land issue was unresolved at independence, continued to bedevil relations between central Government and the islanders for the next decade, and remained far from being properly settled as this book was being written.

•

On 31 July 1981, five weeks after Lester Bird had made his futile trip, the Antigua and Barbuda Constitution Order was signed into law in London, and the future of the two islands as a unitary state was settled. Three months to the day later, at midnight on 31 October, the new country came into being. A connection with Britain which had lasted virtually unbroken for 349 years (the French despoliation of 1666 hardly counted as a change of sovereignty) came to an amicable end. In front of a huge crowd in an overflowing recreation ground the Grand Old Man of Antiguan politics, 'Papa' Bird, received the instruments of independence from Princess Margaret, the royal personage whose turn it was to dispose of another unwanted vestige of empire, and made a short speech.

Not for him any Nehruan reference to 'the midnight hour while the world sleeps', or a diatribe about an end to colonial oppression, but rather a grandfatherly homily quite in keeping with both the unique, widely respected position he held in the community, and the size of the state he had almost single-handedly been responsible for bringing into being:

> My people, we are free this night. But freedom cannot exist without responsibility. The full burden of our freedom now rests squarely upon our shoulders. What we do with that freedom is our responsibility, we can blame no other.
>
> Part of the responsibility of freedom is its protection. As a small developing country with little resources other than beaches, land and people, we have to safeguard our freedom by ensuring that we never become dependent again.
>
> The ultimate safeguard of independence is productivity. This nation, born again tonight, must commit itself to work and to work hard. For if we fail to do so, the consequence of our failure will be dependence on a

new master who will, once again, dictate our policies and direct our affairs.

We must not have struggled so long and with such fortitude to exchange one master for another.[19]

Although, had either the speaker or his audience realised it, the content of the speech was not so very different from that of the proclamation with which Governor McGregor had welcomed the slaves of Antigua to freedom in 1834, the people of the new state needed nothing more. Under Bird's leadership for all but five of the previous thirty-odd years, the island had been transformed: as had the population, ALP supporters and opponents alike. Influenced whether they appreciated it or not by his self-assurance and his ability to more than hold his own in a white man's world, the people of Antigua – who even in colonial times were considered, and considered themselves, a distinct cut above their neighbours – were unjustifiably proud and confident about the future.

When the sun rose on 1 November Prime Minister Bird had another thirteen years to go before he retired and, to quote the words which an envious visitor from another island had uttered over 130 years earlier, 'there was a metropolitan air about Antigua and its inhabitants . . . even the very hills lifted up their heads and tried to look like mountains.'[20]

Notes

Details of books and articles given here in abbreviated form will be found in the Bibliography.

Chapter 1: Prelude

1. The term Leeward Islands is misleading because, given the prevailing north-easterly wind these islands are – as was recognised by the early Spanish explorers who called them *Las islas de Barlovento* (the islands to the windward) – to leeward of nothing but Europe and Africa. When some of the more northerly of them were claimed by England in the seventeenth century, they were called the Leeward Caribbees, probably because they were to leeward, just, of Barbados, England's only other Caribbean possession at the time. That the name remains in use today as a geographical term, long after its usefulness as a political expression has ended, is just another relic of colonial times, reflecting the past overwhelming British influence in the region. The present day Dutch political group of Windward Islands – St Maarten, St Eustatius and Saba – remains firmly in the middle of a geographical area known to the world as the Leeward Islands.
2. 'The River', a name found on maps of Barbuda near the landing place on the south coast, is a misnomer. During periods of heavy rain, water drains from a swampy area in the hinterland across the beach to form a very shallow, and very temporary, stream: perhaps the only place on the island where running water is to be seen at any time.

Chapter 2: Discovery

1. Morison, p. 410.
2. Cameron, p. 8.
3. Ibid., p. 9.
4. Burns, p. 115.
5. Harris, p. 70.
6. *Antigua and the Antiguans*, II, p. 306.
7. Williams, p. 279.
8. Burns, p. 194.

Chapter 3: Proprietary Rule

1. Bridenbaugh, p. 27.
2. Bennett, p. 374.

Chapter 4: Hewing out New Fortunes

1. Oliver, *Caribbeana*, p. 110.
2. Brown, p. 65.
3. *Antigua and the Antiguans*, I, p. 35.
4. Brown, p. 66.
5. Ibid., p. 66.
6. The first Quaker to arrive in Antigua was Jonas Langford, who bought a large tract of land in the north of the island in 1660, and became a successful merchant as well as a planter. He and others of his faith suffered persecution from time to time because of their refusal to bear arms or to swear oaths, and later because of their determination to save the souls of their slaves in the absence of any interest among the Anglican clergy in this aspect of their ministry.
7. Harris, p. 86.
8. Burns, p. 340.
9. Higham, p. 194.
10. It was not until 1709 that the Codrington family acknowledged that others had a legitimate claim to Betty's Hope, by transferring estates in the Bermudian Valley to Valentine Morris, who had acquired the Keynell rights through marriage. 'Hope' in this context is used in its archaic sense as an area of enclosed land; and Elizabeth ('Betty') was a common name in the Keynell family.

Chapter 5: The Codrington Years

1. Higham, p. 152.
2. Gaspar, *Bondmen and Rebels*, p. 177.
3. The Board of Trade and Plantations (usually referred to as the Board of Trade) was an advisory body reporting to the Privy Council through a royally appointed Secretary of State for the Southern Department. Both the Board and the secretaryship were abolished in 1782, when control of the colonies passed first to the Secretary of State for Home Affairs, and then to the Secretary of State for War. The first Secretary of State for the Colonies was not appointed until 1854. The Board of Trade, after being revived in 1786, continued to advise on colonial laws for some years but eventually ceased to have any connection with colonial affairs.
4. Harlow, p. 114.
5. Tiffin's Regiment was raised in 1690 and named, as was the custom of the day, after its Colonel, Zachariah Tiffin. In 1751 it became the 27th Foot, in 1881 the Royal Inniskilling Fusiliers, in 1968 the Royal Irish Rangers, now the Royal Irish Regiment.
6. Gaspar, *Working the System*, p. 140.
7. *Antigua and the Antiguans*, II, p. 78.
8. Gaspar, *Working the System*, p. 140.
9. Gaspar, 'A Mockery of Freedom', p. 136.

Chapter 6: An Unfortunate Divel

1. Gaspar, *Bondmen and Rebels*, p.115.
2. Ibid., p. 117.
3. Hall, *Five of the Leewards*, p. 59.
4. Lillingston's Regiment, which was raised in 1705, became the 38th Foot in 1751, the 1st Battalion of the South Staffordshire Regiment in 1881, and is now The Staffordshire Regiment (The Prince of Wales's).

5. Burns, p. 420.
6. Bourne, p. 228.
7. Savage, p. 5.
8. Ibid., p. 5.
9. Ibid., p. 6.
10. Bourne, p. 223.
11. *Antigua and the Antiguans*, I, p. 76.
12. Ibid., p. 81.
13. Not too much should be read into Watkins's title. The first Chief Justice of Antigua who had any legal training was not appointed until 1786. Prior to this it was just one of the many positions filled from among Council and Assembly members or their associates.

Chapter 7: Prospering at a Price

1. Gaspar, *Bondmen and Rebels*, p. 78.
2. Sheridan, *The Rise of a Colonial Gentry*, p. 350.
3. Lieutenant-General William Mathew (?–1752), professional soldier. Lieutenant-Governor of St Kitts 1714–1733; Governor of Leeward Islands 1733–1752.
4. Pitman, p. 58.
5. Deerr, I, p. 172.
6. Pitman, p. 76.
7. Pares, 'Merchants and Planters', p. 23.
8. The crossing from West Africa to the Caribbean took an average of seven to eight weeks, although just as there was an odd ship which took only four weeks, there were others that took perhaps ten or twelve.
9. Berlin and Morgan, p. 112.
10. John Hart (?–1740) Governor of Maryland 1714–1720; Governor of Leeward Islands 1721–1727.
11. Gaspar, *Bondmen and Rebels*, p. 141.
12. Sir George Thomas (1693–1772) one time Governor of Pennsylvania, and Governor of the Leeward Islands from 1753–1766.
13. Sheridan, *Letters from a Sugar Plantation*, p. 14.
14. Ibid., p. 18.
15. Ibid., p. 19.
16. Gaspar, *Bondmen and Rebels*, p. 159.

Chapter 8: A Great Deal of Trouble in this Island

1. Gaspar, *Bondmen and Rebels*, p. 159.
2. Edward Byam (?–1741) The youngest son of William Byam and Lieutenant-Governor of Antigua 1711–1735.
3. A particularly unpleasant form of execution much used in England in the sixteenth and seventeenth centuries, and less so in the eighteenth century. It was not used after 1781, but not abolished until 1870. It involved the victim being hanged until about to expire, then being disembowelled while still breathing, before being hacked into four pieces.
4. Thomas Pitt, first Earl of Londonderry (1688?–1729); an English MP 1713–1728. Created Baron Londonderry in 1719 and Earl of Londonderry in 1726. Governor

of the Leeward Islands 1727–1729, when he died in St Kitts. He was the uncle of Pitt the Elder, first Earl of Chatham and British Prime Minister 1766–1768.
5. Gaspar, *Bondmen and Rebels*, p. 3.
6. This ghastly form of execution was used in France and other European countries until the end of the eighteenth century, but was never allowed in Great Britain at any time. The victim was spreadeagled under a cartwheel, which was then struck repeatedly until his limbs were broken, before being turned over to have his chest and neck hit until he died.
7. Gaspar, *Bondmen and Rebels*, p. 22.
8. Court, who was probably brought to the island as a ten-year-old child, is remembered as a folk hero in Antigua today, but by the name of Klass or Prince Klass. Although based on no other evidence that the present author has been able to find than its use in the fictionalised account of the 1736 plot contained in Mrs Lanaghan's *Antigua and the Antiguans*, this is thought to be an approximation of his true African name.
9. *Antigua and the Antiguans*, I, p. 108.

Chapter 9: In the Service of their Country

1. This was the same regiment which, then called Lillingston's, had arrived in 1707. Up until 1751 it was always known by the name of its current colonel, of whom there were no less than nine between 1705 and 1750. The regiment's long sojourn in the Leeward Islands was by no means intended from the beginning. In March 1712 orders were received for the regiment to return to England to be disbanded. Unfortunately by then the regiment was already so heavily in debt that the commanding officer was informed by the Legislature that neither he nor his men would be permitted to leave Antigua until the debt had been discharged. As the authorities in London had no intention of assisting in any way it was decided it was easier and cheaper to leave the regiment where it was – a view which prevailed until 1764 when the 38th Foot was finally relieved and sent to Ireland.
2. *Antigua and the Antiguans*, I, p. 87.
3. Gaspar, *Bondmen and Rebels*, p. 119.
4. The same Sir George Thomas for whom Walter Tullideph had acted as attorney in the 1740s (see Chapter 7).
5. Gaspar, *Bondmen and Rebels*, p. 123.
6. Vale, p. 17.
7. Blackburne, *The Romance of English Harbour*, p. 9.
8. Fort Berkeley, named after Admiral James Berkeley, the third Earl of Berkeley, who was First Lord Commissioner of the Admiralty from 1717 to 1727.
9. *Dictionary of National Biography*, XLVII p. 73.

Chapter 10: Every Foolish Extravagance

1. Sir Ralph Payne, first Baron Lavington (1738?–1807). An English MP 1768–1771; Governor of Leeward Islands 1771–1775; English MP 1776–1795; re-appointed Governor of Leeward Islands 1799–1807.
2. Ragatz, *Absentee Landlordism in the British Caribbean*, p. 24.
3. Sheridan, *The Rise of a Colonial Gentry*, p. 353.
4. Lowe, p. 25.
5. *Antigua and the Antiguans*, I, p. 112.
6. Berlin and Morgan, p. 112.

7. Goveia, p. 159.
8. Luffman, p. 53.
9. Ibid., p. 52.
10. *Antigua and the Antiguans*, II, p. 80.
11. Walker, F.D., p. 32.
12. The Anglican Church, which both then and later might be considered 'the planters at prayer', took no part in attempting to enlighten the slaves until 1792, when the Society for the Conversion and Religious Instruction and Education of the Negro Slaves in the West Indian Islands was established in England. Formed with an ambitious plan to provide clerical and lay missionaries to assist the resident clergy in converting the slaves, it failed to live up to its ponderous title. The few missionaries who could be persuaded to undertake the work met with such suspicion and obstruction, from both planters and clergy, that within a few years the Conversion Society, as it had by then become, decided to concentrate solely on sending out schoolmasters. This too failed to make any impact, as not enough qualified men could be found who were willing to go to the West Indies, and many who did proved quite unfit for the work.
13. Luffman, p. 21.
14. *Antigua and the Antiguans*, I, p. 121.
15. Luffman, p. 31.
16. Sir William Mathew Burt (?–1781). Born in St Kitts, where he subsequently became a member of the Council. Appointed Governor of Leeward Islands in 1776. Died *en poste* under slightly mysterious circumstances, probably from a severe bout of delirium tremens.
17. *Antigua and the Antiguans*, I, p. 114.
18. Blackburne, *The Romance of English Harbour*, p. 15.
19. General Sir Thomas Shirley, Bt. (1727–1800). Professional soldier, born in the Bahamas; Lieutenant-Governor of Dominica 1774–1781; Governor of Leeward Islands 1781–1795. Created baronet 1786 and promoted general 1798.
20. *Dictionary of National Biography*, XXVIII, p. 186.
21. Warner, p. 39.
22. *Antigua and the Antiguans*, I, p. 119.
23. Warner, p. 48.
24. *Antigua and the Antiguans*, I, p. 120.
25. The house, which still stands, was used as the official residence of the Senior Naval Officer until 1820, when it became the Commissioner's House, occupied by the civilian head of the dockyard. From some time in the 1860s, and for a hundred years thereafter, it was used as the Governor's country residence and known as Clarence House.
26. In his maiden speech in the House of Lords, made in 1792 as part of a debate on a motion already passed in the House of Commons 'that the slave trade ought to be *gradually* abolished', he argued that he had seen for himself that slaves were not as a rule mistreated, but rather lived in a state of humble happiness, and voted against the proposal. Fortunately his views did not prevail and the motion was passed regardless. He and others of his ilk were still arguing for the retention of the slave trade in 1804, causing a fellow peer to comment that 'it was truly humiliating to see, in the House of Lords, four of the Royal Family come down to vote against the poor, helpless, friendless slaves.'
27. Harlow, p. 328.

28. Jane, p. 21.
29. *Antigua and the Antiguans*, I, p. 124.

Chapter 11: Matters of Consequence

1. Goveia, p. 56.
2. Martinique had been captured at the beginning of 1794, and its main town, Fort Royal, was to remain the headquarters of the British forces in the eastern Caribbean until the island was returned to the French in 1802.
3. Tolstoy, p. 46.
4. *Dictionary of National Biography*, XIV, p. 352.
5. *Antigua and the Antiguans*, I, p. 132.
6. *Dictionary of National Biography*, XLIV, p. 119.
7. Lowe, p. 50.
8. Ragatz, *The Fall of the Planter Class in the British Caribbean*, p. 306.
9. *Antigua and the Antiguans*, I, p. 138.
10. It is perhaps not without interest to note that, out of the 211 names handed out to the men, women and children liberated from the *San José y Anemas* in 1811, no less than 107 were still to be seen in the Antigua telephone directory at the end of the twentieth century.
11. Hugh Elliot (1752–1830), diplomat. Minister plenipotentiary in Germany, Denmark and Italy 1774–1803; Governor of Leeward Islands 1809–1813; Governor of Madras 1814.
12. Burns, p. 595.
13. Leach, p. 20.
14. This experiment did not last beyond November 1832, when new Letters Patent restored one government, and a single governor, for all the Leeward Islands.
15. Ferguson, p. 169.
16. Ibid., p. 170.
17. Andrews, p. 112.
18. Coleridge, p. 252.
19. Shyllon, p. 218.
20. Prince, Mary, *The History of Mary Prince, a West Indian Slave, Related by Herself*, London (1831).

Chapter 12: Immediate, Entire and Universal Freedom

1. The appointment of Bathurst as the first Colonial Secretary marked the end of the patent system. From then on as the patentees died off they were replaced by men who had to serve in person, and who could be replaced if they performed badly. Colonial administration then began to become an acceptable career, with the Colonial Service as such coming into existence within twenty years.
2. Lieutenant-General Sir Benjamin D'Urban (1777–1849), professional soldier and colonial administrator. Governor of Leeward Islands 1820–1824; Governor of British Guiana 1824–1831; Governor of Cape Colony (where he founded the city of Durban) 1842–1847.
3. *Antigua and the Antiguans*, I, p. 146.
4. Gaspar, *Slavery, Amelioration, and the Sunday Markets in Antigua*, p. 21.
5. *Antigua and the Antiguans*, I, p. 147.
6. Lowe, p. 70.

7. Ibid., p. 71.
8. Ibid., p. 71.
9. Loving, p. 2.
10. Ibid., p. 3.
11. Ibid., p. 4.
12. Ibid., p. 4.
13. Ibid., p. 9.
14. Hall, *Five of the Leewards*, p. 23.
15. Augier and Gordon, p. 199.
16. Sir Evan John Murray McGregor, Bt. Governor of Antigua, Barbuda and Montserrat 1832–1833; Governor of Leeward Islands 1834–1836; Governor of Barbados 1836–1841.
17. Horsford, p. 81.
18. Davy, p. 388.
19. Hovey, p. 59.
20. Mathieson, *British Slavery and its Abolition*, p. 246.
21. Walker, F.D., p. 83.
22. *Antigua and the Antiguans*, II, p. 164.
23. Lowe, p. 78.

Chapter 13: A Private Governmency

1. Lowe, p. 51.
2. Ibid., p. 29.
3. Goveia, p. 54.
4. Lowe, p. 28.
5. Ibid., p. 49.
6. Hall, *Five of the Leewards*, p. 60.
7. Lowe, p. 52.
8. Ibid., p. 52.
9. Ibid., p. 53.
10. Norie, p. 34.
11. Coleridge, p. 268.
12. Lowenthal and Clarke, *Slave-Breeding in Barbuda*, p. 515.
13. Lowe, p. 77.
14. Lowenthal and Clarke, *Slave-Breeding in Barbuda*, p. 518.
15. Ibid., p. 77.
16. Ibid., p. 77.
17. Hall, *Five of the Leewards*, p. 61.
18. Ibid., p. 63.
19. Ibid., p. 70.

Chapter 14: Their Natural Portion

1. Hovey, p. 85.
2. Boromé, p. 56.
3. Sturge and Harvey, I, p. 19.
4. *Antigua and the Antiguans*, I, p. 151.
5. Ibid., p. 152.
6. Sturge and Harvey, I, p. 22.

7. Colonial Office Report (1848), p. 218.
8. Lowe, p. 79.
9. Sturge and Harvey, I, p. 13.
10. Sir William MacBean George Colebrook (1787–1870), professional soldier 1803–1832. Lieutenant-Governor of the Bahamas 1834–1837; Governor of Leeward Islands 1837–1841; Lieutenant-Governor of New Brunswick 1841–1846; Governor of Barbados and Windward Islands 1848–1856. Colonel Commanding Royal Artillery 1859–1870.
11. Hall, *Five of the Leewards*, p. 43.
12. Sturge and Harvey, I, p. 29.
13. Baird, p. 52.
14. *Antigua and the Antiguans*, II, p. 289.
15. Day, p. 270.
16. Sir James Macaulay Higginson (1805–1885), professional soldier in India 1824–1834. Private Secretary to Lord Metcalfe in India, Jamaica and Canada 1835–1846. Governor of Leeward Islands 1846–1850; Governor of Mauritius 1850–1857.
17. Boromé, p. 52.
18. Bishop Daniel Gateward Davis (1788–1857), born in St Kitts and ordained in England in 1812. Parish priest in Nevis and St Kitts 1812–1838; Archdeacon of Antigua 1838–1842; Bishop of Antigua 1842–1857.
19. Hovey, p. 68.
20. Thome and Kimbell, p. 31.
21. Ibid., p. 31.
22. Hovey, p. 69.
23. Colonial Office Report (1846), p. 48.
24. Colonial Office Report (1854), p. 119.
25. Hall, *Five of the Leewards*, p. 45.
26. Colonial Office Report (1845), p. 97.
27. Colonial Office Report (1846), p. 48.
28. Over 30 000 went to British Guiana alone.
29. Colonial Office Report (1847), p. 218.
30. Ker Baillie Hamilton (1804–1889) entered the Honourable East India Company's Service 1822. Lieutenant-Governor of Grenada 1846–1852; Governor of Newfoundland 1852–1855; Governor of Leeward Islands 1855–1863.
31. Burns, p. 666.
32. Colonial Office Report (1861), p. 77.
33. Sewell, p. 154.
34. Colonial Office Report (1864), p. 111.
35. Day, p. 300.

Chapter 15: The Fortunes of the Planter

1. Colonial Office Report (1851), p. 123.
2. Colonial Office Report (1854), p. 121.
3. Colonial Office Report (1850), p. 102.
4. Colonial Office Report (1855), p. 181.
5. Colonial Office Report (1860), p. 63.
6. Colonel Sir Stephen John Hill (1809–1891), professional soldier 1823–1850. Held various West African governorships 1851–1862. Governor of Leeward Islands

1863–1869; Governor of Newfoundland 1869–1876.
7. Sir Benjamin Chilley Campbell Pine (1809–1891), called to the Bar 1841 and entered Colonial Service the same year. Served in West Africa 1841–1848. Governor of Natal 1849–1856 and of Gold Coast 1856–1859. Lieutenant-Governor of St Kitts 1859–1869. Governor of Leeward Islands 1869–1873; Governor of Natal 1873–1875.
8. Colonial Office Report (1866), p. 91.
9. Madden and Fieldhouse, p. 246.
10. Ibid., p. 246.

Chapter 16: Great Misery and Distress
1. Colonial Office Report (1863), p. 68.
2. Ibid., p. 69.
3. Colonial Office Report (1864), p. 108.
4. Colonial Office Report (1861), p. 76.
5. Colonial Office Report (1865), p. 69.
6. Colonial Office Report (1878, p. 103.
7. Ibid., p. 103.
8. Ibid., p. 105.
9. Ibid., p. 105.
10. Ibid., p. 105.
11. Ibid., p. 105.
12. Colonial Office Report (1882), p. 73.
13. Colonial Office Report (1885), p. 68. The West Indian Province of the Church of England had been disestablished on 1 January 1875.
14. Colonial Office Report (1852), p. 96.
15. Colonial Office Report (1864), p. 117.
16. Colonial Office Report (1875), p. 204.
17. Ibid., p. 200.
18. Captain Sir John Hawley Glover (1829–1885), Royal Navy officer who served as a colonial administrator in West Africa 1841–1875. Governor of Newfoundland 1875–1881; Governor of Leeward Islands 1881–1883; Governor of Newfoundland 1883–1884.
19. Glover, p. 273.
20. Jenico William Joseph Preston, fourteenth Viscount Gormanston (1837–1907). Served in the Army 1857–1859. Governor of Leeward Islands 1885–1887; Governor of British Guiana 1887–1893.
21. Harper, p. 15.
22. Boromé p. 52.
23. Lowes, p. 44.
24. Glover, p. 281.
25. Sir Charles Cameron Lees (1837–1898), professional soldier 1854–1866. Colonial Secretary of the Gold Coast 1873–1874. Governor of Borneo 1879–1881; Governor of the Bahamas 1881–1883; Governor of Leeward Islands 1884–1885; Governor of Barbados 1885–1889; Governor of Mauritius 1889–1893; Governor of British Guiana 1893–1896.
26. Colonial Office Report (1883), p. 167.
27. Smith and Smith, *To Shoot Hard Labour*, p. 102.

Chapter 17: Deemed to be a Dependency

1. Lowe, p. 80.
2. Sir Francis Fleming (1842–1922). Pursued a legal career in the Colonial Service until 1883. Governor of Sierra Leone 1892–1894; Governor of Leeward Islands 1895–1901.
3. Morse, F.W., p. 81.
4. *Montserrat Mirror*, 8 March 1985, p. 6.
5. Morse, F.W., p. 80.
6. Ibid., p. 86.

Chapter 18: Always Incapable and Frequently Corrupt

1. Sir George Berkeley (1819–1905). Born in Barbados and entered Colonial Service 1843. Lieutenant-Governor of St Vincent 1864–1872; Governor-in-Chief of West Africa settlements 1873–1874; Governor of Leeward Islands 1874–1881.
2. Sir William Frederick Haynes Smith (1839–1928). Governor of British Guiana 1884–1887; Governor of Leeward Islands 1888–1895; Governor of the Bahamas 1895–1897; Governor of Cyprus 1897–1904.
3. Lowes, p. 45.
4. Colonial Office Report (1899), p. 5.
5. Colonial Office Report (1905–6), p. 41.
6. Sir Henry Hesketh Bell (1864–1952) entered Colonial Service 1882. Served in West Indies, Gold Coast and Bahamas until 1896. Administrator of Dominica 1899–1905. Governor of Uganda 1906–1909; Governor of Northern Nigeria 1909–1912; Governor of Leeward Islands 1912–1915; Governor of Mauritius 1916–1924.
7. Sir Ernest Bickham Sweet-Escott (1857–1941). Governor of the Seychelles 1903–1904; Governor of British Honduras 1904–1906; Governor of Leeward Islands 1906–1912; Governor of Fiji and High Commissioner for Western Pacific 1912–1918.
8. Watkins, p. 59.
9. Smith, *No Easy Push-o-ver*, p. 28.
10. Sir Edward Marsh Merewether (1858–1938) entered Colonial Service 1880 and served in Malaya until 1901 and then Malta until 1911. Governor of Sierra Leone 1911–1915; Governor of Leeward Islands 1919–1921.
11. Colonial Office Report (1916–17), p. 11.
12. Colonial Office Report (1917–18), p. 8.
13. Watkins, p. 57.

Chapter 19: Bound to Succeed

1. Sir Thomas Vans Best (1870–1941) served in Africa 1896–1908 and in Falkland Islands 1909–1912. Colonial Secretary of Leeward Islands 1913–1915 and Acting Governor 1915–1919. Colonial Secretary of Trinidad 1919–1924; Lieutenant-Governor of Malta 1925–1930; Governor of Windward Islands 1930–1933.
2. Franck, p. 344.
3. Nutting, p. 76.
4. Sir Reginald St Johnston (1881–1950) qualified as a doctor before joining Colonial Service in 1906, and soon afterwards as a barrister-at-law. Filled various judicial, medical and administrative posts in Fiji 1907–1917. Served with Fijian contingent

in France in First World War. Acting Governor of Falkland Islands 1919–20. Colonial Secretary of Leeward Islands 1920–1925. Administrator of Dominica 1925; Administrator of St Kitts–Nevis 1925–1929; Governor of Leeward Islands 1929–1936.
5. St Johnston, *From a Colonial Governor's Notebook*, p. 80.
6. Sir Eustace Fiennes, Bt. (1864–1943), professional soldier 1885–1918, and English MP 1906–1918. Governor of the Seychelles 1918–1921; Governor of Leeward Islands 1921–1929.
7. St Johnston, *From a Colonial Governor's Notebook*, p. 68.
8. Smith and Smith, p. 134.
9. St Johnston, *From a Colonial Governor's Notebook*, p. 165.
10. Ibid., p. 176.
11. Ibid., p. 179.
12. Marshall, p. 11.
13. Ibid., p. 13.
14. St Johnston, *From a Colonial Governor's Notebook*, p. 235.
15. Sir Gordon Lethem (1886–1962) entered Colonial Service 1911, and qualified as a barrister-at-law 1920. Served in Africa, mostly Nigeria 1911–1933. Governor of the Seychelles 1933–1935; Governor of Leeward Islands 1936–1941; Governor of British Guiana 1941–1946.

Chapter 20: Unrest in the Graveyard

1. The airfield was named in honour of Captain Hamilton Coolidge of the US Army who was killed in France in 1918. The name was retained when the airfield was turned over to the Government of Antigua after the war, and not changed until 1985 when it became the V.C. Bird International Airport.
2. Colonial Office Report (1938–1946), p. 25.
3. Colonial Office Report (1948), p. 4.
4. Sir Leslie Brian Freeston (1892–1958) served as an army officer 1914–1918. Entered Colonial Service 1919 and worked mostly in London until 1938. Chief Secretary of Tanganyika 1939–1943. Governor Leeward Islands 1944–1948; Governor of Fiji and High Commissioner Western Pacific 1948–1951; Secretary-General South Pacific Commission 1952–1954.
5. Smith, *No Easy Push-o-ver*, p. 77.
6. Oliver Ridsdale Baldwin, second Earl Baldwin of Bewdley (1899–1958) served in the First World War 1916–1919. Took part in Armeno-Turkish War 1920 and in Armeno-Russian War 1921. Imprisoned by Bolsheviks 1921. Correspondent in East Africa 1922. English MP 1929–1931 and 1945–1947. Governor of Leeward Islands 1948–1950.
7. Report of Soulbury Commission, p. 78.
8. Ibid., p. 118.
9. Ibid., p. 122.
10. Blackburne, *Lasting Legacy*, p. 133. Sir Kenneth William Blackburne (1907–1980) entered the Colonial Service in 1929. Served in Nigeria, Palestine, London and the Gambia 1930–1943. Administrative Secretary to Comptroller for Development and Welfare in British West Indies 1943–1947. Director of Information Services in Colonial Office 1947–1950. Governor of Leeward Islands 1950–1956; Governor of Jamaica 1957–1962; Governor-General of Jamaica 1962–1963.
11. Smith, *No Easy Push-o-ver*, p. 96.

12. The cotton industry remained marginal to the economy throughout the inter-war years, receiving a boost during the Second World War and again in 1945 when the Empire Cotton Growers' Association chose Antigua for its Central Cotton Station. By 1951 there were about 2000 acres under cotton, much the same as there had been in 1903.
13. Blackburne, *Lasting Legacy*, p. 142.
14. Richards, I, p. 50.
15. Ibid., p. 54.
16. Blackburne, *Lasting Legacy*, p. 143.
17. Colonial Office Report (1953–54), p. 5.
18. Colonial Office Report (1955–56), p. 20.
19. Neither the cornmeal factory nor the cotton gin and factory ever added very much to the economy. In spite of every effort the island's cornmeal never achieved the quality of that which was imported, and output and sales suffered accordingly. The acreage under cotton increased each year until 1958, and then fell dramatically to less than 1000 acres by 1962. The edible oil factory closed down three years later.
20. Colonial Office Report (1953–54), p. 4.
21. *Antigua, Montserrat and Virgin Islands Gazette*, Vol. I, No. 28, 27 December 1956.

Chapter 21: In No Mood to be Dictated to

1. Sir Alexander Williams (1903–1984) entered Colonial Service in 1928 and served in Northern Rhodesia until 1957. Governor of Leeward Islands 1957–1959.
2. Smith, *No Easy Push-o-ver*, p. 118.
3. Lewis, G.K., p. 385.
4. In spite of the party's lack of success in the only election it ever fought, the ABDM deserves to be remembered for its efforts in making Antiguans aware of the dangers inherent in one-party rule, and of introducing the concept of a 'loyal opposition' into Antiguan politics – even if it never had the chance to put the theory into practice before it was dissolved in the early 1970s.
5. Report on the Sugar Industry (1966), p. 3.
6. Ibid., p. 2 of covering letter.
7. Ibid., p. 3. of covering letter.
8. Ibid., p. 2 of covering letter.
9. Lewis, W.A. p. 32.
10. Sanders, *Transition, Trial, Triumph*, p. 2.
11. Antigua–Barbuda Democratic Movement Newsletter, S5, No. 19, 12 November 1966.
12. Ibid.
13. Ibid.
14. Antigua–Barbuda Democratic Movement Newsletter, S5, No. 21, 26 November 1966.
15. Richards, II, p. 22.

Chapter 22: Removing the Pillars

1. Richards, II,. p. 37.
2. Ibid., p. 49.
3. Letter dated 18 December 1967, copy in author's possession.
4. Ibid.

5. *Antigua Star*, 6 March 1968.
6. Richards, II, p. 59.
7. Bird, p. 27.
8. Antigua 'Independence in Association' official Independence Magazine, p. 3.
9. Richards II, p. 71.
10. Lewis, G.K. p. 140.

Chapter 23: For Good, or Come What May

1. Richards, II, p. 74.
2. Smith, *No Easy Push-o-ver*, p. 330.
3. Richards, II, p. 94.
4. Smith, *No Easy Push-o-ver*, p. 243.
5. Richards, II, p. 94.
6. Ibid., p. 101.
7. Ibid., p. 101.
8. Smith, *No Easy Push-o-ver*, p. 293.
9. After his return Halstead was arrested, jailed briefly before being released on bail, and soon released unconditionally. No charges relating to his period as a minister of government have ever been brought.
10. Walter attempted a comeback in 1982, when he formed the United People's Movement as the political arm of the AWU, after the union had parted company with the PLM. This had no success and he retired from politics three years later.
11. Smith, *No Easy Push-o-ver*, p. 286.
12. The ACLM journal, *Outlet*, commenced publication in 1968 when the Afro-Caribbean Movement was founded. Until the early 1990s it was Antigua's only true opposition newspaper, surviving many determined attempts to close it down and to silence the outpourings of its editor, and the ACLM's chairman, Leonard 'Tim' Hector, whose 'Fan the Flames' column earned a well-deserved Caribbean-wide reputation.
13. Coram, p. 84.
14. Lowenthal and Clarke, *Island Orphans*, p. 299.
15. Sanders, *Transition, Trial, Triumph*, p. 28.
16. Ibid., p. 29.
17. Ibid., p. 10.
18. Ibid., p. 10.
19. Ibid., p. 30.
20. Baird, p. 68. V.C. Bird retired in 1994, when his son Lester took over as Prime Minister. He died on 28 June 1999 as the final chapter of this book was being written.

Bibliography

Andrews, E.W. (ed.). *Journal of a Lady of Quality; Being the Narrative of a Journey from Scotland to the West Indies, North Carolina and Portugal, in the years 1774 to 1776.* New Haven (1921).
Anon [Mrs Lanaghan]. *Antigua and the Antiguans,* 2 vols. London (1844).
Augier, F.R. and Gordon, S.C. *Sources of West Indian History.* London (1962).
Ayearst, M. *The British West Indies: The Search for Self-Government.* London (1960).
Baird, R. *Impressions and Experiences of the West Indies and North America in 1849.* Philadelphia (1850).
Baker, G.S. *Three Hundred Years of Witness.* (Alan Pooley, England, 1973).
Baptiste, F.A. *War, Cooperation and Conflict: The European Possessions in the Caribbean, 1939–1945.* Westport (1988).
Beachey, R.W. *The British West Indies Sugar Industry in the Late 19th Century.* Oxford (1957).
Bennett, J.H. 'The English Caribbees in the period of the Civil War, 1642–1646'. *William & Mary Quarterly,* 3rd series, 24, 1967, pp. 359–377.
Berleant-Schiller, R. 'Hidden places and creole forms: naming the Barbudan Landscape'. *Professional Geographer,* 43(1), 1991, pp. 92–101.
Berleant-Schiller, R. 'Statehood, the commons, and the landscape in Barbuda'. *Caribbean Geography,* vol. 3, (1990), pp. 43–52.
Berleant-Schiller, R. and Lowes, S. with Benjamin M. *Antigua and Barbuda* (World Bibliographical Series Vol. 182). Oxford (1995).
Berlin, I. and Morgan, P.D. (eds). *Cultivation and Culture: Labour and the Shaping of Slave Life in the Americas.* Charlottesville (1993).
Bird, E.L. 'The Development of Education in Antigua and Barbuda'. *Bulletin of Eastern Caribbean Affairs,* vol. 7, no. 5 (November/December 1981), pp. 25–29.
Blackburne, K. *Lasting Legacy: A Story of British Colonialism.* London (1976).
Blackburne, K. *The Romance of English Harbour.* Antigua, 4th edn., (1969).
Boromé, J. (ed.) 'John Candler's Diary'. *Caribbean Studies,* vol. 5, no. 3, 1965, pp. 51–57.
Bourne, R. *Queen Anne's Navy in the West Indies.* New Haven (Yale Historical Publication Miscellany 33), (1939).
Bridenbaugh, C. and R. *No Peace Beyond the Line: The English in the Caribbean 1624–1690.* New York (1972).

Brown, J. *Leewards: Writings, Past and Present, about the Leeward Islands*. Barbados (1961).
Buisseret, D. 'The Elusive Deodand: a study of the fortified refuges of the Lesser Antilles'. *Journal of Caribbean History*, 6&7, 1973, pp. 43–80.
Bulkeley, O.T., *The Lesser Antilles: A Guide for Settlers in the British West Indies, and Tourists' Companion*. London (1889).
Burn, W.L. *Emancipation and Apprenticeship in the British West Indies*. London (1937).
Burns, A. *History of the British West Indies*. London (1954).
Cameron, T.W.M. 'The early history of the Caribbee Islands (1493 to 1530)'. *Scottish Geographic Magazine*, vol. 50, no. 1, 1934, pp. 1–18 and 92–100.
Carrington, S.H.H. *The British West Indies during the American Revolution*. Dordrecht (1988).
Carstensen, B. *Betty's Hope: An Antiguan Sugar Plantation*. Antigua (1993).
Challenger, B. 'The Antiguan Economy 1967–1981'. *Bulletin of Eastern Caribbean Affairs*, vol. 7, no. 5, November/December 1981, pp. 12–19.
Coad, J.G., *The Royal Dockyards 1690–1850: Architecture and Engineering Works of the Sailing Navy*. Aldershot (1989).
Coleridge, H.N. *Six Months in the West Indies in 1825*. London (1832).
Coram, R. 'A reporter at large: Ancient rights'. *New Yorker*, 6 February 1989.
Crouse, N.M. *The French Struggle for the West Indies, 1665–1713*. New York (1943).
Davis, G. *Antigua Black: Portrait of an Island People*. San Francisco (1973).
Davy, J. *The West Indies, Before and Since Slave Emancipation*. London (1854).
Day, C.W. *Five Years' Residence in the West Indies*. 2 vols. London (1852).
Deerr, N. *The History of Sugar*. 2 vols. London (1949–50).
Department of the Navy. *US Naval Administrative History of World War II: Caribbean Sea Frontier to VE Day*. Washington DC (n.d.).
Dunn, R.S. *Sugar and Slaves: the Rise of the Planter Class in the English West Indies 1624–1713*. London (1972).
Ferguson, M. (ed.) *The Hart Sisters: Early African Caribbean Writers, Evangelists, and Radicals*. Lincoln, Nebraska (1993).
Flax, O. *Antigua Grammar School: One Hundred Years of Service to Antigua, 1884–1984*. Antigua (1984).
Forbes, U. 'The West Indies Associated States: some aspects of the constitutional arrangements'. *Social and Economic Studies*, vol. 19, 1970, pp. 57–88.
Franck, H.A. *Roaming Through the West Indies*. New York (1920).
French, G. *The History of Col. Parke's Administration, Whilst he was Captain-General and Chief Governor of the Leeward Islands; with an Account of the Rebellion in Antegoa: Wherein he, with Several Others, were Murther'd on 7th of December, 1710*. London (1717).
Galenson, D. 'Servants bound for Antigua, 1752–1756'. *Genealogists' Magazine*, 19, 1978, pp. 277–279.

Gaspar, D.B. 'The Antiguan Slave Conspiracy of 1736: a case study of collective resistance'. *William & Mary Quarterly*, 3rd series, 35, 1978, pp. 308–323.
Gaspar, D.B. *Bondmen and Rebels: A Study of Master-Slave Relations in Antigua with Implications for Colonial British America*. Baltimore (1985).
Gaspar, D.B. '"A Mockery of Freedom": the status of freedmen in Antigua slave society before 1760'. *New West Indian Guide*, vol. 59, nos. 3–4, 1985, pp. 135–148.
Gaspar, D.B. 'Slavery, amelioration, and the Sunday markets in Antigua, 1823–1831'. *Slavery and Abolition*, vol. 9, no. 1, May 1988, pp. 1–28.
Gaspar, D.B. 'Sugar cultivation and slave life in Antigua before 1800'. *Cultivation and Culture*, edited by Berlin and Morgan (1993).
Gaspar, D.B. '"To bring their offending slaves to justice": compensation and slave resistance in Antigua, 1699–1763'. *Caribbean Quarterly*, vol. 30, nos. 3–4, September/December 1984, pp. 45–59.
Gaspar, D.B. 'Working the system: Antigua slaves and their struggle to live'. *Slavery and Abolition*, vol. 13, no. 3, December 1992, pp. 131–155.
Glover, Lady *Life of Sir John Hawley Glover, RN, CGMG*. London (1897).
Goveia, E.V. *Slave Society in the British Leeward Islands at the End of the Eighteenth Century*. New Haven (1965).
Government of Antigua *Antigua: 'Independence in Association*. (1967).
Government of Antigua. *From Bondage to Freedom 1834–1984: Antigua and Barbuda Commemorative Magazine*. (1984).
Government of Antigua. *Historical Notes on Education in Antigua 1837–1984*. (1984).
Government of Antigua. *Mico in Antigua*. (1984).
Government of Antigua. *Space Research in Antigua: a Government Statement* (1978).
Great Britain, Annual Report: Leeward Islands. London (1938 to 1956).
Great Britain Colonial Reports: Annual. London 1897–1919.
Great Britain Reports Exhibiting the Past and Present State of Her Majesty's Colonial Possessions. London (1845–1885).
Great Britain Report of the Royal Commission Appointed in December 1882, Part III: The Leeward Islands. London (1884).
Great Britain Report of the West India Royal Commission. London (1897).
Great Britain Report of the West India Royal Commission (Moyne) 1938–39. London (1945).
Great Britain Report of the Commission appointed to Enquire into the Organization of the Sugar Industry of Antigua (Soulbury). London (1949).
Great Britain Report on the Sugar Industry and Agriculture of Antigua. London (1966).
Green, W.A. *British Slave Emancipation: The Sugar Colonies and the Great Experiment 1830–1865*. Oxford (1976).
Gurney, J.J. *A Winter in the West Indies described in Familiar Letters to Henry Clay, of Kentucky*. London (1840).

Haggard, J. *The Judgment of the Right Hon. Lord Stowell, Respecting the Slavery of the Mongrel Woman, Grace, on Appeal from the Vice-Admiralty Court of Antigua.* London (1827).

Hall, D. *Five of the Leewards, 1834–1870: The Major Problems of the Post-Emancipation Period in Antigua, Barbuda, Montserrat, Nevis and St Kitts.* Barbados (1971).

Hall, D. 'The flight from the estates reconsidered: the British West Indies 1838–42'. *Journal of Caribbean History*, X–XI, 1978.

Harlow, V.T. *Christopher Codrington 1668–1710.* Oxford (1928).

Harlow, V. and Madden, F. *British Colonial Developments 1774–1834: Select Documents.* Oxford (1953).

Harper, B. *A Short History of the Heads of Government of the Island of Antigua.* Antigua (1962).

Harris, D.R. *Plants, Animals, and Man in the Outer Leeward Islands, West Indies: An Ecological Study of Antigua, Barbuda and Anguilla.* Berkeley (1965).

Henry, P. 'C.L.R. James and the Antiguan Left'. *C.L.R. James's Caribbean*, edited by Henry and Buhle (1992).

Henry, P. *Peripheral Capitalism and Undevelopment in Antigua.* New Jersey (1985).

Henry, P. and Buhle, P. *C.L.R. James's Caribbean.* Durham, North Carolina (1992).

Higham, C.S.S. *The Development of the Leeward Islands under the Restoration 1660–1688.* Cambridge (1921).

Hitchcock, C.H. 'The Redonda Phosphate'. *Geological Society of America*, vol. 2, 1891, pp. 6–9.

Horsford, J. *A Voice From the West Indies: Being a Review of the Character and Results of Missionary Efforts in the British and other Colonies of the Caribbean Sea.* London (1856).

Hovey, S. *Letters from the West Indies: Relating Especially to the Danish Island St Croix and to the British islands Antigua, Barbadoes and Jamaica.* New York (1838).

Hulme, P. and Whitehead, N.L. (eds.) *Wild Majesty: Encounters with Caribs from Columbus to the Present Day.* Oxford (1992).

Jane, C.W.E. *Shirley Heights: The Story of the Redcoats in Antigua.* Antigua (1982).

Kelly, W.C. *Coco Point Lodge 1960–1996.* Privately printed (1996).

Kiple, K.F. *The Caribbean Slave: A Biological History.* Cambridge (1984).

Laurence, K.O. *Immigration into the West Indies in the 19th Century.* Barbados (1971).

Layman, A. *Antigua: The Story of the Cathedral and Parish Church of St John 1678–1932.* Guildford (1933).

Leach, J. *Rough Sketches of the Life of an Old Soldier; during a service in The West Indies.* London (1831).

Lewis, G.K. *The Growth of the Modern West Indies.* London (1968).

Lewis, W.A. *The Agony of the Eight.* Barbados (1965).

Loving H. *Correspondence with the Rt. Hon. Viscount Goderich, Secretary of State for the Colonies, on the Subject of the Political Rights of the Free Coloured and Black Inhabitants of the Island of Antigua.* London (1832).

Lowe, R. (ed.). *The Codrington Correspondence 1743–1851*. London (1951).
Lowenthal, D. (ed.), *The West Indies Federation: Perspectives of a New Nation*. London (1961).
Lowenthal, D. and Clarke, C.G. 'Barbuda alone'. *Geographical Magazine*, vol. LIII, no. 7, April 1981, pp. 465–470.
Lowenthal, D. and Clarke, C.G. 'Slave-breeding in Barbuda: The past of a negro myth'. *Annals of the New York Academy of Sciences*, 292, pp. 510–525.
Lowes, S. 'They couldn't mash ants: the decline of the white and nonwhite elites in Antigua, West Indies, 1834–1900'. In: *Small Islands, Large Questions; Society, Culture and Resistance in the Post-Emancipation Caribbean*, Olwig (1995).
Lucas, C. *The Empire at War*. Vol. II, Oxford (1923).
Luffman, J. *A Brief Account of the Island of Antigua*. London (1789).
Madden, F. and Fieldhouse, D. *The Dependent Empire and Ireland, 1840–1900: Advance and Retreat in Representative Self-Government*. Vol. V, New York (1991).
Marshall, B.A. 'Attempts at Windward/Leeward Federation'. *Caribbean Quarterly*, vol. 18, no. 2, June 1972, pp. 9–15.
Mathieson, W.L. *British Slave Emancipation 1838–1849*. London (1932).
Mathieson, W.L. *British Slavery and its Abolition 1828–38*. London (1926).
Mordecai, J. *The West Indies: the Federal Negotiations*. London (1968).
Morison, S.E. *Admiral of the Ocean Sea: A Life of Christopher Columbus*. Boston (1983).
Morse, A.R. *The Quest for M.P. Shiel's Realm of Redonda*. Cleveland (1979).
Morse, F.W. 'Redonda and its Phosphates'. *Popular Science Monthly*, vol. 46, November 1894, pp. 78–87.
Multer, H.G., Weiss, M.P. and Nicholson, D.V. *Antigua: Reefs, Rocks and Highroads of History*. Antigua (1986).
Munroe, T. and Lewis, R. (eds) *Readings in Government and Politics of the West Indies*. Jamaica (1971).
Nicholson, D.V. *Antigua, Barbuda and Redonda: A Historical Sketch*. Antigua (n.d.).
Nicholson, D.V. *Heritage Landmarks: Antigua and Barbuda*. Antigua (n.d.).
Nicholson, D.V. *The Story of the Arawaks in Antigua and Barbuda*. London (1983).
Norie, J.W. *West India Directory: Part I The Caribbee Islands*. London (1836).
Nutting, C.C. 'English Harbour'. *The Scientific Monthly*, July 1920, pp. 72–91.
Oliver, V.L. *Caribbeana, Being Miscellaneous Papers Relating to the History, Genealogy, Topography and Antiquities of the British West Indies*. 6 vols. London (1910–1919).
Oliver, V.L. *The History of the Island of Antigua, one of the Leeward Caribbees in the West Indies, from the First Settlement in 1635 to the Present Time*. 3 vols. London (1894–1899).
Olwig, K.F. *Small Islands, Large Questions; Society, Culture and Resistance in the Post-Emancipation Caribbean*. London (1995).
Pares, R. 'Merchants and planters'. *Economic History Review*, 4 (Supplement), 1960.
Pares, R. *War and Trade in the West Indies 1739–1763*. London (1963).

Penson, L.M. *The Colonial Agents of the British West Indies: A Study in Colonial Administration, mainly in the Eighteenth Century.* London (1971).
Pitman, F.W. *The Development of the British West Indies, 1700–1763.* New Haven (1917).
Prince, M. (Ferguson, M., ed.), *The History of Mary Prince, a West Indian Slave, Related by Herself.* Ann Arbor (1993).
Purdon, H.G. *An Historical Sketch of the 64th (Second Staffordshire)Regiment, and of the Campaigns through which they passed.* Preston (n.d.).
Ragatz, L.J. 'Absentee landlordism in the British Caribbean, 1750–1833'. *Agricultural History,* vol. V, 1931, pp.7–24.
Ragatz, L.J. *The Fall of the Planter Class in the British Caribbean, 1764–1833.* New York (1963).
Regimental History Committee, *Royal Inniskilling Fusiliers 1688–1914.* London (1928).
Richards, N.H. *The Struggle and the Conquest: Twenty-five years of Social Democracy in Antigua.* Antigua (1964).
Richards, N.H. *The Struggle and the Conquest*, Part II. Antigua (1981).
Roberts, G.W. and Byrne, J. 'Summary statistics on indenture and associated migration affecting the West Indies, 1834–1918'. *Population Studies,* vol. XX, 1966–7, pp. 125–134.
Ross, C. *From an Antiguan's Notebook.* Antigua (1962).
Ross, W.G. 'English Harbour, Antigua'. *Canadian Geographical Journal,* vol. LXII, no. 3, 1961, pp. 94–99.
St Johnston, R. *From a Colonial Governor's Notebook.* London (1936).
St Johnston, R. *The Leeward Islands during the French Wars.* Antigua (1933).
Sanders, R. (ed.) *Antigua and Barbuda Independence.* Antigua (1981).
Sanders, R. (ed.) *Antigua and Barbuda 1966–1981: Transition, Trial Triumph.* Antigua (1984).
Saul, S.B. 'The British West Indies in Depression 1880–1914'. *Inter-American Economic Affairs,* XII, 1958.
Savage, M. 'The 38th Foot in the West Indies, Part I 1707–11'. *United Empire,* Oct 1936.
Sewell, W.G. *The Ordeal of Free Labour in the British West Indies.* London (1968).
Sheridan, R. *The Development of Plantations to 1750: An Era of West Indian Propriety 1750–1775.* Barbados (1970).
Sheridan, R. 'Letters from a sugar plantation in Antigua, 1737–1758'. *Agricultural History,* vol. 31, no. 3, July 1957, pp. 3–23.
Sheridan, R. 'Planters and merchants: The Oliver family of Antigua and London'. *Business History,* vol. 13, no. 2, 1971, pp. 104–13.
Sheridan, R. 'The rise of a colonial gentry: a case study of Antigua, 1730–1775'. *Economic History Review,* 2nd Series, vol. 13, nos. 1–3, 1960–61, pp. 342–357.

Sheridan, R. 'Samuel Martin: Innovating sugar planter of Antigua, 1750–1776'. *Agricultural History*, 34, 1960, pp. 126–139.
Sheridan, R. *Sugar and Slavery: an Economic History of the British West Indies, 1623–1775*. Barbados (1974).
Shyllon, F.O. *Black Slaves in Britain*. Oxford (1974).
Smith, K.B. *No Easy push-o-ver: A History of the Working People of Antigua and Barbuda 1836–1994*. Scarborough, Ontario (1994).
Smith, K.B. and Smith, F.C. *To Shoot Hard Labour: the Life and Times of Samuel Smith an Antiguan Workingman 1877–1982*. Scarborough, Ontario (1986).
Sturge, J. and Harvey, T. *The West Indies in 1837, Being the Journal of a Visit to Antigua [etc] for the Purpose of Ascertaining the Actual Condition of the Negro Population of those Islands*. London (reprint 1968).
Thome, J.A. and Kimbell, J.H. *Emancipation in the West Indies: a six-months' tour in Antigua, Barbados and Jamaica in the year 1837*. New York (1838).
Tolstoy, N. *The Half-Mad Lord: Thomas Pitt, 2nd Baron Camelford (1775–1804)*. London (1978).
Vale, W.L. *History of the South Staffordshire Regiment*. Aldershot (1969).
Walker, F.D. *The Call of the West Indies: The Romance of Methodist Work and Opportunity in the West Indies and Adjacent Regions*. London (c. 1927).
Walker, G.P.J. *The Life of Daniel Gateward Davis: First Bishop of Antigua*. St Kitts (1992).
Waller, J.A. *A Voyage in the West Indies, Containing Various Observations made During a Residence in Barbadoes, and Several of the Leeward Islands*. London (1820).
Ward, J.R. *British West Indian Slavery 1750–1834*. Oxford (1988).
Warner, O. *A Portrait of Lord Nelson*. London (1958).
Waters, I. *The Unfortunate Valentine Morris*. Chepstow (1964).
Watkins, F.H. *Handbook of the Leeward Islands*. London (1924).
Watts, F. *Report on the Sugar Industry in Antigua and St Kitts–Nevis, 1881 to 1905*. Barbados (1905).
Webb, E.A.H. *History of the 12th (The Suffolk) Regiment 1685–1913*. London (1914).
Wentworth, T. *The West India Sketch Book*. 2 vols. London (1834).
Will, H.A. *Constitutional Change in the British West Indies, 1880–1903*. Oxford (1970).
Williams, E. *Documents of West Indian History Vol I 1492–1655*. Trinidad (1963).
Williamson, J.A. *The Caribbee Islands under the Proprietary Patents*. Oxford (1926).

Index

Abolitionist movement 100, 102, 113, 114, 123
absentee landlords 65, 69, 88, 96, 111, 137, 167, 169
air travel 219, 236, 256
Amelioration Act (1978) 46, 103, 106, 107, 112, 113, 158
Anglican Church 34, 56, 117, 119, 125, 130, 144, 151, 159, 298, 301
    in Barbuda 144, 190, 191, 193
    schools 151, 184
Anguilla 26, 113, 252, 267
Antigua and the Antiguans 20, 44, 71, 91, 296, 297
Antigua–Barbuda Democratic Movement (**ABDM**) 248, 250, 258, 262, 267, 271, 275, 305
Antigua Caribbean Liberation Movement (**ACLM**) 285, 289, 306
Antigua Employers' Federation 244, 245, 259, 264
'Antigua Freedom Fighters' 278, 279
Antigua Girls' High School 185, 273
Antigua Grammar School 185, 209, 273
Antigua Labour Party (ALP) 275–293 passim
    founded 275
    electoral defeat (1971) 275
    electoral victory (1976) 281
    electoral victory (1980) 289
    and colour red 283
    and independence 288
Antigua National Party (ANP) 248, 253, 275

Antigua Peoples' Party 275
Antigua Star 264, 268
Antigua Sugar Factory 206, 207, 208, 225, 229, 234, 260, 264, 278, 283
Antigua Sugar Planters' Association 225, 229, 233
Antigua Syndicate Estates 234, 239, 246, 247, 257, 260, 264
Antigua Trades and Labour Union (ATLU) 228–279 passim
    founded 228
    political committee 237
    split with Walter 265
Antigua Workers' Union (AWU) 271
    founded 265
    general strike 265–267
Anti-Slavery Society 123, 124, 157, 158
Arawaks 3, 6, 14
Ashton, Henry 15, 16, 17, 26
Assembly, House of, 17–173 passim
    founded 17
    membership 17
Athill, John 134, 159

Baldwin, Earl 238–243, 304
Barbados 13, 17, 19, 20, 24, 25, 26, 37, 50, 52, 56, 84, 134, 163, 165, 186, 223, 252, 260, 266, 294
Barbuda 3, 88, 137–147, 163, 189–200, 254, 264, 282
    description 4, 5, 268–270
    pre-Columbian settlement 7

European discovery 11
English claim 12
settlement 37
Codrington family 7, 8, 50, 137
leases 37, 38, 50, 137, 191, 192
slavery 38, 88, 139, 143–145
wrecks and salvage 38, 139–142, 190–191, 193
emancipation 136, 144, 145
relations with Antigua 139, 145, 146, 147, 163, 192, 193, 267, 282, 286, 288, 291
Crown estate 194
Local Government Council 281, 286, 287, 290
Bathurst, Earl 125, 126, 299
Baxter, John 93, 95, 116
Bell, Hesketh 206, 212, 303
Bendals village 206
sugar factory 206, 207, 225
Berkeley, George 201, 202, 303
Best, Thomas 216, 303
Bethell-Codrington, Sir Christopher 103, 128, 136, 137, 141, 143, 147, 189
Bethell-Codrington, Sir William 189, 192
Bethesda village 117
Betty's Hope estate 29, 30, 32, 37, 38, 39, 51, 63, 67, 117, 210, 295
Bird, Lester 275, 277, 279, 285, 286, 288, 289, 290, 292
Bird, Vere Cornwall 231–293 passim
president, ATLU 234
elected to Legislative Council 234
appointed to Executive Council 237
on Soulbury Commission 238, 239
Member for Trade and Production 247
Minister for Trade and Production 248
Montego Bay Conference 251
WI Federation Labour Party 252
Chief Minister 253
London Conference 1961 255–256
Premier 263

resigns as president of ATLU 274
loses 1971 election 275
wins 1976 election 281
Prime Minister 292
resignation and death 306
Blackburne, Kenneth 243, 244, 245, 246, 247, 253, 256, 304
Board of Trade 26, 30, 40, 44, 47, 49, 53, 55, 59, 63, 68, 73, 78, 97, 295
British troops 37, 43, 79, 245
Burt, William 96, 298
Burton, Eric 276, 287, 289, 290, 291

Camelford, Baron 104–105
Caribs 9, 11, 15, 41
arrival 6
assistance to slaves 24, 34, 35
in Barbuda 27, 37
in Dominica 27
raids 16, 17, 22, 24, 26, 37
Carlisle, 1st Earl of 13, 15, 16, 19
Carlisle, 2nd Earl of 15, 19
Chinese immigrants 165, 187, 188
Church of England *see* Anglican Church
Citrine, Walter 227, 228, 232
Closer Union Commission 223, 224, 226
Codrington, Christopher (elder) 29, 30, 31, 32, 37, 38, 39, 50, 51, 65, 137
Codrington, Christopher (younger) 40, 41, 43, 44, 45, 46, 50, 51, 137
Codrington, Sir William (elder) 50, 65, 137
Codrington, Sir William (younger) 65, 67, 73, 88, 137
Codrington village 139, 142, 268, 286, 291
Colebrook, William 156, 159, 301
Colonial Development and Welfare Acts 229, 235, 242, 247, 252
coloured population (post-1834) 159, 160, 186, 187, 188, 204, 221, 223

Columbus, Christopher 8, 11
constitutional reform
    post-1834 170–174, 204
    1937 224–225
    1951 246–247
    1967 261–262
    1981 288–292
Contract Act 134, 151, 154, 161, 215
Coolidge airport 232, 237, 256, 304
cotton 31, 180, 205, 211, 212, 247, 303
Court (Coromantee slave) 73–75, 296
Crabbs Peninsula 230, 278, 283
Crown Colony rule 172, 174, 187, 205, 242

Daily Meal Society 119, 151, 158, 162, 179
Davis, Bishop Daniel 158, 301
deep-water port 257, 271
Defence Force 210, 211, 216, 233, 266, 277
de la Bastide Inquiry (1976) 282, 283
dockyard *see* English Harbour
Dominica 8, 12, 100, 109, 175, 211, 212, 219, 223
Douglas, Walter 57–59, 79
droughts 3, 5, 16, 68, 69, 96, 109, 173, 206, 212, 215, 236, 247
D'Urban, Benjamin 125, 299

earthquakes 30, 156, 168, 280
education 151, 183–184, 202, 209, 235, 273
    Acts 183, 208
Emancipation 131–136
Elliot, Hugh 110, 111, 298
emigration 155, 208
Encumbered Estates Act (1854) 173, 174, 176, 185, 187
English Harbour 78, 82, 83, 99, 109, 134, 201, 202, 256
    dockyard 82, 93, 97, 116, 163, 201, 202, 256
    fortifications 80
European discovery 11, 12

Executive Council 171, 173–187, 236
export duty 19, 106, 132, 154, 168

Falmouth town 14, 30, 34, 36, 42, 170
federation attempts 222, 223, 251, 255, 256
Federation of West Indies *see* West Indies, Federation of
Field, Revd James 34, 52, 56
Fiennes, Sir Eustace 219, 220, 240, 304
Fiennes Institute 220, 227, 240
Five Islands Harbour 21, 42, 206
Fleming, Francis 194, 199, 205, 303
fortifications 41, 42, 100, 101
    Fort George 42, 43, 79
    Fort James 79, 218
    Fort Shirley 101, 127, 134
franchise 169, 170, 205, 246
free coloured people 45, 46, 76, 94, 95, 115, 117, 118, 124, 128, 134
free labourers 124, 132, 150, 151, 154, 155
Freeston, Brian 236, 304
French invasion (1666) 21–24

garrison 79, 100, 108, 114, 127, 134, 163, 164, 201
    barracks 79, 94
General Assembly of Leeward Islands 26, 104, 106, 107
George, McChesney 254, 262, 263, 264, 267, 277, 290
Gilbert, Anne 115, 116, 118
Gilbert, Francis 93
Gilbert, John 116
Gilbert, Nathaniel 93, 116
Glover, John 185, 186, 302
Golden Grove College 273
Gormanston, Viscount 186, 188, 302
Guadeloupe 3, 8, 13, 15, 21, 43, 47, 69, 81, 109, 163, 180, 191
Gunthorpes sugar factory *see* Antigua Sugar Factory
Hall, Robert 258, 271, 274, 276, 283, 290, 291

Halstead, Donald 265, 271, 274, 277, 278, 279, 280, 306
Hamilton, Ker 163, 169, 171, 179, 301
Hart, John 68, 70, 73, 296
Hart sisters, the 115–117
health and welfare 179, 180, 181, 182, 208, 235, 247
Henry Rowan 248, 253
Higginson, James 157, 160, 162, 167, 191, 301
Hill, Stephen 172, 173, 177, 301
Holberton Institution 179, 208
Holberton, Revd Robert 119, 158, 208
housing 217, 235, 244
    early settlement 15, 30
    free villages 155, 156, 160, 161, 177
    hurricanes 217, 243, 244

immigrant workers 162, 165, 171
indentured servants 14, 17, 19, 25, 27, 28, 29, 33, 41, 62, 78, 88, 89, 129
'Independence in Association' 261, 262
independence negotiations 281, 284, 285, 286, 288, 289
Irving, Henry 182
Isles, Samuel 92

Jacobs, Wilfred 263, 266
Johnson, Nathaniel 36
Jones, Grace 120–121, 123

Keynell, Christopher 17, 18, 19, 295
Klass, Prince *see* Court

'Lady boats' 218
land settlement schemes 41, 155, 160, 161, 209, 238, 245, 247, 248
Lavington, Lord 87, 108, 109, 110, 140, 297
Le Nouveau Justin 190
Lees, Charles 188, 302
Leeward Islands 3, 25, 29, 31, 37, 83, 294
Leeward Islands Federation (1871) 175, 176, 196, 248

Leeward Islands Air Transport (LIAT) 279
Leeward Islands Naval Squadron 83, 84
Legislative Council 17, 26, 40, 86, 170, 203, 229
Leigh, Charles 101, 102
Lethem, Gordon 229, 231, 304
Lewis, Arthur 250, 260
Liberta village 92, 156, 218
Londonderry, Lord 73, 76, 79, 296
Loving Henry 118, 128, 129, 130, 134, 135, 147, 159, 186
Lynch, Elizabeth 118

MacKintosh, Robert 191
Madeira 162, 164
Malone Inquiry (1951) 244–245
maroons 34, 35, 36, 45, 46, 92
Martin, Samuel (elder) 44, 72
Martin, Samuel (younger) 87, 88, 92
Mathew, William (elder) 47, 48
Mathew, William (younger) 62, 63, 73, 76, 78, 80, 81, 83, 296
McGregor, Sir Evan 133, 134, 135, 145, 146, 159, 293, 300
Merewether, Edward 211, 219, 303
Methodist Church 92, 93, 115, 118, 119, 158
    schools 116, 151, 152, 185
Mico Charity School 152
Militia 35, 42, 56, 58, 62, 78, 79, 81, 86, 101, 109, 116, 118, 127, 129, 134, 152, 153, 210
Mill Reef Club 241, 245
Monks Hill 42, 43, 49, 134, 155
Montserrat 8, 12, 24, 37, 58, 69, 80, 109, 113, 155, 175, 194, 212, 221, 241, 246
Moody-Stuart, Alexander 229, 234, 235, 237, 241, 244, 247, 249, 254
Moravian Church 34, 92, 95, 115, 119, 122, 123, 155, 158, 225
    schools 151, 152, 184, 185

Navigation Acts 18, 20, 39, 97

Nelson, Horatio 97–100
Nevis 31, 37, 47, 48, 55, 57, 80, 109, 112, 113, 194
Newfield village 155

oil refinery 254, 256, 271, 279, 284
Old Road village 14, 30

Parham town 30, 93, 170, 230
Parke, Daniel 48–50, 72
Payne, Ralph *see* Lavington, Lord
peasant farming 133, 213, 215, 225
phosphates 194, 196, 198, 199, 200
Pine, Benjamin 172, 173, 175, 185, 192, 301
police and policing 120, 152, 153, 163, 210, 211, 216, 266, 277
  in Barbuda 268, 291
Portuguese immigrants 162, 165, 166, 187
Potworks reservoir *see* water
Prince, Mary 122–123, 124, 126
prison *see* punishment
privateers 12, 41, 55, 58, 83, 84, 96
Progressive Labour Movement (PLM) 271–290 passim
  founded 271
  electoral victory (1971) 275
  electoral defeat (1976) 281
  and colour blue 283
  and independence 281
punishment 43, 44, 153, 297

Quakers 24, 34, 157, 158, 295

Ramsay, George 113, 114
Rat Island 79, 84, 94, 179
'Re-captives' 110
Redonda 3, 8, 13, 194–200, 263
regiments
  British West Indies 211
  Caribbean 233
  Royal Inniskilling Fusiliers 43, 49, 51, 295
  Royal Irish Rifles 127

South Staffordshire 51, 53, 54, 55, 57, 79, 80, 81, 295, 297
Worcestershire 134, 145
Richards, Novelle 253, 263, 276, 290
riots
  1831 127
  1858 163, 192
  1918 212, 216–217
  1968 266–267
Robinson, Nellie 183
Roseau Conference (1932) 223, 251
Ross, Patrick 125, 127, 128, 130, 131, 133
Royal Commissions
  Moyne (1939) 227, 228, 250
  Norman (1896) 203
Royal Navy 54, 55, 80, 81, 82, 83, 84, 97, 98, 99, 104, 163, 202
  in English Harbour 78, 82, 83, 84, 202
runaways 34, 35, 44, 69, 70

Saint Christophe 23, 24, 26
St John's 22, 30, 52, 56, 73, 76, 77, 93, 99, 105, 115, 120, 128, 135, 146, 157, 170, 206, 210, 211, 248
  as capital 43
  Cathedral 94, 157, 158, 206, 207, 280
  churches 34, 92, 118, 157
  housing 156, 178, 235
  Point, The 94, 284
  schools 184, 185
  'Scotch Row' 165
  Sunday market 95, 125, 126, 128
St John's Harbour 22, 79, 90, 98, 188, 202, 219, 236, 257, 272
St Johnston, Reginald 218, 219, 220, 222, 223, 224, 256, 303, 304
St Kitts 8, 12, 15, 20, 21, 24, 37, 47, 48, 55, 59, 73, 80, 104, 106, 108, 109, 113, 155, 165, 172, 175, 202, 212, 218, 221, 241, 267
Sawcolts estate 179, 203, 209

Senate 261, 263, 271, 277, 282
settlement
   pre-Columbian 5–7
   English 14, 24–25
Shekerley Mountains 4, 6, 24, 35, 46, 72, 92, 179, 202
Shirley, Thomas 98, 100, 140, 298
slaves and slavery 23, 24, 82, 87, 89, 90
   abolition of trade 103, 109, 110
   Acts 25, 35, 47, 70, 71, 77, 91, 106, 107
   arming of 81
   Christmas holidays 44, 91
   clothing 68, 87, 91, 108
   conspiracy (1736) 73–77, 78
   domestics 68, 69, 108
   drivers 67, 112
   Emancipation 124, 125, 131–136
   females 32, 66, 67, 68
   field work 32, 66
   foods 68, 69, 90, 96
   introduction of 17, 18
   mistreatment 44, 49, 115
   origin of 31
   population 31, 41, 65, 89
   punishments 34, 35, 36, 45, 66, 67, 69, 70, 72, 74, 75, 76, 106, 112
   registration of 25, 113, 114, 120
   religion 87, 93, 106, 107, 119
   resistance of 34, 35, 36, 44, 71, 72
   skilled workers 34, 67, 82, 83, 89, 90, 99
   trade in 20, 31, 65, 66, 296
Smith, Samuel 220
Smith, William 202, 303
Society for the Propagation of the Gospel 34, 151
soil conditions 4, 85, 86
Soulbury Commission 238, 239
Space Research Corportion 283
Spring Gardens 92, 122, 152, 273
Standing Closer Association Committee 251
Stapleton, William 26, 30, 34, 36

Stevens, Reginald St Clair 214, 226, 227, 228, 231, 232, 233, 234
sugar 20, 21, 22, 28, 32–33, 62–68, 85–96 passim, 167–168, 201, 203–217 passim
   introduction 20, 27
   as payment 22, 23, 28, 35, 42
sugar industry 204, 222, 256, 258
   depression in 174, 185, 201, 203, 258, 272
   collapse of 278
   nationalisation 264
   attempt to revive 284
Sugar Industry Commission (1965) 257, 258, 260, 277, 278
sugar plantations 30, 44, 66, 85, 87, 89, 156, 157, 160, 172
   central factory 204
   field equipment 167, 168
   harvesting 32
   mills 32, 33, 67, 156, 157, 203
   planting 32
   supplies 96
Sunday markets 95, 125, 126, 128
Sweet-Escott, Bickham 208, 303
Syrian immigrants 221

telegraph 201–202
telephone 236, 248
Thomas, George 69, 81, 296
Thwaites, Charles 116, 119
Thwaites, Elizabeth 115, 116
tobacco 13, 16, 18, 20, 28, 31
tourism 219, 256, 272, 279, 280, 283
Tullideph, Walter 64, 66, 70, 72

United States leased bases 230, 231, 232, 233
Walter, George 253, 258, 259, 263–266, 271 passim, 274, 282 passim, 306
   general secretary ATLU 253, 264
   dismissed as general secretary 265
   founds AWU 265

resigns as general secretary AWU 274
  leader of PLM 274
  Premier 276–282
  charged with corruption 283
Warner, Edward 14, 15, 20, 26, 42
Warner, Philip 26, 31
Warner, Thomas 12, 13, 14, 15, 26
Warner, Thomas 'Indian' 27
Warrener, William 92, 94, 116
Wars
  British Civil Wars (1639–60) 16–18
  Second Dutch War (1665–67) 21
  King William's War (1689–97) 36–37, 42, 59
  Spanish Succession, War of (1702–13) 41, 43, 47
  Jenkins' Ear, War of (1739–48) 78, 80, 83
  Seven Years War (1756–63) 81
  American War of Independence (1775–83) 86, 96, 100
  French Revolutionary and Napoleonic Wars (1793–1815) 101, 102, 108, 113, 114
  First World War (1914–18) 199, 210, 221
  Second World War (1939–45) 220, 229, 230
water
  desalination 273

reservoirs 203, 206, 208, 273
  in St John's 172, 178, 179, 248
  schemes 178, 202, 203, 206, 208, 219
  shortages 177, 178, 181, 182, 183, 206, 236, 272
  springs 5, 12, 14, 203
West Indies, Federation of the 252, 253, 255, 256, 260
West Indies Federal Labour Party 252, 256, 260
Weston, George 216
Wheler, Charles 26, 34
white population 14, 16, 17, 25, 30, 41, 62, 63, 86, 88, 117, 186
William Henry, Prince 99, 100, 108, 131, 297
Williams, Alexander 253, 305
Williams, Eric 213, 255
Willoughby, Francis 17, 18, 19, 21, 24, 25
Willoughby, Henry 21, 23, 24
Willoughby, William 24, 29
Willoughby Bay 29, 58, 116
Wilson, Harold 223, 224, 225, 227, 229, 251
Winter, John 137, 143, 190
Wood Report 221, 222, 223
Workers' Voice 242

Yeomanry Cavalry 164, 210